MW01036441

CAMBRIDGE TE.... ...
HISTORY OF PHILOSOPHY

———

ANTOINE ARNAULD AND PIERRE NICOLE
Logic or the Art of Thinking

CAMBRIDGE TEXTS IN THE
HISTORY OF PHILOSOPHY

Series editors

KARL AMERIKS
Professor of Philosophy at the University of Notre Dame

DESMOND M. CLARKE
Professor of Philosophy at University College Cork

The main objective of Cambridge Texts in the History of Philosophy is to expand the range, variety and quality of texts in the history of philosophy which are available in English. The series includes texts by familiar names (such as Descartes and Kant) and also by less well-known authors. Wherever possible, texts are published in complete and unabridged form, and translations are specially commissioned for the series. Each volume contains a critical introduction together with a guide to further reading and any necessary glossaries and textual apparatus. The volumes are designed for student use at undergraduate and postgraduate level and will be of interest not only to students of philosophy, but also to a wider audience of readers in the history of science, the history of theology and the history of ideas.

For a list of titles published in the series, please see end of book.

ANTOINE ARNAULD AND PIERRE NICOLE

Logic or the Art of Thinking

Containing, besides common rules, several new
observations appropriate for forming judgment

TRANSLATED AND EDITED BY
JILL VANCE BUROKER
California State University, San Bernardino

CAMBRIDGE
UNIVERSITY PRESS

Published by the Press Syndicate of the University of Cambridge
The Pitt Building, Trumpington Street, Cambridge CB2 1RP
40 West 20th Street, New York, NY 10011–4211, USA
10 Stamford Road, Oakleigh, Melbourne 3166, Australia

First published 1996

Printed in Great Britain at Bell & Bain Ltd, Glasgow

A catalogue record for this book is available from the British Library

Library of Congress cataloguing in publication data
Arnauld, Antoine, 1612–1694.
Logic, or, The art of thinking: containing, besides common rules, several new observations
appropriate for forming judgment / Antoine Arnauld and Pierre Nicole:
edited by Jill Vance Buroker. – 5th ed., rev. and newly augmented.
p.   cm. – (Cambridge texts in the history of philosophy)
Includes bibliographical references.
1. Logic – early works to 1800.   I. Nicole, Pierre, 1625–1695.
II. Buroker, Jill Vance, 1945– .   III. Title.   IV. Series.
BC62.A713   1996
160–dc20   95-23146   CIP

ISBN 0 521 48249 6 hardback
ISBN 0 521 48394 8 paperback

CE

This book is dedicated to my mother Phyllis,
and the memory of my father Don.

Contents

Acknowledgments

The work on this translation began in 1985–6, while I was supported by a grant from the National Endowment for the Humanities to study Cartesian theories of judgment and perception. Since that time many persons have helped me with the translation. I owe special thanks to my former colleague Don Adams for his cheerful aid in translating the Latin quotations. Bruce Golden, Tom Lennon, John Vickers, and an anonymous reader for the Press made helpful suggestions on parts or all of the manuscript. While I continued working on the translation during a sabbatical in Paris in 1990, Philippe de Rouilhan generously provided computer support and office space at his laboratory at the L'Institut d'Histoire et Philosophie des Sciences et des Techniques of the Centre National de Recherche Scientifique. My greatest debt, however, is to Desmond Clarke who, while establishing this series with the Cambridge University Press, gave me constant encouragement, made painstaking comments on the entire text, and showed me a paradigm example of world-renowned Irish hospitality during a visit to Cork in 1990.

Introduction

La Logique ou l'art de penser, better known as the *Port-Royal Logic*, was written by Antoine Arnauld and Pierre Nicole. Arnauld and Nicole were philosophers and theologians associated with the Port-Royal Abbey, a center of the Catholic Jansenist movement in seventeenth-century France. The first edition of the *Logic* appeared in 1662; during the authors' lifetimes four major revisions were published, the last and most important in 1683. This work is a companion to *General and Rational Grammar: The Port-Royal Grammar*, written primarily by Arnauld and "edited" by Claude Lancelot, which appeared two years before the *Logic*. The *Logic* incorporates some theory from the *Grammar*, but develops an account of knowledge and meaning of much greater scope and richness. The *Grammar* is important because it represents a classical "rational" account of language as opposed to recent behavioristic theories. In the last twenty-five years it has received renewed attention, largely due to Noam Chomsky's claims in *Cartesian Linguistics* and elsewhere that it prefigured modern transformational generative grammar. For example, Arnauld and Lancelot recognize that the "surface structure" of a sentence (the organization of the written or spoken sentence) need not mirror its "deep structure" (the aspects relevant to semantic interpretation). There are, however, reasons to question how systematically or self-consciously the *Grammar* develops this view, as well as whether the theory contains other features required to classify it as a transformational generative grammar.[1] Regardless of the historical accuracy of Chomsky's claims, they have raised new interest in the *Grammar*, which prompted a new and

---

[1]   These questions are discussed in Robin Lakoff's review of Herbert Brekle's critical edition of the *Grammar* in *Language*, 45 (1969), 343–64; Karl E. Zimmer's review of *Cartesian Linguistics* in *International Journal of American Linguistics*, 33–4 (1967–8), 290–303; Vivian Salmon's review of *Cartesian Linguistics* in *Journal of Linguistics*, 5–6 (1969–70), 165–87; Hans Aarsleff, "The History of Linguistics and Professor Chomsky," *Language*, 46 (1970), 570–85; Jan Miel, "Pascal, Port-Royal and Cartesian Linguistics," *Journal of the History of Ideas*, 30 (1969), 261–71; Norman Kretzmann, "Transformationalism and the Port-Royal *Grammar*" in *General and Rational Grammar: The Port-Royal Grammar*, ed. and trans. Jacques Rieux and Bernard E. Rollin (Hague: Mouton, 1975); and Jean-Claude Pariente, *L'Analyse du langage à Port-Royal* (Paris: Les Éditions de Minuit, 1985), especially chapters 1 and 2.

lucid translation by Jacques Rieux and Bernard E. Rollin, published in 1975.[2] Meanwhile, philosophers were rediscovering the companion volume, the *Port-Royal Logic*, in many respects a work of greater historical influence. Although the *Logic* borrows some material from the *Grammar*, its most significant contributions to the history of logic and semantics are absent from the earlier work. In general the semantics of the *Port-Royal Logic* are situated in the context of the Cartesian theory of ideas. Its value to us today resides in its curious combination of deep insights and confusions. For if any single work embodies the standpoint from which to understand the major shifts taking place in logic and in theories of language from the seventeenth century to the present, it is the *Port-Royal Logic*.

In this Introduction I explain briefly the historical and philosophical context of the work. The first part sketches the history of the Port-Royal Abbey and Jansenism, and the lives of the authors Antoine Arnauld and Pierre Nicole.[3] The second part discusses the major philosophical themes in the text, focusing on the influence of Augustine, Descartes, and Pascal, as well as on the criticisms of Aristotle, Montaigne, Gassendi, and others. Finally, I comment on the place of the *Logic* in the history of logic and semantics, and the features of greatest philosophical interest.

Port-Royal and Jansenism

Jansenism was a radical reform movement within French Catholicism based on Augustine's views of the relation between free will and the efficacy of grace. To appreciate its controversial nature we must understand it against the backdrop of the Counter-Reformation. This was the response of the Catholic Church to the growth of Protestantism, in which the Church attempted to redefine its doctrine and make institutional reforms. Following the Council of Trent (1545–63), civil war broke out in France from 1562 to 1595, during which Catholicism suffered a serious decline. During the first half of the seventeenth century, churches and abbeys were rebuilt, and new convents and seminaries were established throughout France. Although reforms took place in older orders such as the Benedictines and Franciscans, and new orders came into being, the Society of Jesus remained the most politically influential order. Because of the enmity they aroused in other orders, the Jesuits were expelled both from the Sorbonne and from France in 1594 by a decree of Parliament. The lawyer Antoine Arnauld, father of the author of the *Port-Royal Logic*, played a key role in prosecuting the case against the Jesuits. In 1603, however, the Jesuits were readmitted to France by order of Henri IV, who took a Jesuit confessor.

Seventeenth-century France was marked by conflicts between the Catholic

---

[2] *General and Rational Grammar: The Port-Royal Grammar.*

[3] The history and biographical information relies heavily on Sainte-Beuve's monumental history of Port-Royal, Alexander Sedgwick's *Jansenism in Seventeenth-Century France*, and A. Bailly's introduction to the Slatkine edition of the *Grammaire générale et raisonnée de Port-Royal*.

Church and French Protestants, the Huguenots, who had been protected by the Edict of Nantes of 1598. But even within Catholicism there were opposing movements. Other religious orders criticized the Jesuits for their interest in the pagan culture of antiquity, their tolerance of liberal thought, and their view that one can act morally of one's own free will. Guided by Luis Molina's work on the compatibility of free will and divine grace, *De Concordia Liberi Arbitrii cum Divinae Gratiae Donis* of 1588, the Jesuits maintained that it is possible to reject God's grace, thereby asserting the priority of human freedom over the efficacy of grace. By contrast, Catholics influenced by the writings of St. Augustine saw humans as powerless to redeem themselves without divine grace. In his writings against the Pelagian heresy (which had denied original sin), Augustine had argued for a form of predestination in which the elect were redeemed by divine grace, which they could not refuse. He claimed, however, that this divine necessity was compatible with human freedom to choose between good and evil. This doctrine of grace attracted scholars at the University of Louvain, in Belgium, where two figures central to Jansenism, Cornelius Jansenius and the Abbot of Saint-Cyran, were later to study theology.

Jansenism was named after Cornelius Jansenius (or Cornelis Jansen), who was born in 1585 in the Dutch Netherlands. He studied theology first at the University of Louvain and later at the Sorbonne. He returned to the Spanish Netherlands where he was ordained a priest, and in 1619 he received his doctorate at Louvain and was admitted to the faculty there. He began his major work *Augustinus* in 1628, envisioning it as the definitive treatise on St. Augustine's theology of grace and free will, but did not complete the work until 1636, when he became the Bishop of Ypres in the Spanish Netherlands. It was not published until 1640, two years after his death from the plague. The treatise *Augustinus* was divided into three parts. The first set the background for understanding Augustine's concept of grace by examining the Pelagian heresy. In rejecting the doctrine of original sin, the Pelagians had argued that one who was untainted by corruption at birth, and who never had the opportunity to know God, could not be condemned. In their view people could attain salvation on their own merits, whether or not they were Christians. In the second part Jansenius argued that Augustine was the best theological authority on matters pertaining to grace. The third part examined the relation between free will and divine grace, and reaffirmed Augustine's view that humans are naturally capable only of evil unless aided by divine grace. These issues – the efficacy of grace, the role of free will in salvation, and the nature of penitence – became the focus of the conflict between Jansenism and more orthodox Catholicism. In fact Jansenism appeared closer to Protestantism than to Catholicism in emphasizing predestination, in putting the spiritual interests of the individual above social interests, and in promoting an elitism in which ordinary individuals do not have access to salvation.

The second major figure in Jansenism was the Abbot of Saint-Cyran, born Jean

Duvergier de Hauranne at Bayonne in 1581. He received his M.A. in theology in 1600 at the Sorbonne. He met Cornelius Jansenius while continuing his studies at the University of Louvain, and the two worked together from about 1611 to 1617 on Scriptural questions and plans for reforming the church. In 1620, two years after being ordained, Duvergier became abbot of the Benedictine monastery of Saint-Cyran. His first controversy took place six years later with the Jesuit scholar Garasse over the efficacy of reason in man's redemption. Christian Pyrrhonists argued that one should suspend judgment on questions on which there was conflicting evidence. Some Catholics used this skeptical position against the Protestant idea that the individual was competent to interpret Scripture. In defending Pyrrhonism, Saint-Cyran portrayed human reason as even more dangerous than the senses, since it is the source of vanity and ignorance. In his claim that wisdom and redemption depend solely on faith, Saint-Cyran articulated a suspicion of reason that was to become prominent in one strain of Jansenism.

The movement named after Jansenius had already begun early in the century, led largely by Angélique Arnauld and the Abbot of Saint-Cyran. Angélique Arnauld, born Jacqueline Arnauld, was the oldest daughter of Antoine and Catherine Arnauld, and older sister of the philosopher Antoine Arnauld. In 1602, at the age of thirteen, she became abbess of the convent of Port-Royal (later known as Port-Royal-des-Champs), a Cistercian abbey founded in the thirteenth century, near Versailles in the valley of the Chevreuse. Six years later she underwent a "conversion," and set about reforming the abbey, instituting monastic rules and closing it off from the outside world. Because of lack of space and unhealthy conditions – the abbey was surrounded by swamps which gave rise to serious epidemics – in 1626 the nuns relocated to Paris, in the Faubourg Saint-Jacques (the men moved nearby about 1637). The following year the Vatican removed Port-Royal from the Cistercian order and placed it under the jurisdiction of the Bishop of Langres and the Archbishops of Paris and Sens.

Angélique Arnauld had met the Abbot of Saint-Cyran in 1625, but they did not develop a close relationship until ten years later. In 1633 the Bishop of Langres, Sébastien Zamet, called upon Saint-Cyran to adjudicate a dispute over the affair of the prayer book. This concerned a special prayer book, the *Chapelet du Saint-Sacrement*, which Angélique's sister Agnès (the former Jeanne Arnauld) had written for the nuns of Port-Royal. The Archbishop of Sens denounced the prayer book as heretical, and eight theologians agreed with him. In response, Saint-Cyran wrote a defense of the prayer book (*Apologie du Chapelet*), which prevented its condemnation. This incident marked an important point in the history of Jansenism, since it was both the first accusation of heresy against Port-Royal as well as Saint-Cyran's first contact with the abbey.

In 1636 Saint-Cyran became the spiritual director of Port-Royal. At about this time he also became associated with a group of men who were to become known as the *solitaires* of Port-Royal. The first and most influential of the *solitaires* was

Antoine Le Maistre, the son of the philosopher Antoine Arnauld's sister, Catherine Le Maistre. Reputed to be one of the best lawyers in Paris, he feared his worldly ambitions. After consulting with Saint-Cyran, he abandoned his career and retired to a little house near the abbey in the Faubourg Saint-Jacques in 1637. He was soon joined by his younger brother, Le Maistre de Sacy, as well as Claude Lancelot and Antoine Singlin. Later *solitaires* included, besides Antoine Arnauld, Arnauld's older brother Robert Arnauld d'Andilly, Pierre Nicole, and Nicolas Fontaine. Although some of the *solitaires* remained laymen, Singlin and Le Maistre de Sacy became priests and served as confessors to the nuns of Port-Royal. In addition to performing manual tasks for the convent, the *solitaires* spent their time reading Scripture and patristic theology, and translating devotional works into French. Perhaps their most important project was founding the Little Schools of Port-Royal.

During the 1630s Saint-Cyran came into conflict with the Jesuits, the Bishop of Langres, and Father Joseph, confidential agent to Cardinal Richelieu. In 1630, Saint-Cyran had refused to endorse the annulment of the King's brother. Then in 1633 there was the affair of the prayer book. He also was identified in 1636 with Jansenius's criticism of France's alliance with Sweden and the Netherlands against Spain. Finally, he opposed Richelieu over the question of penitential discipline. According to the Abbot, genuine repentance required *contrition*, which emanates from a love of God, rather than *attrition*, or fear of punishment, really a form of self-love. Since contrition is much rarer, very few souls are redeemed. For Richelieu, however, the Church had the power to reconcile self-love with God's commandments. Thus the ordinary sinner could be absolved as long as he confessed. Only saints were genuinely contrite, and they were automatically absolved by God without needing to confess.

In 1638 Richelieu had had enough. Declaring that Saint-Cyran was "more dangerous than six armies," he had him arrested and imprisoned at Vincennes on charges of heresy. Although the charges were never substantiated, Saint-Cyran remained in prison for four years, writing letters to the nuns of Port-Royal as well as to Church figures, emphasizing the effects of original sin and the need to isolate oneself from worldly values and temptations. This was the doctrine that inspired the *solitaires* of Port-Royal to leave their secular careers. In early 1643, shortly after Richelieu's death, Saint-Cyran was released from prison. As a result of poor health, exacerbated by his imprisonment, he died later that year. He was buried at Saint Jacques-du-Haut-Pas, a little church near Port-Royal in Paris.

The primary author of the *Port-Royal Logic* was Antoine Arnauld. He was the youngest of Antoine and Catherine Arnauld's twenty children, of whom only ten survived infancy. The Arnauld family was largely responsible for supporting the Port-Royal Abbey. The son Antoine was born on 8 February, 1612, in Paris. His father, one of the most famous lawyers of his time, died in 1619, and the son was raised largely by his mother and his older sister, Catherine Le Maistre. After studying philosophy with distinction, Arnauld originally wanted to follow his father's footsteps in the study of law. But out of respect for his mother's wishes he decided to study theology. He entered the Sorbonne and became the disciple of Lescot, the confessor of Cardinal Richelieu and later the Bishop of Chartres.

In the four theses he defended from 1638 to 1641, Arnauld exhibited Augustinian views entirely opposed to those of Lescot. This put them in conflict from then on. Even though Arnauld had not fulfilled the conditions normally required for entrance to the Society of the Sorbonne, the Society wanted to admit him because of his rare piety, his extraordinary talent, and the brilliance of his dissertation. Despite Richelieu's opposition, Arnauld was finally admitted in 1641. In preaching the usual sermon in the Church of Notre-Dame, he swore "to defend the truth until my blood flows," an oath which all the professors have since taken. In the same year he was ordained a priest, after having given all his worldly goods to the Port-Royal Abbey.

Arnauld's most important theological work was *On Frequent Communion* (*De la fréquente communion*) of 1643. Although approved by the ecclesiastical province of Auch, several bishops, and twenty-four professors of the Sorbonne, the book became the basis of the persecutions Arnauld would subsequently undergo. In it he argued for the necessity of interior conversion before taking the sacraments. This required true repentance before confession, contrition of the heart (based on love of God) before absolution, and contrite penitence before communion. In general he claimed that one was more likely to achieve redemption by taking communion less frequently. The Jesuits, led by Father Nouet, mounted a furious attack on the work. Unfortunately for Nouet, he had been among the clerics to approve the work, and he later had to undergo the humiliation of disavowing his sermons against Arnauld. Despite this setback, the Jesuits had Arnauld ordered to Rome to defend himself before the Inquisition. Arnauld was saved only because the Parliament and the Sorbonne objected to Rome's interference in a matter they thought concerned only the Church of France. Arnauld went into hiding until 1648, the first of many flights he was to experience. In spite of the original controversy, however, Arnauld's views eventually became generally accepted, even among the Jesuits. The work marked a turning point in the Church. By virtue of the reforms it produced in the administration of sacraments as well as in the method of argument, the book earned Arnauld the name The Great Arnauld (*Le Grand Arnauld*). In describing his style of argumentation, Sainte-Beuve calls Arnauld a "logician without pity" who "erected a dike against the flood of false and subtle theology."[4]

Pierre Nicole, the secondary author of the *Logic*, was born at Chartres in 1625. His father was a prominent lawyer with ties to literary circles in Paris. Nicole studied theology at the Sorbonne, where he came into contact with teachers inclined towards Jansenism, and his bachelor's thesis on grace was suspected of

---

[4]   Sainte-Beuve, *Port-Royal*, vol. 1, p. 285.

heretical implications. When Jansenism came under attack at the Sorbonne, he withdrew and went to Port-Royal-des-Champs. While teaching at the Little Schools of Port-Royal, in 1654 he became Arnauld's secretary, helping translate Latin texts. Nicole eventually became one of the most prominent Jansenist writers of the seventeenth century. His most famous work was the *Moral Essays* (1671–8).

The religious disputes marking the history of Jansenism centered around Jansenius's *Augustinus*, and Arnauld's *On Frequent Communion*. The attack against *Augustinus* began with Isaac Habert's sermons during 1643 and his *Defense of the Faith* of 1644. Focusing on eight propositions which he claimed were heretical, Habert attacked both Jansenius for relying too heavily on Augustine's views concerning grace and Port-Royal for propagating these heretical beliefs. These accusations inspired Arnauld to write his *Defense of Monsieur Jansenius* in 1644 and a *Second Defense* in 1645. In 1649 the issue was again raised when Nicolas Cornet, of the theological faculty of the Sorbonne, selected seven propositions from bachelors' theses which he claimed had heretical implications. Although Cornet denied that these propositions had anything to do with *Augustinus*, they were remarkably similar to the ones attacked earlier by Habert. When the faculty would not rule against the propositions, in 1651 Habert wrote a letter to Pope Innocent X, endorsed by seventy-eight French bishops, urging him to condemn the propositions. After heavy lobbying by representatives of Cardinal Mazarin, who wanted the propositions condemned, in 1653 the Pope issued an encyclical, *Cum occasione*, declaring four propositions to be heretical and a fifth false. The four heretical propositions were these:[5]

1. Some commandments [of God] are impossible to the just, who may wish [to obey them] and may exert all their efforts in that direction; they lack the grace necessary to carry them out.
2. In the state of corrupt nature, one can never resist interior grace.
3. In order to act meritoriously or to be blameworthy, it is not necessary that there be in man a liberty that is exempt from necessity. It suffices that liberty be exempt from constraint.
4. The semi-Pelagians admit to the necessity of an inner prevenient grace for each action, even the act of faith. They are heretics insofar as they believe that man's will may resist or accept that grace.

The false proposition was the following:

5. It is a semi-Pelagian sentiment to say that Jesus Christ died or that he shed his blood for all men without exception.

The encyclical hardly settled the matter, however. In the first place, it never referred explicitly to Jansenius's work. And second, it stated the propositions in a way that allowed for differences of interpretation. The Pope was in fact trying to

---

[5] These five propositions are given in Sedgwick, *Jansenism*, p. 68.

walk a fine line between the Jansenists and the Jesuits since he did not want to be seen as condemning either St. Augustine's or St. Thomas's teachings on grace. Under pressure from bishops brought together by Mazarin, however, Innocent X wrote a letter to the French bishops stating that the five propositions were maintained by Jansenius.

Arnauld kept his silence until 1656, when the parish of Saint-Sulpice refused absolution to the Duke of Liancourt if he would not withdraw his granddaughter from Port-Royal. Arnauld published two letters, one "To a Person of Condition," the other "To a Duke and a Peer," which contained two propositions censured by the Sorbonne. The first proposition, raising what was called a question of faith (*question de droit*), was this: "The Fathers show us a just man in the person of St. Peter, to whom the grace without which one can do nothing was lacking on one occasion, when we could not say that he had not sinned." The second proposition opened up a question of fact (*question de fait*) in stating: "One may doubt whether the five propositions condemned by Innocent X and by Alexander VII, as those of Jansenius, the Bishop of Ypres, are in this orator's book."[6] While Arnauld agreed that only the Pope could decide whether the five propositions were heretical, he argued that whether they were actually expressed in Jansenius's work was an empirical question to be investigated by each individual. Judging Arnauld for the Sorbonne were Lescot and other professors against whom he had written. When he refused to subscribe to the censure, Arnauld was excluded from the faculty along with seventy-two other professors and several other faculty. In 1656 Arnauld retired to Port-Royal-des-Champs, where he remained until 1669, after the Peace of the Church was declared in 1668.

Following the censure, Arnauld in effect became the oracle of his party, carrying on an extensive and widely read correspondence, directed mostly against the Jesuits. Arnauld furnished the main ideas for Pascal's *Provincial Letters,* written from 1656 to 1657 in support of the Jansenists, as well as publishing several other theological tracts against the Jesuits. His most famous polemics were *Five Writings in Favor of the Paris Curates Against the Remiss Casuists,* the *New Heresy* and the *Illusions of the Jesuits, Remarks on the Papal Bull of Alexander VII, Five Denunciations* of philosophical sins, and the *Practical Ethics of the Jesuits* in eight volumes. While these works were appearing, Arnauld published works of such philosophical significance that many commentators have regretted he ever devoted his time to theological disputes. In addition to the *General and Rational Grammar* and the *Logic,* he wrote the *New Elements of Geometry,* the fourth set of objections to Descartes' *Meditations,* and *On True and False Ideas* against Malebranche. His complete works, which were published at Lausanne in 1780, comprise no less than forty-four volumes.

In 1656, following Arnauld's exclusion from the Sorbonne, Cardinal Mazarin

---

[6] See Bailly, "Introduction" in *Grammaire générale,* p. xii.

asked the assembly of the clergy to endorse both the encyclical *Cum occasione* and Pope Innocent X's letter attributing the five propositions to the *Augustinus*. The assembly drew up a formulary for all members of the French clergy to sign, promising to obey the papal decrees. In 1655, Innocent X was succeeded by Pope Alexander VII. Although the new Pope did not want to strengthen Mazarin's position, Alexander finally issued a third papal encyclical, *Ad sacram*, in 1657. Here he stated explicitly that the five condemned propositions were found in *Augustinus*, and he condemned them as Jansenius had interpreted them. Mazarin carried out his final act against the Jansenists when he closed the Little Schools in 1659. Although the Little Schools had never enrolled more than fifty students at a time, they exerted a disproportionate influence because of the reputations of both the faculty and students, and the publication of such treatises as *Rules for Educating Children*. Teachers included Claude Lancelot and Pierre Nicole. The most famous students were undoubtedly Jean Racine and the historian Sébastien Le Nain de Tillemont.

In April 1661 the Council of State decreed that all churchmen must sign the formulary drawn up in 1657. Even nuns and lay schoolteachers were required to sign. The text of the formulary read:

> I submit sincerely to the constitution of Innocent X of May 31, 1653 [*Cum occasione*], according to its proper meaning as set forth in the constitution of our Holy Father Alexander VII of October 16, 1656 [*Ad sacram*].
>   I recognize that I am obliged to obey these constitutions, and I condemn with heart and mouth the doctrine contained in the five propositions of Jansenius in his book entitled *Augustinus* that two popes and the bishops have condemned, the doctrine that is not at all that of Saint Augustine, entirely misinterpreted by Jansenius.[7]

The Jansenists responded by appealing to Arnauld's distinction between questions of faith and questions of fact: whether a doctrine was heretical was a matter of faith, but whether it was found in a book or held by a certain person was a matter of fact. Although the Church was infallible in questions of faith, the truth of questions of fact depended on human judgment, which is not infallible. The Jansenists, and particularly the nuns, were divided on whether they should sign the formulary. Shortly before her death in 1661, Angélique Arnauld expressed the view that the appropriate response to persecution is humility and submission in silence. Others agreed that although the Church did not have the right to demand submission on questions of fact, those who disagreed on these matters should maintain silence. They thought one should sign the formulary, while maintaining mental reservations about the Church's position on questions of fact.

A more intransigent position was outlined by Blaise Pascal's sister, Jacqueline (Sister Euphémie of Port-Royal), who argued that a signature of any kind was

---

[7] See Sedgwick, *Jansenism*, p. 108.

incompatible with Christian sincerity. She also challenged the view that women should yield to their superiors, stating that if bishops had the courage of women, then women ought to have the courage of bishops.[8] In her view, endorsed by her brother, anyone who signed the formulary, even while holding mental reservations, was condemning the sacred doctrine of efficacious grace.

Arnauld and Nicole took a third, intermediate position on the formulary, namely that the five propositions were heretical but did not appear in the *Augustinus*. Although Arnauld thought the propositions were highly ambiguous and could be interpreted in both heretical and orthodox ways, he reasoned that the best way to defend Jansenius was to submit on the question of faith. Hence he argued for signing the formulary while appending a statement maintaining a respectful silence on the question of fact. Le Maistre de Sacy, Lancelot, and Le Nain de Tillemont also adopted this position.

In June 1664 the new Archibishop of Paris personally appeared at Port-Royal-de-Paris to interrogate the nuns who had to decide individually whether to sign. Twelve intransigeant nuns were removed to other convents, and the nuns who remained at Port-Royal were put under the supervision of another order. The intransigeant nuns who signed only with express reservations, including Agnès Arnauld, were deprived of the sacraments and confessors, and many experienced severe psychological hardships. In July 1665 the nuns who had been dispersed from Port-Royal-de-Paris were permitted to go to Port-Royal-des-Champs.

After the Peace of the Church in 1668, Pope Clement IX forbade further discussion of the issues connected with the formulary. He permitted the nuns of Port-Royal to participate in the sacraments, and released Le Maistre de Sacy and Fontaine from the Bastille, where they had been imprisoned in 1666. Also in 1669 Arnauld emerged from Port-Royal, announcing his intention to cease defending Jansenism. Both Pope Clement IX, his secret protector, and Louis XIV received him as a man of great distinction and a defender of the Church. Despite these honors he was never able to return to the Sorbonne. During the 1670s, Port-Royal-des-Champs experienced a few years of tranquillity. It re-admitted boarders and postulants, and the *solitaires* returned to their religious tracts. Arnauld and Nicole wrote against the Huguenots and in support of the revocation of the Edict of Nantes. Arnauld also published *The Perpetuity of the Faith of the Catholic Church Concerning the Eucharist* in 1669 in which he attempted to mark Jansenism off from Protestantism, and to smooth over relations with the Church. In 1670 Arnauld, Nicole, and others published the notes Pascal had made for his work defending Christianity, under the title *Thoughts of Monsieur Pascal on Religion and Several Other Subjects* (*Pensées*). Many of the ideas contained in Pascal's writings also appeared in Nicole's important *Moral Essays*, which appeared during the 1670s.

[8]   Ibid., p. 117.

Although after the Peace of the Church Arnauld wrote primarily against the Protestants, he eventually returned to attacking the Jesuits. This finally provoked the mistrust of the King, and Arnauld was once again forced into hiding. In 1679, with the conclusion of the war against the Dutch and the death of their patroness the Duchess of Longueville, Port-Royal again found itself under siege, this time by King Louis XIV. The confessors, postulants, and pensioners of Port-Royal were expelled by decree of the archbishop of Paris. Arnauld went into exile in the Austrian Netherlands in 1679, and wandered from city to city, writing with an ardor that never abated. He continued to criticize both Protestants and ecclesiastical officials for interfering with free inquiry into natural phenomena. In part this defense was based on a fear of the effects of free thinking, since drawing a firm line between religious and scientific matters would protect divine authority in questions of theology. When Pierre Nicole, who had joined him in exile, admitted one day that he was tired of waging war, Arnauld remarked that he would have all of eternity to rest. But unlike Arnauld, Nicole yearned for peace. So he returned to Paris in 1683 where he was reconciled with the authorities. He died in Paris in 1695. Antoine Arnauld died at Brussels on 8 August 1694, at the age of 82. His body was buried in the Church of Saint Catherine at Brussels. His heart was taken to Port-Royal, and in 1710 was moved from there to Palaiseau.

Following Arnauld's death, Jansenists continued to circulate polemical tracts and to feud with the Jesuits. The issue of the formulary was again raised in 1701 before the faculty of the Sorbonne. This case concerned Pascal's nephew, the priest Louis Périer, who had continued to proclaim the doctrines of efficacious grace and contrition. The question was whether he was entitled to final absolution on his deathbed. When forty professors affirmed his rights, Louis XIV again decided to take action against the Jansenists. He had the Jansenist leaders Pasquier Quesnel and Gabriel Gerberon arrested in the Spanish Netherlands by his nephew King Philip V of Spain in 1703. Gerberon was eventually imprisoned at Vincennes, and was released in 1710 after signing the formulary. Quesnel escaped from prison, but his papers and correspondence were confiscated by the Spanish authorities. Aided by the Jesuits, Louis XIV persuaded Pope Clement XI to promulgate another encyclical, *Vineam Domini*, against the Jansenists. Arriving in France in 1705, it specifically condemned maintaining a silence on the question of fact concerning the five propositions of Jansenius. In 1703 the nuns had again been ordered to sign the formulary, and again they refused to sign without noting their reservations. Finally Louis received the Pope's permission to suppress the convent, and in 1709 he dispersed the nuns. He had the bodies of the more prominent *solitaires* and nuns moved elsewhere or thrown into a common grave, and in 1711 the buildings were leveled. A final encyclical, *Unigenitus*, promulgated in 1713 by Pope Clement XI, condemned 101 propositions from Quesnel's *Moral Reflections* including, among other ideas, the doctrine of efficacious grace, Saint-Cyran's notion of contrition, the right to translate Scripture into the vernacular, and the right of informed Christians to interpret Scripture on their own. Despite these attacks and the end of Port-Royal, Jansenism survived until the Revolution of 1789.

Philosophical themes and influences

Although St. Augustine shaped the theology of Jansenism, René Descartes was the true philosophical father of the *Port-Royal Logic*. In contrast to Jansenists such as Saint-Cyran and Le Maistre de Sacy, who suspected the efficacy of reason, Arnauld and Nicole wholeheartedly embraced Descartes' rationalism. In fact, the Port-Royal theory of knowledge is taken almost verbatim from Descartes. But Cartesian rationalism is, in its broad outlines, compatible with Augustinian views, and so Arnauld and Nicole often cite the authority of both philosophers. The philosophy of the *Logic* is not confined, however, to epistemological questions. For Descartes the theory of knowledge is inextricably linked with his views of mental and physical reality. Hence we also find Arnauld and Nicole espousing Cartesian dualism as well as the principles of Descartes' mechanistic physics.

In endorsing Cartesian thought the authors of the *Logic* stand squarely opposed to Aristotle and the Scholastics on most philosophical issues. Hence the *Logic* contains criticisms of practically all of Aristotle's fundamental ideas, most borrowed directly from Descartes. Arnauld and Nicole also attack their empiricist contemporaries – especially Thomas Hobbes and Pierre Gassendi – not only for their erroneous views about knowledge, but also for their mistaken metaphysical and physical theories. A third major target is Montaigne, first, for his skeptical arguments, and second for his libertine tendencies. In what follows I shall summarize these main themes in the *Logic*.

As we have seen, the Port-Royal theology is based on St. Augustine's doctrines of original sin, the natural incapacity of humans to act morally of their own free will, and the irresistible efficacy of grace. Moreover, although Arnauld and Nicole accept the Augustinian view that faith and reason each has its own proper domain – religious matters for faith, natural phenomena for reason – they emphasize the importance of human reason in supplementing faith in theological matters. In chapter 12 of Part IV, citing Augustine, they maintain that faith always presupposes some reason, since reason persuades us that there are things we ought to believe, even though we lack the appropriate evidence.

In setting out their philosophical foundations, the authors borrow whole arguments from Descartes' *Rules for the Direction of the Mind, Discourse on the Method*, and *Meditations*, occasionally acknowledging their source. The issues most addressed concern the nature and sources of ideas, the analysis of mental faculties, and the primacy of reason or the understanding in attaining certainty. Underlying the entire text is Descartes' anti-empiricist principle that certainty depends solely on the intellect. In Parts I and IV of the *Logic*, Arnauld and Nicole argue that it is possible to attain certainty concerning the nature of both mental and physical reality. This indubitable knowledge is based on self-evident propositions intuited by the understanding. Following Descartes, the authors label these perceptions "clear and distinct," although their analysis, in chapter 9 of Part I, differs somewhat from Descartes' account. The authors also cite Descartes' famous *cogito* argument ("I think, therefore I am") as the primary example of knowledge by intellectual intuition. As Arnauld and Nicole recognize, a version of this argument appeared in Augustine, who also claimed that it is impossible to doubt that one is thinking and existing (or is alive, as Augustine but not Descartes would have it). In Augustine this is referred to as the "interiorization principle," and it coincides exactly with Descartes' view that truths about one's own mental states are self-evident and self-verifying. Like Descartes, Arnauld and Nicole regard mathematics, and in particular geometry, as the paradigm of knowledge. Despite their criticisms in Part IV of Euclid's definitions and the order of his proofs, they maintain that only mathematics exhibits the essential features of a true science, in the simplicity of its concepts and the rigor of its demonstrations.

On the other side of the same coin, the authors share Descartes' mistrust of sensory experience and his evaluation of sensory states as obscure and confused. They cite the usual cases of deception by the senses and agree with Descartes that such sensible qualities as color, sound, odor, taste, hot and cold, are merely the content of sensations in the mind and not real properties of corporeal substances. Even though sense perception plays a role in developing scientific hypotheses, and spatial images are occasionally useful in geometry, a true understanding of reality is based on purely intellectual representation. In fact, the empiricist reliance on the senses, characteristic of Aristotelian and Scholastic thought, is an infantile form of epistemology. Just as the child assumes that the world really is the way it appears, empiricists are misled by a naive trust in sense experience. By means of the correct use of "natural reason" and the Cartesian method of doubt, however, the knower can overcome these childhood prejudices and can attain a scientific understanding of the world.

The rationalism of the *Port-Royal Logic* is also partly responsible for its anti-rhetorical polemics. Combined with the puritanical nature of Jansenism, their rationalism leads the authors to condemn writing that relies heavily on metaphorical or figurative styles. Following the line that sensory experience interferes with clear and distinct perceptions of reality, Arnauld and Nicole argue that philosophical writing should avoid appeals to the passions. Now when one's purpose is to arouse emotion in the reader – for example, to inspire love of God – then a more figurative style may be appropriate. But whenever the subject concerns speculative matters that ought not affect the emotions, an ornate style only leads to sophisms and fallacious reasoning.

In addition to the empiricists, a second target of Port-Royal's criticisms are the skeptics, and particularly ancient Pyrrhonism as revived by Montaigne. The Cartesians were not threatened by skeptical arguments concerning the senses, because they denied that the senses played any significant role in producing certain knowledge. But the matter is quite different concerning skepticism with regard to reason. So the authors are particularly harsh against philosophers who question the capacity of reason to produce knowledge about oneself, God, and the external world. In fact they accuse Montaigne and other skeptics of insincerity and hypocrisy because they deny the self-validating nature of clear and distinct perception.

Cartesian metaphysics and physics are also well represented in the *Logic*. Descartes' major contribution to metaphysics was his dualism, his account of the mind and the body as two distinct kinds of substance. The defining attribute of a mind or soul is thinking, whereas the feature essential to corporeal substance is being extended spatially. Since Descartes thought there was no necessary connection between thinking and being extended, he maintained that minds and bodies share no properties in common and are capable of existing independently. Among existing things, human beings are unique in being a composite of mental and corporeal substances. As states of consciousness, experiences are mental states, although they may be causally related to states of physical substances. Aristotle, by contrast, had a non-dualistic or functional conception of the soul as the principle of life in all living things. For him even plants and nonhuman animals are endowed with souls. Only humans, however, are capable of higher rational activities. Thus Aristotle and Descartes differ radically over the conception of the soul and its relation to physical substance. It is no surprise, then, to find attacks on Aristotle's view of the soul throughout the *Logic*. Their dualism also leads Arnauld and Nicole to object to the view that all reality is physical, whether espoused by ancient philosophers such as Lucretius, the Epicureans, and the Stoics, or their contemporaries Hobbes and Gassendi. Many of these arguments occur in the discussions of definition, and the types of confusions that can take place in defining words.

Equally prominent is Port-Royal's espousal of Descartes' mechanistic physics. As we saw above, Arnauld and Nicole agree with Descartes that sensory qualities cannot be real properties of physical things. The only properties belonging to bodies are extension, motion, and shape. In consequence, all changes in physical states can be accounted for in terms of the motions and impacts of particles on one another. In endorsing Cartesian physics, the authors of the *Logic* condemn as "occult" explanations in terms of "natural motion" or "attractive" powers acting at a distance, such as magnetism and gravity. They also share Descartes' objection to the Scholastic theory of substantial forms. According to this theory one body transmits a quality such as heat, for example, to another by transmitting the "form" of heat from the first to the second body. From the mechanistic point of view, these substantial forms are every bit as mysterious and unintelligible as forces acting at a distance. Now one peculiarity of Descartes' mechanism is his identification of matter with extension. Unlike atomists, who distinguish between the space a particle occupies and the matter making up the particle, Descartes thought matter is constituted solely by extension. Hence there is no such thing as empty space.

Following this line of reasoning, Arnauld and Nicole also argue against theories postulating a void, whether advocated by the ancients or their contemporary Gassendi.

Finally, the *Logic* is indebted to Blaise Pascal for the theory of definition in chapters 12 through 15 of Part I, as well as the account in Part IV of the relation of definitions to axioms and demonstrations. Although Aristotle had distinguished nominal from real definitions (that is, definitions of words from definitions of things), Pascal extended this analysis in *On the Geometrical Mind and the Art of Persuasion* (probably written between 1657 and 1658). His treatment is noteworthy for rejecting the earlier theory of definitions in terms of genus and difference, and for substituting a Cartesian account in terms of the ideas naturally available to all. Pascal also argued that it is impossible to define all terms, since some ideas are so simple that words expressing them cannot be defined. Many of these views are imported wholesale into the Port-Royal theory of scientific method.

The place of the *Port-Royal Logic* in history

The *Port-Royal Logic* was the most influential logic from Aristotle to the end of the nineteenth century. The 1981 critical edition by Pierre Clair and François Girbal lists 63 French editions and 10 English editions, one of which (1818) served as a text in the course of education at the Universities of Cambridge and Oxford. The work treats topics in logic, grammar, philosophy of language, theory of knowledge, and metaphysics.

As I mentioned earlier, the semantics of the *Logic* is an interesting amalgam of medieval and seventeenth-century theories. Arnauld and Nicole attempt to force a Cartesian view of judgment, none too happily, onto the traditional theory of categorical propositions and a medieval term logic. Similarly, in spite of their Cartesian views of intellectual intuition and the nature of inference, the authors devote Part III on reasoning to the medieval theory of syllogism. So problems are raised, inevitably, by the attempt to graft a new theory of knowledge onto an existing logical framework.

Descartes' influence is evident in two basic features of the semantics. First is the view that thought is prior to language, that words are merely external, conventional signs of independent, private mental states. On this view, strictly speaking, linguistic utterances signify the thoughts occurring in the speaker's mind. Although the association between words and ideas is conventional and thus arbitrary, language can signify thought insofar as both are articulated systems: there is a correlation between the structure of a complex linguistic expression and the natural structure of the ideas it expresses.

The second feature is the general framework of the Cartesian theory of ideas, including both a philosophy of mind as well as an epistemology. Although Arnauld and Nicole depart from Descartes in some of the details of this theory, by and large they accept its general assumptions. First is the traditional view that there are four mental operations required for scientific knowledge: conceiving, judging, reasoning, and ordering. These operations must occur in this order, since each operation has for its elements the product of the preceding operation. Arnauld and Nicole agree with Descartes that conceiving consists in a simple apprehension of ideas by the understanding, whereas judging is an action of the will. It is possible to operate on ideas without making judgments, for example, to form complex ideas out of simpler ideas, and to analyze complex ideas into their parts. The Port-Royal authors differ from Descartes in identifying forming a proposition with the act of judgment. Descartes himself drew a sharp line between making a judgment and merely apprehending a proposition, since in mere apprehension the mind is passive, and Descartes thought it possible for an idea to take a propositional form. The Port-Royal treatment of the verb unfortunately makes it impossible to distinguish between simply apprehending a proposition and judging its truth. In the *Logic* the verb both connects the subject and predicate, and has assertive force; hence, forming a proposition is equivalent to judging it.

Another classical aspect of the *Logic* is the treatment of negation. Port-Royal follows the tradition in treating affirmation and denial as two polar forms of judgment. On their account, propositions containing negative particles such as "not" constitute denials as opposed to affirmations. Further, denial is an action opposite to affirming. Since in affirming one connects the subject- and predicate-ideas to form a propositional unity, in denying one must separate the subject from the predicate. Hence negation belongs to the action rather than to the propositional content of the act.

The Port-Royal semantics is a good example of the traditional "two-name" theory of the proposition. Every simple proposition is composed of the same elements: a subject, a predicate, and a copula. Following the theory of categorical propositions, the authors classify all propositions by quantity as universal, particular, or singular, and as affirmative or negative by quality. They also follow the tradition in treating singular propositions as universals. Hence they use the standard A, E, I, O designations for universal affirmative, universal negative, particular affirmative, and particular negative propositions. In trying to force more complex forms of proposition into this categorical framework, Arnauld and Nicole run into the difficulties which motivated the development of modern logic at the end of the nineteenth century.

Despite their traditional view of the proposition, the Port-Royal semantics is based on Descartes' metaphysics. Without using the terminology, they recognize the medieval distinction between categorematic and syncategorematic expressions. Categorematic expressions, or "terms," are those which can serve as a subject or predicate of a proposition. Syncategorematic expressions include verbs and quantifiers, since they signify operations on ideas (such as judgment) rather than the ideas themselves. Undoubtedly the most significant contribution of the *Port-Royal Logic* to semantics is the analysis of general terms. General terms are categorematic words such as "man" and "philosopher" that signify ideas representing more than one individual. In chapters 6 and 7 of Part I, the authors recognize two aspects of the significance of general terms: the comprehension and the extension. The comprehension of a general term consists of the set of attributes essential to the idea it expresses; the extension is constituted by the "subjects to which this idea applies." Unlike the modern view, which identifies the extension of a predicate with the individuals to which the term applies, Port-Royal conceives the extension as including the species (or subsets) of the general idea as well as the individuals (members of the set) possessing the relevant attributes. Despite this ambiguity, the analysis marks an important simplification of the medieval theory of supposition, which attempted to account for all the varieties of reference. Although the distinction was prefigured in both ancient and Scholastic works and was also formulated by Leibniz, the Port-Royal account represents the clearest treatment up to that time.

A second important contribution to the history of semantics is the authors' analysis of the difference between restrictive or "determinative" and nonrestrictive or "explicative" subordinate clauses, developed in the discussions of complex terms and complex propositions. Although their theory of embedded propositions runs into difficulty with their view of the difference between ideas and propositions, their treatment is noteworthy for foreshadowing the distinction between analytic and synthetic propositions.

To appreciate the place of the *Port-Royal Logic* in history, it might be helpful to recall the major developments in logic and philosophy of language after the seventeenth century. Perhaps the first important shift came with Kant's theory of judgment as a synthetic activity in *The Critique of Pure Reason* (1781). Although Kant accepted the traditional logic, he rejected both Descartes' notion of passive intellectual intuition of the truth, and the priority of conceiving to judging. Gottlob Frege inaugurated modern logic by discarding the traditional theory of the proposition. First he did away with the subject-predicate analysis, including the traditional theory of the copula. In its place he substituted a sharp distinction between expressions for objects, which he characterized as "complete," and function-expressions, which are "incomplete" in the sense that they contain gaps for other expressions. Here the unity of the proposition depends not on a linking term such as the copula, but on the fit between complete and incomplete expressions. This syntactical basis allowed him to lay the framework for both sentential and quantificational logic. Negation was analyzed as a sentential function, part of the content of a proposition, rather than the act of denial. At one stroke Frege dismantled the traditional classification scheme of affirmative and negative propositions. The invention of quantifiers replaced the classification of universal, particular, and singular propositions, and permitted an account of embedded generality that was not possible on the traditional subject-predicate analysis.

Subsequent developments in the philosophy of language and philosophy of mind have led to a view of meaning as more holistic and socially dependent than the Cartesian view. Wittgenstein's private language argument posed a serious challenge to the account of language as a merely external expression of private, independent thought. Speech act theory has generalized the notion of the force of an utterance, already present in Frege's account of assertion, and brought into relief the contextual aspects of meaning. With a few exceptions, most philosophers regard these developments as putting a definitive end to the Cartesian views that thought is prior to language, and conceiving prior to judging.

There are, of course, many other aspects of the *Port-Royal Logic* of interest to philosophers, linguists, theologians, and rhetoricians. In this introduction I have concentrated only on the features having the most general philosophical import. My hope is that this translation will arouse a new interest among English-speaking scholars in the complex constellation of views presented in the *Logic*.

Chronology

1679	Arnauld goes into exile in Flanders, then the Netherlands
1683	Nicole returns to Paris; fifth edition of *Logic*
1694	Arnauld dies, Brussels, 8 August
1695	Nicole dies, Paris, 16 November

Further reading

The classical history of the Port-Royal Abbey and the development of Jansenism in France is available in French in C. A. Sainte-Beuve, *Port Royal* (3 vols., Paris, Bibliothèque de la Pléiade, 1961–5). Alexander Sedgwick's more recent history, *Jansenism in Seventeenth-Century France* (Charlottesville, University Press of Virginia, 1977), presents a clear account of the theological and political controversies in which Jansenists engaged. Ruth Clark's *Strangers and Sojourners at Port Royal* (New York, Octagon Books, 1932; reprint 1972) details the connections between the British Isles and the Jansenists of France and Holland.

Very little of Arnauld's work has been translated into English. In addition to the Dickoff and James translation of the *Logic* and the translation of *The General and Rational Grammar* by Rieux and Rollin, his best known writings have been the *Fourth Objections to the "Meditations on First Philosophy"* in *The Philosophical Writings of Descartes*, trans. by John Cottingham, Robert Stoothoff, and Dugald Murdoch (3 vols., Cambridge, Cambridge University Press, 1985–91), vol. 2; and his correspondence with Leibniz, in *Leibniz: Discourse on Metaphysics, Correspondence with Arnauld and Monadology*, trans. by G. R. Montgomery (Lasalle, IL, Open Court, 1968). Two English translations of Arnauld's *On True and False Ideas* appeared in 1990. The more accurate one is Elmar J. Kremer's *On True and False Ideas, New Objections to Descartes' Meditations and Descartes' Replies* (Lewiston, NY, Edwin Mellen Press). Also available is Stephen Gaukroger's *On True and False Ideas* (Manchester, Manchester University Press).

Until recently, few books were published on the philosophical views of Arnauld and the Port-Royalists. An earlier text was Jean Laporte's *La Doctrine de Port-Royal* (2 vols., Paris, Presses Universitaires de France, 1923). Another is L. Marin's *La Critique du discours: Sur la "logique de Port-Royal" et les "Pensées" de Pascal* (Paris, Les Éditions de Minuit, 1975). In the past several years, new interest in Arnauld's work and his connections to other thinkers of his time has resulted in several volumes. An overview of Arnauld's thought is available in A. R. Ndiaye's *La Philosophie d'Antoine Arnauld* (Paris, J. Vrin, 1991). Steven Nadler's *Arnauld and the Cartesian Philosophy of Ideas* (Princeton, Princeton University Press, 1989) studies Arnauld's controversy with Malebranche over the status of ideas. R. C. Sleigh, Jr., examines Arnauld's relations to Leibniz in *Leibniz and Arnauld: A Commentary on Their Correspondence* (New Haven, CT, Yale University Press, 1990). Toronto Studies in Philosophy has published a collection of articles on various aspects of Arnauld's thought, *The Great Arnauld and Some of His Philosophical Correspondents*, ed. Elmar J. Kremer (Toronto, University of Toronto Press, 1994). The last four volumes have fairly detailed bibliographies.

Even among Arnauld's commentators, relatively little attention has been paid to his logic and linguistic theory. Marc Dominicy's *La Naissance de la grammaire moderne* (Brussels, Pierre Mardaga, 1985) examines the formal aspects of the Port-Royal semantics and pragmatics. Jean-Claude Pariente's *L'Analyse du langage à Port-Royal* (Paris, Les Éditions de Minuit, 1985) presents a less technical discussion in six essays. Two earlier articles are Jan Miel's "Pascal, Port-Royal and Cartesian Linguistics," *Journal of the History of Ideas*, 30 (1969), 261–71, and Dragan Stoianovici, "Definite Descriptions in *Port-Royal Logic*," *Revue Roumaine des Sciences Sociales, Série de Philosophie et Logique*, 20 (1976), 145–54. Finally, I discuss the Port-Royal semantics and its relations to modern semantic theory since Frege in two essays, "The Port-Royal Semantics of Terms," *Synthese*, 96 (1993), 455–75, and "Judgment and Predication in the Port-Royal Logic" in *The Great Arnauld*, ed. Kremer, pp. 3–27.

Works cited in the text and notes

Aquinas, St. Thomas. *Summa Theologiae* in *Injustice*, ed. and trans. M. Lefébure in *St. Thomas Aquinas: Summa Theologiae*, Oxford, Blackfriars, vol. 38, 1975

Aristotle. *The Complete Works of Aristotle*, ed. Jonathan Barnes, The Revised Oxford Translation, 2 vols., Princeton, Princeton University Press, 1984

Arnauld, Antoine. *La Perpétuité de la foi de l'Église Catholique touchant l'Eucharistie, défendue contre les livres du Sieur Claude Ministre de Charenton*, 3 vols., Paris, Ch. Savreux, 1672

and Claude Lancelot. *General and Rational Grammar: The Port Royal Grammar*, ed. and trans. Jacques Rieux and Bernard E. Rollin, The Hague, Mouton, 1975

and Claude Lancelot. *Grammaire générale et raisonnée de Port-Royal*, Geneva, Slatkine Reprints, 1968

and Pierre Nicole. *La Logique ou l'art de penser*, édition par Pierre Clair et François Girbal, Paris, J. Vrin, 1981

and Pierre Nicole. *L'Art de penser: La Logique de Port-Royal*, édition par B. von Freytag Löringhoff et H. E. Brekle, Stuttgart-Bad Cannstatt, Friedrich Frommann Verlag, 1967

St. Augustine. *Basic Writings of Saint Augustine*, ed. Whitney J. Oates, 2 vols., New York, Random House, 1948

Contra Cresconium Grammaticum Partis Donati, Migne, *Patrologia Latina*, vol. 43

The Literal Meaning of Genesis, trans. John Hammond Taylor, S.J., 2 vols., New York, Newman Press, 1982

The Teacher, the Free Choice of the Will, Grace and Free Will in *The Fathers of the Church*, trans. Robert P. Russell, Washington, D. C., Catholic University of America Press, 1968

Treatises on Various Subjects, ed. Roy J. Deferrari in *The Fathers of the Church*, Washington, D. C., Catholic University of America Press, vol. 14, 1965

The Works of Aurelius Augustine, Bishop of Hippo, ed. Rev. Marcus Dods, 15 vols., Edinburgh, T. & T. Clark, 1872

Writings of Saint Augustine, ed. Ludwig Schopp, 18 vols., New York, CIMA Publishing Co., 1948

Balzac, Jean-Louis Guez de. *Œuvres*, 2 vols., Geneva, Slatkine Reprints, 1971

Baronius, Caesar. *Annalium Ecclesiasticarum Caes. Baronii*, I–XII, Antwerp, 1610–58

Buxtorf, Johann. *Epistome Grammaticae Hebraeae, breviter et methodice ad publicam scholarum usum proposita* ..., Basileae, typis Comadi Waldkirchii, 1613

Campanella, Thomas. *De sensu rerum et magia*, libri quatuor, Tobias Adami rec. Frankfurt, 1620

Cicero. *De Finibus Bonorum et Malorum*, trans. H. Rackham, Loeb Classical Library, Cambridge, Harvard University Press, 1951

    De Natura Deorum, Academica, trans. H. Rackham, in *Cicero in 28 Volumes*, Loeb Classical Library, Cambridge, Harvard University Press, vol. 19, 1967

    De Oratore, trans. E. W. Sutton, in *Cicero in 28 Volumes*, Loeb Classical Library, Cambridge, Harvard University Press, vol. 3, 1979

    The Letters to His Friends, trans. W. Glynn Williams, 3 vols., Loeb Classical Library, Cambridge, Harvard University Press, 1965

    The Speeches, trans. N. H. Watts, Loeb Classical Library, Cambridge, Harvard University Press, 1958

    Tusculan Disputations, trans. J. E. King, Loeb Classical Library, Cambridge, Harvard University Press, 1960

    The Verrine Orations, trans. L. H. G. Greenwood, Loeb Classical Library, 2 vols., Cambridge, Harvard University Press, 1953

Claudianus, Claudius. *Claudian*, trans. Maurice Platnauer, 2 vols., New York, G. P. Putnam's Sons, 1922

Cordemoy, Gerauld de. *Discours physique de la parole*, ed. Pierre Clair et François Girbal, Paris, Presses Universitaires de France, 1968

Descartes, René. *Œuvres de Descartes*, ed. Ch. Adam and P. Tannery, rev. ed. Paris, Vrin/CNRS, 1964–76

    The Philosophical Writings of Descartes, trans. John Cottingham, Robert Stoothoff and Dugald Murdoch, volume 3 also translated by Anthony Kenny, 3 vols., Cambridge, Cambridge University Press, 1985–91

Euclid. *Euclid's Elements*, ed. Isaac Todhunter, London, J. M. Dent & Sons, Ltd., 1955

Eustachio a Sancto Paulo. *Summa philosophica quadripartita, de rebus Dialecticis, Moralibus, Physicis et Metaphysicis, Fr. Eustachio a Sancto Paulo, a congregatione Fuliensi*, 2 vols., Paris, 1609

Gassendi, Pierre. *Institutio Logica (1658)*, trans. Howard Jones, Assen, Netherlands, Van Gorcum, 1981

    Opera Omnia, 6 vols., Lyon, 1658

Horace. *The Complete Works of Horace (Quintus Horatius Flaccus)*, trans. with notes by Charles E. Passage, New York, Frederick Ungar Pub. Co., 1983

The Odes and Epodes, trans. C. E. Bennett, Loeb Classical Library, Cambridge, Harvard University Press, 1960

Satires, Epistles and Ars Poetica, trans. H. Rushton Fairclough, Loeb Classical Library, Cambridge, Harvard University Press, 1978

Juvenal. *Satires in Juvenal and Persius*, trans. G. G. Ramsay, Loeb Classical Library, Cambridge, Harvard University Press, 1961

Launoy, Jean de. *De Varia Aristotelis Fortuna in Academia Parisiensi*, 2nd ed. Hagaecomitum, Adrianum Vlacq, 1656

Lortie, André. *Traité de la Sainte Cène ... où sont examinées les nouvelles subtilités de Monsieur Arnauld, sur les paroles "Ceci est mon corps"*, Saumur, R. Pean, 1675

Lucan. *The Civil War (Pharsalia)*, trans. J. D. Duff, Loeb Classical Library, Cambridge, Harvard University Press, 1977

Malebranche, Nicolas. *The Search After Truth*, trans. Thomas M. Lennon and Paul J. Olscamp, Columbus, Ohio State University Press, 1980

Martial. *Epigrams*, trans. Walter C. A. Ker, Loeb Classical Library, 2 vols., Cambridge, Harvard University Press, 1961

Montaigne, Michel de. *The Complete Works of Montaigne*, trans. Donald M. Frame, Stanford, Stanford University Press, 1957

Ovid. *Metamorphoses*, trans. Rolfe Humphries, Bloomington, Indiana University Press, 1955

Pascal, Blaise. *Œuvres Complètes*, Paris, Éditions de Seuil, 1963

Pascal, Selections, ed. by Richard H. Popkin, New York, Macmillan Publishing Company, 1989

Pascal's Pensées, trans. by Martin Turnell, New York, Harper & Brothers, 1962

Pensées and the Provincial Letters, trans. W. F. Trotter and Thomas M'Crie, Modern Library, New York, Random House, 1941

The Physical Treatises of Pascal: The Equilibrium of Liquids and The Weight of the Mass of the Air, trans. I. H. B. and A. G. H. Spiers, New York, Farrar, Straus and Giroux, 1973

Plato. *Theaetetus*, trans. John McDowell, Oxford, Clarendon Press, 1973

Publius Syrus. *Publii Syri sententiae; ad fidem codicum optiorum primum recensuit Eduardus Weolfflin*. Accedit incerti autoris liber qui vulgo dicitur de moribus, Lipsiae, in aedibus B. G. Teubneri, 1869

Quintilianus, Marcus Fabius. *The Institutio Oratoria of Quintilian*, trans. H. E. Butler, Loeb Classical Library, 4 vols., Cambridge, Harvard University Press, 1959

Scaliger, Julius Caesar. *De Causis linguae latinae libri tredecim*, Lugdunum apud Seb. Gryphium, 1540

Iul. Caes. Scaligeri adversus Desid. Erasmum orationes duae, Eloquentiae Romanae vindices ... Tolosae apud *Dominicum Bosc, et Petrum Posc*, 1621

Seneca. *Ad Lucilium Epistulae Morales*, trans. Richard M. Gummere, Loeb Classical Library, 3 vols., Cambridge, Harvard University Press, 1961

Seneca's Tragedies, trans. Frank Justus Miller, Loeb Classical Library, 2 vols.,
Cambridge, Harvard University Press, 1960

Stevin, Simon. *The Principal Works of Simon Stevin*, ed. D. J. Struik, 4 vols.,
Amsterdam, C. V. Swets & Zeitlinger, 1958

Tacitus. *The Histories*, trans. Clifford H. Moore, Loeb Classical Library, 5 vols.,
Cambridge, Harvard University Press, 1968

Terence. *The Comedies*, trans. Betty Radice, New York, Penguin Books, 1976

Vergilius Maro, P. *Virgil*, trans. H. Rushton Fairclough, Loeb Classical Library, 2
vols., Cambridge, Harvard University Press, 1965

Note on the text and translation

La Logique ou l'art de penser was first published in 1662 and saw four major revisions during the authors' lifetimes. The definitive state of the *Logic* is represented by the final 1683 version. It contains several highly significant additions, notably chapters 4 and 15 of Part I, and chapters 1-2 (taken from the *Grammar*), and 12 and 14 of Part II. The main text is introduced by a Preface (*Avertissement*), a Foreword (*Avis*), and two Discourses. The first Discourse appeared in the first (1662) edition; the second Discourse was added in 1664 and contains replies to criticisms of the previous edition.

This translation is based on the critical edition by Pierre Clair and François Girbal, which first appeared in 1965 and was revised in 1981.[1] Clair and Girbal use the 1683 version of the *Logic* as their basis and indicate textual variations from the four earlier versions in footnotes. Their edition also contains a chronological catalogue of all French, Latin, and English editions, as well as richly detailed annotations, based on notes originally provided by two nineteenth-century editors, Charles Jourdain and Alfred Fouillée. A second major French edition in three volumes was published in 1967 by Bruno von Freytag Löringhoff and Herbert E. Brekle.[2] Volume 1 contains the original (1662) text of the *Logic*, volume 2 lists textual variants from 1664-83, and volume 3 consists of textual variants between the 1662 text and the manuscript Fr. 19915 of the Bibliothèque Nationale, evidently an early handwritten copy of the *Logic*.[3] There are only minor differences between the Clair–Girbal and the Löringhoff–Brekle editions – mostly a few discrepancies in attributing citations.

Until 1964, contemporary English-speaking readers had access only to the nineteenth-century Thomas Spencer Baynes translation. This edition is serviceable although outdated. In 1964 *The Art of Thinking*, translated by James Dickoff and Patricia James, was published. It favors readability and plausibility over accuracy, and

---

[1]   *La logique ou l'art de penser*, édition critique par Pierre Clair et François Girbal (Paris, J. Vrin, 1981).
[2]   *L'art de penser: La Logique de Port-Royal*, édition par B. von Freytag Löringhoff et H. E. Brekle (Stuttgart-Bad Cannstatt, Friedrich Frommann Verlag, 1967).
[3]   See p. 3 n. 3.

may thus be unsuitable for close scholarly work. As the translators mention in their introduction, for example, Arnauld and Nicole do repeatedly conflate theses about thought, language, and the external world, and this cannot fail to strike the modern reader as muddled. But these confusions are themselves of considerable philosophical and historical interest, and the tendency of Dickoff and James to introduce post-Fregean distinctions not found in the original can mislead those without access to the French text. The present translation strives to render the original as faithfully as possible – confusions and all – trusting the reader to sort things out.

Although this is a work on logic and language, the reader should keep in mind that the vocabulary of the seventeenth century does not approach ours in precision. While the authors clearly recognize the difference between the validity and the soundness of an argument, for example, they typically evaluate arguments in rather general, nontechnical terms. Thus an argument may be "good" (*bon*) or "bad" (*mauvais*), and even "true" (*vrai*) or "false" (*faux*). Fallacious arguments may be labelled "vicious" (*vicieux*) or "defective" (*défectueux*). In analyzing syllogisms their term most closely approaching "valid" is *concluan*, but since some "concluding moods" (*modes concluans*) of syllogisms violate the rules of logic, the translation here cannot be exact. In short, the reader is cautioned not to take occurrences of English terms such as "valid" and "sound" in this translation to represent technical equivalents in the French. I have generally tried to avoid literal translations such as "true argument" which would be jarring to a modern reader.

A second case where caution is advised concerns the French verb *convenir à* which literally means "to agree with or to conform to." The difficulty arises because the authors use the term widely and indifferently to express a relation sometimes between ideas, sometimes between ideas or words and the things they signify, and occasionally even between genus and species. The term is translated here variously, depending on the context. Where it expresses a logical relation between ideas, for example, this text may say one idea "conforms to" or "is compatible with" another. Where the term indicates a semantic relation between a word and a thing, it may say the word "applies to" the thing. Again the reader is warned not to assume that these differences represent technical distinctions in the French. My aim throughout has been to make the translation both accurate and sufficiently general to avoid anachronism, while rendering the French into smooth and idiomatic English.

This translation follows the Clair and Girbal format, and thus chapters are organized as in the fifth edition. (The table below displays the differences among the five major editions.) For readers who wish to compare this translation with the French, the page numbers from the Clair and Girbal 1981 edition are given in brackets in the text. I have maintained the paragraph breaks in the original while translating sentences more freely, since the authors' sentences are extremely long. Also, the French text includes many Latin quotations, only some of which were translated into French. Where Arnauld and Nicole did not provide a translation, an English translation appears in brackets following the Latin quotation.

The annotations rely heavily on those of Clair and Girbal, and fall into three types. The first, marked by letters, give textual variants from the first four editions. Those which quote exactly from an earlier edition begin with three dots, and end with roman numerals in parentheses specifying the editions in which the variant occurred. Others simply indicate the edition in which a passage first appeared. A second type of note gives sources of works cited in the text, where possible listing a readily available English translation. In cases where the authors' quotations from other works are not exact, the note identifies the discrepancy. The last type contains biographical information on less well-known figures referred to in the text as well as sources of some of the Port-Royal views. For the sake of brevity I have not reproduced all the Clair and Girbal references to works of other philosophers, particularly Descartes, from which Arnauld and Nicole borrow; readers who are interested in this information should consult their edition.

ORGANIZATION OF CHAPTERS IN THE FIVE EDITIONS

	I (1662)	II (1664)	III (1668)	IV (1671)	V (1683)
	...	...	...	...	Preface
	Foreword	Foreword	Foreword	Foreword	Foreword
	Discourse	1st Discourse	1st Discourse	1st Discourse	1st Discourse
	...	2nd Discourse	2nd Discourse	2nd Discourse	2nd Discourse
Part I	I–III	I–III	I–III	I– III	I–III
	...	...	...	...	IV
	IV	IV	IV	IV	V
	V	V	V	V	VI
	VI	VI	VI	VI	VII
	VII	VII	VII	VII	VIII
	VIII	VIII	VIII	VIII	IX
	...	IX	IX	IX	X
	IX	X	X	X	XI
	X	XI	XI	XI	XII
	XI	XII	XII	XII	XIII
	XII	XIII	XIII	XIII	XIV
	...	...	...	...	XV
Part II	...	...	...	...	I
	...	...	...	...	II
	I	I	I	I	III
	II	II	II	II	IV
	III	III	III	III	V
	IV	IV	IV	IV	VI
	V	V	V	V	VII
	VI	VI	VI	VI	VIII
	VII	VII	VII	VII	IX

ORGANIZATION OF CHAPTERS IN THE FIVE EDITIONS (*contd*)

	I (1662)	II (1664)	III (1668)	IV (1671)	V (1683)
	VIII	VIII	VIII	VIII	X
	IX	IX	IX	IX	XI
	…	…	…	…	XII
	X	X	X	X	XIII
	…	…	…	…	XIV
	XI	XI	XI	XI	XV
	XII	XII	XII	XII	XVI
	XIII	XIII	XIII	XIII	XVII
	XIV	XIV	XIV	XIV	XVIII
	XV	XV	XV	XV	XIX
	XVI	XVI	XVI	XVI	XX
Part III	I-VIII	I-VIII	I-VIII	I-VIII	I-VIII
	IX	…	…	…	…
	X	IX	IX	IX	IX
	XI	X	X	X	X
	XII	XI	XI	XI	XI
	XIV	XII	XII	XII	XII
	…	XIII	XIII	XIII	XIII
	…	XIV	XIV	XIV	XIV
	…	XV	XV	XV	XV
	XIII	XV-2	XV-2	XV-2	XVI
	XV	XVI	XVI	XVI	XVII
	XVI	XVII	XVII	XVII	XVIII
	XVII	XVIII	XVIII	XVIII	XIX
	XVIII	XIX	XIX	XIX	XX
Part IV	…	I	I	I	I
	I	II	II	II	II
	II	III	III	III	III
	III	IV	IV	IV	IV
	IV	V	V	V	V
	V	VI	VI	VI	VI
	VI	VII	VII	VII	VII
	VII	VIII	VIII	VIII	VIII
	VIII	IX	IX	IX	IX
	IX	IX-2	IX-2	IX-2	X
	X	X	X	X	XI
	XI	XI	XI	XI	XII
	XII	XII	XII	XII	XIII
	XIII	XIII	XIII	XIII	XIV
	XIV	XIV	XIV	XIV	XV
	XV	XV	XV	XV	XVI

Logic or the Art of Thinking
Containing, besides common rules, several new
observations appropriate for forming judgment

Fifth edition, revised and newly augmented

Preface to this new edition (1683)

We have made several important additions to this new edition of the *Logic*, which resulted from objections some ministers made to some of our remarks, thereby obliging us to clarify and defend the rights they wanted to attack. These clarifications will show that reason and faith are in perfect agreement, like streams from the same source, and that we can scarcely distance ourselves from one without removing ourselves from the other. But although these additions were prompted by theological disputes, they are no less appropriate or natural to logic.[1] We could have made them even had there never been ministers in the world who wanted to obscure the truths of faith with false subtleties. [13]

---

[1] This refers to chapters 4 and 15 of Part I, and chapters 12 and 14 of Part II, which concern the controversies with the Calvinists over the Eucharist.

Foreword

The birth of this little work is due entirely to chance, and more to a kind of entertainment than to a serious plan. While conversing with a young nobleman[1] who, at a tender age, displayed a very sound and discerning mind, a gentleman told him that when he was young he had found a man who helped him master part of logic in two weeks. This speech prompted another person who was present, and who had no great esteem for this science,[2] to reply in jest that if the young nobleman wanted to take the trouble, he would take it upon himself to teach him everything useful about logic in four or five days. After discussing this extravagant proposal for a while, they resolved to make the attempt. But since ordinary logic books were thought to be neither short nor precise enough, they decided to create an abridged version just for the young nobleman.

This was our sole aim when we began the work, and we thought it would not take us more than a day. But once the work was under way, so many new thoughts came to mind that we had to write them down to unburden ourselves. So instead of one day it took us four or five to write the body of this *Logic*, to which we have since made various additions.

Now although we included much more material than we had originally intended, the attempt nevertheless succeeded as promised. For, after the young nobleman reduced the material to four tables, he learned it easily, one table a day, requiring practically no help from anyone to understand it. Of course we should not expect others to learn it so easily, since he had an extraordinary mind for intellectual matters.

Such was the chance encounter which brought about this work. But whatever one thinks of it, no one can justly disapprove [14] of its publication, which was more forced than voluntary. For several persons had made handwritten copies, which as everyone knows cannot be done without introducing many errors, and we were warned that the bookstores were getting ready to print it.[3] Given these circumstances, we decided it was better to give it to the public correct and whole rather than letting it be printed from defective copies. But this also obliged us to

---

[1] Charles-Honoré d'Albert (1646–1712), the future Duke of Chevreuse, was the son of the Duke of Luynes, who translated Descartes' *Meditations* into French.

[2] Probably Arnauld himself.

[3] The Bibliothèque Nationale contains a manuscript numbered Fr. 19915, which is attributed to Arnauld but which is undoubtedly only a copy. It bears the catalogue number 2663 from the library of St. Germain-des-Prés, and the inscription *Ex dono D. Vallant ex biblioth. S. Germani a pratis 1683*. Brekle conjectures that it was made by a curé named Vallant from St. Germain-des-Prés. Based on references in the text, he argues that it was based on a draft of the *Logic* dating from 1659 or 1660. When compared to the first edition this text is incomplete, missing several chapters from each part. For a detailed comparison of the text of the manuscript with the first edition see volume 3 of Löringhoff and Brekle.

make various additions which increased its size by nearly a third, because we thought we should extend our views beyond the original version. This is the subject of the following discourse, in which we explain our proposed aim and the rationale for the material treated here. [15]

First discourse

Where the plan of this new logic is presented

Nothing is more praiseworthy than good sense and mental accuracy in discerning the true and the false. All the other mental qualities have limited uses, but an exact reason is generally useful in all aspects and all walks of life. It is difficult to distinguish truth from error not only in the sciences, but also in the majority of subjects people discuss and affairs they conduct. There are different routes practically everywhere, some true, others false. It is up to reason to choose among them. Those who choose well are those who are mentally acute; those who take the wrong path have faulty minds. This is the first and most important difference we can note in the qualities of people's minds.

Thus our main concern ought to be educating our judgment and making it as precise as possible. This ought to be the goal of the greatest part of our studies. We use reason as an instrument for acquiring scientific knowledge, when, on the contrary, we should use the sciences as an instrument for perfecting reason, since mental accuracy is infinitely more important than all the speculative knowledge to be attained by means of the truest and most reliable sciences. This should move wise persons to engage in speculation only to the extent that it serves this purpose, to make it merely the test and not the main use of their mental powers. [16]

If we do not follow this plan, we will not see that the study of speculative sciences, such as geometry, astronomy, and physics, is more than merely idle amusement, nor that they are much more valuable than ignorance of all these things. Ignorance at least has the advantage of being less painful and not giving rise to the foolish vanity often produced by these sterile and fruitless sciences.

Not only do these sciences have nooks and crannies of very little use, but they are completely worthless considered in and for themselves. People are not born to spend their time measuring lines, examining the relations between angles, or contemplating different motions of matter. The mind is too large, life too short, time too precious to occupy oneself with such trivial objects. But they are obligated to be just, fair, and judicious in all their speech, their actions, and the business they conduct. Above all they ought to train and educate themselves for this.

This care and study are even more necessary given how rare a quality is precise judgment. Everywhere we encounter nothing but faulty minds, who have practically no ability to discern the truth. They view everything from the wrong angle; they are satisfied by the worst reasons and want to satisfy others with them. They let themselves be carried away by the slightest appearances; they are always in excess and extremes; they have no grasp for holding firmly to the truths they know because they are attached to them more by chance than solid enlightenment. Or else they insist on nonsense with such obstinacy that they hear nothing that could set them straight. They decide boldly about what they do not know, what they do not understand, and what perhaps no one has ever understood. They fail to distinguish one statement from another, or they judge the truth of things only by the tone of one's voice: whoever speaks easily and soberly is right; anyone who has some trouble explaining himself or who exhibits some passion is wrong. This is all they know.

This is why there are no absurdities so unacceptable that they do not find approval. Anyone who sets out to [17] trick the world is sure to find people who will be happy to be tricked, and the most ridiculous idiocies always encounter minds suited to them. After seeing so many people infatuated with the follies of judicial astrology, and sober people taking this subject seriously, we should no longer be amazed at anything.[1] There is a constellation in the heavens which some people were pleased to name the Balance, which resembles a windmill as much as a balance. The balance is the symbol of justice; therefore those who are born under this constellation will be just and fair. There are three other signs of the zodiac, one called the Ram, another the Bull, a third the Goat, which could just as easily have been called the Elephant, the Crocodile, and the Rhinoceros. The ram, the bull, and the goat are animals that ruminate. Therefore those who take medicine when the moon is in these constellations are in danger of vomiting it up. However extravagant these reasonings, there are people who peddle them and others who let themselves be persuaded by them.

This defect of the mind causes not only scientific errors, but also the majority of mistakes committed in civil life: unjust quarrels, ill-founded lawsuits, hasty opinions, and badly organized enterprises. All but a handful of these have their source in some error or mistake in judgment, so that there is no fault we have more interest in correcting.

But this correction is as difficult to achieve as it is desirable, because it depends largely on the amount of intelligence we have at birth. Common sense is not so common a quality as people think. There are countless unrefined and stupid minds which can be reformed, not by giving them knowledge of the truth, but only by restricting them to matters within their grasp and by preventing them from judging about what they are not capable of knowing. It is true, however, that most false judgments do not arise from this principle, and that they are caused only by impetuosity and lack of attention, which make us judge recklessly about things we know only confusedly and obscurely. The little love people have for the truth causes them not to take the trouble most of the time to distinguish what is true

---

[1] Judicial astrology concerned judgments about human affairs, as opposed to judgments about natural or physical processes. The latter, known as natural or scientific astrology, was used in medicine, meteorology, and alchemy. It was considered unobjectionable by most medieval writers, because Aristotelian physics assumed that the heavenly bodies influenced sublunary processes. But both Christian and Moslem writers denied the validity of judicial astrology, primarily because it was incompatible with free will. Augustine made extended attacks on judicial astrology in *The City of God*, Bk v, chs. 1–7, and in *The Confessions*, Bk iv, ch. 3, *Writings*, vol. 6, pp. 241–51 and vol. 5, pp. 76–8. St. Thomas made a similar argument in *Summa Theologiae*, Ia, quest. 115, art. 4, pp. 7–11.

from what is false. [18] They let all sorts of pronouncements and maxims enter their souls; they would rather suppose them true than examine them. If they do not understand them, they like to believe that someone else does. So they fill their memories with innumerable false, obscure, and misunderstood ideas, and then they reason following these principles without considering in the least what they are saying or thinking.

Vanity and presumption contribute even more to this defect. People believe it is shameful to doubt and to be ignorant, and they would rather speak and decide haphazardly than admit that they are not well enough informed about something to render a judgment. We are all full of ignorance and errors, and yet it is the most difficult thing in the world to draw from our mouths this admission which is so accurate and describes our natural condition so well: "I am mistaken, and I know nothing about it."

There are others who, by contrast, are enlightened enough to know that a great many matters are obscure and uncertain. Wanting from a different kind of vanity to show that they are not swayed by popular credulity, they take pride in maintaining that nothing is certain. Thus they relieve themselves of the burden of examining these matters, and based on this unsound principle they call into doubt the most constant truths, including religion itself. This is the source of Pyrrhonism, another extravagance of the human mind. Although it appears contrary to the recklessness of those who believe and decide everything, it nevertheless comes from the same source, namely lack of attention. Whereas the believers do not want to take the trouble to identify errors, the skeptics do not want to bother to contemplate the truth with enough care to recognize its evidence. The least glimmer is enough to persuade the former of completely mistaken views; it suffices to make the latter doubt the most certain things. But the different effects in these two cases result from the same lack of attention.

Right reason accords all things their appropriate status. It makes us doubt those that are doubtful, reject those that are false, and recognize in good faith those that are evident. It is not influenced by the Pyrrhonists' vain arguments, which do not destroy our reasonable assurance [19] in matters that are certain, not even in the minds of those who present them. No one ever seriously doubted whether there is an earth, a sun, or a moon, or whether the whole is greater than its part. Of course people can bring themselves to say outwardly – orally – that they doubt these things, because they can lie. But they cannot assert them in their minds. Thus Pyrrhonism is not a sect of persons convinced of what they say, but a sect of liars. And so they often contradict themselves in expressing their views, since their hearts do not agree with their tongues. This is evident in Montaigne, who tried to revive Pyrrhonism in the last century.

For after saying that the Academics differed from the Pyrrhonists in admitting that some things were more likely than others, which the Pyrrhonists would not acknowledge, Montaigne declares for the Pyrrhonists in these terms: "The

Pyrrhonists' view," he says, "is bolder and at the same time more likely."[2] Thus some things are more likely than others. He is not just stretching the point in saying this, since these words slipped out without his thinking about them, arising from the depths of his nature, which the lie in his opinions cannot stifle.

But the harm is that, in matters that are not directly tied to the senses, people who take pleasure in doubting everything either prevent the mind from focusing on what could persuade them, or they apply themselves to it only imperfectly. Consequently they fall into a voluntary uncertainty with respect to religious matters, because the murky state they achieve for themselves is pleasant and convenient for alleviating the remorse of their consciences and for freely satisfying their passions.

These mental disorders which appear opposed to one another – one leading people to believe easily what is obscure and uncertain, the other to doubt what is clear and certain – nevertheless arise from the same principle, namely a failure to make oneself attentive enough to discern the truth. Obviously they must be remedied in the same way, and the only guaranteed method is to pay strict attention to our judgments and thoughts. This is the only thing which is absolutely necessary to protect ourselves against being taken by surprise. For the Academics' view – that it is as impossible to find the truth if one has no marks of it, as it would be to recognize a fugitive slave for whom one was searching if there were no signs to distinguish him [20] from others in case one encountered him – is only a vain subtlety. Just as no other marks are needed to distinguish light from darkness except the light itself which makes itself sensed sufficiently, so no marks are necessary to recognize the truth but the very brightness which surrounds it and to which the mind submits, persuading it in spite of itself. Accordingly, all these philosophers' arguments can no more prevent the soul from surrendering to the truth whenever it is strongly penetrated by it, than they can prevent the eyes from seeing when they are open and struck by sunlight.

But because the mind sometimes lets itself be misled by false glimmers when it does not pay enough attention, and because clearly some things are known only by long and difficult examination, it would certainly be useful to have rules for conducting oneself so as to make the search for truth both easier and surer.

[2] *Essays*, Bk II, ch. 12, *Complete Works*, p. 422. The Academics were leaders of Plato's Academy in the third century BC, among them Arcesilaus (c. 315–240 BC), who took to heart Socrates' remark: "All that I know is that I know nothing." The most influential Academic was Carneades (213–128 BC), who attacked the Stoic view that there are cataleptic impressions, that is, mental states that are indubitable and compel assent. The Academics argued that there was no sure criterion distinguishing true from false impressions, although they admitted that some beliefs were more probable than others. By contrast, the Pyrrhonists claimed that there was no basis for distinguishing even the probable from the improbable. Tracing their origins to Pyrrho of Elis (c. 360–c. 270 BC), they argued that every possible criterion of knowledge was open to question, and hence the only reasonable attitude was to suspend judgment on the nature of reality in order to attain *ataraxia*, a state of mental tranquillity. These arguments are presented most fully in the *Outlines of Pyrrhonism* of Sextus Empiricus (c. 150–250 AD).

Moreover, these rules are doubtless not impossible to find. After all, people are sometimes mistaken and sometimes not mistaken in their judgments, they reason well at times and badly at others, and when they reason badly they can recognize their mistakes. By reflecting on their thoughts, they can notice which method they used when they were reasoning well and which was the cause of error when they were mistaken. They can then form rules based on these reflections to avoid being caught off guard in the future.

This is properly speaking what philosophers engage in, which is the basis of their magnificent promises to us. Were we to believe them, they provide us in the branch of philosophy meant to serve this purpose, which they call logic, a light capable of dissipating all the darkness of the mind. They would correct all the errors in our thoughts and give us rules so sure that they lead infallibly to the truth, and so necessary, taken together, that without them it is impossible to know it with complete certainty. Such are the praises philosophers themselves bestow on their precepts. But if we consider what experience shows about how philosophers have used these rules, in logic as well as other branches of philosophy, there are plenty of grounds for suspecting those promises to be empty.

Nevertheless, because it is not right to reject absolutely [21] what is good in logic because of the ways it can be misused, and since it is not likely that so many great minds who devoted themselves with such care to the rules of reasoning could have found nothing worthwhile, and, finally, because custom has introduced a certain need to know what logic is, at least in a rough way, we thought it would be generally useful to take from it what is most helpful for educating our judgment. This is properly speaking the plan proposed in this work, along with several new reflections that came to mind while we were writing, which make up the largest and perhaps the most valuable part.

For it seems that ordinary philosophers hardly ever apply themselves to logic except to give rules of good and bad reasoning. Now we cannot say that these rules are useless, since they are sometimes helpful for revealing flaws in certain confused arguments and for arranging our thoughts in a more convincing manner. We should not, however, also believe that this usefulness extends much further, given that most human errors consist not in letting oneself be deceived by faulty inferences, but in granting false judgments from which mistaken conclusions are inferred.[3] Until now those who have treated logic have rarely tried to remedy this. So this is the main topic of the new reflections which will be found throughout this book.

We must acknowledge, however, that the reflections we call new because they do not appear in typical logic books, are not completely due to the author of this work,

---

[3]   The notion that the attentive thinker cannot make mistaken inferences, but that faulty reasoning generally consists in accepting false premises, is an important part of Descartes' theory of error and his criticism of syllogistic reasoning as circular reasoning. See Rules Two and Ten of *Rules for the Direction of the Mind*, *Philosophical Writings*, vol. 1, pp. 12, 36–7.

and that he borrowed several of them from the books of a famous philosopher of this century, whose mind is as sharp as those of others are confused.[4] Several others were also taken from a small unpublished essay by the late Pascal which he titled *On the Geometrical Mind*. These are found in chapter 9 of Part I,[5] on the difference between nominal and real definitions, and in the five rules explained in Part IV, which are much more developed than in his essay. [22]

As for what was taken from ordinary logic books, this is our thinking:

First, our plan was to include in this work everything truly useful from other works, such as rules for figures of syllogisms, the classification of terms and ideas, and some reflections on propositions. There were other things we judged fairly useless, such as the categories and topics, but because they are short, easy, and common, we thought we should not omit them, while warning, however, about how to evaluate them so that they will not be thought to be more useful than they are.

We had more doubts about certain rather thorny and less useful material, such as the conversion of propositions,[a] and demonstrations of the rules for figures. But we finally decided not to take them out, given that their very difficulty has some merit. For it is true that when something difficult does not lead to knowledge of any truth, we have grounds for saying *Stultum est difficiles habere nugas*.[6] [It is stupid to waste time on useless difficulties.] But we should not avoid difficulty when it leads to some truth, because it is beneficial to practice understanding difficult truths.

Some stomachs can digest only light and delicate food; likewise some minds can be applied only to simple truths or truths ornately garbed in eloquence. Both have a blameworthy delicacy, or rather a genuine weakness.[b] The mind must be made capable of discovering the truth, even when it is hidden and covered up, and of respecting it in whatever form it appears. Everyone is naturally repelled and disgusted by what seems subtle and Scholastic. If this aversion is not overcome, the mind narrows and, unbeknownst to itself, becomes incapable of comprehending what can be known only by connecting several propositions. So when a truth depends on three or four principles that must be considered all at once, we become overwhelmed and discouraged, and thereby deprive ourselves of much useful knowledge. This is a considerable shortcoming.

Practice expands or contracts the mind's capacities. This is the main benefit of mathematics and, generally, of all difficult things, such as those we have mentioned. For they stretch the mind in a certain way [23] and exercise it to greater application and a firmer grasp of what it knows.

These are the reasons we did not omit these thorny subjects, and even discussed

---

[4] Descartes.

[5] Chapter 12 in the 1683 edition, and actually chapter 10 in the earlier editions.

[a] ... propositions, the reduction of syllogisms, and ... (I)

[6] Martial, Bk II, epigram 86: *Turpe est difficiles habere nugas, et stultus labor est ineptiarum* [It is bad to waste time on useless difficulties, and labor spent on foolishness is stupid], vol. I, p. 159.

[b] ... weakness. We must sometimes be able to eat dry bread; the mind ... (I)

them in as much detail as any other logic text. Those who object to this can spare themselves by not reading them. This is why we were careful to indicate these subjects in the chapter titles themselves so that no one would have grounds to object. If anyone reads them they do so voluntarily.

We also thought we should not be deterred by the aversion of some people who are horrified by certain artificial terms created for remembering different argument forms more easily, as if they were magical incantations, and who often make derisory comments about *Baroco* and *Baralipton* having a pedantic character, because we judged that the derision was more contemptible than the words. Right reason and good sense do not allow us to treat as ridiculous what is not so. Now there is nothing ridiculous about these terms provided we do not make too great a mystery of them. Since they were created only to aid the memory, no one would want to use them in ordinary speech, for example, saying one was going to reason in *Bocardo* or *Felapton*, which would be truly ridiculous.[7]

This charge of pedantry is sometimes quite unfounded. Indeed, those who attribute pedantry to others often fall into it themselves. Pedantry is a vice of the mind, not of any particular profession. There are pedants of all stripes, all conditions, and all walks of life. To appeal to lowly and trivial things; to make a vain display of learning; to pile up Greek and Latin sayings mindlessly; to grow heated over the order of Attic months, the Macedonians' dress, and similar useless disputes; to plunder an author while insulting him; to tear outrageously into those who do not share our opinions on the meaning of a passage in Suetonius or the etymology of a word, as if it were a question of religion or the state; to want to incite everyone against a person who does not admire Cicero sufficiently, as against a disturber of the public peace, which Julius Scaliger tried to do against Erasmus;[8] to be concerned for the reputation of an ancient philosopher as if he were a close relative: this is properly speaking pedantry. But there is none in understanding or explaining artificial words that were rather cleverly [24] invented for the sole purpose of aiding the memory, provided one takes the precautions indicated here.

It remains only to explain why we omitted a great number of topics found in ordinary logic books, such as those treated in the prolegomenas: the universal *à parte rei*,[9] relations, and several others of this sort. It would almost do to reply that they belong more to metaphysics than to logic. But this was not a major

---

[7] From the sixteenth century, the battle against the syllogism symbolized the innovative spirit of the Renaissance. Among the thinkers attacking traditional syllogistic were Luther, Erasmus, Rabelais (see ch. 19 of *Gargantua*), Montaigne (Bk I, ch. 26, of the *Essays*), and even Pascal (*On the Geometrical Mind and the Art of Persuasion*, *Pascal, Selections*, pp. 193–4). For the artificial words, see p. 146 and n. 1.

[8] Giulio Cesare Scaligero (1484–1558), known more generally as Julius Caesar Scaliger, was an Italian physician and humanist who opposed the thinking of many humanists of the period, in particular Erasmus. Scaliger was the author of many scientific works on Hippocrates, Aristotle, and Theophrastus, as well as several literary works. This reference concerns his attack in *Iul. Caes. Scaligeri adversus Desid. Erasmum orationes duae*.

[9] From the perspective of things.

consideration. For once we decided that a method could be useful for educating judgment, we paid little attention to the science to which it belonged. Knowledge can be organized as freely as letters in a printer's shop. Each of us has the right to form different orders according to our needs, although in forming them we ought to arrange them in the most natural manner. It is enough for some material to be useful for us to use it, and to view it not as alien but as appropriate. This is why a number of things are found here from physics and morals, and almost as much metaphysics as one ought to know, although we do not claim not to have borrowed from anyone. Everything that is useful to logic belongs to it. It is thoroughly ridiculous to subject oneself to the torments certain otherwise very capable authors put themselves through, such as Ramus and the Ramists,[10] who take as much trouble to mark the jurisdiction of each science and ensure that one does not infringe on another, as is taken in marking the boundaries of kingdoms and settling the sovereignty of parliaments.

What also convinced us to leave these Scholastic topics out entirely is not merely that they are difficult and of little use; we have treated several topics of this nature. But since they have all these bad qualities, we thought we could avoid mentioning them without offending anyone, because no one cares about them.

An important distinction must be drawn among the useless questions that fill philosophy books. Some are scorned even by those who discuss them while, on the other hand, others are famous and well thought of, and are very popular in the writings of otherwise admirable persons.

It seems we have a duty with respect [25] to these common and well-known views, however false we believe them, not to ignore what is said about them. We owe this civility, or rather this justice, not to their falsity, because it certainly does not deserve it, but to the persons who are so taken by these views, so as not to reject what they value without examining it. So by taking the trouble to study these topics, we can reasonably purchase the right to hold them in contempt.

But we have more freedom with the first kind of question, and the topics in logic that we decided to omit are of this sort. They have the advantage of not being highly regarded, not only in the world where they are unknown, but even by those who teach them. No one, thank heavens, is interested in the universal *à parte rei*, beings of reason, or second intentions. Thus we had no grounds to fear that anyone would be offended if we did not mention them. Besides, these matters are so inappropriate to being expressed in French that they would have been more suitable for disparaging Scholastic philosophy than for making it admired.

We should also warn that we exempted ourselves from always strictly following

---

10   Pierre de la Ramée (1515–72), better known under his Latin name Petrus Ramus, was a French humanist, mathematician, and philosopher. More familiar today to historians of rhetoric, he was hostile to the Scholastic tradition and wrote two works against Aristotle which earned him the opposition of the Sorbonne. Nevertheless, he became the first Professor of Mathematics of the Collège Royal (Collège de France). Among his mathematical works, his treatment of negative numbers deserves mention.

the rules of method, since we put many things in Part IV which could have been discussed in Parts II and III. But we did this on purpose[c] because we thought it useful to see everything required for perfecting knowledge in one place, which is the main point of the work on method treated in Part IV. This is why we reserved the discussion of axioms and demonstrations for that section.

These are nearly all the aims we had in creating this *Logic*. Even with all this perhaps few persons will profit from it or recognize the benefits they will derive from it, because people usually pay less explicit attention to putting rules into practice. But still we hope that those who read it with some care might take a tincture of it, making them more precise and reliable in their judgments without their even being aware of it, just as certain remedies cure diseases by increasing vigor and strengthening the parts of the body. In any case, at least [26] no one will be inconvenienced for long, since anyone who is even slightly advanced can read and understand it in seven or eight days. Because it contains a great variety of topics, it is difficult to believe that not everyone will find some compensation for the trouble of reading it.

---

[c] ... purpose, as much because we thought it useful to see everything required for perfecting knowledge in one place, as because we thought there would be many persons who could be satisfied with the first and last parts of this work, since there are few things in the other two parts that good sense could not supply, without having to make a special study of them. – These are ... .(I)

Second discourse

Containing a reply to the principal objections made to this logic

All who share their work with the public should be reconciled to having as many judges as readers, and this should appear neither unjust nor onerous. For genuinely disinterested authors give up rights of ownership in publishing their writings, and they will thenceforth consider them with the same indifference they bring to the works of others.

Authors can reserve for themselves only the right to correct whatever is defective, for which various criticisms of books are extremely helpful. They are always useful when they are fair, and they cause no harm when they are unfair because one may ignore them.

Prudence will have it, however, that we occasionally accommodate ourselves to criticisms that do not seem fair, because even if they do not show that what is faulted is bad, they at least show that it is not congenial to the minds of those who criticize it. Now it is doubtless better, whenever we can do it without falling into some greater difficulty, to try to be so just that in satisfying judicious persons we do not displease those who have less precise judgment, since we should not assume that we will have only capable and intelligent readers.

So it would be desirable to view the first editions of books as first drafts which their authors present to educated persons to learn their opinions. Afterwards, based on the different [27] views expressed in these different opinions, they should rewrite everything to make their works as excellent as possible.

This is the course we would like to have followed in the second edition of this logic, had we learned more from the world about the first edition. Nevertheless, we did what we could: we added, deleted, and corrected several things, following the advice of those who were good enough to tell us what ought to be revised.

First, as for the language, we followed almost to the letter the advice of two persons[1] who took the trouble to note some errors which slid in through carelessness, as well as certain expressions they thought were not good usage. We excused ourselves from following their views only when, after consulting others, we found opinion divided. In that case we believed it was permissible to do as we liked.

With respect to the content, there are more additions than changes or deletions, because we had less advice about what was being criticized. It is true, however, that we know of several general objections to this book that we thought we could ignore, because we were convinced that even those who made them would be easily

---

[1] This has traditionally been taken to refer to de Sacy and Lancelot. Isaac Le Maistre de Sacy (1613–84) was the son of Isaac Le Maistre and Catherine Arnauld, the sister of Antoine Arnauld; he became a priest and a *solitaire* of Port-Royal. Claude Lancelot (1615–95) was a French grammarian and a Port-Royal Jansenist, and co-author with Arnauld of the *Port-Royal Grammar* (1660); he was one of the founders of the Little Schools of Port-Royal, and an educator of the Duke of Chevreuse and the two Princes of Conti from 1669 to 1672.

satisfied if we explained the reasons for the things they criticized. This is why it will be useful to reply to their main objections here.

Some people were offended by the title, *The Art of Thinking*, which they would have replaced by *The Art of Reasoning Well*. But we ask them to consider that since the purpose of logic is to give rules for all actions of the mind, and for simple ideas as well as for judgments and inferences, there is practically no other word which covers all these different acts. Certainly "thinking" includes all of them, for simple ideas are thoughts, judgments are thoughts, and inferences are thoughts. It is true that we could have said *The Art of Thinking Well*, but this addition was not necessary, being sufficiently indicated by the word *Art* which in itself signifies a method of doing something well, as Aristotle himself remarks.[2] This is why we say the art of painting and the art of counting, because we assume that no art is needed to paint or count badly.

A more important objection was raised against [28] the large number of examples from different sciences included in this logic. Since this objection attacks the entire plan and so gives us an opportunity to explain it, we should examine the objection more closely. To what purpose, they say, this patchwork of rhetoric, ethics, physics, metaphysics, and geometry? When we think we are dealing with precepts of logic, all of a sudden the authors carry us off into the loftiest sciences without knowing whether we have learned them. Should they not assume, to the contrary, that if we already had all this knowledge we would not need this logic? Would it not be better to give us a pure and simple logic text which explains the rules by everyday examples rather than one complicated by all this material that smothers them?

But anyone who reasons this way has not taken into consideration that a book can hardly have a greater fault than not being read, since it is useful only to those who read it. So everything that contributes to a book's readability also contributes to its usefulness. Now it is certain that if we had followed their thinking and had produced a completely dry logic text with the usual examples of animals and horses, however exact and methodical it might have been, it would only have added to the many texts filling the world which are never read. On the contrary, it is just this collection of different examples that has given some vogue to this logic and causes it to be read with a bit less irritation than others.

Attracting the world to read this text by making it more amusing than the usual logic book was not, however, the main point of this assortment of examples. We claim, in addition, to have followed the most natural and advantageous path in treating this art, by remedying as much as possible a drawback that can make its study useless.

For experience shows that of a thousand young persons who learn logic, there are not ten who know anything about it six months after they have finished the

---

[2] *Nicomachean Ethics*, Bk I, ch. 1, *Complete Works*, vol. 2, p. 1729.

course. Now it seems that the real cause of this widespread forgetfulness or neglect is that all the material treated in logic, which is itself quite abstract and removed from practical matters, is on top of that combined with uninteresting examples that are never discussed elsewhere. So, grasping these subjects only with difficulty, the mind has no basis for retaining them, and easily loses hold of its ideas of them because they are never reinforced by practice. [29]

In addition, since the usual examples do not make the usefulness of this art clear, students are accustomed to thinking of logic in narrow terms, without seeing its larger implications. In fact it exists only to serve as an instrument for other sciences. So because students have never seen it put into practice, they do not use it themselves and are quite happy to dismiss it as trivial and worthless learning.

Thus we thought that the best remedy for this problem was not to separate logic from the other sciences for which it is intended, as is usually done, but to combine it with established knowledge by means of examples so that the rules and the practice can be seen simultaneously. In this way we might learn to evaluate the sciences through logic and retain the logic by means of the sciences.

So rather than stifling these precepts, nothing is better for making them understood and retained than all these examples. The rules alone are too subtle to make an impression on the mind if they are not combined with something more pleasing and obvious.

To make this assortment more useful, we did not borrow examples from the sciences at random. Instead we selected the most important points that could best serve as rules and principles for finding the truth in other matters we could not discuss here.

For example, we thought that rhetoric is not very helpful for finding thoughts, expressions, and embellishments. The mind furnishes enough thoughts, and usage provides the expressions. And usually there are too many metaphors and figures of speech. So the main idea is to avoid certain bad styles of writing and speaking, and above all the artificial rhetorical style made up of false and exaggerated thoughts and forced metaphors, which is the worst vice. Now the reader may find in this logic as many useful points for recognizing and avoiding these defects as in books dedicated to the subject. The last chapter of Part I, on metaphorical style, also teaches how to use it, and explains the real rule for distinguishing good from bad metaphors. The chapter treating Topics in general could be very helpful for eliminating an excess of common thoughts. By teaching never to take for beautiful what is false, the section [30] discussing arguments where reason is sacrificed to eloquence presents in passing one of the most important rules of true rhetoric. More than any other it can educate the mind to a simple, natural, and judicious way of writing. Finally, in the same chapter, what we say about how to avoid offending the reader warns against many faults that are even more dangerous, being harder to detect.

Our main subject did not permit us to include very much about ethics. I believe, however, that the reader will see that the chapters on false ideas of good and evil in Part I, and on bad inferences drawn in everyday life, have a broad scope and help identify a great many human foibles.

Nothing is more important in metaphysics than the origin of our ideas, the separation of mental ideas from corporeal images, the distinction of the soul from the body, and the proofs of its immortality based on this distinction. These are fully treated in Parts I and IV.

We have even included, scattered throughout, most of the general principles of physics, which can be easily collected. The reader may learn enough from what is said about weight, sensible qualities, actions, the senses, attractive faculties, occult powers, and substantial forms to disabuse himself of the countless false ideas left in the mind by childhood preconceptions.

This is not to say that one should avoid the more careful study of these matters in books that treat them explicitly. But we thought that many people who are not destined for theology, which requires a precise knowledge of Scholastic philosophy – since it is, as it were, the language of theology – would be satisfied with a more general acquaintance with these sciences. Now even if they cannot find in this book everything they ought to learn about them, still, we can truthfully say that they will find here nearly everything they ought to remember about them.

The objection that several of these examples are not simple enough for beginners [31] is true only for the geometric examples. As for the others, they can be understood by those whose minds are at all open, even if they have never studied any philosophy. They might even be more intelligible to those who as yet have no prejudices than to those whose minds are filled with maxims of common philosophy.

As for the geometric examples, though they may not be understood by everyone, this is no great flaw. For they occur either in isolated and independent passages that can be safely bypassed, or in contexts which are sufficiently clear on their own or which are clarified enough by other examples so that they do not need the geometrical examples.

Furthermore, anyone who examines the passages where we use these examples will recognize that it would be difficult to find others that are as appropriate. Geometry is virtually the only science that can furnish clear ideas and indisputable propositions.

In speaking of reciprocal properties, for example, we said that it was reciprocal to right triangles that the square of the hypotenuse is equal to the sum of the squares of the other two sides. This is clear and certain to everyone who understands it, and those who do not can assume it without failing to understand the idea to which this example is applied.

But if we had wanted to use the example usually given, namely that laughter is essential to humans, we would have asserted something both obscure and question-able. For if the word "laughter" is understood to mean the ability to make a certain grimace while laughing, it is not clear why brutes could not be trained to make this grimace, and perhaps there even are some that do so. If this word includes not only the change the laugh causes in one's facial expression, but also the thought that accompanies and produces it, so that "laughter" means the ability to laugh while thinking, then all human actions will become essential properties in this way, since there are no properties that are not distinctive to humans alone if thought is added to them. So we could say that walking, drinking, and eating are essential to humans because only humans walk, drink, and eat while thinking. Provided these attributes are understood this way, there is no shortage of essential properties. But these examples will still not be conclusive in the minds of those who attribute thoughts to brutes, and who could as easily attribute laughter along with thinking to them, whereas the example [32] we use is conclusive in everyone's mind.

Similarly we wanted to show at one point that there are corporeal things that can be conceived in a mental form without being imagined. For this we used the example of a figure of a thousand angles, which is clearly conceived by the mind although no one can form a distinct image representing its properties. We said in passing that one of the properties of this figure is that all of its angles are equal to 1996 right angles. It is obvious that this example demonstrates quite well what we wanted to show in that passage.

It remains only to answer a more disagreeable objection several persons have raised, concerning examples of faulty definitions and fallacious arguments taken from Aristotle. This appears to them to arise from a secret desire to discredit that philosopher.

But they would never have made such an unfair judgment if they had thought sufficiently about the true rules one ought to follow when giving examples of mistakes, which are those we had in mind in quoting Aristotle.

First, experience shows that the usual examples of errors are worthless and hard to remember because they are made up intentionally. They are so obvious and crude that it seems impossible to make them. So to remember what is said about these errors and how to avoid them, it is better to choose real examples from some highly regarded author, whose reputation will cause us to be more on guard against such mistakes, given that the greatest minds are capable of them.

In addition, just as we ought to strive to make everything we write as useful as possible, we should try to choose examples of errors that are worth knowing about, for it would be quite useless to burden the memory with all the reveries of Fludd, Van Helmont, and Paracelsus.[3] Thus it is better to look for examples in authors

---

[3] Robert Fludd (or Flud) (1574–1637) was an English physician, author, and occultist. As a philosopher he exemplified the Hermetic tradition, taking seriously the claims of astrology, chiromancy, and alchemy against the scientific spirit of Aristotle and Galen. Fludd was attacked by both Marin Mersenne and Gassendi, and engaged in a controversy with Johannes Kepler. Jan Baptista Van Helmont (1577–1644) was a Flemish physician and chemist. For a time he supported the Hippocratic empirical approach to medicine in opposition to the prevailing Aristotelian and Galenic doctrines. Even after coming under the influence of Paracelsus and the Hermetic writings, he continued his

who are so famous that everyone is in some way required to know them, including their faults.

Now Aristotle supplies all this perfectly. Nothing is more effective in helping us avoid a mistake than to be shown that such a great mind made it. Moreover, due to the great number of respectable persons who have embraced his philosophy, it has become so famous that one ought to know it even to the extent of knowing its defects. Thus, since we thought it would be very useful for those who read this book to learn, in passing, various aspects of his philosophy, and since, however, it [33] is never good to be mistaken, we discussed these examples to make them known, and we indicated their defects while on the subject, to prevent others from making the same mistakes.

So it was not to discredit Aristotle but, on the contrary, to honor him as much as possible where we did not share his views, that we took examples from his books. Besides, it is obvious that the points we criticized are not very important and do not get at the heart of his philosophy, which we had no intention of attacking.

If we did not similarly discuss the many excellent things found in Aristotle's works, it is because they were not relevant to the discussion. But had we found the opportunity, we would gladly have done so, and we would not have failed to give him the praise he justly deserves. For it is certain that Aristotle is truly a thinker of extraordinary vastness and scope, who develops many of the implications and consequences of the views he discusses. This is why what he says about the passions in the second book of the *Rhetoric* is so brilliant.

There are also several fine things in his *Politics* and *Ethics*, in the *Problems* and the history of animals. Whatever confusion there is in his *Analytics*, still we must admit that nearly everything we know about the rules of logic comes from there. Indeed there is no author from whom we borrowed more for this *Logic* than Aristotle, since the body of precepts belongs to him.

It is true that the least perfect of his works seems to be the *Physics*, and it was also the one condemned and forbidden by the Church for the longest time,[4] as a learned man has shown in a book intended for this purpose.[5] Yet its main defect is not that it is false, but, on the contrary, that it is too true and teaches us only things of which we cannot be ignorant. Who can doubt that everything is composed of matter and a certain form of this matter? Who can doubt that in order for matter to

experimental approach, which led to important discoveries in physiological chemistry, medicine, and the chemistry of gases, including the discovery of carbon dioxide. Philippus Aureolus Theophrastus Bombastus von Hohenheim, known as Paracelsus, (c. 1493–1541) was a Swiss physician and alchemist. He caused a scandal at Basel by criticizing the theories of Galen and Avicenna. His medical theory was based on the ancient faculty psychology and the alchemical and astrological idea of a correspondence between the different parts of the human body (microcosm) and those of the universe as a whole (macrocosm). He nevertheless contributed to the development of chemistry and perhaps homeopathy.

[4] Aristotle's physics, accompanied by his metaphysics, was condemned by the Council of Paris which met in 1209 or 1210, under the papacy of Innocent III and the reign of Philippe Auguste.

[5] This refers to Jean de Launoy (1603–78), *De Varia Aristotelis Fortuna in Academia Parisiensi*.

acquire a new manner and form, it must not have had it previously, that is, it must have had its privation? Who can doubt, finally, based on these other metaphysical principles, that everything depends on the form, that matter alone does nothing, that there are places, motions, qualities, and faculties? But after having learned all these things, we seem not to have learned anything new, nor to be in a better position to make sense of any of the effects of nature. [34]

Were someone to claim that it is absolutely forbidden to declare oneself opposed to Aristotelian views, it would be easy to show him that this scrupulosity is unreasonable.

Surely if some philosophers are owed deference, it can only be for two reasons: either because they advocate the truth, or because some people approve of them.

From the standpoint of truth, we owe them respect whenever they are right, but the truth cannot oblige us to respect falsity, regardless of where it is found.

As for the consensus of those who approve of a philosopher, certainly it too deserves some respect, and it would be unwise to offend it without taking great precautions. This is because in attacking received opinions we cause others to suspect us of presuming to think ourselves more enlightened than they are.

But when the world is divided over an author's views, and when there are important persons on both sides of the issue, we no longer need to be so reserved. We can freely declare what we do or do not accept in books about which learned persons disagree. This is not so much to prefer our own view to that of the author and those who accept it, as to take the side of those who oppose it on this point.

Strictly speaking, this is the state of Aristotle's philosophy today. It has had various fortunes, having been generally rejected at one time and generally accepted at another; now it is reduced to a state between these two extremes. It is defended by several learned persons and attacked by others who are equally reputable. Every day in France, Flanders, England, Germany, and Holland, people write freely for and against Aristotle's philosophy. The conferences in Paris are as divided as the books, and no one is offended if someone declares himself against him. The most famous professors are no longer bound to the slavishness of blindly accepting everything found in his books. Some of his opinions are even generally abandoned. What physician wants to maintain these days that the nerves come from the heart, as Aristotle thought,[6] since anatomy shows clearly [35] that they originate in the brain? As Saint Augustine said: *qui ex puncto cerebri et quasi centro sensus omnes quinaria distributione diffudit.*[7] [[God] diffuses all five senses from a somewhat central point of the brain.] And what philosopher is so stubborn as to say that the speed of heavy things increases proportionally to their weight? Anyone can disabuse himself of this opinion of Aristotle's[8] by letting two things unequal in weight fall from a high place, where we see only a very slight inequality in speed.

---

6   *The History of Animals*, Bk III, ch. 5, *Complete Works*, vol. 1. p. 818.
7   *Letters*, Letter no. 137, ch. 2, *Writings*, vol. 11, p. 24.
8   *On the Heavens*, Bk III, ch. 2, *Complete Works*, vol. 1, pp. 493–4.

Violent states do not usually last long, and all extremes are violent.[9] It is too hard to condemn Aristotle's philosophy generally, as was done formerly, and it is a great discomfort to think ourselves obliged to accept it completely and take it for the standard of truth in philosophy, as people apparently thought subsequently. The world cannot remain under this constraint for long. Imperceptibly it takes possession of the natural and reasonable liberty that consists in accepting what is thought to be true and rejecting what is thought to be false.

Reason does not find it strange to be subjected to authority in the sciences that treat matters that transcend reason, which ought to follow another light, namely divine authority. But in human sciences that profess to rely only on reason, it seems reason would be justified in not submitting to an authority against reason.

This is the rule we followed in speaking of the views of ancient as well as contemporary philosophers. In both cases we took into consideration only the truth, generally without espousing the opinions of anyone in particular and, equally generally, without declaring ourselves against anyone.

Given this, all anyone ought to conclude when we reject an opinion of Aristotle or some other philosopher is that we do not share that author's view on that matter. But certainly no one should conclude that we do not share his view on other matters, much less that we have some aversion to him or some desire to discredit him. We think all fair-minded persons will approve of this attitude, and they will recognize in the whole of this work only a sincere desire to contribute to the common good, as much as a book of this nature can, without any passion against anyone. [37]

---

[9] This is an indirect reference to Aristotle's theory of motion, which distinguishes between natural and violent motions. The cause of the former is internal to objects, and returns them to their natural places. The latter are caused externally, and move objects from their natural places.

LOGIC OR THE ART OF THINKING

Logic is the art of conducting reason well in knowing things, as much to instruct ourselves about them as to instruct others.

This art consists in reflections that have been made on the four principal operations of the mind: *conceiving, judging, reasoning,* and *ordering.*

The simple view we have of things that present themselves to the mind is called *conceiving*, as when we represent to ourselves a sun, an earth, a tree, a circle, a square, thought, and being, without forming any explicit judgment about them. The form by which we represent these things is called an *idea.*

Judging is the action in which the mind, bringing together different ideas, affirms of one that it is the other, or denies of one that it is the other. This occurs when, for example, having the idea of the earth and the idea of round, I affirm or deny of the earth that it is round.

The action of the mind in which it forms a judgment from several others is called *reasoning*. So, after judging that true virtue should be attributed to God, and that the pagans' virtue was not attributed to him, from this we conclude that the pagans' virtue was not true virtue. [38]

Here we call *ordering* the mental action in which different ideas, judgments, and reasonings are arranged on the same subject, such as the human body, in the manner best suited for knowing the subject. This is also called *method.*

All this is done naturally and sometimes better by those who have never studied any rules of logic than by those who have.

Thus this art does not consist in finding the means to perform these operations, since nature alone furnishes them in giving us reason, but in reflecting on what nature makes us do, which serves three purposes.

The first is to assure us that we are using reason well, since thinking about the rule makes us pay new attention to it.

The second is to reveal and explain more easily the errors or defects that can occur in mental operations. For we frequently discover by the natural light of reason alone that some reasoning is fallacious without, however, knowing why it is so, just as people who do not know painting can be offended by the defect in a canvas without being able to explain what it is that offends them.

The third purpose is to make us better acquainted with the nature of the mind by reflecting on its actions. This is more excellent in itself, considering the case of pure speculation alone, than knowing all about corporeal things, which are infinitely lower than spiritual things.

If reflections on our thoughts never concerned anyone but ourselves, it would be enough to examine them in themselves, unclothed in words or other signs. But because we can make our thoughts known to others only by accompanying them with external signs, and since this habit is so strong that even when we think to ourselves, things are presented to the mind only in the words in which we usually clothe them in speaking to others, logic must examine how ideas are joined to words and words to ideas.

From all we have just said it follows that logic can be divided into four parts, according to the different reflections that can be made on these four operations of the mind. [39]

First part

Containing reflections on ideas, or the first action of the mind, which is called conceiving

As we can have no knowledge of what is outside us except by means of the ideas in us, the reflections we can make on our ideas are perhaps the most important part of logic, since they are the foundation of everything else.

These reflections can be reduced to five headings, according to the five ways we shall consider ideas.

The first is according to their nature and origin.

The second, according to the main difference between the objects they represent.

The third, according to their simplicity or composition, where we will treat abstractions and specifications of the mind.

The fourth, according to their extension or restriction, that is, their universality, particularity, or singularity.

The fifth, according to their clearness and obscurity, or distinctness and confusion.

CHAPTER 1

Ideas according to their nature and origin

The word "idea" is one of those that are so clear that they cannot be explained by others, because none is more clear and simple. [40]

All we can do to avoid mistakes is to note the false interpretation we could give this word by restricting it merely to that form of conceiving things that consists in applying the mind to images formed in the brain, which is called imagining.

For, as St. Augustine often remarks,[1] since the Fall we have been so accustomed to thinking only about corporeal things, whose images enter the brain by the senses, that the majority believe themselves unable to conceive something if they cannot imagine it, that is, represent it under a corporeal image. It is as if this were the only way we had of thinking and conceiving.

On the contrary, we cannot reflect on what happens in the mind without recognizing that we conceive a great number of things without any such images, and without becoming aware of the difference between imagination and pure intellection. When I imagine a triangle, for example, I do not conceive it merely as a figure bounded by three straight lines. Beyond that I consider these three lines as present by the force and internal application of my mind. Properly speaking, this is

---

[1] *City of God*, Bks. XIII and XIV, *Writings*, vol. 7, pp. 299–412; *The Literal Meaning of Genesis*, Bk. XII, chs. 1–26, vol. 2, pp. 178–217.

imagining. But if I wish to think of a figure of a thousand angles, I certainly conceive the truth that it is a figure composed of a thousand sides as easily as I conceive that a triangle is a figure composed of only three sides. But I cannot imagine the thousand sides of that figure nor, so to speak, regard them as present before the mind's eye.[2]

It is true, however, that our habit of using the imagination when we think of corporeal things often causes us, in conceiving a figure of a thousand angles, to represent some figure confusedly. But obviously the figure thereby represented in the imagination cannot be a figure of a thousand angles, since it is no different from what I would represent if I were thinking of a figure of ten thousand angles, and it is no aid to discovering the properties that differentiate between a figure of a thousand angles and any other polygon.

Strictly speaking, then, I cannot imagine a figure of a thousand angles, since any image I might try to form of it in my imagination could as easily represent another figure of a great many angles as one of a thousand angles. Nevertheless, I can conceive it very clearly and distinctly, since [41] I can demonstrate all its properties, such as that all its angles taken together are equal to 1996 right angles. Consequently imagining is one thing and conceiving is another.

This becomes even clearer when we consider several things we conceive very clearly although they certainly cannot be imagined. For what do we conceive more clearly than our thought when we are thinking? Yet it is impossible to imagine a thought or to form an image of it in the brain. "Yes" and "No" also have no images: someone who judges that the earth is round and someone who judges that it is not round both have the same things depicted in the brain, namely the earth and roundness, but the first person adds an affirmation to them, an action the mind conceives without any corporeal image, and the other adds the contrary action, negation, which allows even less of an image.

Whenever we speak of ideas, then, we are not referring to images painted in the fantasy, but to anything in the mind when we can truthfully say that we are conceiving something, however we conceive it.

It follows that we can express nothing by our words when we understand what we are saying unless, by the same token, it were certain that we had in us the idea of the thing we were signifying by our words, although this idea is at times more clear and distinct, and at others more obscure and confused, as we shall explain below.[3] For there would be a contradiction in maintaining that I know what I am saying in uttering a word, and yet that I am conceiving nothing in uttering it except the sound itself of the word.

This allows us to see the falsity of two very dangerous views that have recently been advanced by philosophers.

---

[2] This example is borrowed from Descartes. See Sixth Meditation, *Philosophical Writings*, vol. 2, pp. 50–1.

[3] Cf. Descartes to Mersenne, July 1641, *Philosophical Writings*, vol. 3, p. 185.

The first is that we have no idea of God.[4] For if we had no idea of God, in uttering the name "God" we would conceive only these three letters, "G," "o," "d."[a] And a Frenchman would have nothing more in his mind on hearing the name *Dieu* than when, in entering a synagogue and being entirely ignorant of Hebrew, he heard *Adonai* or *Elohim* uttered in Hebrew.

Moreover, when men such as Caligula and Domitian called themselves God, they would not have committed any impiety since there [42] is nothing in these letters or the two syllables *Deus* which could not be attributed to a man if no idea were connected to them. This is why a Dutchman could not be accused of impiety for calling himself *Ludovicus Dieu*.[5] What, then, did the impiety of these princes consist in if not that, retaining at least part of the idea in the word *Deus*, such as having an excellent nature worthy of adoration, they appropriated the name with this idea for themselves?

If we had no idea of God, on what could we base everything we say about God, such as that there is only one, that he is eternal, all powerful, all good, all wise? None of this is contained in the sound "God," but only in the idea of God connected to this sound.

This is also the only reason we refuse to give the name "God" to all the false divinities. It is not because this word taken materially could not be attributed to them, since the pagans in fact did so, but because the idea of a sovereign being connected by usage to this word "God" conforms only to the one true God.

The second of these false views is maintained by an Englishman: "that reasoning is simply joining together and linking names by the word 'is.' It would follow that in reasoning our inferences do not touch the nature of things, but merely their labels; that is, we simply see whether we are combining the names of things well or badly according to the arbitrary conventions we have laid down concerning their meaning."

To which that author adds: "If this is so, as may well be the case, reasoning will depend on words, words on the imagination, and the imagination will depend, as I believe it does, on the motions of bodily organs; and so the mind will be nothing more than motion occurring in various parts of an organic body."[6]

We have to believe that these words express an objection far removed from their author's real opinion. But since, taken literally, they would deny the immortality of the soul, it is important to make their falsity evident, which will not be difficult. For the conventions this philosopher mentions could be nothing but agreements we have made to take certain sounds as signs of ideas in the mind. So if we did not have ideas of things in addition to these names, [43] these conventions would have

---

4   Cf. Hobbes, *Third Set of Objections to Descartes' Meditations* and Gassendi, *Fifth Set of Objections to Descartes' Meditations, Philosophical Writings*, vol. 2, pp. 127, 199–200.

5   This refers to the Protestant minister, Louis de Dieu (1590–1642).

6   Cf. Hobbes, *Third Set of Objections to Descartes' Meditations, Philosophical Writings*, vol. 2, pp. 125–6.

a   The French text reads: "si nous n'en avions aucune idée, en prononçant le nom de Dieu, nous n'en concevrions que ces quatres lettres D, i, e, u ..."

been impossible, just as it is impossible to make blind people understand what the words "red," "green," and "blue" mean by any convention because, lacking these ideas altogether, they cannot connect them to any sounds.

Furthermore, because different nations have given different names to things, even to the clearest and simplest, such as the objects of geometry, they could not make the same inferences about the same truths if reasoning were merely connecting names by the word "is."

Moreover, as it appears from their different vocabularies that the Arabs, for example, do not give the same meanings to sounds as the French, likewise they could not agree in their judgments and inferences if reasoning depended on this convention.

Finally, there is a considerable equivocation in this word "arbitrary" when it is said that the meaning of words is arbitrary. For it is true that it is purely arbitrary to connect a certain idea to one particular sound rather than another. But ideas – at least those that are clear and distinct – are not at all arbitrary things depending on our fancy. This is shown by the absurdity of imagining that very real effects could depend on purely arbitrary things. Now when someone has concluded by reasoning that the iron axle that goes through two grindstones of a mill could turn without making the one below turn if, being round, it went through a round hole; but that it could not turn without making the one above turn if, being square, it were embedded in a square hole in the upper stone, the claimed effect follows infallibly. Consequently reasoning is not a collection of names according to a convention depending entirely on human fancy, but a solid and practical judgment about the nature of things by considering ideas in the mind that people chose to mark by certain names.

Thus it is sufficiently clear what we mean by the word "idea." It remains only to say a word about the origin of our ideas.

The issue comes down to whether all our ideas come from the senses, and whether this common maxim should be considered true: *Nihil est in intellectu quod non prius fuerit in sensu.*[7] [Nothing is in the intellect which was not previously in the senses.]

This is the opinion of a widely admired philosopher, [44] who begins his logic with this proposition: *Omnis idea orsum ducit à sensibus.* Every idea originates in the senses.[8] He admits, however, that not all our ideas exist in the mind exactly as they were in the senses, but he claims that at least they are formed from those which passed through the senses. This happens either by composition, as when we form a golden mountain from separate images of gold and a mountain; or by amplification and diminution, when we form a giant or a pygmy from the image of a person of

---

[7]   Cited by Etienne Gilson, *Index scolastico-cartésien* (Paris, Alcan), 1913, p. 203, as an extract from *Eustachio a Sancto Paulo, Summa philosophica quadripartita,* 1st ed., vol. 3, pp. 427–9.

[8]   Gassendi, *Institutio Logica,* Canon II, p. 84. See also Canon III: "Every idea either comes through the senses, or is formed from those which come through the senses." Cf. p. 85. (Clair and Girbal attribute this text to the English mathematician and logician, John Wallis.)

ordinary height; or by accommodation and analogy, when we form the image of a house we have not seen from the idea of one we have seen. Thus, he says, we conceive God, who cannot fall under the senses, under the image of a venerable old man.

According to[b] this view, although not all our ideas are like some particular body we have seen or which has struck our senses, they would all nonetheless be corporeal and would represent nothing which had not entered our senses at least in a piecemeal way. So we will conceive nothing except by images like those formed in the brain when we see or imagine bodies.

Although his opinion is shared by several Scholastic philosophers, I shall not hesitate to point out that it is absurd and as contrary to religion as to true philosophy. For, just to say the obvious, there is nothing we conceive more distinctly than our thought itself, nor any proposition clearer to us than this: "I think, therefore I am." Now we could not have any certainty regarding this proposition if we did not distinctly conceive what *being* is, and what *thinking* is. No one needs to ask for an explanation of these terms because they are among those everyone understands so well that trying to explain them only obscures them. If it is undeniable, then, that we have in us the ideas of being and thought, I ask, by what senses did they enter? Are they luminous or colored for entering by sight? Low-pitched or high-pitched, for entering by hearing? Do they have a good or [45] bad odor for entering by smell? A good or bad flavor for entering by taste? Are they cold or hot, hard or soft, for entering by touch? If someone says they are formed from other sensible images, let him tell us from which other sensible images the ideas of being and thought have been formed and how they could have been formed from them, whether by composition, amplification, diminution, or analogy. If there are no reasonable answers to all these questions, it must be admitted that the ideas of being and thought in no way originate in the senses. Instead, the soul has the faculty to form them from itself, although often it is prompted to do so by something striking the senses, just as a painter can be brought to produce a canvas by the money promised him, without our thereby being able to say that the money was the origin of the painting.

But the thought added by these same authors, that our idea of God originates in the senses because we conceive him under the idea of a venerable old man, is worthy only of the anthropomorphites or those who confuse our true ideas of mental things with the false images we are led to form of them by the bad habit of wanting to imagine everything. Rather, it is as absurd to try to imagine what is in no way corporeal as to try to hear colors and see sounds.

To refute this view it is only necessary to consider that if we had no other idea of God than that of a venerable old man, all our judgments about God[c] would have to

---

[b] This paragraph was added in II.

[c] ... God would be false to us whenever they conflict with this idea. For we have no other rule for the truth of our judgments than when they conform to the ideas we have of things. Thus it would be false to say that God has no parts ... (I)

appear false to us whenever they conflict with this idea. For we are naturally led to believe that our judgments are false when we see clearly that they are contrary to our ideas of things. Thus we could not judge with certainty that God has no parts, that he is incorporeal, that he is everywhere, and that he is invisible, since none of this agrees with the idea of a venerable old man. That God is sometimes represented under this form does not imply that this is the idea we ought [46] to have of him. For it would also follow that we had no other idea of the Holy Ghost than that of a dove, because he is represented under the form of a dove, and that we conceive God as a sound because the sound of the name "God" awakens the idea of him in us.

It is thus false that all our ideas originate in the senses. On the contrary, one can say that no idea in the mind originates in the senses, although motions in the brain, which is all the senses can bring about, may provide the occasion for the soul to form various ideas that might not have been formed without this occasion. Indeed, even these ideas almost never resemble what is in the senses and the brain. Furthermore, it would be absurd to attribute the many ideas that have nothing whatever to do with corporeal images to the senses.

If[d] someone objects that while we are having an idea of something mental like thought we continue to form some corporeal image, at least of the sound which signifies the idea, this in no way conflicts with what has been proved. For the image of the sound of the thought we imagine is not the image of the thought itself, but only of a sound. It can make us conceive it only inasmuch as the soul, being accustomed when it conceives this sound to conceive the thought too, forms at the same time a completely mental idea of the thought. This idea has no relation to the idea of the sound, but is connected to it only by habit. This is seen in the fact that deaf people who lack images of sounds nonetheless have ideas of their thoughts, at least when they reflect on what they are thinking.

CHAPTER 2

Ideas considered according to their objects

Everything we conceive is represented to the mind either as a thing, a manner of a thing, or a modified thing. [47]

I call whatever is conceived as subsisting by itself and as the subject of everything conceived about it, a thing. It is otherwise called a substance.

I call a manner of a thing, or mode, or attribute, or quality, that which, conceived as in the thing and not able to subsist without it, determines it to be in a certain way and causes it to be so named.

I call a modified thing whatever is considered a substance determined by a certain manner or mode.

---

[d]   This paragraph was added in II.

This will be made clearer by some examples.

When I think of a body, my idea of it represents a thing or a substance, because I consider it as a thing subsisting by itself and needing no other subject to exist.

But when I think that this body is round, the idea I have of roundness represents only a manner of being or a mode which I conceive as incapable of subsisting naturally without the body whose roundness it is.

Finally, when I join the mode to the thing and consider a round body, this idea represents a modified thing.

Nouns used to express things are called substantives or absolutes, such as "earth," "sun," "mind," "God."

Nouns that signify modes primarily and directly, such as "hardness," "heat," "justice," and "prudence," are also called substantives or absolutes because their signification has some relation to substances.

Nouns that signify things as modified, indicating the thing primarily and directly although more confusedly, and the mode indirectly although more distinctly, are called adjectives or connotatives. Examples are "round," "hard," "just," "prudent."

We should remark, however, that the mind, accustomed to knowing most things as modified since it knows them almost always by accidents or qualities that strike the senses, often divides the essence of the substance itself into two ideas, viewing one as subject and the other as mode. For example, although everything in God is God himself, this does not prevent us from conceiving him as an infinite being, regarding infinity as an attribute of God and being as the subject of this attribute. Thus a human being is often considered as the subject of humanity *habens humanitatem* [possessing humanity], and consequently as a modified thing.

In these cases the essential attribute, which is the thing itself, is taken for a mode because it is conceived as in a subject. This is [48] properly speaking an abstraction of substance, such as humanity, corporeality, and reason.

Nevertheless, it is very important to know a real mode from an apparent mode, because one of the main causes of error is confusing modes with substances and substances with modes. Thus it is the nature of a true mode that one can clearly and distinctly conceive the substance of which it is a mode without it, while not being able, conversely, to conceive the mode clearly without conceiving at the same time its relation to the substance[a] without which it could not exist naturally.

It is not impossible to conceive the mode without paying distinct and explicit attention to its subject. But the fact that we cannot deny this relation of the mode without destroying our idea of it shows that the[b] relation to the substance is included at least confusedly in the idea of the mode. On the other hand, when we conceive two things or two substances, we can deny one of the other without destroying either idea.

[a] ... substance of which it is a mode, and without ... (I)
[b] ... the notion of the relation ... (I)

31

For example, I can easily deny prudence without paying distinct attention to someone who is prudent, but I cannot conceive prudence while denying its relation to some person or other intelligent nature having this virtue.

By contrast, when I have considered everything that pertains to an extended substance called body, such as extension, shape, mobility, and divisibility, and, on the other hand, everything pertaining to mind or thinking substance, such as thinking, doubting, remembering, willing, and reasoning, I can deny of extended substance everything I conceive of thinking substance without thereby ceasing to conceive distinctly extended substance and all the other attributes joined to it. And conversely, I can deny of thinking substance everything I have conceived about extended substance without thereby ceasing to conceive quite distinctly everything I conceive in thinking substance.

This also shows that thought is not a mode of extended substance, because we can deny extension and all the properties depending on it of thought without ceasing to conceive thought clearly.

On[c] this subject of modes, we should note that some [49] may be called internal because they are conceived in the substance, such as "round" and "square." Others may be called external because they are taken from something that is not in the substance, such as "loved," "seen," and "desired," names derived from the actions of something else. In the Schools these are called *external denominations*. When these words are based on the way things are conceived, they are called second intentions. So, for example, to be a subject and to be an attribute are second intentions because these are ways of conceiving things taken from the mental action that connects two ideas by affirming one of the other.

We should note further that some modes can be called substantial because they represent true substances applied to other substances as modes and manners. Being clothed and being armed are modes of this sort.

Other modes can be called simply real. These are true modes which are not substances but manners of a substance.

Finally, some can be called negative because they represent the substance with a negation of some real or substantial mode.

Whether they are substances or modes, if the objects represented by these ideas actually are as they are represented, the ideas are called true. If they are not such, the ideas are false in the way they can be. The latter, which the Schoolmen call beings of reason, ordinarily arise when the mind combines two ideas that are real in themselves but not joined in truth, to form a single idea. For example, the idea we can form of a golden mountain is a being of reason, because it is composed of the two ideas of a mountain and of gold, which it represents as united although they are not so in reality.

---

[c]   The text from here to the end of the chapter was added in II.

CHAPTER 3

Aristotle's ten categories

We can relate this discussion of ideas according to their objects to Aristotle's ten categories, since they are only different classes to which this philosopher wanted to reduce all the objects of our thoughts, by putting all [50] substances in the first class and all accidents in the other nine. They are as follows.[1]

I. SUBSTANCE, which is either mental or corporeal, etc.

II. QUANTITY, which is called discrete when the parts are not connected, as in number, and continuous when they are connected. In the latter case they are either successive, for example in time and motion, or permanent, otherwise called space or extension in length, width, and depth. Length alone produces lines, length and width produce surfaces, and the three together produce solids.

III. QUALITY, which Aristotle divides into four kinds:

The first includes *habits*, that is, dispositions of the mind or body that are acquired by repeated acts, such as the sciences, the virtues, the vices, skill in painting or writing or dancing.

The second are *natural powers*, such as the faculties of the soul or body, for example, understanding, will, memory, the five senses, and the power to walk.

The third are *sensible qualities*, such as hardness, softness, heaviness, cold, heat, colors, sounds, odors, or different tastes.

The fourth is form or shape, which is the external determination of quantity, such as being round, square, spherical, or cubic.

IV. RELATION. Either the connection between one thing and another, such as father, son, master, servant, king, subject; or between the power and its object, such as of sight to the visible. This includes anything indicating a comparison, such as similar, equal, greater, smaller.

V. ACTIVITY. Either in itself, such as to walk, to dance, to know, or to love; or outside itself, such as to beat, to cut, to break, to illuminate, or to heat.

VI. PASSIVITY. To be beaten, to be broken, to be illuminated, to be heated.

VII. PLACE. That is, the answer to questions concerning place, such as to be in Rome, in Paris, in one's study, in bed, in one's chair.

VIII. TIME. That is, the answer to questions concerning time, such as when did he live? one hundred years ago; when did it happen? yesterday. [51]

IX. POSITION. To be seated, standing, lying down, in front of, behind, to the right, to the left.

X. STATE. That is, to have something around oneself serving as clothing, ornaments, or armor, such as to be dressed, to be crowned, to be shod, to be armed.

These are Aristotle's ten categories of which so much mystery is made,[a] although

---

[1] Here the authors are condensing Aristotle's list of categories, although not in the order he presents them. See *Categories*, ch. 4, *Complete Works*, vol. 1, p. 4.

[a] ... made in the Schools, and which take so long to learn, although ... (I)

to tell the truth, in themselves they are fairly useless. Not only are they hardly helpful in forming judgments, which is the goal of a true logic, but they are often harmful for two reasons which are important to note.

The first is that these categories are viewed as based on reason and truth, when in fact they are completely arbitrary, having no foundation but the imagination of one man who had no authority to prescribe laws to others. Each of us has as much right as he has to arrange the objects of our thoughts in other ways, according to our own manner of philosophizing. In fact, others have included everything in the world, viewed from the standpoint of a new philosophy, in the following couplet:

> *Mens, mensura, quies, motus, positura, figura:*
> *Sunt cum materia cunctarum exordia rerum.*[2]
> [Mind, measure, rest, motion, position, shape:
> Are with matter the beginning of all things.]

That is, these people are persuaded that all of nature can be explained by considering only these seven things or modes:

1. *Mens,* the mind or substance that thinks.
2. *Materia,* body or extended substance.
3. *Mensura,* the largeness or smallness of each part of matter.
4. *Positura,* their position with respect to each other.
5. *Figura,* their shape.
6. *Motus,* their motion.
7. *Quies,* their rest or least motion.

The second reason that makes studying the categories dangerous is that it accustoms people to be satisfied with words, and to imagine that they know everything when they know only their arbitrary labels. These do not produce any clear and distinct ideas in the mind, as we shall show elsewhere. [52]

We could also mention here the attributes of the Lullists,[3] e.g., *goodness, power, greatness, etc.* But it is so ridiculous for them to think they can explain everything by applying metaphysical words to whatever is proposed to them, that it does not even deserve to be refuted.

A contemporary author has quite reasonably said that Aristotle's rules of logic serve merely to prove what one person already knows to another, but Lull's art is useful only for producing an unreasonable discourse about something one does not know.[4] Ignorance is worth much more than this spurious knowledge, which makes us imagine that we know what we do not know at all. For, as St. Augustine wisely

---

[2] It appears that Regius, the author of *Fundamenta Physices* (Amsterdam, 1646), created this verse according to the Aristotelian mnemonic technique, but for the Cartesian cause.

[3] Raymond Lully (Ramon Lull) (c. 1232–1316) was a Catalan philosopher, poet, and author of the complex *Arts of Memory* which he believed would convert Moslems to Christianity. Lull maintained that every article of faith could be perfectly demonstrated by logic.

[4] Descartes, *Discourse on the Method*, Pt. II, *Philosophical Writings*, vol. 1, p. 119.

remarks in his book on the usefulness of belief, this tendency of the mind is blameworthy for two reasons. First, he who is falsely persuaded that he knows the truth thereby makes himself incapable of learning about it. The other is that this presumption and rashness are marks of a mind which is not well formed: *Opinari, duas ob res turpissimum est: quod discere non potest qui sibi jam se scire persuasit: et per se ipsa temeritas non bene`affecti animi signum est.*[5] [To be opinionated is very bad for two reasons. First, whoever has convinced himself that he already knows cannot learn. Second, the recklessness itself reveals a mind which is not well disposed.] For in the purity of the Latin tongue, the word *Opinari* signifies the tendency of a mind to consent too readily to uncertain things and thus to believe that it knows what it does not. This is why all the philosophers maintained: *Sapientem nihil opinari.* [A wise person has no opinions.] And Cicero, reproaching himself for this vice, said he was *magnus opinator* [highly opinionated].[6]

CHAPTER 4

Ideas of things and ideas of signs

When we consider an object in itself and in its own being, without carrying the view of the mind to what it can represent, our idea of it is an idea of a thing, such as the idea of the earth [53] or the sun. But when we view a certain object merely as representing another, our idea of it is an idea of a sign, and the first object is called a sign.[1] This is how we ordinarily think of maps and paintings. Consequently the sign includes two ideas, one of the thing which represents, the other of the thing represented. Its nature consists in prompting the second by the first.

Signs can be classified in various ways, but we will content ourselves here with three which are the most useful.

First, there are certain signs, which in Greek are called τεχμήρια, as breathing is a sign of life in animals. And there are signs that are only probable, which are called σημεῖα in Greek, as pallor is only a probable sign of pregnancy in women.[2]

Most hasty judgments arise from confusing these two types of signs, and attributing an effect to a particular cause, even though it could also arise from other causes, and hence is only a probable sign of that cause.

Second, there are signs joined to things. For example, facial expressions, which are signs of movements in the soul, are joined to the emotions they signify; symptoms, signs of diseases, are joined to these diseases; and to use some nobler examples, as the ark, the sign of the Church, was joined to Noah and his children,

---

[5]   *The Advantage of Believing*, ch. 11, *Writings*, vol. 2, p. 425.
[6]   *Academica*, Bk II, ch. 20, *De Natura Deorum, Academica*, p. 551.
[1]   St. Augustine, *On Christian Instruction*, Bk. II, ch. 1, *Writings*, vol. 4, p. 61.
[2]   Aristotle, *Prior Analytics*, Bk. II, ch. 27, *Complete Works*, vol. 1, p. 112.

who were the true Church at that time. So our material temples, signs of the faithful, are often joined to the faithful; the dove, symbol of the Holy Ghost, was joined to the Holy Ghost; and the cleansing of baptism, symbol of spiritual birth, is joined to this rebirth.[3]

There are also signs separated from things, as the sacrifices of the ancient law, signs of Jesus Christ immolated, were separated from what they represented.

This classification of signs allows us to establish these maxims:

1. We can never reason strictly either from the presence of a sign to the presence of the thing signified, since there are signs of things that are absent, or from the presence of a sign to the absence of the thing signified, since some signs are of present things. This matter has to be decided, then, by the particular nature of the sign.

2. Although something in a given state cannot be a sign of itself in the same state, since every sign requires a distinction between the thing representing and the thing represented, it is certainly possible for something in a [54] given state to represent itself in another state, just as it is possible for someone in his room to represent himself preaching. Hence the mere difference in state is enough to distinguish the symbol from the thing symbolized. In other words, the same thing can in a particular state be the symbol and in another state be the thing symbolized.

3. It is quite possible for the same thing both to conceal and to reveal another thing at the same time. So those who say "nothing appears by means of that which conceals" have asserted a highly questionable maxim. For since the same thing can be both a thing and a sign at the same time, it can as a thing conceal what it reveals as a sign. Thus the hot cinder, as a thing, hides the fire and, as a sign, reveals it. So also the forms borrowed by angels concealed them as things and revealed them as signs. As things, the Eucharistic symbols conceal the body of Jesus Christ and reveal it as symbols.

4. Since the nature of the sign consists in prompting in the senses the idea of the thing symbolized by means of the idea of the symbol, we can conclude that the sign lasts as long as this effect lasts. That is, it lasts as long as this double idea is prompted, even if the thing in its own nature is destroyed. Hence it does not matter whether the colors of the rainbow which God took as the sign he would never again destroy the human race by flood are real and true, provided that the senses always have the same impression, and that this impression enables them to conceive God's promise.

By the same token, it does not matter whether the bread of the Eucharist remains in its own nature, provided that it still prompts in our senses an image of bread that somehow allows us to conceive that the body of Christ is nourishment for the soul and the way the faithful are united.

The third classification of signs is between natural signs, which do not depend

---

[3] Much of the analysis in this chapter comes from Arnauld's *La Perpétuité de la foi*, vol. 3.

on human fancy, as an image that appears in a mirror is a natural sign of what it represents, and others that are only instituted or conventional, whether they bear some distant relation to the thing symbolized or none at all.[4] Thus words are conventional signs of thoughts, and characters are conventional signs of words. In discussing propositions we shall explain an important truth about this sort of sign, namely that on some occasions the things signified can be affirmed of the signs. [55]

CHAPTER 5

Ideas considered according to their composition or simplicity, including a discussion of knowledge by abstraction or specification

The remark we made in passing in chapter 2, that it is possible to consider a mode without reflecting distinctly on the substance of which it is a mode, provides an opportunity to explain what are called *abstractions of the mind*.

Because of its small scope, the mind cannot perfectly understand things that are even slightly composite unless it considers them a part at a time, as if by the different faces they can assume. This is generally called knowing by abstraction.

But there are different kinds of composition. Some things are composed of really distinct parts, called integral parts, such as the human body and different parts of a number. In this case it is quite easy to conceive how the mind can be applied so as to consider one part independently of another, because the parts are really distinct. This is not what we mean by "abstraction."

Now in these same cases, it is so useful to consider the parts separately rather than the whole that without it we would have almost no distinct knowledge. How could we know the human body, for example, except by dividing it into all its similar and dissimilar parts and giving them different names? All arithmetic is also based on this. No skill is needed to calculate small numbers because the mind can grasp them in their entirety. The art consists entirely in calculating by parts what cannot be calculated as wholes. For example, it would be impossible, whatever the scope of one's mind, to multiply two numbers of eight or nine digits each, taken as wholes.

The second kind of knowledge by parts arises when we consider a mode without paying attention to its substance, or two modes which [56] are joined together in the same substance, taking each one separately. This is what geometers do who take the object of their science to be the body extended in length, width, and depth. In order to know it better they first consider it according to a single dimension, namely length, which they call a line. Next they consider it according to two dimensions, length and width, which they call a surface. And finally, considering all three dimensions together, length, width, and depth, they call it a solid or a body.

---

[4]   St. Augustine, *On Christian Instruction*, Bk. II, ch. I, *Writings*, vol. 4, pp. 61–2.

This shows how ridiculous is the argument of some skeptics who try to call into question the certainty of geometry, on the grounds that it presupposes lines and surfaces which are not found in nature. For geometers by no means assume that there are lines without width or surfaces without depth. They only think that it is possible to consider the length without paying attention to the width. This is indubitable, just as when, in measuring the distance from one city to another, we measure only the length of a path without bothering about its width.

Now the more we can separate the different modes of things, the more easily the mind can know them. It is obvious, for example, that no clear account of reflection and refraction was possible until the analysis of motion distinguished its determination in a particular direction from the motion itself, and even separated various aspects within this determination. Given these distinctions, the account follows easily, as is seen in chapter 2 of Descartes' *Dioptrics*.[1]

The third way of conceiving things by abstraction takes place when, in the case of a single thing having different attributes, we think of one attribute without the other even though they differ only by a distinction of reason. Here is how this happens. Suppose, for example, I reflect that I am thinking, and, in consequence, that I am the I who thinks. In my idea of the I who thinks, I can consider a thinking thing without noticing that it is I, although in me the I and the one who thinks are one and the same thing. The idea I thereby conceive of a person who thinks can represent not only me but all other thinking persons. By the same token, if I draw an equilateral triangle on a piece of paper, and if I concentrate on examining it on this paper along with all the accidental circumstances determining it, [57] I shall have an idea of only a single triangle. But if I ignore all the particular circumstances and focus on the thought that the triangle is a figure bounded by three equal lines, the idea I form will, on the one hand, represent more clearly the equality of lines and, on the other, be able to represent all equilateral triangles. Suppose I go further and, ignoring the equality of lines, I consider it only as a figure bounded by three straight lines. I will then form an idea that can represent all kinds of triangles. If, subsequently, I do not attend to the number of lines, and I consider it only as a flat surface bounded by straight lines, the idea I form can represent all straight-lined figures. Thus I can rise by degrees to extension itself. Now in these abstractions it is clear that the lower degree includes the higher degree along with some particular determination, just as the I includes that which thinks, the equilateral triangle includes the triangle, and the triangle the straight-lined figure. But since the higher degree is less determinate, it can represent more things.

Finally, it is obvious that through these sorts of abstractions, ideas of individuals become common, and common ideas become more common. Accordingly, this gives us the opportunity to proceed to what we have to say about the universality or particularity of ideas.

---

[1] *Optics*, Discourse Two, *Philosophical Writings*, vol. 1, pp. 156–64.

CHAPTER 6

Ideas considered according to their generality, particularity, or singularity

Although everything that exists is singular, nevertheless, by means of the abstractions we have just explained, we all have several sorts of ideas. Some of these represent only a single thing, such as the idea each person has of himself. Others are capable of representing several things equally. For example, when we conceive a triangle without considering anything except that it is a [58] figure having three lines and three angles, our idea allows us to conceive all other triangles.

Ideas that represent only a single thing are called singular or individual, and what they represent are called individuals. Those representing several things are called universal, common, or general.

Nouns used to indicate the first are called proper: "Socrates," "Rome," "Bucephalus." Those which we use to indicate the latter are called common and appellative, such as "man," "city," and "horse." Both universal ideas and common nouns may be called general terms.

But we should note that a word can be general in two ways. The first, called *univocal*, occurs when words are connected with general ideas so that the same word applies to several things, in terms of both the sound and a single idea joined to it. Such are the words just mentioned, "man," "city," and "horse."

The other way is called *equivocal* and occurs when, through usage, different ideas are connected to a single sound so that the same sound applies to several things, not according to a single idea but by different ideas. Thus in French the word *canon* signifies an instrument of war, a decree of a council, and a kind of regulation. But it signifies them only with respect to completely different ideas.

This equivocal universality, however, is of two kinds. Either the different ideas joined to the same sound have no natural relation between them, as in the case of the word *canon*, or there is some relation, as when a word connected primarily to a given idea is joined to another idea merely because there is some relation between the ideas, such as cause, effect, sign, or resemblance. Equivocal words of this sort are called *analogues*. An example is the word "healthy" when attributed to animals, the air, and food. The main idea joined to this word is health, which applies only to animals. But it is connected to another idea close to that one, namely the cause of health, which makes us say that air and food are healthy, because they help us conserve our health.

When we speak of general words here we mean the univocals which are joined to universal or general ideas. [59]

Now in these universal ideas there are two things which it is most important to distinguish clearly, *the comprehension* and *the extension*.

I call the *comprehension* of an idea the attributes that it contains in itself, and that cannot be removed without destroying the idea. For example, the comprehension of the idea of a triangle contains extension, shape, three lines, three angles, and the equality of these three angles to two right angles, etc.

I call the *extension* of an idea the subjects to which this idea applies. These are also called the inferiors of a general term, which is superior with respect to them. For example, the idea of a triangle in general extends to all the different species of triangles.

Although the general idea extends indistinctly to all the subjects to which it applies, that is, to all its inferiors, and the common noun signifies all of them, there is nevertheless this difference between the attributes it includes and the subjects to which it extends: none of its attributes can be removed without destroying the idea, as we have already said, whereas we can restrict its extension by applying it only to some of the subjects to which it conforms without thereby destroying it.

Now the extension of a general idea can be restricted or narrowed in two ways.

The first is by joining another distinct or determinate idea to it, as when I join the idea of having a right angle to the general idea of a triangle. Then I narrow this idea to a single species of triangle, namely the right triangle.

The other is by joining to it merely an indistinct and indeterminate idea of a part, as when I say "some triangle." In that case the common term is said to become particular because it now extends only to a part of the subjects to which it formerly extended, without, however, the part to which it is narrowed being determined.

CHAPTER 7

The five kinds of universal ideas: genus, species, difference, property, and accident

What has been said in the preceding chapters allows us to clarify briefly the five universals usually explained in the Schools. [60]

For when general ideas represent their objects as things and are indicated by terms called substantive or absolute, they are called *genus* or *species*.

The genus

An idea is called a genus when it is so common that it extends to other ideas that are also universal, as the quadrilateral is a genus with respect to the parallelogram and the trapezoid. Substance is a genus with respect to the extended substance called body and the thinking substance called mind.

The species

Common ideas that fall under a more common and general idea are called species, just as the parallelogram and the trapezoid are species of the quadrilateral, and body and mind are species of substance.

Thus the same idea can be a genus with respect to the ideas to which it extends, and a species when compared to another, more general idea. For example, body is a genus with respect to animate and inanimate bodies, and a species with respect to substance. The quadrilateral is a genus compared to the parallelogram and the trapezoid, and a species with respect to shape.

But there is another notion of the word "species" that applies only to ideas that cannot be genera. This occurs when an idea has under it only individuals and particulars, just as the circle has under it only individual circles, which are all of the same species. This is called the lowest species, *species infima*.

There is also a genus that is not a species, namely the highest of all the genera. Whether this genus is being or substance is unimportant, and is more a question for metaphysics than logic.

I have said that general ideas that represent their objects as things are called genera or species. For it is not necessary for the objects of these ideas actually to be things or substances, but it suffices for us to consider them as things. In that case even when they are modes we relate them not to their substances, but to other ideas of modes which are more or less general. Thus shape, which is only a mode with respect to a body having shape, is [61] a genus with respect to curved and straight-lined figures, etc.

By contrast, if ideas that represent their objects as modified things, and that are indicated by adjectival or connotative terms, are compared with the substances these connotative terms signify confusedly although directly, then they are called not genera or species, but *differences*, *properties*, or *accidents*. This is true whether in fact these connotative terms signify essential attributes, which are actually only the thing itself, or true modes.

These ideas are called *differences* when their object is an essential attribute distinguishing one species from another, such as extended, thinking,[a] and rational.

An idea is called a *property* when its object is an attribute actually belonging to the essence of the thing as long as it is not the primary attribute considered in the essence. These are merely attributes dependent on the primary attribute, such as divisible, immortal, and docile.

Finally, an idea is called a *common accident* when its object is a true mode which can be separated, at least by the mind, from the thing whose accident it is said to be, without destroying the idea of this thing in the mind. Examples are round, hard, just, and prudent. All this must be explained in more detail.

The difference

When a genus has two species, it is necessary for the idea of each species to include something not contained in the idea of the genus. Otherwise, if each idea included

---

[a] Two versions of the text are available: *pesant* = heavy, *pensant* = thinking. I have chosen *pensant* as the more likely, and the other seems to be a misprint.

only what is included in the genus, it would be merely the genus. Since the genus applies to each species, each species would apply to the other. Hence the primary essential attribute which each species includes over and above the genus is called its difference. Our idea of it is a universal idea because one and the same idea can represent this difference everywhere it is found, that is, in all the inferiors of the species.

Example. Body and mind are the two species of substance. Therefore the idea of a body must have something more in it than the idea of substance, and the same is true for the idea of a mind. Now the first additional thing we see in the body is extension, and the first additional thing we see in the mind is thought. Thus the difference of body will be extension and that of mind will be thought, [62] that is, the body will be an extended substance and the mind a thinking substance.

From this we can see, first, that the difference has two aspects, one with respect to the genus it divides and separates, the other the species it constitutes and forms, making up the principal part of the comprehension of the idea of the species. From this it follows that every species can be expressed by a single noun, such as "mind" or "body"; or by two words, namely one for the genus and one for the difference, joined together; this is called a definition, such as "thinking substance," "extended substance."

Second, it is clear that since the difference constitutes the species and distinguishes it from other species, it must have the same extension as the species. Thus they must be able to be said reciprocally of each other, for example, that everything that thinks is mind, and everything that is mind thinks.

Often, however, we can see in certain things no attribute that applies to the whole species and only that species. In those cases we join several attributes together whose combination, found only in this species, constitutes its difference. Thus the Platonists, viewing demons as well as humans as rational animals, did not consider the difference rational, reciprocal to human. This is why they added another attribute to it, such as mortal, which is also not reciprocal to human since it applies to brutes. But the two together apply only to humans. This is what we do in the ideas we form of most animals.

Finally, we should note that it is not always necessary for the two differences dividing a genus both to be positive, but it is enough if one is, just as two people are distinguished from each other if one has a burden the other lacks, although the one who does not have the burden has nothing the other one does not have. This is how humans are distinguished from brutes in general, since a human is an animal with a mind, *animal mente praeditum*, and a brute is a pure animal, *animal merum*. For the idea of a brute in general includes nothing [63] positive which is not in a human, but is joined only to the negation of what is in a human, namely the mind. So the entire difference between the idea of an animal and the idea of a brute is that the comprehension of the idea of an animal neither includes nor excludes thought – the idea even includes it in its extension because it applies to an animal that thinks – whereas the idea of a brute excludes thought from its comprehension and thus cannot apply to an animal that thinks.

The property

When we have found the difference constituting a species, that is, the principal essential attribute that distinguishes it from all other species, if, considering its nature in more detail, we find yet another attribute necessarily connected to this primary attribute, that therefore applies to all and only this species, *omni et soli* [to all and only], we call it a property. Because it is signified by a connotative term, we attribute it to the species as its property. And because it also applies to all the inferiors of the species, and the sole idea we have of it, once formed, can represent this property everywhere it exists, it is considered the fourth of the common and universal terms.

Example. Having a right angle is the essential difference of the right triangle. Since it is a necessary consequence of the right angle that the square of the hypotenuse is equal to the squares of the two sides which enclose it, the equality of these squares is considered a property of the right triangle, applying to all and only right triangles.

The term "property," however, is sometimes extended further, and divided into four kinds.

The first is the one just explained, *quod convenit omni soli, et semper* [that applies to all exclusively at all times]. For example, it is a property of all and only circles, and always, that lines drawn from the center to the circumference are equal.

The second *quod convenit omni, sed non soli* [that applies to all, but not exclusively], as it is said to be proper to extension to be divisible because every extension can be divided, although duration, number, and force can also be divided.

The third is *quod convenit soli, sed non omni* [that applies exclusively but not to all], just as it applies only to a human to be a doctor or a philosopher, although not all humans are such. [64]

The fourth *quod convenit omni et soli, sed non semper* [that applies to all exclusively, but not at all times], where we cite the example of hair becoming gray, *canescere*, which applies to all and only humans, but only in old age.

The accident

We said previously in the second chapter that a mode is that which can exist naturally only through a substance, and which is in no way necessarily connected to the idea of a thing, so that one can easily conceive the thing without conceiving the mode. For example, we can easily conceive a human without conceiving prudence, but we cannot conceive prudence without conceiving either a human or another intelligent nature which is prudent.

Now when the confused and indeterminate idea of substance is joined to a distinct idea of some mode, this idea can represent everything that has the mode, as the idea of prudent represents all prudent people, and the idea of round represents all round bodies. In that case, this idea, expressed by a connotative term such as "prudent" or "round," constitutes the fifth universal, which is called an accident because it is not essential to the thing to which it is attributed. If it were essential it would be a difference or a property.

But we must remark here, as was said previously, that when two substances are considered together, one can be viewed as a mode of the other. Thus a clothed person could be considered as a whole composed of the person and the clothing. But with respect to the person, being clothed is only a mode or a manner of being under which one is considered, although the clothes are substances. This is why being clothed is only a fifth universal.

This is more than anyone needs to know about the five universals treated so extensively in the Schools. Knowing that there are genera, species, differences, properties, and accidents is not very useful. The important point is to recognize the true genera of things, the true species of each genus, their true differences, their true properties, and the accidents that apply to them. This is what we shall elucidate in the following chapters, after first saying something about complex terms. [65]

CHAPTER 8

Complex terms and their universality or particularity

Occasionally we join a term to various other terms, composing in the mind a complete idea, of which one can often affirm or deny what could not be affirmed or denied of each of these terms taken separately. For example, these are complex terms: "a prudent person," "a transparent body," "Alexander son of Philip."

This addition is sometimes made by the relative pronoun, as when I say: "a body that is transparent," "Alexander who is the son of Philip," "the Pope who is the Vicar of Jesus Christ."

Moreover, it can be said that even if the relative pronoun is not always expressed, it is in some way always implicitly understood because we can express it if we like without changing the proposition.

For it is the same thing to say "a transparent body" or "a body that is transparent."

What is more noteworthy about complex terms is that the addition made to a term is of two sorts: one can be called an *explication*, the other a *determination*.

An addition is merely an *explication* when it only develops either what is contained in the comprehension of the idea of the first term, or at least what applies to it as one of its accidents, provided that it applies generally and throughout its extension. Suppose I say, for example: "a human who is an animal endowed with reason," or "a human who naturally desires to be happy," or "a human who is mortal." These additions are only explications because they in no way change the idea of the term "human" or restrict it to signifying only some humans. They indicate merely what applies to all humans.

All the additions made to names that distinctly indicate an individual are of this sort, as when we say "Paris which is the largest city of Europe," "Julius Caesar who was the greatest military leader of the world," "Aristotle the prince of philosophers," "Louis XIV King of France." For these individual terms, distinctly expressed, are always taken in their entire extension, being as determinate as possible. [66]

The other sort of addition, which can be called a *determination*, occurs when the addition to a general word restricts its signification and causes it no longer to be taken through its entire extension, but only for a part of it, as when I say, "transparent bodies," "knowledgeable people," "a rational animal." These additions are not simple explications but determinations, because they restrict the extension of the first term, causing the word "body" to signify no more than some bodies, the word "people" only some people, and the word "animal" only some animals.

When these added conditions are individual, they make a general word individual. When I say, for example, "the present Pope," this determines the general word "Pope" to the unique and singular person Alexander VII.[a]

Two sorts of complex terms can be further distinguished: those that are complex in expression, and others that are complex only in meaning.

The first kind are those in which the addition is expressed. Such are all the examples mentioned up to now.

The latter kind are those in which one of the terms is not expressed but only implicitly understood. In France when we say "the King," for example, this term is complex in meaning, because in uttering the word "King" we do not have in mind merely the general idea which answers to this word, but we mentally join to it the idea of Louis XIV, who is presently King of France. There are countless terms in ordinary speech that are complex in this way, such as the name "Sir" in each family, and so on.

There are even words that are complex in expression for one thing and yet complex in meaning for others. When we say "the prince of philosophers," for example, this term is complex in expression since the word "prince" is determined

---

[a]   . . . Alexander VII; the father of Alexander the Great, this determines the general word "father" to a unique man, since there could only be one who was the father of Alexander. – Two . . . (I)

by the word "philosopher." But with respect to Aristotle, whom the Schoolmen indicate by this term, it is complex only in meaning, since the idea of Aristotle is only in the mind without being expressed by any sound that distinguishes it in particular.

All connotative or adjectival terms either are parts of a complex term when their substantive is expressed, or are [67] complex in meaning when it is implicit. For, as we said in chapter 2, these connotative terms indicate a subject directly although more confusedly, and a form or mode indirectly although more distinctly. Hence the subject is only a very general and confused idea, sometimes of a being, sometimes of a body, which is usually determined by the distinct idea of the form joined to it. *Album* [white], for example, signifies a thing that has whiteness, which determines the confused idea of a thing to represent only those things having this quality.

What is even more remarkable about these complex terms is that some actually are determined to a single individual, but still retain a certain equivocal universality, which could be called equivocation by error. In these cases everyone has agreed that this term signifies just one unique thing, but for lack of identifying what this unique thing really is, some apply it to one thing and others to another. This means the exact signification of the term still needs to be determined, either by different circumstances or by the subsequent discourse.

Thus the words "true religion" signify but a single and unique religion, which is in fact the Catholic religion, since that is the only true one. But because each nation and each sect believes that its religion is the true religion, these words are highly equivocal in people's mouths, if only by error. If we read in a history book that a prince was zealous about the true religion, we could not know what was meant unless we knew the historian's religion. For if he were a Protestant, it would mean the Protestant religion; if he were an Arab Moslem who spoke this way about his prince, it would mean the Moslem religion; and we could judge that it was the Catholic religion only if we knew that the historian was Catholic.

Complex terms that are thus equivocal by error are primarily those containing qualities that are judged not by the senses but only by the mind, about which people can easily disagree.

If I say, for example, "Only men six feet tall were enlisted in Marius's army," this complex term "men six feet tall" would not be subject to equivocation by error, because it is very easy to measure men in order to decide whether they are six feet tall. But if it were said that one ought to enlist only valiant men, the term "valiant men" [68] would be more susceptible to equivocation by error, that is, to being attributed to men believed to be valiant who in fact were not so.

Comparative terms are also highly subject to equivocation by error: "the greatest geometer of Paris," "the most knowledgeable person," "the most adroit," "the richest," etc. For although these terms are determined by individual conditions, since there is only one person who is the greatest geometer of Paris, these words nonetheless could easily be attributed to several individuals, although in fact they apply to only one, because people are easily divided in their opinions on this subject. Thus several people give this name to whoever each believes is superior in this respect to others.

The words "an author's meaning," "an author's doctrine on such-and-such a subject," are also of this sort, especially when an author is not very clear. In that case the opinion is a matter of dispute, just as we see philosophers arguing constantly about Aristotle's opinions, all claiming support for their view. For even though Aristotle had only a single and unique view on any given subject, since these views have been interpreted differently, the words "Aristotle's opinion" are equivocal by error, because people call Aristotle's opinion what they understand his true opinion to be. Since one person understands one thing and others another, these terms "Aristotle's opinion on such-and-such a subject," however individual they are in themselves, could apply to several things, namely to all the different opinions that have been attributed to him. In each person's mouth they signify what that person conceives this philosopher's opinion to be.

But to understand better the nature of equivocation in these terms, which we have called equivocation by error, we should notice that these words are connotative either explicitly or in meaning. Now as we have already said, in connotative words one has to consider the subject which is directly but confusedly expressed, and the form or mode which is distinctly although indirectly expressed. So "white" signifies a body confusedly and whiteness distinctly; "Aristotle's opinion" signifies some opinion or thought or doctrine confusedly, and it signifies distinctly the relation of this thought to Aristotle, to whom it is attributed. [69]

Now when there is some equivocation in these words, it is not properly speaking by virtue of this form or mode, which being distinct is invariable. It is also not by virtue of the confused subject, when it remains confused. The words "prince of philosophers," for example, can never be equivocal as long as the idea of the prince of philosophers is not applied to some distinctly known individual. The equivocation occurs only because the mind often substitutes for the confused subject a distinct or determinate subject to which it attributes the form or mode. Having different opinions on the matter, people may impute this quality to different persons, and subsequently indicate them by these words which they think apply to them, just as the name "prince of philosophers" was used to mean Plato and now means Aristotle.

The words "true religion" are not at all equivocal as long as they are joined to a confused idea, and not to the distinct idea of any particular religion, since they signify only what is in fact the true religion. But whenever the mind joins the idea of the true religion to a distinct idea of a particular cult that is known distinctly, these words become highly equivocal and signify in the mouths of each nation the cult they take to be the true one.

The same is true of the words "such-and-such a philosopher's view on such-

and-such a topic." As long as they remain in a general idea, they signify simply or in general the doctrine that philosopher taught on that subject, such as that taught by Aristotle on the nature of the soul: *id quod sensit talis scriptor* [that which a certain writer means]. As long as this *id*, that is, this doctrine, remains in its confused idea without being applied to a distinct idea, these words are by no means equivocal. But when the mind substitutes a distinct doctrine and a distinct subject in place of this confused *id*, namely this doctrine conceived confusedly, then this term will become equivocal, depending on the different distinct ideas which may be substituted for it. Thus "Aristotle's view concerning the nature of the soul" is equivocal in the mouth of Pomponazzi,[1] who claims that Aristotle thought it was mortal, and equally when said by several other of his interpreters who claim, to the contrary, that along with his masters Plato and Socrates, he thought it immortal. Consequently these sorts of words can often signify a thing to which the form indirectly expressed does not apply. Suppose, for example, that Philip was not really Alexander's father, as Alexander himself wanted him to believe. When applied erroneously to Alexander, the words "son of Philip," which in general signify [70] a male engendered by Philip, would signify a person who was not really the son of Philip.

The words "the meaning of Scripture," as applied by heretics to an erroneous view contrary to Scripture, would signify in their mouths the mistaken views they believe to be the meaning of Scripture, and which in this thought they would have called the meaning of Scripture. This is why Calvinists are not more Catholic for protesting that they follow only the word of God. For these words "the word of God" signify in their mouths all the errors they mistakenly take for the word of God.

CHAPTER 9

The clarity and distinctness of ideas, and their obscurity and confusion

In an idea we can distinguish the clarity from the distinctness, and the obscurity from the confusion. For we can say that an idea is clear to us when it strikes us in a lively manner, even though it is not distinct. The idea of pain, for example, strikes us very vividly, and accordingly can be called clear, and yet it is very confused since it represents pain as in the wounded hand although it is only in the mind.

Nevertheless we can say that all ideas are distinct insofar as they are clear, and that their obscurity derives only from their confusion, just as in pain the single sensation which strikes us is clear and also distinct. But what is confused, namely that the sensation is in the hand, is by no means clear to us.

---

[1]   Pietro Pomponazzi (1462–1525) was an Italian philosopher; a neo–Aristotelian from the Padua school, he made a clear distinction between philosophical reflection and dogmas of faith. In his *Tractatus de immortalitate animae* (1516), which was condemned by Rome, he called into question the immortality of the soul.

Taking the clarity and distinctness of ideas for the same thing, then, it is very important to examine why some ideas are clear and others obscure.

But this is shown better by examples than any other way, so we are going to enumerate the main ideas that are clear and distinct and those that are confused and obscure.

The idea each of us has of ourselves as a thing that thinks is very clear, and similarly the ideas of everything that [71] depends[a] on thinking, such as judging, reasoning, doubting, willing, desiring, sensing, and imagining.

We also have very clear ideas of extended substance and whatever belongs to it, such as shape, motion, and rest. For although we can pretend that there is neither body nor shape – something we cannot pretend about thinking substance as long as we are thinking – we cannot, however, deceive ourselves into thinking that we do not conceive extension and shape clearly.

We conceive being, existence, duration, order, and number just as clearly, provided that we think that the duration of each thing is only a mode or manner of considering the thing as long as it continues to exist. Similarly, order and number are not actually different from the things being ordered and numbered.

All these ideas are so clear that we often obscure them when we try to make them clearer and are not satisfied with the ideas formed naturally.

We can also say that the idea we have of God in this life is clear in one sense, although in another sense it is obscure and quite imperfect.

It is clear in being sufficient to make us know a great many attributes in God which we are sure of finding in God alone. It is obscure, however, when compared to the idea had by the blessed in heaven. And it is imperfect because the mind, being finite, can conceive of an infinite object only very imperfectly. But being perfect and being clear are different conditions in an idea. For it is perfect when it represents everything in its object, and it is clear when it represents enough of it to conceive of the object clearly and distinctly.

Confused and obscure ideas are those we have of sensible qualities, such as colors, sounds, odors, tastes, cold, heat, weight, and so on, and also of our appetites, hunger, thirst, bodily pain, etc. Here is what makes these ideas confused.

Because we were children before we became adults, and because external things acted on us, causing various sensations in the soul by the impressions they made on the body, the soul saw that these [72] sensations were not caused in it at will, but only on the occasion of certain bodies, for example, when it sensed heat in approaching the fire. But it was not content to judge merely that there was something outside it that caused its sensations, in which case it would not have been mistaken. It went further, believing that what was in these objects was exactly like the sensations or ideas it had on these occasions. From these judgments the soul formed ideas of these things, transporting the sensations of heat, color, and so on, to the things themselves outside the soul. These are the obscure and confused

[a]   ... depends only ... (I)

ideas we have of sensible qualities, the soul adding its false judgments to what nature caused it to know.

Since these ideas are in no way natural, but arbitrary, we are behaving in a very bizarre fashion. For although heat and burning are merely two sensations, one weaker and the other stronger, we impute the heat to the fire and say that the fire is hot. But we do not put the burning there or the pain we feel when we get too close, and we never say that the fire is in pain.[b]

Even though people realized that the pain is not in the fire that burns the hand, they may well have been mistaken in thinking it is in the hand burned by the fire. Instead, to consider it more carefully, it is only in the mind, although occasioned by what happens in the hand, because bodily pain is nothing more than a feeling of aversion in the soul to some motion contrary to the natural constitution of its body.

This was recognized not only by several ancient philosophers, such as the Cyrenaics,[1] but also by St. Augustine in various places. He says in Book 14, chapter 15, of *The City of God*, that the pains we call corporeal are not of the body, but of the soul which is in the body, and because of the body. *Dolores qui dicuntur carnis, animae sunt in carne, et ex carne.*[2] For corporeal pain, he adds, is nothing other than the distress of the soul caused by the body and the opposition the soul has to what takes place in the body, just as the pain of the soul called sadness is the opposition the soul has to things that happen against our will. *Dolor carnis tantummodo offensio est animae ex carne, et quaedam ab ejus passione dissensio;* [73] *sicuti animae dolor, quae tristitia nuncupatur, dissensio est ab his rebus, quae nobis nolentibus acciderunt.*[3]

Further, in Book 7, chapter 19 of *The Literal Meaning of Genesis*, he says that what we call pain is the repugnance the soul feels on seeing the action by which it governs the body hindered by the disorder occurring in its temperament. *Cùm afflictiones corporis molestè sentit (anima) actionem suam qua illi regendo adest turbato ejus temperamento impediri offenditur, et haec offensio dolor vocatur.*[4] [And when the soul is distressed because of a bodily affliction, it discovers that its activity of ruling the body is impeded by a disturbance in the body, and this affliction is called pain.]

What actually shows that the pain called corporeal is in the soul rather than the body, is that the same things that cause us pain when we think about them cause none when the mind is intensely occupied elsewhere. For example, in Book 14, chapter 24 of the *City of God*, St. Augustine mentions the priest from Calame in Africa who, every time he wished, withdrew from his senses as if he were dead. He felt nothing, not only when he was pinched or jabbed, but even when he was

---

[1] The Cyrenaics were philosophers of the school of Cyrene founded by Aristippus around the fourth century BC. Their moral philosophy was essentially hedonistic, affirming the identity of happiness, pleasure, and virtue.

[2] *Writings*, vol. 7, p. 387.

[3] Ibid.

[4] *The Literal Meaning of Genesis*, Bk. VII, ch. 19, vol. 2, p. 19.

[b] ... pain. – The same thing happened on the subject of weight. For when children see ... (I) The next six paragraphs were added in II.

burned. *Qui quando ei placebat ad imitatas quasi lamentantis hominis voces, ita se auferebat à sensibus, et jacebat simillimus mortuo, ut non solùm vellicantes atque pungentes minimè sentiret, sed aliquando etiam igne ureretur admoto, sine ullo doloris sensu, nisi postmodum ex vulnere.*[5] [There was a man who could cut himself off from his senses when he was near people imitating the lamentation of human voices, so that he would lie down exactly like a dead man. Not only did he feel nothing when he was pinched or poked, but even when he was burned by fire he had no sensation of pain, except afterward from the wound.]

We should also note that it is not, properly speaking, the bad disposition of the hand or the motion caused in it by burning which makes the soul feel pain. Rather, this motion must be communicated to the brain by means of tiny fibers enclosed in the nerves, like pipes, which extend like little ropes from the brain to the hand and other parts of the body. This makes it impossible to move these little fibers without also moving the part of the brain where they originate. This is why, if some obstruction prevents these fibers in the nerves from communicating their motion to the brain, as happens in paralysis, a person could see his hand cut and burned without feeling pain. And conversely, what seems even stranger, one could feel what is called pain in the hand without having a hand. This frequently happens to those who have had a hand amputated, because when the fibers in the nerves extending from the hand to the brain are moved [74] by some impulse towards the elbow, where they end when the arm is amputated there, they can pull the part of the brain to which they are attached just as they pull it when they extend to the hand. In the same way the end of a rope can be moved equally well by pulling it from the middle as by pulling it from the other end. This then causes the soul to feel the same pain it felt when it had a hand, because its attention is directed to the place where the motion of the brain usually begins, just as what we see in the mirror appears to be located where it would be if it were seen by straight light rays, because that is the usual way of seeing objects.

This can help us understand how it is quite possible for a soul separated from the body to be tormented by the fires of hell or purgatory, and to feel the same pain we feel when burned, since even while it was in the body the pain of burning was in the soul and not the body. This pain is nothing other than a thought of the sadness it feels when something happens in the body that God united to it. Is it not conceivable, then, for divine justice to arrange a certain portion of matter to be related to a mind so that the motion of this matter is an occasion for the mind to have afflicting thoughts, which is all that happens to the soul in corporeal pain?

But to return to confused ideas, the idea of weight which seems so clear is no less confused than the others we have just mentioned. For when children see rocks and similar things fall as soon as they are no longer supported, they form the idea of a thing that falls, which idea is natural and true, as well as the idea of some cause of

---

[5]   *Writings*, vol. 7, pp. 403–4.

this fall, which is also true. But since they see nothing but the rock, and they see nothing at all pushing it down, they jump to the hasty conclusion that what they do not see does not exist. Hence they think the rock falls by itself, by virtue of an internal principle, without anything else pushing it down. This confused idea, which arises only by mistake, they label gravity or weight.

Moreover,[c] they end up making completely different judgments [75] about things they ought to judge in the same way. For just as they see rocks falling toward the earth, they see straws moving towards amber, and pieces of iron or steel moving towards a magnet. So they have as much reason to put a quality in the straw or the iron to carry it towards the amber or the magnet, as in rocks to carry them towards the earth. Nonetheless, they do not choose to do so. Instead they put a quality in the amber for attracting the straw and one in the magnet for attracting iron, which they call attractive qualities, as if it were not just as easy to put one in the earth for attracting heavy things. But whatever they are, these attractive qualities originate in the same way as weight, merely from fallacious reasoning that makes people think the iron must attract the magnet because they see nothing pushing the magnet towards the iron. It is impossible, however, to conceive that one body can attract another if the attracting body is not itself moved, and if the attracted body is not connected or attached to it by some tie.[d]

We should also relate these judgments of childhood to the idea that represents hard and heavy things as more material or solid than light and delicate things. This makes us believe that there is much more matter in a box filled with gold than in another box filled only with air. For these ideas come only from our childhood judgments about all external things, based only on the impressions they made on our senses. Hence, because hard and heavy bodies act on us much more than do light and subtle bodies, we imagine that they contain more matter, whereas reason ought to make us judge that since each part of matter never occupies more than its place, an equal space is always filled by the same quantity of matter.

Consequently a vessel of a cubic foot does not contain more matter when it is full of gold than when it is full of air. It is even true in one sense that when it is full of air it contains more solid matter, for a reason which would take too long to explain here.[6]

One could say that the imagination gives rise to all these extravagant opinions of those who think that the soul is either a very subtle air composed of atoms,

---

6   In Part II of the *Principles of Philosophy*, Descartes discusses rarefaction in articles 6–7 and 17–19. In article 19 he says: "Similarly, there cannot be more matter or corporeal substance in a vessel filled with lead or gold or any other body, no matter how heavy and hard, than there is when it contains only air and is thought of as empty" (*Philosophical Writings*, vol. 1, p. 231). It is not clear how this theory supports the authors' statement that a vessel full of air contains more solid matter than one full of gold, unless they are thinking of the case in which the pores in the gold are filled by particles of some liquid or less solid matter, whereas there are no gaps in the air in the "empty" vessel.

c   ... Moreover, the same thing happens as in the other example, namely, they end ... (I)

d   ... tie. – We could take this ... (I) The next three paragraphs were added in II.

such as Democritus and the Epicureans; or an ignited air, such as the [76]
Stoics; or a bit of celestial light, such as the ancient Manichaeans and even
Fludd in our time; or a delicate wind, such as the Socinians. For none of these
persons ever believed that a rock or wood or mud was capable of thinking. This
is why although, like the Stoics, Cicero thought that the soul is a subtle flame,
he rejected as an untenable absurdity the idea that it was made of earth or coarse
air: *Quid enim, obsecro te, terrá ne tibi aut hoc nebuloso aut caliginoso caelo, sata aut
concreta esse videtur tanta vis memoriae?*[7] [I ask you, do you really think that the
power of memory grew from earth or condensed out of the misty and foggy air?]
But these philosophers were convinced that in making matter more subtle they
would make it less material, less coarse, and less corporeal, and that eventually it
would become capable of thinking, which is ridiculous. For one piece of matter
is more subtle than another only because, in being divided into smaller and more
agitated parts, on the one hand it has less resistance to other bodies and, on the
other, it insinuates itself more easily into their pores. But divided or not, agitated
or not, it is no less matter, no less corporeal, no more capable of thinking. For it
is impossible to imagine that there is any relation of the motion or shape of
subtle or coarse matter to thinking, or that a piece of matter which does not
think when it is at rest like the earth, or in moderate motion like water, could
succeed in knowing itself if one just shook it more or made it boil three or four
times faster.

We could take this much further, but this is enough to explain all the other
confused ideas, which nearly all have causes similar to those we have just discussed.

The sole remedy for this problem is to undo the prejudices of childhood, and to
believe nothing issuing from reason based on our previous judgments, but only on
our present judgments. And so we will be brought to our natural ideas. As for
confused ideas, we will retain only what is clear in them, such as that there is
something in the fire which causes us to feel heat, and that all things called heavy
are pushed down by some cause, not determining anything about what could be in
the fire which causes this sensation in us, or about the cause making a rock fall,
unless we have clear reasons yielding knowledge of them. [77]

CHAPTER 10

Some examples of confused and obscure ideas taken from morals

In the preceding chapter we cited various examples of confused ideas, which could
also be called false for the reason mentioned. But because they are all taken from
physics, it may be useful to add several examples taken from morals, since the false
ideas we form about good and evil are infinitely more dangerous.

[7] *Tusculan Disputations*, I, xxv.60, p. 71.

Whether we have a true or false idea, clear or obscure, of weight or sensible qualities or actions of the senses, we are neither more nor less happy because of it. We are neither better nor worse because we are more or less knowledgeable about them. Whatever opinion we have about all these things, they will not change for us. Their being is independent of our knowledge, and the way we conduct our lives does not depend on our knowledge of them. Thus everyone is allowed to defer judgment on these matters to the next life, and generally to entrust the order of the world to the goodness and wisdom of those who govern it.

But no one is exempted from forming judgments about good and evil, since these judgments are necessary for conducting our lives, directing our actions, and making ourselves eternally happy or miserable. Because false ideas about all these things are the source of the bad judgments we make about them, it is infinitely more important to apply ourselves to knowing and correcting these ideas, rather than reforming those which our hasty judgments or the prejudices of childhood make us conceive about things in nature, which are merely objects of sterile speculation.

We would have to create a complete ethics to reveal all these false ideas. But here we intend only to present some examples of the way they are formed, by putting together different ideas which are not joined in reality, from which we compose the vain phantoms people chase after and which repay them with misery all their lives. [78]

We find in ourselves the idea of happiness and unhappiness, and this idea is neither false nor confused as long as it remains general. We also have ideas of smallness, greatness, lowliness, and excellence. We desire happiness and flee from unhappiness; we admire excellence and scorn lowliness.

True happiness can be found in God alone, and consequently we should attach the idea of happiness to him alone. But the corruption of sin separating us from God impels us to join this idea to countless things we lust after, seeking the bliss we have lost. So we create innumerable false and obscure ideas, representing the objects of our love as capable of making us happy and things that deprive us of it as making us miserable. By sinning we have similarly lost true greatness and excellence. So to love ourselves we are forced to represent ourselves as other than we really are, to hide our miseries and poverty from ourselves, and to include in our ideas of ourselves a great many things that are completely separate from this idea, in order to enlarge it and make it grander. Here is the usual course of these false ideas.

The first and main inclination of lust is towards the sensual pleasure that arises from certain external objects. Aware that the pleasure it adores is derived from these things, the soul immediately connects them with the idea of good, and whatever deprives it of pleasure with the idea of evil. Next, seeing that riches and human power are the usual means for mastering these objects of human lust, the soul begins to regard them as a great good. Consequently, it judges the rich and great who possess them to be happy, and the poor who are deprived of them to be unhappy.

Now since there is a certain excellence in happiness, the soul never separates these two ideas, always regarding everyone it considers happy as great, and those it considers poor and unhappy as lowly. This is why people scorn the poor and admire the rich. These judgments are so unjust and false, that St. Thomas believes it is this attitude of esteem and admiration for the rich that the Apostle St. James condemns so severely when he forbids giving a more elevated seat to the rich than to the poor in church assemblies.[1] Now it is not possible to interpret this passage literally as prohibiting the fulfillment of certain external duties more to the rich than the poor, since the worldly order which [79] religion in no way disturbs permits these preferences, and even the saints practiced them. So it seems we ought to understand the passage as referring to the internal preference that makes us view the poor as beneath the feet of the rich, and the rich as infinitely better than the poor.

Even though these ideas and the judgments resulting from them are false and unreasonable, they are nevertheless common among those who have not corrected them, because they arise from the lust infecting all of us. Not only do people create these ideas of the rich, but they know that others feel the same esteem and admiration for them. So their lot is judged not only by all the pomp and luxuries surrounding them, but also by these favorable judgments made about them, which we know of from ordinary speech and our own experience.

Properly speaking it is this vision of all the admirers of the rich and the great, imagined as surrounding their thrones and regarding them with internal feelings of fear, respect, and humiliation, which the ambitious idolize. This is why they work all their lives and expose themselves to so many dangers.

To show that this is what people seek and worship, we only have to suppose that there were just one person in the world who could think, and that everyone else with a human shape was only a mechanical statue. Suppose further that this lone rational individual knew perfectly well that all these statues that resembled him outwardly were entirely devoid of reason and thought, and also knew the secret for moving them by various inner springs, and obtaining from them all the services we obtain from people. It is easy to imagine him amusing himself occasionally with the different motions he could impart to these statues, but certainly his pleasure and glory would never depend on the external respect he would make them show him. He would never be flattered by their reverence, and he would even get tired of them as people soon tire of marionettes. Ordinarily he would be satisfied with the services he required from them, and would not worry about acquiring more than he needed for his use.

Thus ambitious people desire not merely the simple external effects of others'

---

[1] Aquinas, *Summa Theologiae*, Ia IIae, quest. 63, art. 2, pp. 7–11. The biblical reference is to James 2:1.

obedience, disconnected from any insight into their thoughts. They want to command people [80] and not machines; their pleasure consists in imagining the feelings of fear, esteem, and admiration they arouse in others.

This shows that the idea that preoccupies them is as vain and insubstantial as the idea people have who are properly called vain, who reward themselves with praises, acclaim, eulogies, titles, and other things of this nature. The only things distinguishing them are the different emotions and judgments they like to cause in others. Whereas vain people try to arouse emotions of love and esteem for their knowledge, eloquence, minds, skill, and goodness, the ambitious want to arouse emotions of terror, respect, and humiliation before their greatness, along with the judgment that they are intimidating, elevated, and powerful. Thus both the ambitious and the vain invest their happiness in the thoughts of others. But the former choose certain thoughts, and the latter choose others.

Nothing is more common than to see these vain phantoms which arise from people's false judgments impelling them to the greatest undertakings, and serving as their main aim in conducting their lives.

The valor so admired in the world, which makes those who pass for brave fearlessly place themselves in the greatest danger, often results only from fixing on these empty and hollow images which fill their minds. Few persons seriously scorn life, and those who seem to face death with such boldness at the breach or in battle tremble like others, and often more so, when it attacks them in bed. What produces the abandon apparent on some occasions is that they imagine, on the one hand, the mockery made of cowards and, on the other, the praises made of the valiant. Preoccupied by this double specter, they are distracted from thinking about dangers and death.

For this reason people who are most subject to thinking they are observed by others, being more concerned by their judgments, are more valiant and more courageous. Thus officers are usually more courageous than soldiers, and gentlemen more courageous than those who are not, because having more honor to gain or lose, they are also more keenly affected by it. The same tasks, said a great military leader, are not as difficult for a general in the army as for a [81] soldier. A general is sustained by the judgments of an entire army which has their eyes on him, while a soldier has nothing to sustain him but the hope of a small reward and the lowly reputation of a good soldier, which often does not extend beyond his own company.

What are people thinking about who build superb houses far beyond their station and means? They are not pursuing simple comfort; this excessive magnificence interferes with comfort more than it promotes it. It is also obvious that were they alone in the world, they would never go to these lengths, no more than if they thought that everyone who saw their houses felt only contempt for them. They are, then, working for others, and for others who approve of them. They imagine that everyone who sees their palaces will feel respect and admiration for whoever owns them. So they imagine themselves in the middle of their palaces, surrounded by a troop of people who look up to them from below, and who judge them great, powerful, happy, and magnificent. This is the idea that takes hold of them, and the reason they make all these great expenditures and go to all this trouble.

People might wonder why carriages are filled with so many servants. It is not for the service one gets from them – they are more trouble than they are worth. It is rather to arouse, in those who watch them passing by, the idea that this is a person of high station. The idea that people have this notion when they see these carriages satisfies the vanity of their owners.

Similarly, if we examine all the conditions, occupations, and professions respected in the world, we shall find that what makes them pleasing and soothes the pains and fatigues accompanying them, is that they often present to the mind the idea of feelings of respect, esteem, fear, and admiration others have for us.

Conversely, what makes solitude annoying to most people is that, by separating them from the sight of others, it also separates them from their judgments and thoughts. Thus the heart remains empty and famished, being deprived of its usual nourishment and not finding in itself the means to satisfy it. This is why pagan philosophers judged solitary life so unbearable that they did not hesitate to say that their sage would not want to possess all the bodily and mental goods if he had to live alone and could tell [82] no one about his happiness. Only the Christian religion has been able to make solitude pleasing, by bringing people to scorn these vain ideas, and at the same time giving them other objects better for occupying the mind and more worthy of filling the heart, for which they do not need the regard of or dealings with others.

But we must note that human love does not, properly speaking, end at knowing the thoughts and feelings of others. People use these thoughts only to enlarge and elevate their ideas of themselves, by incorporating all these alien ideas. They imagine by some rude illusion that they really are greater because they live in a larger house and more people admire them, although all these external things and the thoughts of others add nothing to them, leaving them as poor and miserable as they were before.

This explains why people are pleased by things that seem, in themselves, incapable of amusing and pleasing them. The reason they take pleasure in them is because these things connect their idea of themselves to some vain circumstance representing them as greater than usual.

We enjoy speaking of the dangers we have run because, based on these adventures, we form an idea of ourselves as either prudent or especially favored by God. We like to speak of illnesses of which we have been cured because we depict ourselves as having the fortitude to resist great evils.

People want to gain the advantage in all things, even in games of chance where there is no skill, and even when one is not playing for stakes, because this is connected to the idea of happiness. It seems that fortune has chosen us and has favored us on account of our merit. This so-called happiness is even conceived as a permanent quality that entitles one to hope for the same success in the future. This is why players choose to associate with certain people rather than others, which is completely ridiculous. For we can say that someone was happy up to a certain moment, but at the next moment has no greater probability of being happy than have the most unfortunate.

Thus the minds of those who love only the world actually have as aims only the vain phantoms that amuse them and [83] unfortunately preoccupy them. Those who pass for the wisest reward themselves, as do others, merely by illusions and dreams. Only those who relate their lives and actions to eternal things can be said to have solid, real, and substantial ends. The truth about all the others is that they love vanity and trifles, and they chase after falsity and lies.

CHAPTER 11

Another cause of confusion in our thoughts and discourse, which is that we connect our thoughts to words

We have already said that our need to use external signs to make ourselves understood causes us to connect our ideas to words in such a way that we often pay more attention to the words than to the things. Now this is one of the most common causes of confusion in our thoughts and discourse.

We should note that while people often have different ideas about the same things, still they use the same words to express them. For example, a pagan philosopher's idea of virtue differs from a theologian's idea, and yet each expresses his idea by the same word, "virtue."

Moreover, people in different ages have viewed the same things quite differently, and yet they have always collected all these ideas under the same name. This causes us to become easily confused when uttering a word or hearing it uttered, since we take it sometimes for one idea, sometimes for another. For example, once people recognized that there was something in themselves, whatever it was, that caused them to be nourished and to grow, they called this the *soul*, and they extended this idea to what is similar, not only in animals, but even in plants. Furthermore, when they noticed that they thought, they again called the principle of thought in themselves the *soul*. Based on the resemblance in the name, they came to take the thinking thing and the thing that causes the body to be nourished and grow to be the same thing. Similarly, the word "life" was extended to the cause [84] of activity in animals, as well as to what makes us think, which are two entirely different things.

The words "senses" and "sensations" are also highly equivocal, even when they are applied only to one of the five bodily senses. For three things usually take place in us when we use our senses, for example, when we see something. The first consists of certain motions in the bodily organs such as the eye and the brain. The second is that these motions are the occasion for the soul to conceive something, as when following the motion produced in the eye by the reflection of light in raindrops facing the sun, the soul has the ideas of red, blue, and orange. The third is the judgment we make about what we see, such as the rainbow to which we attribute these colors, and which we conceive as having a certain size, a certain shape, and being at a certain distance. The first of these three things exists uniquely in the body. The other two exist only in the soul, although on the occasion of what happens in the body. And yet we include all three, albeit so different, under the same name "sense" or "sensation," or "sight," "hearing," etc. For when we say that the eye sees or the ear hears, that can be understood only in terms of the motion of the bodily organ, since it is clear that the eye has no perception of objects striking it and does not judge them. On the other hand, we say that when we were not paying attention we did not see a person who was present before us and who made an impression on our eyes. In that case we take the word "see" for the thought formed in the soul after what happens in the eye and the brain. According to this meaning of the word "see," it is the soul that sees and not the body, as Plato maintained,[1] and later Cicero, in these words: *Nos enim ne nunc quidem oculis cernimus ea quae videmus. Neque enim est ullus sensus in corpore. Viae quasi quaedam sunt ad oculos, ad aures, ad nares à sede animi perforatae, itaque saepè aut cogitatione aut aliqua vi morbi impediti apertis atque integris et oculis et auribus, nec videmus, nec audimus: ut facile intelligi possit, animum et videre et audire, non eas partes quae quasi fenestrae sunt animi.*[2] [We do not even now distinguish the things we see with our eyes. For there is no perception in the body, but, as is taught not only by natural philosophers but also by medical experts who have seen clear evidence, there are, as it were, passages bored from the seat of the soul to the eye, ear, and nose. Often, therefore, we are hindered by absorption in thought or by some attack of an illness, and although our eyes and ears are open and uninjured, we neither see nor hear. So it is easy to understand that it is the soul that both sees and hears, and not those parts of us which serve as windows to the soul.] Finally, the words "senses," "sight," "hearing," etc. are taken [85] for the last of these three things, that is, for the judgments the soul makes following the perceptions it has on the occasion of what occurs in the bodily organs. This happens whenever we say that the senses are mistaken, as when we see a curved stick in water and when the sun appears to be only two feet in diameter. For it is certain that there can be neither error nor falsity in whatever takes place in the bodily organ, nor in the mere perception of the soul, which is only a simple apprehension. But all error derives only from judging badly, in concluding, for example, that the sun is only two feet in diameter because the

---

[1]   *Theaetetus*, 184b–187b.
[2]   *Tusculan Disputations*, I, xx.46, pp. 55–7.

great distance causes the image it forms in the back of the eye to be almost the same size as the one produced by an object of two feet at a distance more proportional to our usual manner of seeing. But because we have made this judgment since childhood and we are so accustomed to it that we do it at the very instant we see the sun, practically without reflecting, we attribute it to sight, and we say that we see small or large objects depending on whether they are nearer to or farther from us. Despite this, it is the mind and not the eye which judges their smallness or largeness.

Every language is full of countless similar words that share only the same sound, but are nevertheless signs of completely different ideas.

We must point out that when an equivocal name signifies two unrelated things that people have never confused in their thoughts, then it is almost impossible for us to be mistaken and to commit errors. For example, no one with a bit of common sense will be misled by the equivocation in the word "ram" which signifies both an animal and a sign of the zodiac. By contrast, when the equivocation comes from the error itself of people who contemptuously confuse different ideas, as in the case of the word "soul," it is difficult to clear it up, because we assume that the people who first used these words understood them very well. Thus we are often content to utter a word without ever examining whether the idea we have of it is clear and distinct. We even attribute to things having the same name what is appropriate only to ideas of incompatible things, without realizing that this inconsistency derives only from confusing two different things under the same name. [86]

CHAPTER 12

The remedy for the confusion arising in our thoughts and discourse from the confusion in words: where we discuss the necessity and utility of defining the nouns we use, and the difference between real and nominal definitions

The best way to avoid the confusion in words encountered in ordinary language is to create a new language and new words that are connected only to the ideas we want them to represent. But in order to do that it is not necessary to create new sounds, because we can avail ourselves of those already in use, viewing them as if they had no meaning. Then we can give them the meaning we want them to have, designating the idea we want them to express by other simple words that are not at all equivocal. Suppose, for example, I want to prove that the soul is immortal. Since the word "soul" is equivocal, as we have shown, it could easily cause confusion in what I want to say. To avoid this confusion I will view the word "soul" as if it were a sound that does not yet have a meaning, and I will apply it uniquely to the principle of thought in us, saying: "By 'soul' I mean the principle of thought in us."

This is called a nominal definition, *definitio nominis*, which geometers use so frequently, and which must be clearly distinguished from a real definition, *definitio rei*.[1]

For in a real definition, perhaps such as these: "Man is a rational animal," or "Time is the measure of motion," we leave the term being defined, such as "man" or "time," its usual idea, which we claim contains other ideas, such as rational animal, and measure of motion. Whereas in a nominal definition, as we said previously, we consider only the sound,[a] and then determine this sound to be the sign of an idea we designate by other words.

We must also be careful not to confuse the nominal definition we are discussing here with what some [87] philosophers speak of, who mean the explanation of a word's meaning according to ordinary linguistic practice or etymology. We will discuss this elsewhere. Here, however, we are concerned only with the particular way the person defining a word wants us to take it in order to conceive his thought clearly, without taking the trouble to see if others understand it in the same sense.

From this it follows: first, that nominal definitions are arbitrary, and real definitions are not. Since each sound is indifferent in itself and by its nature able to signify all sorts of ideas, I am permitted for my own particular use, provided I warn others, to determine a sound to signify precisely one certain thing, without mingling it with anything else. But it is entirely otherwise with real definitions. For whether ideas contain what people want them to contain does not depend at all on our wills. So if in trying to define them we attribute to these ideas something they do not contain, we are necessarily mistaken.

So, to give some examples of each: if I strip the word "parallelogram" of all meaning and use it to signify a triangle, this is permitted and I commit no error in doing so, as long as I use it in only this way. I could then say that a parallelogram has three angles equal to two right angles. But suppose I leave this word its ordinary meaning and idea, which signifies a figure with parallel sides, and I go on to say that a parallelogram is a figure of three lines. Since that would then be a real definition, it would be quite false, because it is impossible for a figure of three lines to have parallel sides.

Second, it follows from their arbitrariness that nominal definitions cannot be contested. For you cannot deny that people have given a sound the meaning they said they gave it, nor that the sound has this meaning only in their use of it, once they have warned us about it. But we often have the right to contest real definitions, since they can be false, as we have shown.

It follows, third, that every nominal definition [88] can be taken for a principle, since it is not contestable, whereas real definitions can never be taken for principles,

---

[1] The analysis in this chapter is largely taken from Pascal's *On the Geometrical Mind*, see *Pascal, Selections*, pp. 173–85. The distinction between real and nominal definitions is set out in Aristotle's *Posterior Analytics*, Bk. II, ch. 7, *Complete Works*, vol. 1, pp. 152–3.

[a] ... sound in the name being defined, and ... (I)

and are genuine propositions which can be denied by anyone who finds some obscurity in them. Consequently, they need to be proved like other propositions, and should never be assumed unless they are in themselves as clear as axioms.

Nevertheless, I need to explain what I have just said, that nominal definitions can be taken as principles. For this is true only because we should not deny that a designated idea can be called by the name someone has given it. But nothing further should be concluded to the advantage of this idea, nor should we believe that merely because someone has given it a name, it signifies something real. I can define the word "chimera," for example, by saying: "I call a chimera whatever implies a contradiction." It does not follow from this, however, that a chimera is something. Similarly, if a philosopher tells me, "I call weight the internal principle which causes a rock to fall without being pushed by anything," I will not dispute this definition. On the contrary, I will welcome it because it makes me understand what he means. But I will deny that what he means by the word "weight" is something real, because there is no such principle in rocks.

I wanted to explain this at some length, because in ordinary philosophy two important abuses are committed on this subject. The first is confusing a real definition with a nominal definition, and attributing to the first what belongs only to the second. For philosophers have capriciously created a hundred definitions, not of names but of things, that are quite false and do not at all explain the real nature of things or the ideas we naturally have of them. Subsequently they wished to have these definitions considered as principles that could not be contradicted.[b] If someone does deny them, since they are highly questionable, they claim that it is not worth discussing.

The second abuse is leaving these names in confusion, since people hardly ever use nominal definitions to remove the obscurity from names and to fix them to certain clearly designated ideas. [89] As a result, the majority of their disagreements are only verbal. Further, they use what is clear and true in confused ideas to establish something obscure and false, which would be easily recognized if the names had been defined. Thus philosophers usually believe that the clearest thing in the world is that fire is hot and a rock is heavy, and that it would be foolish to deny it. Indeed, they would convince everyone of this as long as the names are not defined. But once they are defined, we easily discover whether what is denied on the subject is clear or obscure. For we must ask them what they mean by the words "hot" and "heavy." If they reply that by "hot" they mean only what properly speaking causes the sensation of heat in us, and by "heavy" whatever falls when not supported in any way, they are right to say that it would be unreasonable to deny that fire is hot and that a rock is heavy. But if they mean by "hot" what has in it a quality similar to what we imagine when we feel heat, and by "heavy" whatever has

b   ... be contested. If someone does deny them, since they are highly questionable, they claim that it is not worth discussing, following this rule, *contra negantem principia non est disputandum.* – The second ... (I) an internal principle making it move towards the center of the earth without being pushed by anything whatever, then it will be easy to show them that it is not denying something clear but very obscure, not to say quite false, to deny that fire is hot and a rock is heavy in the senses just mentioned. For it is quite clear that fire causes us to have the sensation of heat by the impression it makes on the body, but it is not at all obvious that fire has anything in it resembling what we feel when we are near the fire. Likewise, clearly a rock falls when it is dropped, but it is not at all clear that it falls by itself without anything pushing it down.

Here, therefore, is the great utility of nominal definitions, to make the matter clearly understood in order to avoid useless disputes over words that one person understands one way and another in another way, as so often happens even in ordinary speech.

But besides this advantage, there is yet another. Often we can have a distinct idea of something only by using many words to designate it. Now it would be inconvenient, especially in scientific texts, to repeat constantly this long series of words. This is why, once we have explained [90] something by means of all these words, we connect the idea we have conceived to a single word, which thereby takes the place of all the others. Thus, when we understand that some numbers are divisible into two equal parts, we give a name to this property to avoid repeating all these terms frequently, saying: "I call every number which is divisible into two equal parts an even number." This shows that every time we use a word we have defined, we mentally have to substitute the definition for the defined word, and to have this definition present. As soon as we call a number even, for example, we will understand precisely that it is divisible into two equal parts, and that these two things are so connected and inseparable in thought that as soon as one is expressed, the mind immediately connects it to the other. Those who define terms, as geometers do so carefully, do it only to abbreviate their discourse, which would be irritating if it included so many circumlocutions. *Ne assiduè circumloquendo moras faciamus* [We make a work tiresome by circumlocution], as St. Augustine said.[2] But they do not do it to abbreviate the ideas of the things they are discussing, because they claim that the mind supplies the entire definition to the shortened expression, which they use only to avoid the complication produced by a great many words.

CHAPTER 13

Important observations concerning nominal definitions

After having explained nominal definitions and how useful and necessary they are, it is important to make some observations about the way to use them, so as not to abuse them.

---

[2]   *The Literal Meaning of Genesis*, Bk. xii, ch. 7, no. 16, vol. 2, p. 186.

The first is that we should not try to define all words, because this would often be useless. It is even impossible to do so. I say that it would often be useless to define certain names. For when people have a distinct idea of something, and when everyone who understands a language forms the same idea upon hearing a word uttered, it would be useless to define it since the goal of the definition has already been attained, [91] which is to connect the word to a clear and distinct idea. This is what happens with very simple matters about which people naturally have the same idea. The words signifying these ideas are understood in the same way by everyone who uses them, or, if they sometimes mix in something obscure, still their principal attention is always directed to what is clear in them. Thus those who use them only to indicate clear ideas have no reason to fear that they will not be understood. Words such as "being," "thought," "extension," "equality," "duration," or "time," and similar ones are of this sort. For even though some people obscure the idea of time by forming various propositions about it which they call definitions – such as that time is the measure of motion according to before and after[1] – they do not attend to this definition when they hear time mentioned, nor do they conceive anything beyond what everyone else naturally conceives about it. And so the learned and the ignorant alike just as easily understand the same thing when they are told that a horse takes less time to travel a league than a tortoise does.

Furthermore, I say it would be impossible to define every word. For in order to define a word it is necessary to use other words designating the idea we want to connect to the word being defined. And if we again wished to define the words used to explain that word, we would need still others, and so on to infinity. Consequently, we necessarily have to stop at primitive terms which are undefined. It would be as great a mistake to try to define too many words as not to define enough, because in both cases we would fall into the confusion we are claiming to avoid.

The second observation is that we should not change accepted definitions when nothing needs to be restated. For it is always easier to make a word understood when accepted practice, at least among the educated, has connected it to an idea, than when it has to be disassociated from some idea to which it is usually joined and reconnected to another one. This is why it would be a mistake to change definitions accepted by mathematicians, unless they are muddled or their ideas are not clearly enough designated, as may be the case with Euclid's definitions of angle and proportion. [92]

The third observation is that when we are obliged to define a word, we should accommodate ourselves to usage as much as possible. We should not give words meanings completely removed from those they have, or meanings which might even be incompatible with their etymology, as would someone who says: "I call a figure bounded by three lines a 'parallelogram.'" But in the case of words with two

---

[1]   Aristotle, *Physics*, Bk. IV, ch. 11, *Complete Works*, vol. 1, p. 373.

meanings, we should usually be satisfied to remove one meaning and to connect the word uniquely to the other. For example, in everyday speech "heat" signifies both the sensation we have, and a quality we imagine to be in the fire, completely similar to what we feel. To avoid this ambiguity, I can apply the name "heat" to one of these ideas and detach it from the other, by saying "I call the sensation I have when I approach the fire 'heat.'" In that case I would give the cause of this sensation either a completely different name such as "ardor," or the same name with something added to determine it and to distinguish it from heat taken as the sensation, as does someone who says "virtual heat."

The reason behind this observation is that once people have connected an idea to a word, it is not easily undone. Hence their previous idea always comes back, making them quickly forget the new one you want to give them in defining the word. It would be easier to accustom them to a word that signifies nothing at all, as would someone who says, "I call a figure bounded by three lines a 'bara,'" than to accustom them to strip the word "parallelogram" of the idea of a figure whose opposite sides are parallel, and make it signify a figure whose sides cannot be parallel.

This is an error chemists fall into who enjoy changing the names of most of the things they talk about, to no purpose, and giving them names that already signify other things that have no real connection to the new ideas with which they are linked. This even gives some people the opportunity to construct ridiculous inferences, like the person who imagined that the plague was an evil from Saturn. He claimed to have cured the afflicted by hanging around their necks a piece of lead, which chemists call Saturn, on which someone engraved the day Saturday – which also has the name of Saturn and is the figure used by astronomers to indicate this planet – as if the [93] arbitrary and irrational connections between lead, the planet Saturn, the little mark that designates it, and the day Saturday, could have real effects and actually cure diseases!

But[a] what is even more unacceptable in the chemists' language is the way they profane the most sacred mysteries of religion in order to veil their so-called secrets. Some even go so far as to commit the impiety of applying what Scripture says about true Christians to the chimerical brotherhood of the Rosicrucians, namely that they are the chosen race, the royal priesthood, the holy nation, the people God has chosen and whom he has called from the shadows to his marvelous light. According to them, this brotherhood is composed of wise men who have attained blessed immortality by using the philosopher's stone to fix their souls in their bodies in such a way, they claim, that no body except gold is more immutable and incorruptible. These and many other similar reveries are exposed in Gassendi's study of Fludd's philosophy,[2] which shows that there is hardly a worse mental trait

---

[2]   *Examen Roberti Fluddi Medici in quo et ad illius libros adversus R. P. F. Marinum Mersennum ... respondetur, Opera Omnia*, vol. 3, pp. 213–68.
[a]   This paragraph was added in II.

than that had by these enigmatic writers; they imagine that the most frivolous thoughts, not to say the most false and impious, will pass for the greatest mysteries if they are reworded so that they are unintelligible to common people.

CHAPTER 14

Another sort of nominal definition, which indicates what words signify in common use

Everything we have said about nominal definitions should be understood to concern only those in which words are defined according to an individual's use: this is what makes them free and arbitrary, because people are permitted to use whatever sound they like to express their ideas, provided they warn others about it. But as we are masters only of our own language and not that of others, each of us has the right to create a dictionary for ourselves, but not to create one for others, nor to explain their words by the particular meanings we [94] would connect to them. This is why whenever we not only intend to explain the sense in which we take a word, but claim to explain the way it is commonly used, our definitions are not at all arbitrary, but are bound and constrained to represent the truth of usage rather than the truth of things. Such definitions should be considered false if they do not genuinely express that usage, that is, if they do not connect sounds to the same ideas to which those who use them in ordinary speech connect them. This also shows that these definitions are by no means exempt from being contested, since people argue every day over the meanings given to terms in practice.

Now these sorts of definitions of words would seem to be the province of grammarians, since they are the ones who write dictionaries which do nothing but explain ideas people have agreed to connect to certain sounds. We can, however, make several observations on this subject which are important for making our judgments exact.

The first, which is the foundation of the others, is that people often do not consider the entire meaning of words. That is, words often signify more than they appear to, and when people try to explain their meaning, they do not represent the entire impression made in the mind.

This is so because for an uttered or written sound to signify is nothing other than to prompt an idea connected to this sound in the mind by striking our ears or eyes. Now, frequently, in addition to the main idea which is considered its proper meaning, a word may prompt several other ideas – which may be called incidental ideas – without our realizing it, although the mind receives their impressions.

For example, if we say to someone, "You lied about it," and we consider only the principal meaning of this expression, this is the same as saying: "You know that the contrary of what you say is true." But in common use these words carry an additional idea of contempt and outrage. They make us think that the person who says them does not care whether they injure us, and this makes the words insulting and offensive.

Sometimes these incidental ideas are connected to [95] words not by common practice, but only by the person who is using them. These are the ideas, properly speaking, prompted by the speaker's tone of voice, facial expression, gestures, and other natural signs which connect to our words countless ideas diversifying, changing, diminishing, and augmenting their meaning, by joining to them the image of the speaker's emotions, judgments, and opinions.

This is why if whoever said that one ought to measure the tone of voice by the ears of the listener meant that it is enough to speak fairly loudly to make oneself understood, that person was ignorant of part of the use of the voice, since the tone often signifies more than the words themselves. There is a tone for teaching, one for flattering, and one for disapproving. Often we want it not just to reach our listeners' ears, but to strike them and wound them. No one would approve of a servant who was being reprimanded and who replied: "Sir, speak more softly, I can hear you very well." The tone is part of the reprimand and is necessary for imprinting the desired idea in the mind.

But sometimes these incidental ideas are connected to the words themselves, because they are normally prompted by everyone who utters them. This is why, among expressions that appear to mean the same thing, some are insulting and others are polite, some are modest and others immodest, some decent and others indecent. Because in addition to the principal idea which they share, people have connected them to other ideas which cause this diversity.

This remark could help to explain a rather common mistake – of changing substantives into adjectives – to people who complain about the way they are criticized. Thus if someone accuses them of ignorance or deception, they say they were called ignorant or deceitful. This is unreasonable, for these words do not mean the same thing. The adjectives "ignorant" and "deceitful," besides signifying a defect, include further the idea of contempt, whereas the words "ignorance" and "deception" indicate the thing such as it is, making it neither polite nor offensive. Other words could be found signifying the same thing but adding a mollifying idea, which [96] would show that one wanted to spare the feelings of the person being criticized. These expressions are chosen by wise and temperate persons, unless they have a particular reason to speak more forcefully.

This also explains how to recognize the difference between a plain and a metaphorical style, and why the same thoughts appear to be much more vivid when they are expressed metaphorically than in a straightforward way. For in addition to their principal meaning, metaphors signify the speaker's emotion and passion, and thus imprint both ideas in the mind, whereas plain expressions indicate only the unvarnished truth.

For example, if this half verse of Virgil: *Usque adeone mori miserum est!* [1] [And after all, is death so sad a thing?] were expressed simply and literally in this way: *Non est usque adeo mori miserum* [It is not so very wretched to die], it would doubtless be less forceful. The reason is that the first expression signifies much more than the second: it expresses not only the thought that death is not such a great evil as one thinks, but also the idea of someone who stands firm against death and who envisages it without dread, an image much more vivid than the thought itself to which it is joined. So it is not strange that the first expression is more striking, because the soul is taught by images of truth but it is scarcely ever moved except by images of emotions.

Si vis me flere, dolendum est
Primum ipse tibi. [2]
[If you would have me weep, you must first feel grief yourself.]

Since metaphors usually signify not only things but the emotions we feel in conceiving and discussing them, we can judge by this how we ought to use them and the subjects for which they are appropriate. Obviously it is ridiculous to use them in purely speculative matters which are viewed with a calm eye and which do not produce any emotion in the mind. Metaphors express emotions in the soul: when they are mixed with subjects that do not move the soul at all, they are emotions contrary to nature and a kind of convulsion. This is why there is nothing more annoying than those preachers who [97] exclaim indifferently about everything, and who are no less agitated about philosophical reasonings than about the most amazing truths that are necessary for salvation.

By contrast, when the matter being treated is such that it ought reasonably affect us, it is a mistake to speak about it in a dry, cold manner, without emotion. It is a defect not to be affected when one ought to be.

Thus since divine truths are not merely to be known, but even more to be loved, revered, and adored by people, the noble, elevated, and metaphorical manner in which the Holy Fathers treated them is doubtless much more suitable than a simple and nonmetaphorical style such as that of the Schoolmen. The former not only teaches us the truths, but also represents the feelings of love and reverence with which the Fathers spoke of them. By bringing the image of this holy disposition into our minds, it can contribute greatly to imprinting a similar disposition in us. Whereas the Scholastic style, since it is simple and contains only the ideas of the unvarnished truth, is less able to produce in the soul the emotions of respect and love one ought to have for Christian truths. To this extent it is not only less useful, but also less pleasing, since the soul's pleasure consists more in feeling emotion than in acquiring knowledge.

Finally, this same remark allows us to resolve the famous question raised by

---

[1]   *Aeneid,* XII.646, *Virgil,* vol. 2, p. 343.
[2]   Horace, *Ars Poetica,* verses 102–3, *Odes and Epodes,* p. 459.

ancient philosophers, whether there are indecent words. We can also refute the arguments of the Stoics, who maintained that expressions normally considered disgraceful and immodest can be used neutrally.

They claim, says Cicero in a letter he wrote on the subject, that there are no obscene or shameful words.[3] For (they say) disgrace is derived either from things or from words. It is not derived from things alone, because they can always be expressed in other words that are not considered at all indecent. It also does not exist in words viewed merely as sounds since, as Cicero shows, when the same sound signifies different things, it is often deemed indecent in one meaning but not at all indecent in another. [98]

But all that is only vain subtlety which arises only because philosophers have not paid enough attention to the incidental ideas the mind connects to the principal ideas of things. As a result, the same thing can be expressed decently by one sound and indecently by another, if one of these sounds is connected to some other idea that conceals the shame, and if the other, by contrast, presents it to the mind in an immodest manner. Hence the words "adultery," "incest," and "abominable sin" are not shameful, although they represent extremely shameful actions, because they only represent them as covered by a veil of horror which causes them to be viewed simply as crimes. These words thereby signify the crime of these actions more than the actions themselves. On the other hand, certain words express these actions without the sense of horror, as being somewhat pleasant rather than criminal, and even join to them an idea of immodesty and effrontery. These are the shameful and indecent words.

The same is true of certain phrases by which we politely express actions that, although lawful, carry some sense of the corruption of nature. These phrases are actually decent because they express not only these things, but also the attitude of the people speaking this way, who testify by their reserve that they envisage these things with pain, and try to conceal them as much as possible from others and themselves. On the other hand, those who speak about them another way make it obvious that they take pleasure in viewing these sorts of objects. Given the shamefulness of this pleasure, it is not strange that the words that leave this impression are considered contrary to decency.

This is also why the same word is considered decent at some times and indecent at others. This forced Hebrew scholars to substitute Hebrew words in the margin at certain places in the Bible, to be uttered by those reading it in place of the words Scripture uses. This happened because when the prophets used them these words were not at all indecent because they were linked with an idea that made them view the objects with reserve and modesty. But since that time they became separated from this idea and joined by usage to another immodest and insolent idea, thereby becoming shameful. So, to avoid striking the mind with this bad idea, it was

---

[3]   Cicero to L. Papirius Paetus, Rome, July 45 BC, Bk. IX, letter 22, *Letters to His Friends*, vol. 2, pp. 265–71.

reasonable for the rabbis to want people [99] to utter other words when reading the Bible, although they did not thereby change the text.

Thus an author whose religious profession required an exacting modesty, and who had been rightly criticized for using a barely decent word to signify an infamous place, put up a weak defense when he alleged that the Fathers caused no difficulty using the word *lupanar* [brothel], and that we often find in their writings the words *meretrix* [whore], *leno* [pimp], and others that would scarcely be tolerated in our language. For the freedom with which the Fathers used these words should have made it clear to him that they were not considered shameful at that time. That is, usage had not yet joined them to the insolent idea making them shameful. He was wrong to conclude from this that it is permissible to use words considered indecent in our language, because these words do not in fact mean the same thing as those used by the Fathers. Besides the principal idea they share, they also include the image of a mind with libertine and immodest tendencies.

Given, then, that these incidental ideas are so important and change so greatly the principal meanings, it would be useful for people who write dictionaries to indicate them, warning us, for example, whether words are offensive, polite, biting, decent, or indecent. Rather, it would be useful for them to take the latter out entirely, since it is always better not to know them than to know them.

CHAPTER 15

Ideas the mind adds to ideas precisely signified by words

The term "incidental ideas" can also include another sort of idea that the mind adds to the precise meaning of terms, for a specific reason. This often happens when, after it conceives the precise meaning connected to the word, it does not stop there when this meaning is too confused and general. Instead, carrying its view further, the mind takes the opportunity to [100] consider still other attributes and aspects of the object, and thereby to conceive it by means of these more distinct ideas.

This happens in particular with demonstrative pronouns when we use the neuter *hoc*, "this," instead of the proper noun, for it is clear that "this" signifies "this thing," and that *hoc* signifies *haec res, hoc negotium* [this thing, this affair]. Now the word "thing," *res*, indicates a very general and very confused attribute of every object, since there is only nothingness to which it does not apply.

But since the demonstrative pronoun *hoc* does not indicate simply the thing in itself, and since it causes it to be conceived as present, the mind does not stop at this single attribute thing, but usually joins to it several other distinct attributes. So when the word "this" is used to display a diamond, the mind is not satisfied with conceiving it as a present thing, but adds to it the ideas of a hard and sparkling body having a certain shape.

All these ideas, the primary and principal as well as those the mind adds to it, are prompted by the word *hoc* applied to a diamond, but they are not prompted in the same way. For the idea of the attribute a present thing is prompted as the proper meaning of the word. These others are prompted as ideas conceived as connected and identified with this primary and principal idea, but not precisely indicated by the pronoun *hoc*. This is why the additions vary, depending on the subject matter to which the term *hoc* is applied. If I say *hoc* in displaying a diamond, this term always signifies this thing, but the mind supplies and adds to it "which is a diamond," "which is a hard and sparkling body." If it is wine, the mind adds the ideas of a liquid, of the taste and color of wine, and other things of this sort.

Thus it is necessary to distinguish carefully these supplementary ideas from the signified ideas, for although both exist in the same mind, they do not exist there in the same way. When adding these other, more distinct ideas, the mind still conceives that the term *hoc* signifies in itself only a confused idea which always remains confused, even when joined to more distinct ideas.

This is how we ought to resolve a troublesome quarrel which the [Calvinist] ministers made famous, on which they based their main argument establishing their metaphorical interpretation of the Eucharist. It should not surprise us to use [101] this remark here to clarify their argument, since it is more worthy of logic than theology.

Their claim is that in Jesus Christ's assertion, "This is my body," the word "this" signifies the bread. Now the bread, they say, cannot really be the body of Christ, and therefore Christ's assertion does not mean "This is really my body."

The point here is not to examine the minor premise to show its falsity; this has been done elsewhere.[1] The issue is only the major premise in which, they maintain, the word "this" signifies the bread. It remains only to be said, following the principle we have established, that the word "bread," indicating a distinct idea, does not correspond exactly to the term *hoc* which indicates only the confused idea of a present thing. Rather it is clear that when Christ uttered this word, and at the same time drew the Apostles' attention to the bread he held in his hands, they probably added to the confused idea of a present thing signified by the term *hoc*, the distinct idea of bread which was only prompted and not precisely signified by this term.

All these ministers' confusion is caused only by lack of attention to this necessary distinction between prompted ideas and precisely signified ideas. They have made a thousand useless attempts to prove that when Christ displayed the bread, and the Apostles saw it and were directed to it by the term *hoc*, they had to conceive of the bread. Everyone agrees that they obviously conceived of the bread and that they

---

[1] Cf. Arnauld, *La Perpétuité de la foi*, vol. 2, Bk. I, ch. 12.

had reason to conceive of it; no one needs to work so hard to prove that. The question is not whether they conceived of the bread, but how they conceived of it.

On this point we say that if they conceived, that is, if they had the distinct idea of bread in the mind, they did not have it as signified by the word *hoc*, which is impossible since this term never signifies anything but a confused idea. But they had it as an idea added to this confused idea, which was prompted by the circumstances.

We shall see the importance of this remark in what follows. But it is worth adding here that this distinction is so unquestionable, that even when the ministers attempt to prove that the term "this" signifies bread, they only reinforce it. " 'This,' " says a minister who spoke most recently on the topic, "signifies not only this present thing, but this present thing which you know is bread."[2] Who cannot see that in this proposition, these terms "which you know is bread" are [102] clearly added to the term "present thing" by means of a subordinate proposition, but are not precisely signified by the term "present thing," since the subject of a proposition does not signify the entire proposition? Consequently in this proposition which has the same meaning, "this which you know is bread," the word "bread" is clearly added to the word "this," but is not signified by the word "this."

But it does not matter, the ministers will say, whether the word "this" signifies the bread precisely, provided it is true that the Apostles conceived that what Christ called "this" was bread.

Here is what matters: namely that the term "this," signifying in itself only the precise idea of a present thing, although linked to the bread by the distinct ideas the Apostles added to it, always remains susceptible of another determination and of being linked to other ideas, without our becoming aware of the change of object. And so when Christ uttered "this," which meant his body, the Apostles only had to subtract the distinct ideas of bread they had added. Retaining this same idea of a present thing, they conceived at the end of Christ's assertion that this present thing was now the body of Jesus Christ. Thus they connected the word *hoc*, "this," which they joined to the bread by means of a subordinate proposition, to the attribute body of Jesus Christ. The attribute body of Jesus Christ clearly requires them to subtract the added ideas, but it in no way makes them change the idea precisely indicated by the word *hoc*, and they simply conceived that it was the body of Jesus Christ. Here is the whole mystery of this assertion, which arises not from the obscurity of terms, but from the change effected by Christ, which caused this subject *hoc* to have two different determinations at the beginning and at the end of the proposition. We will explain this in Part II when we discuss the unity arising from confused subjects. [103]

[2] André Lortie, *Traité de la Sainte Cène*, cf. especially pp. 148 and 410–43.

Second part of the logic,

Containing reflections people have made about their judgments

CHAPTER 1

Words as related to propositions

Since our purpose here is to explain various remarks that have been made about judgments, and since judgments are propositions composed of different parts, we should begin by explaining these parts, which are primarily nouns, pronouns, and verbs.

It is not particularly important to examine whether it is up to grammar[1] or logic to deal with the parts of judgment. It is more concise to say that everything serving the purpose of each art belongs to that art, whether that knowledge is particular to it or is useful to other arts and sciences.

Now certainly it is useful to the aim of logic, which is to think well, to understand the different functions of sounds intended to signify ideas. The mind is accustomed to linking them so closely that we can scarcely conceive one without the other,[2] so

---

[1] The *Logic* borrows its beginning from Part II, chapter 1 and returns here to Part II, chapter 2 of the *General and Rational Grammar Containing the Foundations of the Art of Speaking Explained in a Clear and Natural Manner*, more commonly called the *Port-Royal Grammar*. Arnauld collaborated on this work, and the "first editor," Claude Lancelot, writes this in his preface:

> But having on occasion found difficulties in this endeavor which halted me as I chanced upon them, I related them to one of my friends [in the margin: "Monsieur Arnauld"] who, although he had never applied himself to this sort of science, did not fail to provide me with a great many opportunities for resolving my doubts. My very questions were the cause of his making various reflections upon the true foundations of the art of speaking, which, when he discussed them with me, I found so substantial that I felt obliged not to let them be lost, having seen nothing in either the ancient grammarians nor in the modern ones which was more searching or more accurate concerning this material. That is why I once again drew upon his generosity, so that he dictated them to me during his spare moments; and having thus collected them and put them in order, I composed this small treatise. (*Grammar*, pp. 39–40.)

[2] Cf. Gerauld de Cordemoy, *Discours physique de la parole* (1668). Since chapter 1 was added in V, the authors of the *Logic* had access to this text (pp. 237ff.):

> From the first language we learn, we join the idea of a thing to the sound of a word, which takes place entirely in the soul; for the sensation called sound and the idea of the thing it is made to signify, are entirely in the soul, as we have already recognized. On the side of the body there is a motion of the [animal] spirits and of the brain which each vocal excites, and an impression everything leaves there. Now this motion is always joined to this impression, just as the perception of each sound is always joined to a particular idea of a certain thing in the soul, so that whenever we want to express the idea of this thing, we conceive at the same time the vocal sound which signifies it . . .

See also Descartes, *Principles of Philosophy*, Pt. IV, art. 197; *Optics; The World; Philosophical Writings*, vol. 1, pp. 284, 165, 81–2.

that the idea of the thing prompts the idea of the sound, and the idea of the sound that of the thing.

On this topic we can generally say that words are [104] distinct and articulated sounds that people have made into signs to indicate what takes place in the mind.[3]

Since what takes place in the mind consists in conceiving, judging, reasoning, and ordering, as we have already said, words function to indicate all these operations. Three main kinds essential for this purpose were invented, which we will be content to discuss, namely nouns, pronouns, and the verbs that take the place of nouns but in a different way. This is what we must explain here in more detail.

NOUNS

Since the objects of our thoughts are, as we have already said, either things or manners of things, the words intended to signify things as well as manners are called *nouns*.

Those that signify things are called substantive nouns, such as "earth" and "sun." Those that signify manners, indicating at the same time the subject to which they apply, are called *adjectival nouns*, such as "good," "just," and "round."

This is why whenever these manners are conceived by mental abstraction, without being referred to a particular subject, since they then subsist in the mind by themselves as it were, they are expressed by a substantive word, such as "wisdom," "whiteness," or "color."

By contrast, when what is in itself a substance or a thing comes to be conceived in relation to some subject, the words signifying it this way become adjectives, such as "human" and "carnal." When we strip the adjectives formed from these substantive nouns of this relation, we make new substantives out of them. So after having formed the adjective "human" from the substantive word "man," we form the substantive "humanity" from the adjective "human."

Some nouns that pass for substantives in grammar are really adjectives, such as "king," "philosopher," and "physician," since they indicate a manner of being or mode in a subject. But they pass for substantives since, applying to a single subject, this unique subject is always understood without having to be expressed.

For the same reason the words "the red," "the white," etc. are really adjectives because they indicate the relation. But we do not express the substantive to which they are related because it is a general substantive which includes all the subjects of these modes and which is thereby unique in its generality. Thus [105] "the red" is every red thing, "the white" every white thing; or as it is put in geometry, it is any red thing whatever.

Consequently, adjectives have essentially two significations:[4] one distinct, which

---

[3] *Grammar*, Pt. II, ch. 1, p. 66: "Thus words can be defined as distinct and articulate sounds, which men have made into signs for signifying their thoughts."

[4] *Grammar*, Pt. II, ch. 2, p. 72:

is the signification of the mode or manner, the other confused, which is that of the subject. But although the signification of the mode is more distinct, it is nonetheless indirect; and by contrast, that of the subject, although confused, is direct. The word "white," *candidum*, signifies the subject directly but confusedly, and whiteness indirectly but distinctly.

PRONOUNS

Pronouns are used to take the place of nouns,[5] as a way to avoid repetition, which becomes tedious. But we should not assume that in taking the place of nouns they have exactly the same effect on the mind. That is not true. On the contrary, they relieve our dislike of repetition only because they represent nouns in a confused way. In a sense nouns reveal things to the mind while pronouns present them as veiled, although the mind nevertheless senses that it is the same thing as that signified by the noun. This is why there is no objection to joining a noun with a pronoun: "You, Phaedra,"[6] *Ecce ego Joannes*[7] [Here am I, John].

DIFFERENT KINDS OF PRONOUNS

When people realized that it is often useless and graceless to refer to themselves, they introduced the first-person pronoun to put in the place of the speaker: *Ego*, "me," "I." In order not to have to name the persons being spoken to, they saw fit to indicate them by a word called the second-person pronoun, "thou" and "you."

To avoid repeating the names of other persons and other things being discussed, they invented third-person pronouns, *ille, illa, illud* [he, she, it], among which some indicate, as if by pointing, the thing being spoken about, which is why they are called demonstratives, *hic, iste*, "this one," "that one."

There is also a pronoun called reflexive, because it indicates the relation of a thing to itself. This is the pronoun *sui, sibi, se* [himself, herself, itself], "Cato killed himself."

As we have already said, it is common to all pronouns that they indicate

---

I have said that adjectives have two significations, one distinct, which is that of the form, and the other confused, which is that of the subject. But it must not be concluded from this that they signify the form more directly than the subject, as if the more distinct signification were also the more direct. Because on the contrary, it is certain that they signify the subject directly, and, as the grammarians say, *in recto*, although more confusedly; and that they only signify the form indirectly, what the grammarians call *in obliquo*, however more distinctly. Thus white, *candidus*, signifies directly that which has whiteness, *habens candorem*, but in a most confused manner, marking in particular no one thing which could have whiteness, and it signifies whiteness only indirectly, but in a manner as distinct as the word whiteness itself, *candor*.

5 Ibid., Pt. II, ch. 7, p. 92: "Since men have been compelled to speak often of the same things in the same discourse, and since it was bothersome to repeat the same nouns continually, they invented certain words to take the place of these nouns, and for this reason they named them *pronouns*."
6 Terence, *The Eunuch*, verse 86 (*Tun hic eras, mi Phaedria*), *Comedies*, p. 168.
7 John 1:9. (All translations from *The New English Bible with the Apocrypha* [New York, Oxford University Press, 1961, 1970].)

confusedly the noun whose place they take. But there is something particular about the neuter of these [106] pronouns *illud, hoc* [that, this], when it stands absolutely, that is, without an expressed noun. For the other kinds, *hic, haec, ille, illa* [this (masc.), this (fem.), that (masc.), that (fem.)], can be and nearly always are related to distinct ideas, which they nevertheless indicate only confusedly: *illum expirantem flammas*[8] [as he breathed forth flame], that is, *illum Ajacem* [that Ajax (accusative)]. *His ego nec metas rerum, nec tempora ponam*[9] [I shall set no limits to their fortunes and no time], that is, *Romanis* [to/for the Romans (dative)]. By contrast the neuter always relates to a general and confused noun: *hoc erat in votis*[10] [This is what I prayed for!], that is, *haec res, hoc negotium erat in votis: hoc erat alma parens, etc.*[11] [And was it then, for this, my gracious mother ...] Thus there is a double confusion in the neuter, namely one in the pronoun whose signification is always confused, and one in the word *negotium*, "thing," which is equally general and confused.

THE RELATIVE PRONOUN

There is also another pronoun called relative, *qui, quae, quod,* "who," "which," "that."

This relative pronoun has something in common with other pronouns and something distinctive to itself.

It has in common that it stands in place of the noun and prompts a confused idea of it.[12]

What is distinctive[13] is that the proposition in which it occurs can be part of the subject or the attribute of a proposition, and so can form one of these added or subordinate propositions which we will discuss below in more detail: "God who is good," "the world which is visible."

I assume here that the terms "subject" and "attribute" of a proposition are understood even though we have not yet explained them explicitly, because they are so common that people usually understand them before studying logic. Those who do not understand them need only refer to the place where we explain their meaning.

This is how to solve the problem of the precise meaning of the word "that" when it follows a verb, and appears not to be related to anything: "John answered that he was not Christ." "Pilate said that he found no crime in Jesus Christ."

Some people want to make it an adverb, just like the word *quod* which

---

[8] Virgil, *Aeneid*, 1.44, *Virgil*, vol. 1, p. 245. The exact Latin is *illum expirantem transfixo pectore flammas* [as with pierced breast he breathed forth flame].

[9] Ibid., 1.278, *Virgil*, vol. 1, p. 261.

[10] Horace, *Satires*, II.vi.1, *Satires, Epistles*, p. 211.

[11] Virgil, *Aeneid*, II.664, *Virgil*, vol. 1, p. 339.

[12] "There is also ... in place of the noun" is taken entirely from the *Grammar*, Pt. II, ch. 9, p. 98.

[13] Ibid.: "The second thing which is unique to the relative pronoun and which to my knowledge has never before been noted by anyone is that the proposition into which it enters (and which may be called *subordinate*) can be part of the subject or of the predicate of another proposition which may be called the *principal* proposition."

sometimes, although rarely, is taken in the same sense in Latin as the French *que* [that]: *Non tibi objicio quod hominem spoliasti* [I am not objecting that you robbed the man], Cicero said.[14]

But the truth is that the words "that," *quod* are nothing but relative pronouns, and they retain their meaning.

Thus in the proposition "John answered that he was not Christ," the "that" retains the function of connecting another proposition, [107] namely, "was not Christ," to the attribute embedded in the word "answered," which signifies *fuit respondens*.

The other use, which is to take the place of the noun and to refer to it, appears to be much less obvious here. This has led several astute persons to say that the "that" was completely devoid of this function in this case. We should say, however, that it still performs it. For in saying "John answered," we understand "that he made an answer," and the "that" refers to this confused idea of answer. Similarly when Cicero says: *Non tibi objicio quod hominem spoliasti*; the *quod* refers to the confused idea of the thing objected to, formed by the word *objicio*. This thing objected to, conceived confusedly at first, is later particularized by the subordinate proposition, connected by *quod*: *Quod hominem spoliasti*.

The same thing can be seen in these cases: "I assume that you will be wise"; "I tell you that you are wrong." The term "I tell you" first makes us conceive a thing told confusedly, and the "that" refers to this thing told. "I tell you that," that is, "I tell you a thing which is." By the same token, anyone who says "I assume" produces the confused idea of a thing assumed. For "I assume" means "I make an assumption"; and the "that" refers to this idea of a thing assumed. "I assume that," that is, "I make an assumption which is."

The Greek articles ὅ, ἡ, τό, can be classified as pronouns when they are placed after rather than before the noun. Τοῦτό ἐστι τὸ σῶμά μου τὸ ὑπὲρ ὑμῶν διδόμενον [This is my body which is given for you], said St. Luke.[15] For this τό, "the," represents the body σῶμα to the mind in a confused manner. Hence it has the function of a pronoun.

The only difference between the article employed in this way and the relative pronoun is that, although the article takes the place of the noun, it connects the attribute that follows it to the noun preceding it in a single proposition. But the relative pronoun forms a separate proposition with the attribute following it, although it is joined to the first proposition, ὅ δίδοται, *quod datur*, that is, *quod est datum* [which is given].

We can see from this use of the article that there is little substance to the remark a minister[16] recently made concerning the way these words which we have just

---

[14]   *Verrine Orations*, Bk. IV, ch. 17, vol. 2, p. 325.

[15]   Luke 22:19.

[16]   Löringhoff and Brekle identify this as referring to Jean Claude (1619–87), a Calvinist minister who carried on polemics against Jacques Bossuet, Nicole, and Arnauld. His principal work was the *Reply*

quoted from the Gospel of St. Luke ought to be translated. In the Greek text there is no relative pronoun, but an article: "This is my body (the) given for you," and not "which is given for you," τὸ ὑπὲρ ὑμῶν διδόμενον and not ὅ ὑπὲρ ὑμῶν δίδοται. He claims that in order to express the force of this article, it is absolutely necessary to translate the text this way: "This is my body, my body given for you" or "the body given for you," and that it is not a good translation [108] to express the passage in these terms: "This is my body which is given for you."

But this claim is based solely on the fact that this author has only imperfectly grasped the true nature of the relative pronoun and the article. Certainly, when it takes the place of the noun, the relative pronoun *qui, quae, quod* [who (masc.), who (fem.), which (neut.)] represents it only in a confused way. Similarly the article ὅ, ἡ, τὸ, represents the noun to which it refers only confusedly. Given that this confused representation is intended precisely to avoid repeating exactly the same word, which is annoying, translating it by explicitly repeating the same word in some sense defeats the purpose of the article – "this is my body, my body given for you" – where the article is introduced only to avoid this repetition. On the other hand, translating it by the relative pronoun, "this is my body which is given for you," preserves the essential condition of the article, which is to represent the noun only in a confused manner, and not to strike the mind twice with the same image. But it fails to satisfy another condition that may appear less essential, namely for the article to replace the noun in such a way that the adjective connected to it does not form a new proposition, τὸ ὑπερ ὑμῶν διδόμενον, whereas the relative *qui, quae, quod* separates it a bit more, and becomes the subject of a new proposition, ὅ ὑπέρ ὑμῶν δίδοται. Thus it is true that neither of these two translations, "This is my body which is given for you" and "This is my body, my body given for you," is entirely perfect. One translation changes the confused meaning of the article into a distinct meaning, contrary to the nature of the article; the other preserves this confused meaning, but the relative pronoun separates into two propositions what the article makes into one proposition. Being forced by necessity to use one or the other, however, does not give us the right to choose the first while condemning the other, as this author claimed in his remark.

CHAPTER 2

The verb

Up to now we have borrowed what we have said about nouns and pronouns from a little book published a while ago under the title *A General Grammar*, with the exception of several points we have explained somewhat differently. [109] But with

to the *Perpetuity of the Faith* (*Réponse au traité de la perpétuité de la foi* [Charenton, 1668]) of Arnauld. Clair and Girbal identify the minister as André Lortie; cf. p. 72 n. 2.

respect to the verb, which it discusses in chapter 13, I shall only transcribe what the author says, because it seems to me that nothing more can be added to it.[1] People, he says, have had no less need to invent words indicating affirmation, which is our principal way of thinking, than to invent words indicating the objects of our thoughts.

Properly speaking, this is what the verb consists in. It is nothing other than *a word whose principal function is to signify an affirmation*, that is, to indicate that the discourse where this word is employed is the discourse of a person who not only conceives things, but who judges and makes affirmations about them. This is what distinguishes the verb from several nouns that also signify affirmation, such as *affirmans, affirmatio* [affirming, affirmation], because they signify affirmation only insofar as it has become an object of thought by mental reflection. Hence they do not indicate that the people who use these words are making an affirmation, but only that they conceive of an affirmation.

I said that the *main* function of the verb is to signify affirmation, because we shall see below that it is also used to signify other actions of the soul, such as desiring, requesting, commanding, and so on. But this happens only by changing the inflection and the mood, so in this chapter we will consider the verb only in its principal signification, which is what it has in the indicative. Accordingly, we can say that the verb in itself ought to have no other use than to indicate the connection the mind makes between the two terms of a proposition. Only the verb "to be," however, called the substantive, retains this simplicity, and only in the third person present, "is," and on certain occasions. Since people are naturally led to abbreviate their expressions, they almost always join other significations to affirmation in the same word.

I. They join to it those signifying some attribute, so in that case two words form a proposition, as when I say, for instance, *Petrus vivit*, "Peter lives." Because the single word *vivit* includes both an affirmation and the attribute to be alive, it is thus the same thing to say "Peter lives" as to say "Peter is alive." This gives rise to the great variety of verbs in each language, whereas if we had chosen to give the verb the general significance of affirmation without connecting it to any particular attribute, each language would need only a single verb, namely the one called the substantive. [110]

II. Further, in certain cases they have connected it to the subject of the proposition, so that two words, and even a single word, can form a complete proposition. This is possible with two words, as when I say *sum homo* [I am a man], because *sum* signifies not only affirmation, but also includes the signification of the pronoun *ego* [I], which is the subject of the proposition. It is always expressed in our language: "I am a man." A single word can form a proposition, for instance when I say *vivo, sedeo* [I am living, I am seated]. For these verbs contain in themselves both

---

[1] What follows is taken almost verbatim from Pt. II, ch. 13 of the *Grammar*, "Verbs and What is Proper and Essential to them."

an affirmation and an attribute, as we have already said. Since they are in the first person they also include the subject: "I am living," "I am seated." From this arises the difference of persons which is usually found in all verbs.

III. They have also joined a reference to the time at which the affirmation is made, so that a single word such as *coenasti* [you dined] signifies that I am affirming of the person to whom I am speaking the action of dining, not in the present, but in the past. This is the source of the diversity of tenses which is, again, usually common to all verbs.

The variety of meanings combined in the same word has prevented many otherwise quite astute persons from recognizing the nature of the verb. For they have considered it not in terms of what is essential to it, namely the *affirmation*, but rather in terms of these other relations which are accidental to it as a verb.

Thus Aristotle, focusing on the third of the significations added to the essence of the verb, defined it as *vox significans cum tempore*, a word that signifies with tense.[2]

Others such as Buxtorf, having added the second signification to it, defined it as *vox flexilis cum tempore et persona*, a word having different inflections with tense and person.[3]

Still others, paying attention to the first of these added meanings, namely the attribute, and considering that the attributes joined to affirmation in the same word are usually actions or passions, held that the essence of the verb consisted in *signifying actions or passions*.

Finally, Julius Caesar Scaliger thought he solved a mystery in his book *On the Principles of the Latin Language*,[4] claiming that the distinction between things *in permanentes et fluentes*, between what endures and what happens, was the true origin of the distinction between nouns and verbs: nouns were used to signify what endures, and verbs that which happens.

But it is easy to see that all these definitions are false and fail to explain the true nature of the verb. [111]

The way the first two are stated makes it obvious, since they say nothing about what the verb means, but only what is connected to its meaning, *cum tempore, cum persona.*

The last two are even worse. For they have the two worst defects of a definition, which is to apply neither to all the defined, nor to only the defined, *neque omni, neque soli.*

For there are verbs that signify neither actions nor passions, nor what happens, such as *existit* [it exists], *quiescit* [it rests], *friget* [it is cold], *alget* [it is chilled], *tepet* [it is warm], *calet* [it is hot], *albet* [it is white], *viret* [it is green], *claret* [it is bright], etc.

And some words that are not at all verbs signify actions and passions, and even

[2] *On Interpretation*, ch. 3, *Complete Works*, vol. 1, p. 26.
[3] Johann Buxtorf, *Epistome Grammaticae Hebraeae*, ch. 12, p. 21.
[4] *De Causis linguae latinae libri tredecim*, p. 220.

things that happen, in accordance with Scaliger's definition. Clearly participles are genuine nouns. Yet those formed from active verbs signify actions, and those formed from passive verbs signify passions no less than the verbs themselves that produce them. There is no reason to maintain that *fluens* [flowing] does not signify a thing that happens as well as *fluit* [flows].

To which we may add against the first two definitions of the verb that participles also signify with tense, since among them there are past, present, and future participles, especially in Greek. Those who believe, not without reason, that the vocative case is actually a second person, especially when it has an ending different from the nominative, will find that from this perspective there is only a slight difference of more or less between the vocative and the verb.

So the essential reason a participle is not a verb is that it does not signify an affirmation at all. This is why it can form a proposition, which is the essence of the verb, only by being added to a verb, that is, by replacing what was removed in changing the verb into a participle. Why is *Petrus vivit*, "Peter lives" a proposition, and *Petrus vivens*, "Peter living" not one if you do not add "is" to it, as in *Petrus est vivens*, "Peter is living"? Only because the affirmation contained in *vivit* was removed from it to make it the participle *vivens*. From this it appears that the affirmation that does or does not exist in a word is what makes it a verb or not.

On this topic we can further note something in passing about the infinitive, which is very often a noun, as we will explain – for example, when we say in French *le boire* [drink], *le manger* [food]. In that case it differs from participles in that participles are adjectival nouns, and the infinitive is a substantive noun formed by abstraction from the adjective, just as *candor* is formed from *candidus*, and "whiteness" comes from "white." So the verb *rubet* signifies "is red," containing [112] both the affirmation and the attribute: the participle *rubens* signifies "red" simply without an affirmation; and *rubere* taken as a noun signifies "redness."

It ought therefore be conceded that, considering merely what is essential to the verb, the only true definition is *vox significans affirmationem*, a word that signifies an affirmation. For it is not possible to find a word indicating an affirmation that is not a verb, or a verb that does not function to indicate it, at least in the indicative. It is indubitable that if a word such as "is" had been invented that always indicated an affirmation without any difference in person or tense, so that a difference in person were indicated only by nouns and pronouns, and a difference in tense by adverbs, it would not cease to be a true verb. In fact this occurs in the propositions philosophers call eternal truths, such as "God is infinite," "every body is divisible," "the whole is greater than its part." Here the word "is" signifies only a simple affirmation without any relation to time, since these are true for all times, and without directing the mind to any difference in person.

So in terms of its essence, the verb is a word that signifies an affirmation. But if we wished to include its primary accidents in the definition of the verb, we could define it as follows: *vox significans affirmationem cum designatione personae, numeri, et temporis.* A word that signifies an affirmation while designating person, number, and tense. Properly speaking this is true of the substantive verb.

As for other verbs, inasmuch as they differ from the substantive verb by the way people have combined the affirmation with certain attributes, they can be defined as follows: *vox significans affirmationem alicujus attributi cum designatione personae, numeri, et temporis.* A word that signifies the affirmation of some attribute while designating person, number, and tense.

We can say in passing that in so far as it is conceived, an affirmation can also be an attribute of a verb. For example, the verb *affirmo* [I affirm] signifies two affirmations, one relating to the person who is speaking, the other to the person being spoken of, whether it is oneself or someone else. For when I say *Petrus affirmat* [Peter affirms], *affirmat* is the same thing as *est affirmans* [is affirming]. Then *est* indicates my affirmation, or the judgment I make concerning Peter, and *affirmans* the affirmation I conceive and attribute to Peter. The verb *nego* [I deny], [113] on the other hand, contains an affirmation and a negation by the same reasoning.

Further, we must note that although not all our judgments are affirmative, since there are also negative judgments, verbs nonetheless always signify in themselves only affirmations, negations being indicated only by the particles "not" and "no," or by nouns including them, *nullus, nemo,* "none," "no one." When joined to verbs, these words change them from affirmations to negations: "No person is immortal"; "No body is indivisible."

CHAPTER 3

The proposition, and the four kinds of propositions

After conceiving things by our ideas, we compare these ideas and, finding that some belong together and others do not, we unite or separate them. This is called *affirming* or *denying*, and in general *judging*.

This judgment is also called a *proposition*, and it is easy to see that it must have two terms. One term, of which one affirms or denies something, is called the *subject*; the other term, which is affirmed or denied, is called the *attribute* or *Praedicatum*.

It is not enough to conceive these two terms, but the mind must connect or separate them. As we have already said, this action of the mind is indicated in discourse by the verb "is," either by itself when we make an affirmation, or with a negative particle in a denial. Thus when I say, "God is just," "God" is the subject of this proposition, "just" is its attribute, and the word "is" indicates the action of the mind that affirms, that is, that connects the two ideas "God" and "just" as belonging together. If I say, "God is not unjust," the word "is" when joined to the particle "not" signifies the action contrary to affirming, namely denying, in which I view these ideas as repugnant to one another, because the idea "unjust" contains something contrary to what is contained in the idea "God."

Although every proposition necessarily contains these three things, as we said in the [114] preceding chapter, it could be composed of only two words, or even one.

Wishing to abbreviate their speech, people created an infinity of words all signifying both an affirmation, that is, what is signified by the substantive verb, and in addition a certain attribute to be affirmed. All verbs besides the substantive are like this, such as "God exists," that is, "is existent," "God loves humanity," that is, "God is a lover of humanity." When the substantive verb stands alone, for example when I say, "I think, therefore I am," it ceases to be purely substantive, because then it is united with the most general attribute, namely being. For "I am" means "I am a being," "I am a thing."

There are also other cases in which the subject and the affirmation are contained in a single word, as in the first and second persons of the verb, especially in Latin, for example, when I say, *sum Christianus* [I am a Christian]. For the subject of this proposition is *ego* [I] which is contained in *sum* [I am].

From this it is apparent that in that same language a single word constitutes a proposition in the first and second persons of verbs, which by their nature already contain the affirmation along with the attribute. So *veni, vidi, vici* [I came, I saw, I conquered], are three propositions.

This shows that every proposition is affirmative or negative. This is indicated by the verb which is affirmed or denied.

But there is another difference among propositions which arises from the subject, namely whether it is universal, particular, or singular.

For, as we previously said in Part I, terms are either singular, or common and universal.

On one hand, universal terms may be taken throughout their entire extension by joining them to universal signs, either expressed or implied, such as *omnis*, "every," in the case of affirmation; *nullus*, "no" for negation: "every person," "no person."

Alternatively, they can be taken through an indeterminate part of their extension. This happens when they are joined to the word *aliquis*, "some," as in "some person," "some people," or other words depending on the language in question.

This gives rise to an important difference among propositions. For when the subject of a proposition is a common term taken in its entire extension, the proposition is [115] universal, whether it is affirmative, as in "every impious person is foolish," or negative, as in "no evil person is happy."

When the common term is taken only through an indeterminate part of its extension, because it is restricted by the indeterminate word "some," the proposition is called particular, whether it affirms, as in "some cruel people are cowardly," or whether it denies, as in "some poor people are not unhappy."

A proposition whose subject is singular, as in "Louis XIII took La Rochelle," is called a singular proposition.

Although singular propositions differ from universals in not having a common subject, they should nevertheless be classified with them rather than with particulars, because they have a singular subject which is necessarily taken through its entire extension. This is the essence of universal propositions and distinguishes them from particulars. For it makes no difference to the universality of a proposition whether the subject's extension is large or small, provided that whatever it is, it is taken completely throughout. This is why singular propositions take the place of universals in arguments. Hence all propositions can be reduced to four kinds, which are indicated by the four vowels A, E, I, O to aid the memory.

A. Universal affirmative, as "Every evil person is a slave."
E. Universal negative, as "No evil person is happy."
I. Particular affirmative, as "Some evil people are rich."
O. Particular negative, as "Some evil people are not rich."

And to retain these better, these two verses were formed:

Asserit A, negat E, verum generaliter ambo,
Asserit I, negat O, sed particulariter ambo.
[A asserts, E denies, truly both do so generally.
I asserts, O denies, but both do so particularly.]

The universality or particularity of a proposition is usually called its quantity.

The affirmation or negation, which depends on the verb and is considered the form of the proposition, is called its quality.

Thus A and E agree in quantity and differ in quality, and similarly for I and O. [116]

But A and I agree in quality and differ in quantity, and likewise for E and O.

Propositions are further classified by their content as true or false. It is clear that there cannot be any that are neither true nor false. Since every proposition indicates the judgment we make about things, it is true when this judgment conforms to the truth and false when it does not.

Often, however, we lack the insight to distinguish the true from the false. So aside from propositions that appear to be[a] true and those that appear to be certainly false, there are others that seem true, but whose truth is not so obvious that we do not have some sense that they may be false, or else they seem false to us, but with a falsity we are not sure of. These propositions are called probable: the former are more probable and the latter less probable. We will say something in Part IV about what makes us judge with certainty that a proposition is true.

---

[a]   ... to be certainly true ... (I)

CHAPTER 4

The opposition between propositions having the same subject and the same attribute

We have just said that there are four types of propositions, A, E, I, O. Now we ask how they agree or disagree among themselves when different types of propositions are formed from the same subject and the same attribute. This is called opposition.

It is easy to see that there can be only three kinds of opposition, although one of them is divided into two others.

If they are opposed in both quantity and quality, such as A and O, and E and I, they are called contradictories, [117] such as "Every human is an animal" and "Some humans are not animals"; "No person is without sin" and "Some people are without sin."

If they differ only in quantity and agree in quality, as A and I, E and O, they are called subalterns, for example, "Every human is an animal" and "Some humans are animals"; "No person is without sin" and "Some people are not without sin."

And if they differ in quality and agree in quantity, then they are called *contraries* or *subcontraries*. They are contraries when they are universal, such as "Every human is an animal" and "No human is an animal."

They are *subcontraries* when they are particular, such as "Some humans are animals" and "Some humans are not animals."

Now when we consider these opposed propositions in terms of truth and falsity, it is obvious that:

1. Contradictories are never both true or both false, but if one is true the other is false, and if one is false the other is true. For if it is true that every human is an animal, it could not be true that some humans are not animals, and if on the contrary it is true that some humans are not animals, it is not true that every human is an animal. This is so clear that we would only obscure it by explaining it further.

2. Contraries can never be true together, but they can both be false. They cannot be true because contradictories would be true. For if it is true that every human is an animal, it is false that some humans are not animals, which is its contradictory, and in consequence even more false that no human is an animal, which is the contrary.

But the falsity of one does not imply the truth of the other. For it could be false that all people are just without it thereby being true that no person is just, since there could be some just people, although not all people are just.

3. By virtue of a rule completely opposite that of contraries, subcontraries can be true together, for example these two: "Some people are just" and "Some people are not just," because justice can belong to one group of people and not to another. Thus the affirmation and the negation do not refer to the same subject, since "some people" is taken for one group of people in one of these propositions and for [118] another group in the other. But they cannot both be false, since

otherwise contradictories would both be false. For if it were false that some people are just, it would therefore be true that no person is just, which is its contradictory, and by the same reasoning that some people are not just, which is its subcontrary.

4. For subalterns there is no true opposition, since the particular follows from the general. If every human is an animal, some humans are animals: if no human is a monkey, some humans are not monkeys. This is why the truth of universals entails the truth of particulars, but the truth of particulars does not entail that of universals. For it does not follow that because it is true that some people are just, it is also true that every person is just. By contrast, the falsity of particulars entails the falsity of universals. For if it is false that some people are without sin, it is even more false that every person is without sin. But the falsity of universals does not entail the falsity of particulars. For although it is false that every person is just, it does not follow that it is a falsehood to say that some people are just. Consequently there are several cases where these subalternate propositions are both true, and others where they are both false.

I shall say nothing about reducing propositions opposed in the same sense, because it is completely useless, and the rules given for it are for the most part true only in Latin.

CHAPTER 5

Simple and compound propositions. There are simple propositions that appear compound and are not, and can be called complex. Those which are complex in subject or attribute

We have said that every proposition must have at least one subject and one attribute, but it does not follow from this that it cannot have more than one subject or more than one attribute. Therefore those with only one subject and only one attribute are called *simple*. Those having more than one subject or more than one attribute are called [119] *compound*, for instance when I say, "Good and evil, life and death, poverty and riches come from the Lord." Here the attribute, "coming from the Lord," is affirmed not of a single subject, but of several, namely, "good and evil," etc.

But before explaining compound propositions, we should observe that some appear to be compound but are nevertheless simple. For the simplicity of a proposition is based on the unity of the subject or the attribute. Now there are many propositions that properly speaking have only one subject and one attribute, but whose subject or attribute is a complex term containing other propositions which can be called subordinate. These make up only a part of the subject or attribute, being connected to them by the relative pronoun, "who," "which," or "that," whose proper character is to unite several propositions so that altogether they form only one proposition.

Thus when Jesus Christ said: "He who would do my Father's will, who is in Heaven, will enter the Kingdom of Heaven,"[1] the subject of this proposition contains two propositions, since it includes two verbs. But because they are connected by "who," they constitute only part of the subject. Whereas when I say, "good and evil come from the Lord," there are properly speaking two subjects, because I affirm equally of both of them that they come from God.

The reason is that propositions joined to others by the relative pronoun either are only very imperfect propositions, as we shall see below, or are not considered propositions made at that time so much as propositions that have been previously made and are only conceived at that time, as if they were simple ideas. Consequently it does not matter whether we express these subordinate propositions by adjectival nouns or participles, without verbs and without the relative pronoun, or with verbs and the relative pronoun. For it means the same to say: "The invisible God created the visible world," or "God who is invisible created the world which is visible": "Alexander the most generous of kings defeated Darius," or "Alexander who was the most generous of kings defeated Darius." In either case my primary aim is not to affirm that God is invisible or that Alexander was the most generous of kings, but, assuming both were previously affirmed, I affirm of God conceived as invisible, that he created the visible world, and of Alexander conceived as the most generous of kings, that he defeated Darius.

But if I said: "Alexander was the most generous of kings, and the conqueror of Darius," it is obvious that I would be affirming [120] of Alexander both that he was the most generous of kings and that he was the conqueror of Darius. Thus these latter sorts of propositions are rightly called compound propositions, whereas the others can be called complex propositions.

We should notice that there are two kinds of complex propositions. For the complexity, so to speak, can affect either the content of the proposition, that is, the subject or attribute or both of them, or the form alone.

1. The complexity affects the subject when the subject is a complex term, as in this proposition: "Everyone who fears nothing is king": *Rex est qui metuit nihil.*[2]

Beatus ille qui procul negotiis,
Ut prisca gens mortalium,
Paterna rura bobus exercet suis,
Solutus omni foenore.[3]
[Happy the man who, far from business and affairs,
    Like mortals of the early times,

---

[1] Matthew 7:21.
[2] Seneca, *Thyestes*, verse 388, *Seneca's Tragedies*, vol. 2, p. 123.
[3] Horace, *Epodes*, II.1–4, *Complete Works*, p. 99.

May work his father's fields with oxen of his own,
    Exempt from profit, loss, and fee.]

For the verb "is" is implied in this last proposition, *beatus* [happy] is its attribute, and the rest is the subject.

2. The complexity affects the attribute when the attribute is a complex term, as in:

"Piety is a good that makes a person happy in the greatest adversity."
Sum pius Æneas famâ super aethera notus.[4]
[I am pious Æneas . . . my fame is known in the heavens above.]

But we should especially note here that all propositions formed from active verbs and their objects can be called complex, and that in some sense they contain two propositions. If I say, for example, "Brutus killed a tyrant," this means that Brutus killed someone and the person he killed was a tyrant. So this proposition can be contradicted in two ways, either by saying that Brutus did not kill anyone, or by saying that the person he killed was not a tyrant. This is very important to note, because when these sorts of propositions occur in arguments, we sometimes prove only one part while presupposing the other, so that to reduce these arguments to their most natural form, we often have to change the active verb into a passive verb in order to express the part to be proved directly. We will explain this in more detail when we discuss arguments formed from these complex propositions. [121]

3. Sometimes the complexity affects the subject and the attribute when both are complex terms, as in this proposition: "The mighty who oppress the poor will be punished by God, who is the protector of the oppressed."

Ille ego qui quondam gracili modulatus avenâ
Carmen, et egressus sylvis vicina coëgi
Ut quamvis avido parerent arva colono
Gratum opus agricolis: At nunc horrentia Martis
Arma, virumque cano. Trojae qui primus ab oris,
Italiam fato profugus Lavinaque venit littora.[5]
[I am he who once tuned my song on a slender reed,
    then, leaving the woodland, constrained the neighboring fields
    to serve the husbandmen, however grasping –
a work welcome to farmers: but now of Mars' bristling
    Arms I sing and the man who first from the coasts of Troy,
    exiled by fate, came to Italy and Lavinian shores.]

---

[4]   Virgil, *Aeneid*, 1.378–9, *Virgil*, vol. 1, p. 267. Arnauld omits a relative clause; the text actually reads:

    Sum pius Æneas, raptos qui ex hoste Penatis
    classe veho mecum, famâ super aethera notus.
    [I am pious Æneas, who carry with me in my fleet my household gods,
    snatched from the foe; my fame is known in the heavens above.]

[5]   Virgil, *Aeneid*, 1, the first six verses of the poem, including 1–4 attributed to Virgil but not appearing in all editions: see *Virgil*, vol. 1, pp. 240–1.

The first three verses and half of the fourth make up the subject of this proposition. The remainder makes up the attribute, and the affirmation is contained in the verb *cano* [I sing].

These are the three ways in which propositions can be complex in content, that is, in terms of their subject or attribute.

CHAPTER 6

The nature of subordinate propositions that make up part of complex propositions

Before speaking of propositions whose complexity affects the form, that is, the affirmation or negation, there are several important remarks to make about the nature of subordinate propositions making up part of the subject or attribute of propositions that are complex in content.

1. We have already seen that subordinate propositions are those whose subject is the relative pronoun "that," "which," "who," such as "people who are created to know and love God," or "people who are pious." When the term "people" is removed, the rest is a subordinate proposition.

But we must recall what we said in Part I, chapter 7, that there are two ways to add complex terms. The first, which can be called a simple explication, happens when the addition changes nothing in the idea of the term, because what is added to it applies generally and throughout its extension, as in the first example, "people who are created to know and love God." [122]

The other kind of addition can be called a determination, because what is added to the term does not apply to its entire extension, and thus it restricts it and determines its signification, as in the second example, "people who are pious." As a result, we can say that there is an explicative pronoun and a determinative pronoun.

Now when the pronoun is explicative, the attribute of the subordinate proposition is affirmed of the subject to which the pronoun is related, although this is only incidental to the whole proposition. In this case we can substitute the subject itself for the pronoun, as can be seen in the first example: "People who are created to know and love God." For we can say: "People are created to know and love God."

But when the pronoun is determinative, the attribute of the subordinate proposition is not properly affirmed of the subject to which the pronoun refers. For if after saying "people who are pious are charitable," we wanted to substitute the word "people" for "who" in order to say "people are pious," the proposition would be false, because this would be to affirm the word "pious" of people as people. But when we say "people who are pious are charitable" we affirm neither of people in general, nor of any particular persons, that they are pious. Instead, by connecting the idea "pious" to the idea "people" and making a whole idea of them, the mind judges that the attribute charitable belongs to this whole idea. Thus the entire judgment expressed in the subordinate proposition is only the one in which the mind judges that the idea "pious" is not incompatible with the idea "people," and so we can consider them as joined together and then examine what belongs to them as unified.

Often there are terms that are doubly and triply complex, being composed of several parts each of which is complex. Thus we may encounter different subordinate propositions of various types, the relative pronoun of one being determinative, the relative pronoun of another explicative. This will be clearer from this example: "The doctrine that places the highest good in bodily pleasure, which was taught by Epicurus, is unworthy of a philosopher." This proposition has as its attribute "unworthy of a philosopher," and all the rest as its subject. Hence the subject is a complex term containing two subordinate propositions. The first is "that places the highest good in bodily pleasure." In this subordinate proposition the pronoun is determinative because it determines [123] the word "doctrine," which is general, to the doctrine that affirms that the highest human good is in bodily pleasure. Consequently we could not without absurdity substitute for "that" the word "doctrine," saying: "the doctrine places the highest good in bodily pleasure." The second subordinate proposition is "which was taught by Epicurus," and the subject to which this "which" refers is the entire complex term, "the doctrine that places the highest good in bodily pleasure." This indicates a singular and individual doctrine, capable of various accidents, such as being maintained by different persons, although in itself it is determined always to be taken in the same sense, at least on this precise point, according to its meaning. This is why the "which" of the second subordinate proposition, "which was taught by Epicurus," is not determinative but only explicative. Consequently we can substitute the subject to which this "which" refers in place of the "which" as follows: "the doctrine that places the highest good in bodily pleasure was taught by Epicurus."

3. The last remark is that in order to judge the nature of these propositions, and to decide whether the relative pronoun is determinative or explicative, it is often necessary to pay more attention to the meaning and the speaker's intention than to the expression alone.

For there are complex terms which often appear simple or less complex than they really are, since part of what they contain in the speaker's mind is implicit and not expressed. This follows from what was said in Part I, chapter 7, where we showed that nothing is more common in people's speech than to indicate singular things by common nouns, because the context makes it clear that the common idea which corresponds to the word has been connected to a singular and distinct idea which determines it to signify only a single and unique thing.

I said this is usually clear from the context, for example the way the word "king" signifies Louis XIV in the mouths of French speakers. But here is yet another rule which can help us decide when a common term remains in its general idea and when it is determined by a distinct and particular idea, although not expressed.

When there is a manifest absurdity in connecting an attribute with a subject remaining in its general idea, we ought to think that the person forming the proposition did not take the subject generally. Thus if I hear someone say: *Rex hoc mihi* [124] *imperavit*: "The king ordered me to do that," I am sure that person did not take the word "king" to express the general idea, for the king in general makes no particular commands.

If someone says to me: "The *Brussels Gazette* of 14 January 1662, concerning what happened at Paris, is false," I would be certain that they had something in mind in addition to what these terms signify, because none of that enables me to decide if what the *Gazette* said is true or false. Thus this person must have conceived some distinct and specific news item and judged it to be contrary to the truth, for example, if this gazette had said that the King created one hundred Knights of the Order of the Holy Ghost.

The same is true of judgments about the views of philosophers, whenever someone says that the doctrine of a certain philosopher is false, without expressing the doctrine distinctly, for example, in "the doctrine of Lucretius concerning the nature of the soul is false." The person forming this sort of judgment must conceive a distinct and specific view under the general term "doctrine of a certain philosopher," because the quality of being false does not belong to a doctrine insofar as it belongs to a certain author, but only by being a certain opinion contrary to the truth. So this type of proposition should be analyzed as follows: "A certain opinion taught by a certain author is false"; "the view that the soul is composed of atoms, which was taught by Lucretius, is false." Accordingly, these judgments always include two affirmations, even when they are not distinctly expressed. One is the principal proposition, concerning the truth in itself, which is that it is a great error to hold that the soul is composed of atoms. The other is a subordinate proposition which concerns only a historical point, namely that this error was taught by Lucretius.

CHAPTER 7

The falsity that can exist in complex terms and subordinate propositions

What we have just said can help resolve a famous issue, namely whether falsity can exist only in propositions, or whether it is also found in ideas and simple terms.

I refer to falsity rather than truth, because there is a kind of [125] truth in things with respect to God's mind, whether people think of it or not. But there can be falsity only relative to the human mind or to some other mind subject to error, that falsely judges that a thing is what it is not.

We ask, then, whether this falsity is encountered only in propositions and judgments.

The usual answer is no, which is true in a sense. But this does not preclude falsity from existing sometimes, not in simple ideas, but in complex terms because, for that to happen, it suffices if there is some judgment in the complex term, or some affirmation, either explicit or implicit.

This will be clearer if we look in more detail at the two kinds of complex terms, one in which the relative pronoun is explicative, the other in which it is determinative.

We should not be surprised to find falsity in the first sort of complex term, because the attribute of the subordinate proposition is affirmed of the subject to which the pronoun refers. In "Alexander who is the son of Philip," I affirm of Alexander, albeit only incidentally, that he is the son of Philip, and consequently there is some falsity in that if it is not the case.

But there are two or three important points to make here.

1. That the falsity of the subordinate proposition does not ordinarily preclude the truth of the main proposition. Consider this example, "Alexander who was the son of Philip defeated the Persians." This proposition should be considered true even if Alexander were not the son of Philip, because the affirmation of the principal proposition affects only Alexander, and what is joined to it incidentally, although false, does not prevent it from being true that Alexander defeated the Persians.

If, however, the attribute of the principal proposition were related to the subordinate proposition, for example if I said, "Alexander the son of Philip was the grandson of Amintas," only then would the falsity of the subordinate proposition make the principal proposition false.[a]

2. Titles commonly given to certain [126] dignitaries can be given to all people who possess this office, even if what is signified by the title does not apply to them at all. Thus, because formerly the titles "holy" and "most holy" were given to all bishops, it was clear that the Catholic bishops in the Council of Carthage had no difficulty bestowing this title on Donatist bishops, *sanctissimus Petitianus dixit* [the

---

[a] The following paragraph was deleted from I:

> When these subordinate propositions are used only to designate the subject of the discourse, then for these propositions to be true it is not necessary that the attribute really apply to the subject, but it is enough if it applies to it in people's minds. Thus when we say "Alexander the son of Philip" or "who was the son of Philip," the quality "son of Philip" which is affirmed of Alexander is affirmed only according to men's opinion, and not according to the truth of things, so that the sense is, "Alexander [126] who according to popular opinion was the son of Philip." This is why it could be false that Alexander is the son of Philip although the Scripture gives him this quality: *Alexander Philipi, Rex Macedo.* The First Book of the Maccabees 1:1.

most holy Petitianus said], although they knew quite well that true holiness could not belong to a schismatic bishop. We also see that in Acts,[1] St. Paul gives the title "best" or "most excellent" to Festus, the Governor of Judea, because this was the title ordinarily given to these governors.

3. It is not the same if people are the authors of a title they are bestowing on another, which they bestow speaking for themselves and not for others or from popular error, for they can always rightly be charged with the falsity of these propositions. Thus if someone says: "Aristotle who is the prince of philosophers," or simply "the prince of philosophers thought that the nerves originated in the heart," it would not be right to say that this is false because Aristotle is not the greatest philosopher. For it is enough that he was following common opinion, however false, in speaking thus of Aristotle. But if someone says "Gassendi, who is the most astute of philosophers, believes that there is a void in nature," we would be right to argue with this person about the quality he wanted to attribute to Gassendi, and to hold him responsible for the falsity we could allege in this subordinate proposition. We can thus be accused of falsity in giving the same person a title which is not fitting, and not be accused of it in giving the person another that is in fact even less fitting. For example, "Pope John XII was neither holy nor chaste nor pious," as Baronius recognized.[2] And yet those who called him "most holy" could not be charged with lying, and those who might call him "very chaste" or "very pious" would be very great liars, even were they to do it only by subordinate propositions, as if they said "John XII, a very chaste Pontiff, ordained such-and-such."

This is the case with the first sort of subordinate proposition, in which the relative pronoun is explicative. As for the others, in which the [127] relative pronoun is determinative, such as "people who are pious," "kings who love their people," certainly they are not usually susceptible of falsity, because the attribute of the subordinate proposition is not affirmed of the subject to which the relative pronoun refers. When we say, for example, "Judges who never do anything by prayers and favors are worthy of praise," we are not thereby saying that there are any judges on the earth in this state of perfection. Nevertheless I believe that in these propositions there is always a tacit or virtual affirmation, not of the actual application of the attribute to the subject to which the pronoun refers, but of its possible application. If this is mistaken, then I think we are right to find these subordinate propositions false. For example, suppose someone says, "Minds that are square are more sound than those that are round." Since the ideas "square" and "round" are incompatible with the idea "mind" taken as the principle of thought, I would say these subordinate propositions should be considered false.

We can even say that most of our errors arise from this. For when we have the idea of something, we often connect it to another idea which is incompatible,

---

[1]   Acts of the Apostles, 26:25.
[2]   Caesar Baronius, *Annalium Ecclesiasticarum*, vol. 10, p. 772.

although we mistakenly believe it to be compatible. This makes us attribute to the first idea something that cannot belong to it.

So, finding in ourselves two ideas, one of thinking substance and one of extended substance, often when we consider the soul, which is a thinking substance, we unwittingly mix in something from the idea of extended substance. This happens, for example, when we imagine that the soul must take up some space just as a body does, and that it could not exist if it were not somewhere, which are things that apply only to bodies. This is how the impious error arises of persons who think the soul is mortal. St. Augustine has an excellent passage on this topic in Book 10 of *The Trinity*,[3] where he shows that nothing is easier to know than the nature of the soul. But what confuses people is that in trying to know it, they are not satisfied with what is known without difficulty, which is that it is a substance that thinks, wills, doubts, and knows. But they connect what it is with something it is not, trying to imagine it under one of these images [128] by which they customarily conceive corporeal things.

On the other hand, when we consider the body, we certainly find it hard to keep from mingling in it something from the idea of thinking substance. This causes us to say that heavy bodies want to move to the center, that plants seek the nourishment appropriate for them, that in the crisis of an illness nature is trying to get rid of something harmful, and that nature wants to do this or that about a thousand other things, especially concerning the body. This is true even though we are quite sure that we have not willed it nor thought it in any way, and that it is ridiculous to imagine that there is something else in us besides ourselves that knows what is helpful or harmful, that seeks one and avoids the other.

I think, again, that all the mutterings against God ought to be attributed to this mixture of incompatible ideas. For it would be impossible to mutter against God if he were conceived as he really is, omnipotent, omniscient, and benevolent. But the wicked conceive him as omnipotent and the sovereign master of all, attributing to Him all the evils that befall them, which they are right to do. But because at the same time they conceive him as cruel and unjust, which is incompatible with his goodness, they rail against him as if he were wrong to send them the evils they suffer.

CHAPTER 8

Propositions that are complex in affirmation or negation; one species of this type of proposition which philosophers call modal

Besides propositions whose subject or attribute is a complex term, others are complex because they contain terms or subordinate propositions that affect only the

---

[3] Bk. x, ch. 10, *Writings*, vol. 18, pp. 309-10.

form of the proposition, that is, the affirmation or negation expressed by the verb. When I say, for example, "I maintain [129] that the earth is round," "I maintain" is only a subordinate proposition that must be part of something in the principal proposition. Yet it is obvious that it is part of neither the subject nor the attribute. For it changes nothing at all in them, and they would be conceived in exactly the same way if I simply said, "the earth is round." And so this affects only the affirmation which is expressed in two ways, one in the usual way by the verb "is": "the earth is round"; the other more explicitly by the verb "I maintain."

The same is true when we say "I deny," "it is true," "it is not true," or when we add something supporting its truth to a proposition, as when I say: "The evidence of astronomy convinces us that the sun is much larger than the earth." For the first part is only support for the affirmation.

It is important to notice of this kind of proposition, however, that some are ambiguous and can be taken differently depending on the intentions of the speaker, for example: "All philosophers assure us that heavy things fall to earth of their own accord." If my intent is to show that heavy things fall to earth of their own accord, the first part of this proposition would be merely subordinate, and would only support the affirmation of the last part. But if, to the contrary, I simply intended to report this as an opinion of philosophers without approving of it myself, then the first part would be the principal proposition and the last part would be only part of the attribute. For I would be affirming not that heavy things fall of their own accord, but only that all philosophers assure us of it. It is clear that these two different ways of taking this same proposition change it, so that they are two different propositions with completely different meanings. But it is often easy to tell by the context in which of these two senses to take it. Suppose that after uttering this proposition I added: "Now rocks are heavy; therefore they fall to earth of their own accord." It would be obvious that I was taking it in the first sense and that the first part was only subordinate. But if by contrast I reasoned this way: "Now this is an error; consequently it is possible for all philosophers to teach something erroneous," it would be clear that I was taking it in [130] the second sense, that is, that the first part was the principal proposition and the second part only part of the attribute.

Among these complex propositions where the complexity affects the verb and not the subject or attribute, philosophers have paid particular attention to those called *modal*, because the affirmation or negation is modified by one of these four modes: *possible, contingent, impossible, necessary*. Because each mode can be affirmed or denied, as in "it is possible" or "it is not impossible," and joined in either way to an affirmative or negative proposition, such as "the earth is round" or "the earth is not round," each mode can have four propositions. The four taken together make sixteen, which are indicated by these four words: PURPUREA, ILIACE, AMA-BIMUS, EDENTULI. The whole mystery here is that each syllable marks one of these four modes:

The 1st. possible:
The 2nd. contingent:
The 3rd. impossible:
The 4th. necessary.

The vowel in each syllable, either **A, E, I,** or **U,** indicates whether the mode should be affirmed or denied and whether the proposition, which is called the *dictum*, should be affirmed or denied as follows:

A. Affirmation of the mode and affirmation of the proposition.
E. Affirmation of the mode and negation of the proposition.
I. Negation of the mode and affirmation of the proposition.
U. Negation of the mode and negation of the proposition.

It would be a waste of time to run through examples, which are easy to find. We should only observe that PURPUREA corresponds to **A** of noncomplex propositions, ILIACE to **E**, AMABIMUS to **I**, and EDENTULI to **U**. So if we want the example to be valid, after selecting a subject we must choose an attribute that can be universally affirmed of it for PURPUREA, for ILIACE one that can be universally denied, one that can be particularly affirmed for AMABIMUS, and for EDENTULI one that can be particularly denied.

But whatever attribute we choose, it is always true that all four propositions of the same word have just the same meaning, so that when one is true, all the others are too. [131]

CHAPTER 9

Different kinds of compound propositions

We have already said that compound propositions are those with either a double subject or a double attribute. Now there are two kinds: those in which the composition is explicitly indicated, and others in which it is implied, which logicians call [in Latin] *exponibiles* because they need to be expounded or explained.

The first kind can be reduced to six species: copulatives and disjunctives; conditionals and causals; relatives and discretives.

COPULATIVES

Copulatives are propositions that contain several subjects or attributes united by an affirmative[a] or negative conjunction, namely "and" or "neither/nor." For "neither/nor" does the same thing as "and" in these sorts of propositions,[b]

---

[a]   ... by a copulative or negative conjunction. For ... (I)
[b]   ... propositions: Faith and the good life are necessary for salvation. The wicked are happy neither in this world nor in the other. – The truth [98:3] ... (I)

since "neither/nor" signifies "and" with a negation affecting the verb, rather than the union of the two words it connects. For example when I say "neither knowledge nor wealth makes a person happy," I unite knowledge and wealth, maintaining of each that they do not make a person happy, as if I were to say that knowledge and wealth make a person vain.

Three kinds of these propositions can be distinguished:

1. Those with more than one subject.

Mors et vita in manibus linguae.[1]
Death and life are in the power of language.

2. Those with more than one attribute.

Auream quisquis mediocritatem
Diligit, tutus caret obsoleti
Sordibus tecti, caret invidenda
        Sobrius aula.[2]
[Anyone who prizes the golden mean will
Live secure from ramshackle roof and squalor
And, in wisdom, equally safe from mansions
        Subject to envy.]

Whoever loves the moderation that is so admirable in everything lives neither sordidly nor opulently. [132]

Sperat infaustis, metuit secundis
Alteram sortem, benè praeparatum
Pectus.[3]
[Any well fortified heart hopes in times of
Trouble, and, when fortune is showing favor
Most, will fear the opposite fate.]

A sound mind hopes for prosperity in adversity and fears adversity in prosperity.

3. Those with more than one subject and more than one attribute.

Non domus et fundus, non aeris acervus et auri,
Ægroto Domini deduxit corpore febres,
Non animo curas.[4]
[Never did house or estate, nor the bronze and gold of a treasure
Draw off the fever tormenting the frame of their invalid owner,
Nor have they ever purged cares from his mind.]

Neither houses nor lands, nor the greatest heaps of gold and silver can banish

[1] Proverbs 18:21.
[2] Horace, *Odes*, II.x.5–8, *Complete Works*, p. 193.
[3] Ibid., II.x.13–15, *Complete Works*, p. 193.
[4] Horace, *Epistles*, I.ii.47–9, *Complete Works*, pp. 263–4.

fever from the body of their possessors, nor deliver his mind of cares and sorrow.

The truth of these propositions depends on the truth of both parts.ᶜ Hence if I say that faith and a good life are necessary for salvation, this is true because both are necessary. But if I said a good life and riches are necessary for salvation, this proposition would be false, because even though a good life is necessary, riches are not.

Not all propositions in which negatives occur are considered negations or contradictions of copulatives and other compound propositions, but only those where the negation affects the conjunction. This happens in several ways, such as putting a "not" at the beginning of the proposition. *Non enim amas, et deseris,* says St. Augustine.⁵ That is, you should not believe that you can both love someone and abandon them. [133]

This is also the way to form the contradictory of the copulative, by explicitly denying the conjunction, as we do when we say that it is not possible for the same thing to be this and that at the same time.

That one cannot be both in love and wise.

*Amare et sapere vix Deo conceditur.*⁶

That love and majesty do not go together;

*Non bene conveniunt, nec in una saede morantur majestas et amor.*⁷
[Do majesty and love go together,
Or linger in one dwelling? Hardly.]

---

5 Tractate XLIX, ch. 11, no. 5, *Lectures or Tractates on the Gospel According to St. John,* vol. 2, pp. 126–7, *Works,* vol. 11.

6 Publius Syrus, *Publii Syri sententiae,* sentence 25 as classified by alphabetical order.

7 Ovid, *Metamorphoses,* II.846–7, p. 55. (Clair and Girbal incorrectly locate this verse in Bk. III.)

c ... parts. This is why these two are true, because not only faith, and not only the good life, but both are necessary for salvation. And the wicked are unhappy in this world as well as in the other.

These propositions are considered as negations and contradictories of others only when the negation falls on the conjunction. This is done in Latin by putting the negation at the beginning of the proposition: *Non et fides et bona opera necessaria sunt ad salutem* [Neither faith nor good works are necessary for salvation].

But in our language we get the same effect although we put the negation near the verb:

Knowledge and wealth, neither is necessary for salvation.
The wicked are not at all happy in this world and also not in the other.

Or to indicate it better we can put "it is not true" in place of the Latin negation: It is not true that the wicked are unhappy in this world and in the other.

2. Disjunctives are widely used ... (I)

DISJUNCTIVES

Disjunctives are widely used. These are propositions containing the disjunctive conjunction *vel*, "either/or."[d]

Friendship either finds friends equal or makes them equal;

Amicitia pares aut accipit, aut facit.[8]

A woman either loves or hates: there is no middle ground;

Aut amat aut odit mulier, nihil est tertium.[9]

Whoever lives in complete solitude is either a beast or an angel (says Aristotle).[10]
People are moved only by self-interest or fear.
Either the Earth revolves around the sun or the sun revolves around the Earth.
Every intentional action is either good or bad.

The truth of these propositions depends on the necessary opposition between the parts, which must not permit a middle term. Just as they cannot permit a middle term at all in order to be necessarily true, it is enough that they do not usually allow it to be considered morally true. This is why it is absolutely true that an action done intentionally is good or bad, since theologians have shown that there is not a single action which is indifferent. But when we say that people are moved only by self-interest or fear this is not absolutely true, since [134] some people are moved by neither of these passions, but rather by consideration of their duty. Hence the real truth of the matter is that these are the two motives which influence most people.

Propositions contradicting disjunctions are those where we deny the truth of the disjunction. This happens in Latin, as in all other compound propositions, by putting the negation at the beginning: *Non omnis actio est bona vel mala* [Not every action is good or bad]. And in our language: "It is not true that every action is good or bad."

CONDITIONALS

Conditionals are propositions made up of two parts connected by the condition *if*.[e]
The first part, which contains the condition, is called the antecedent, and the other

---

[8]   Publius Syrus, *Publii Syri sententiae*, sentence 32 as classified by alphabetical order.
[9]   Ibid., sentence 67.
[10] *Politics*, Bk. 1, ch. 2, *Complete Works*, vol. 2, pp. 1987–8.
[d]   . . . or.

Every line is straight or curved.
Every person will be eternally happy or eternally unhappy.
Every intentional action is either good or bad.

The truth of these propositions depends on the necessary opposition between the parts, which must not permit a middle term, but each part taken separately need not be true.

For it is not at all necessary for a person to be happy, nor for him to be unhappy eternally, but it is necessary for him to be one or the other.

They are negated when we deny the necessity of the disjunction. This happens in Latin. . .(I)

[e]   . . . if, as in:

If one does not live according to the Gospel, he will not be saved.
If one loves God, he will find everything in him.

part is called the consequent: "if the soul is spiritual" – this is the antecedent – "it is immortal" – this is the consequent.

This inference is sometimes mediate and sometimes immediate. It is only mediate when there is nothing in the terms of either part that links them, as for instance:

If the earth is immovable, the sun revolves.
If God is just, the wicked will be punished.

These inferences are quite valid, but they are not immediate because the two parts, lacking a common term, are connected only by what one has in mind, which is not expressed. Given that the earth and the sun are constantly in different positions with respect to each other, it follows necessarily that if one is immovable, the other moves.

When the inference is immediate, it must usually be the case that:

1. Either the two parts have the same subject:
   If death is the passage to a happier life, it is desirable. [135]
   If you failed to feed the poor, you killed them.
   Si non pavisti, occidisti.
2. Or they have the same attribute:
   If all the tests of faith from God ought to be dear to us, diseases ought to be so.
3. Or the attribute of the first part is the subject of the second:
   If patience is a virtue, some virtues are painful.
4. Or, finally, the subject of the first part is the attribute of the second, which can happen only when the second part is negative:
   If all true Christians live according to the Gospel, there are practically no true Christians.

To determine the truth of these propositions we consider only the truth of the inference. For even if both parts are false, if the inference from one to the other is valid, the proposition insofar as it is conditional is true. For example:

If a creature's will can obstruct the absolute will of God, God is not omnipotent.

Propositions considered to be negations or contradictories of conditionals are only those that deny the condition. This is done in Latin by putting the negation at the beginning:

Non si miserum fortuna Sinonem
Finxit, vanum etiam mendacemque improba finget.[11]

To determine the truth of these propositions we consider only the truth of the inference. For even if both parts are false, if the inference is true, the proposition insofar as it is a conditional is taken as true. For example: If a monkey is a man, he is rational.
These propositions are taken to be negations or contradictories of affirmatives only when the condition is denied. This is [100:4up] ... (I)

[11] Virgil, *Aeneid*, II.79–80, *Virgil*, vol. I, p. 299.

[Not even if fortune has made Sinon miserable
would it make him deceitful and wicked.]

But in our language we express these contradictories by "although" and a negation,

If you eat the forbidden fruit, you will die.[12]
Although you eat the forbidden fruit, you will not die.

Or equally by "it is not true."

It is not true that if you eat the forbidden fruit, you will die. [136]

CAUSALS

Causals are propositions containing two propositions connected by a word expressing cause, *quia*, "because,"[f] or *ut*, "so that."

Woe to the rich, because their consolation is in this world.[13]
The wicked are raised up so that in falling from on high their fall will be greater;
 Tolluntur in altum.
Ut lapsu graviore ruant.[14]
They can do it because they believe they can;
Possunt quia posse videntur.[15]
A certain prince was unhappy because he was born under a certain sign.

Propositions called *reduplicatives* can also be reduced to this kind of proposition, for example:

A human, as a human, is reasonable.
Kings, as kings, depend on God alone.

For the truth of these propositions it is necessary for one of the parts to be the cause of the other. This entails that both parts must be true, for what is false is not a cause and has no cause. But it is possible for both parts to be true and the causal

---

[12] Genesis 2:17.
[13] Luke 6:24.
[14] Claudius Claudianus, *The First Book Against Rufinus*, verses 22–3, *Claudian*, vol. 1, p. 29.
[15] Virgil, *Aeneid*, v.231, *Virgil*, vol. 1, p. 461.
[f] ... "because," "for the reason that."

He was punished because he committed a crime.
He will be saved because he lives according to God.

For the truth of these propositions it is necessary for both parts to be true, and for one to be the cause of the other.
We contradict them by denying either of the two parts, or both of them, or only that one is the cause of the other, as in:

He was punished, and he committed a crime, but it was not because of it that he was punished. –

5. RELATIVES are ... (I)

to be false, because in that case it is enough if one part is not the cause of the other. Thus a prince could have been unhappy and have been born under a certain sign, which would not prevent its being false that he was unhappy because he was born under that sign.

This is why the contradictories of these propositions, properly speaking, consist in denying that one thing is the cause of another: *Non ideo infœlix, quia sub hoc natus sidere* [It is not the case that he was unhappy because he was born under a certain sign].

RELATIVES

Relatives are propositions that contain some comparison and some relation:

> Where the treasure is, there the heart lies.[16] [137]
> As a person lives, so he dies.
> *Tanti es, quantum habeas.*[17]
> We are admired in the world in proportion to our wealth.

Truth depends on the accuracy of the relation, and relatives are contradicted by denying the relation.[g]

> It is not true that as a person lives, so he dies.
> It is not true that we are admired in the world in proportion to our wealth.

DISCRETIVES

These are propositions in which[h] we make different judgments, indicating this difference by the particles *sed*, but, *tamen*, nevertheless, or similar particles either expressed or implied.

> *Fortuna opes auferre, non animum potest.*[18] Fortune can take away my wealth, but not my heart.
> *Et mihi res, non me rebus submittere conor.*[19] I try to put myself above circumstances, and not to be a slave to them.
> *Caelum non animum mutant qui trans mare currunt.*[20] Those who cross the seas change only their country, and not their minds.

---

[16] Matthew 6:21. Cf. also Luke 12:34.

[17] Seneca, Epistle 115, *Ad Lucilium Epistulae Morales*, vol. 3, p. 329. The exact quotation is *Ubique tanti quisque, quantum habuit, fuit* [All persons are worth as much as what they own].

[18] Seneca, *Medea*, verse 176, *Seneca's Tragedies*, I: 243.

[19] Horace, *Epistles*, Book I, Epistle I, verse 19, *Complete Works*, 259; read: "*...rebus subjungere conor...*"

[20] *Ibid.*, Book I, Epistle XI, verse 27, *Complete Works*, 279.

[g]   ... relation.
    It is not true that as a person lives, so he dies. –
    6. Discretives are propositions ... (I)

[h]   ... in which we express various things about different things, connecting them by *sed*, but, or *tamen*, nevertheless, as in *Non omnis qui dicit mihi, Domine, Domine, intrabit in regnum coelorum, sed qui facit voluntatem Patris mei*:
    Do not believe that whoever would say to me, Lord, Lord, should enter the kingdom of Heaven, but he who would do the will of my Father will enter. The truth .. .(I)

The truth of this kind of proposition depends on the truth of both parts and the separation between them. For even if both parts were true, a proposition of this kind would be ridiculous if there were no contrast between them, for instance:

> Judas was a thief, and nevertheless he could not bear for Mary Magdalene to spread her ointments on Jesus Christ.

There are several ways of contradicting a proposition of this kind, for example:

> Happiness depends not on wealth but on knowledge.

This proposition can be contradicted in all the following ways:

> Happiness depends on wealth and not knowledge.
> Happiness depends neither on wealth nor knowledge.
> Happiness depends on both wealth and knowledge.

Thus we can see that copulatives are contradictories of discretives, for these last two propositions are copulatives. [138]

CHAPTER 10

Propositions with compound meanings[a]

There are other compound propositions whose composition is more implicit. They can be reduced to these four types: 1. Exclusives, 2. Exceptives, 3. Comparatives, and 4. Inceptives or Desitives.

1. EXCLUSIVES

Exclusive propositions are those indicating that an attribute applies to a subject and only to this single subject; in other words, that it does not apply to others. It

---

[a]   State of the chapter in I:

> It remains to say a word about propositions whose composition is more implicit. There are six kinds of them.
> 1. EXCLUSIVES: Virtue alone is admirable. Only virtue is admirable.
> 2. EXCEPTIVES: All persons are miserable except those who belong to God.
> 3. COMPARATIVES: Impiety is the greatest of all blindnesses
> 4. INCEPTIVES: Whoever is converted to God begins to feel the weight of sin.
> 5. DESITIVES: Whoever is justified is no longer under the domination of sin.
> 6. REDUPLICATIVES: Humans insofar as they are animals are similar to beasts.
> It is easy to see that all these propositions contain several propositions in their meaning. We only have to pay attention to them to recognize this. It is necessary to leave something to be discovered by those who are learning, so that they will exercise their minds.
> What is more noteworthy here is that often there are propositions which are exclusive in meaning although the exclusion is not expressed, especially in Latin. So in translating them into our language we cannot completely preserve their meaning without making them exclusive propositions, although the exclusion is not indicated in Latin ... *si tantum tales habet.* [105:7up] ... (I) [This is the end of the chapter in I.]

follows that they contain two different judgments, and consequently they are compound in meaning. This is expressed by the word "only" or something similar. Or in our language: "there is only." There is only God worthy of being loved for His own sake.

> *Deus solus fruendus, reliqua utenda.*[1]
> That is, we should love God for His own sake, and love other things only for God's sake.
> *Quas dederis solas semper habebis opes.*[2] The only riches that will always remain with you are those you have freely given away.
> *Nobilitas sola est atque unica virtus.*[3]
> Virtue is the only true nobility.
> *Hoc unum scio quod nihil scio*, said the Academics.[4] [139]
> It is certain that nothing is certain; there is only obscurity and uncertainty in everything else.

Lucan, speaking of the Druids, forms this disjunctive proposition composed of two exclusives:

> *Solis nosse deos, et caeli numina vobis*
> *Aut solis nescire datum est.*[5]
> [To you alone is granted knowledge – or ignorance, it may be –
> of gods and celestial powers.]
> Either you know the gods, although everyone else is ignorant of them, or you do not know them, although everyone else does.

These propositions are contradicted in three ways:

1. We can deny that what is said to apply to a single subject, applies to it at all.
2. We can maintain that it applies to something else.
3. We can maintain both.

Thus we can say contrary to this sentence, "virtue is the only true nobility":

1. That virtue does not make one noble at all.
2. That birth makes one noble as does virtue.
3. That birth and not virtue makes one noble.

Hence this maxim of the Academics: "It is certain that nothing is certain," was contradicted differently by the Dogmatists and the Pyrrhonists. The Dogmatists argued against it by claiming that it was doubly false, since there are many things we know quite certainly, and so it is not true that it is certain that we know nothing.

---

[1] St. Augustine, *On Christian Instruction*, I, chs. 4–22, *Writings*, vol. 4, pp. 41–2.
[2] Martial, v.xlii.8, *Epigrams*, vol. 1, p. 327.
[3] Juvenal, VIII.20, *Satires*, p. 159.
[4] Cicero, *Academica*, Bk. I, ch. 4, *De Natura Deorum, Academica*, p. 425.
[5] Lucan, *Pharsalia*, Bk. I, verse 452, p. 37.

The Pyrrhonists also said it was false, for a contrary reason, namely that everything is so uncertain that it is even uncertain whether nothing is certain.

This is why what Lucan said of the Druids contains a mistaken judgment, because it is not necessary that only Druids know the truth about the gods, or that they alone are mistaken. Because different errors concerning the nature of God are possible, it could easily have happened that although the Druids had thoughts concerning God's nature that differed from thoughts of other nations, they were as mistaken as other nations.

What is more important is that often propositions of this kind are exclusive in meaning although the exclusion is not expressed. For instance, this verse of Virgil, where the exclusion is indicated: [140]

Una salus victis nullam sperare salutem,[6]

has been happily translated into our language by this verse in which the exclusion is implicit.

The hope of the vanquished is to expect nothing.

Nevertheless implied exclusives are more common in Latin than in our language. So we often find passages whose meaning cannot be completely preserved in translation without making them exclusive propositions, although the exclusion is not indicated in Latin.

For example, 2 Corinthians 10:17: *Qui gloriatur, in Domino glorietur,* should be translated: "Those who boast should boast only in the Lord."

Galatians 6:8:[7] *Quae seminaverit homo, haec et metet*: "Man shall reap only what he has sown."

Ephesians 4:5: *Unus Dominus, una fides, unum baptisma*: "There is only one Lord, one faith, one baptism."

Matthew 5:46: *Si diligitis eos qui vos diligunt, quam mercedem habebitis?* "If you love only those who love you, what reward do you deserve?"

Seneca in his *Troades: Nullas habet spes Troja, si tales habet.*[8] "Troy has no hopes, if she has but these." As if it said *si tantum tales habet* [if she has so little].

2. EXCEPTIVES

Exceptives are propositions in which we affirm something of an entire subject with the exception of some of the inferiors, using an exceptive particle to show that this thing does not apply to them. Obviously these propositions contain two judgments and are thereby compound in meaning. For example:

No ancient philosophers, except the Platonists, recognized God's incorporeality.

---

[6] *Aeneid*, II.354, *Virgil*, vol. 1, p. 319.
[7] The original text has verse 7.
[8] Verse 741, *Seneca's Tragedies* vol. 1, p. 189.

This means two things: first, that ancient philosophers believed God was corporeal; and second, that the Platonists believed the contrary.

Avarus nisi cùm moritur, nihil rectè facit.[9]
The miser does no good except by dying.
Et miser nemo, nisi comparatus.[10]
No one believes he is miserable except by comparing himself to those who are happier.
Nemo laeditur nisi à seipso:
The only harm we suffer, we do to ourselves. [141]
Except for the sage, the Stoics said, all people are truly fools.

These propositions may be contradicted in the same way as exclusives.

1. By maintaining that the sage of the Stoics was as foolish as other people.
2. By maintaining that there were others besides this sage who were not foolish.
3. By claiming that the sage of the Stoics was foolish, and that others were not.

We should note that exclusives and exceptives are almost the same thing, expressed slightly differently, so one is always easily changed into the other. Hence we see that this exceptive of Terence:

Imperitus nisi quod ipse facit, nil rectum putat.[11]
[The ignorant person thinks that nothing is right except what he himself does.]

was changed by Cornelius Gallus into this exclusive:

Hoc tantum rectum quod facit ipse putat.[12]
[He thinks that only what he himself does is right.]

3. COMPARATIVES

Propositions in which we make a comparison contain two judgments because there are two judgments involved in saying that something is such-and-such, and in saying that it is more or less such-and-such than something else. Thus this sort of proposition is compound in meaning.

Amicum perdere, est damnorum maximum.[13]
The greatest of all losses is to lose a friend.

---

[9] Publius Syrus, *Publii Syri sententiae*, sentence 75 as classified by alphabetical order.
[10] Seneca, *Troades*, verse 1023, *Seneca's Tragedies*, vol. 1, p. 211.
[11] *The Brothers*, I.ii.98–9, *Comedies*, p. 343. Arnauld & Nicole misquote this passage, which should read: *Homine imperito nunquam quicquam iniustiust / Qui nisi quod ipse fecit nil rectum putat* [Is anything as unjust as a narrow-minded man! He can only see right in what he has done himself].
[12] Gaius Cornelius Gallus (c. 70–26 BC) was a soldier and poet, and a friend of Virgil and the emperor Augustus. Augustus made him the first prefect of Egypt in 30 BC, but four years later he was recalled in disgrace and committed suicide. He appears to have originated the genre of the elegy, but only one pentameter line and some papyrus fragments of his elegies survive. Virgil incorporated some of Gallus's own lines into his tenth *Eclogue*. Clair and Girbal give as the source *Elegies*, 1.198.
[13] Publius Syrus, *Publii Syri sententiae*, sentence 35 as classified by alphabetical order.

Ridiculum acri
Fortius ac melius magnas plerumque secat res.[14]
[A joke often settles an issue of substance
Better and with a more telling effect than a bitter rejoinder.]
A pleasant joke often makes a greater impression in even the most important
matters than the best reasons.
Meliora sunt vulnera amici, quàm fraudulenta oscula inimici.[15]
A friend's blows are worth more than an enemy's fraudulent kisses.

These propositions are contradicted in several ways, just as this maxim of
Epicurus, "pain is the greatest of all evils," was contradicted in one way by the
Stoics and in another by the Peripatetics. The Peripatetics admitted that pain is an
evil, but they maintained that vices and other disorders of the mind are even
greater evils, whereas the Stoics would not even acknowledge that pain is an evil,
much less that it is the greatest evil.

But here we can discuss an issue, which is whether it [142] is always necessary in
these propositions for the positive of the comparative to apply to both members of
the comparison, for example, whether we must assume that two things are good
before we can say that one is better than another.

At first it seems that this must be so, but practice is to the contrary, since we see
Scripture using the word "better" not just to compare two good things: *Melior est
sapientia quàm vires, et vir prudens quàm fortis.*[16] Wisdom is better than strength,
and the prudent person better than the valiant person.

But Scripture also uses it to compare a good with an evil: *Melior est patiens
arrogante.*[17] A patient person is better than a proud person.

And even to compare two evil things: *Melius est habitare cum dracone, quàm cum
muliere litigiosa.*[18] It is better to live with a dragon than with a quarrelsome woman.
And in the Gospel: it is better to be thrown in the sea with a rock around one's
neck than to scandalize the least of the faithful.

The reason for this practice is that a much greater good is better than a lesser
good, because it has more goodness than a lesser good. Now by the same reasoning
we can say, although less properly, that a good is better than an evil because it has
more goodness than something having none at all. And we can also say that a lesser
evil is better than a greater evil, because when the diminution of evil is substituted
for a good in comparing two evil things, what is less evil has more of this sort of
goodness than what is worse.

Thus we should avoid getting caught up in the heat of the debate, quibbling over

---

[14] Horace, *Satires*, I.x.14–15, *Complete Works*, p. 30.
[15] Proverbs 26:6; read *diligentis* instead of *amici*, and *odientis* instead of *inimici* .
[16] Clair and Girbal give as Wisdom of Solomon 6:1, but the source has not been identified.
[17] Ecclesiastes 7:9.
[18] The exact citation has not been found, but Proverbs 21:9 contains "Better to live in a corner of the
housetop than have a nagging wife and a brawling household"; and Proverbs 21:19 reads "Better to
live alone in the desert than with a nagging and ill-tempered wife."

these forms of speech, as did a Donatist Grammarian named Cresconius when he wrote against St. Augustine. For when this Saint said that Catholics had more reason to criticize the Donatists for abandoning the sacred books than the Donatists had for criticizing the Catholics, *Traditionem nos vobis probabilius objicimus* [We have a more credible objection to you from the teachings that have been handed down], Cresconius thought he had the right to infer from this that St. Augustine thereby acknowledged that the Donatists were right to criticize the Catholics. *Si enim vos probabilius*, he said, *Nos ergo probabiliter: Nam gradus isto quod antè positum est auget, non quod ante dictum est improbat* [If you have a more credible objection, then we have a credible one: for where there is a degree that surpasses something posited, that which is posited cannot be rejected]. But St. Augustine first refutes this worthless subtlety by examples from Scripture, among them the passage from A Letter to the Hebrews, in which St. Paul says that the ground that bears only thistles is cursed and ought to expect only to be burned. He adds: *Confidimus* [143] *autem de vobis fratres charissimi meliora: Non quia*, says this Father, *bona illa erant quae supra dixerat, proferre spinas et tribulos, et ustionem mereri, sed magis quia mala erant, ut illis devitatis meliora eligerent et optarent, hoc est mala tantis bonis contraria.*[19] [But we are sure of better things from you, dearest brothers. Not on the grounds that those were good things which were mentioned above, namely to bring out prickles and thorns and to earn burnings, but rather because they were bad. When these are avoided, better things are selected and chosen, the opposites of such bad things]. Then, referring to the most famous authors of their kind, he shows how fallacious this inference is, since Virgil could similarly be criticized for considering as a good thing a violent disease which causes people to tear themselves apart with their own teeth, because he wishes good people a better fate.

> *Dii meliora piis, erroremque hostibus illum;*
> *Discissos nudis laniabant dentibus artus.*[20]
> [Heaven grant a happier lot to the good, and such madness to our foes!]

Quomodo ergo meliora piis, says this Father, *quasi bona essent istis, ac non potius magna mala qui discissos nudis, laniabant dentibus artus* [In this way he wished them better things, as if the things they had were good things, and not rather very bad things that would lead them to tear themselves apart in a very short time].

4. INCEPTIVES and DESITIVES

Whenever we say that something began or ceased to be such-and-such, we make two judgments, one about what the thing was before the time referred to, the other about what it is since. So these propositions, of which the former are called inceptives and the latter desitives, are compound in meaning. They are so similar

---

[19] *Contra Cresconium grammaticum* , Bk. III, chs. 73–5, Migne, *Patrologia Latina*, vol. 43, pp. 542–3.
[20] *Georgics*, III.513–14, *Virgil*, vol. 1, p. 191.

that it is more appropriate to consider them just one species and discuss them together.

Beginning with their return from captivity in Babylon, the Jews stopped using their ancient characters, which are called Samaritan characters today.
1. *The Latin language ceased to be common in Italy 500 years ago.*
2. *The Jews began to use dots to indicate vowels only in the fifth century after Christ.*

These propositions may be contradicted variously depending on their relation to the two different times. Thus some people contradict this last one by claiming, although falsely, that the Jews always used dots, at least for reading, and that they were kept in the Temple. Others contradict it by claiming, to the contrary, that the use of dots is even more recent than the fifth century.

GENERAL OBSERVATION

Although we have shown that it is possible to contradict these propositions, exclusives, exceptives, etc., in several ways, it is true that when they are simply denied without [144] further explanation, the negation naturally affects the exclusion, or the exception, or the comparison, or the change indicated by the words "begin" and "cease." This is why if people who believe that Epicurus did not place the highest good in bodily pleasure are told "only Epicurus placed the highest good there," and if they simply deny it without adding anything else, they would not express their thought completely. For based on this simple negation we would be right to believe that they agree that Epicurus actually placed the highest good in bodily pleasure, but they think he was not the only one to do so.

Similarly if, knowing the probity of a judge, I were asked if he no longer sells justice, I could not simply reply "no," because "no" would signify that he no longer sells it, but would leave one believing at the same time that I acknowledge that he used to sell it.

This shows that it would be wrong to ask us to respond to some propositions simply by yes or no, because they contain two meanings. So we can answer accurately only by explaining our response to each one.

CHAPTER 11

Observations for recognizing the subject and the attribute in certain
propositions expressed in an unusual manner

It is doubtless a fault of ordinary logic that those who learn it are accustomed to recognizing the nature of propositions or arguments only in terms of the way they are ordered and classified in the Schools. This is often quite different from the way they are formed in real life, or in books on rhetoric, morals, or other sciences.

Thus people have practically no other idea of a subject and an attribute except that one is the first term of a proposition and the other the last. And the only idea of universality and particularity is that the first one has *omnis* or *nullus* in it, "all" or "none," and the other has *aliquis*, "some." [145]

All this is very often misleading, however, and it takes some judgment to make these distinctions in certain propositions. Let us begin with the subject and attribute.

The only authentic rule for telling what the thing is of which one is affirming, and what is being affirmed of it, is by the meaning. For the first is always the subject and the latter the attribute, regardless of the order in which they occur.

So there is nothing more common in Latin than these sorts of propositions: *Turpe est obsequi libidini;* "It is shameful to be a slave of the passions," where it is obvious from the meaning that *turpe*, "shameful" is what is affirmed and is consequently the attribute. And *obsequi libidini*, "to be a slave of the passions," is that of which it is affirmed, that is, what is asserted to be shameful, and is consequently the subject. Similarly, in St. Paul, *Est quaestus magnus pietas cum sufficientia*[1] [A great gain is piety with sufficiency], the true order would be *pietas cum sufficientia est quaestus magnus* [Piety with sufficiency is a great gain].

By the same token, in this verse:

Felix qui potuit rerum cognoscere causas:
Atque metus omnes, et inexorabile fatum
Subjecit pedibus strepitumque Acherontis avari.[2]
[Blessed is he who has been able to win knowledge of the causes of things,
and has cast beneath his feet all fear and unyielding Fate,
and the howls of hungry Acheron!]

Felix [Blessed] is the attribute and the rest is the subject.

It is often even more difficult to recognize the subject and the attribute in complex propositions. We have already seen that sometimes we can decide only by the context or the author's intention which is the principal proposition and which is subordinate in this kind of proposition.

But in addition to what we have said, we may make a further observation about complex propositions in which the first part is only a subordinate proposition and the latter is the principal proposition, such as in the major premise and the conclusion of this argument:

God commands us to honor kings:
Louis XIV is King.
Therefore God commands us to honor Louis XIV.

Here we often have to change the active verb to a passive verb to locate the true

[1] 1 Timothy 6:6.
[2] Virgil, *Georgics*, II.490–2, *Virgil*, vol. 1, p. 151.

subject of the principal proposition, as in the previous example. For it is clear that in reasoning this way, my principal intention in the major premise is to affirm something of kings, from which I can infer that we must honor Louis XIV. Consequently what I say about God's commandment is properly speaking only a subordinate proposition, which confirms the assertion "kings ought to be honored": *Reges sunt honorandi*. From this it follows that "kings" is the subject of the major premise, and "Louis XIV" is the subject of the conclusion, although at first glance both seem to be only part of the attribute. [146]

The following are also quite common propositions in our language: "It is foolish to pay attention to flatterers"; "It is hail which is falling"; "It is God who has redeemed us." Now the meaning ought to make us judge that to arrange them in their natural order, placing the subject before the attribute, they must be expressed this way: "To pay attention to flatterers is foolish"; "What is falling is hail"; "He who has redeemed us is God." And it is almost universally true of propositions beginning with "it is," or in which "that" or "which" appears, that their attribute is at the beginning and their subject at the end. It should be enough to be warned once; all these examples are only to show that we have to decide by the meaning and not by word order. This advice is necessary to avoid the mistake of taking syllogisms that are really sound for unsound, since the failure to distinguish the subject and the attribute in these propositions makes us believe that they are contrary to the rules when they actually conform to them.

CHAPTER 12

Confused subjects that are equivalent to two subjects

To understand better the nature of what is called the *subject* in propositions, it is important to add an observation here which has been made in more eminent works than this one,[1] but which, belonging to logic, is not out of place here.

Whenever two or more things that are similar in some way follow one another in the same place, and usually when there is no visible difference between them, although people can distinguish them when they speak metaphysically, they do not distinguish them in ordinary speech. Instead, they unite them under a common idea that does not make the difference between them clear and indicates only what they have in common. So they discuss them as if they were the same thing.

For example, even though the air is changing at every moment, we still view the air surrounding us as always the same, and we say that it has changed from cold to warm, as if it were the same air. Whereas in reality the air we feel as cold is often not the same as the air we found warm. [147]

---

[1] This refers to Arnauld, *La Perpétuité de la foi* (long version). The next four paragraphs are taken virtually verbatim from Bk III, ch. 4, pp. 171–2 in the 1713 edition.

When we speak about a river, we also say this water was muddy two days ago, and here it is now as clear as crystal. But how much does it take for it not to be the same water? *In idem flumen bis non descendimus*, said Seneca, *manet idem fluminis nomen, aqua transmissa est*[2] [We do not go down into the same river twice; while the river keeps the same name, the water has flowed past].

We consider the bodies of animals, and we talk about them as always being the same, even though we cannot be certain that after several years any part remains of the original matter which composed them. We speak of them as the same bodies, not only when we do not reflect on it, but even when we do. For ordinary language allows us to say: the body of this animal was composed of certain particles of matter ten years ago, and now it is composed of completely different particles. There seems to be a contradiction in this way of speaking, for if the parts are all different, then it is not the same body. This is true, but we still talk about it as the same body. What makes these propositions legitimate is that the same term is taken for different subjects by being applied differently.

Augustus said that he found the city of Rome made of brick and left it made of marble. Similarly, we say about a city, a house, or a church, that it was destroyed at a certain time and rebuilt at another. So which Rome was once made of brick and another time made of marble? Which cities, houses, or churches were destroyed at one time and rebuilt at another? Was the Rome made of brick the same as the Rome made of marble? No, but this does not prevent the mind from forming a certain confused idea of Rome to which it attributes these two qualities, namely being made of brick at one time and of marble at another. When we subsequently form propositions about it and say, for example, that Rome which was made of brick before Augustus was made of marble when he died, the word "Rome," which appears to be only one subject, nonetheless indicates two really distinct subjects, but united under one confused idea of "Rome," which keeps the mind from recognizing the difference between these subjects.

This is how, in the book from which we borrowed this observation,[3] we clarified the bogus perplexity the Calvinist ministers enjoyed finding in this proposition, "this is my body," which no one who has a glimmer of common sense will find there. No one would ever say that it was an extremely confused proposition which was difficult to understand, to say of a church that burned down and was rebuilt: this church burned down ten years ago [148] and has been rebuilt for a year. Likewise, it would not be reasonable to say that this proposition was difficult to understand: "This which is bread at this moment is my body at another moment." It is true that it is not the same "this" at these different moments, just as the burned church and the rebuilt church are not really the same church. But when the

---

[2]   Letter lviii, verse 23, *Ad Lucilium Epistulae Morales*, vol. 1, p. 401. Here Seneca is translating a thought of Heraclitus cited by Plato in the *Cratylus*, 402A. The exact quotation reads: *In idem flumen bis descendimus et non descendimus* ...

[3]   Arnauld, *La Perpétuité de la foi*.

mind conceives both the bread and the body of Jesus Christ under the common idea of a present object, which it expresses by "this," it attributes to this object, which is really double and which is one only by a confusing unity, being both bread at one time and the body of Jesus Christ at another. Similarly, when it forms a common idea of a church from the burned church and the rebuilt church, the mind gives this confused idea two attributes which cannot apply to the same subject.

From this it follows that there is no difficulty in this proposition: "This is my body," taken in the Catholics' sense, since it is only an abbreviation of this other perfectly clear proposition: "This which is bread at this moment is my body at another moment," where the mind supplies everything that is not explicit. For, as we remarked at the end of the first book, when we use the demonstrative pronoun *hoc* [this] to indicate something exhibited to the senses, and when the precise idea formed by the pronoun remains confused, the mind adds to it clear and distinct ideas derived from the senses, in the form of a subordinate proposition. Thus when Jesus Christ uttered the word "this," in their minds the Apostles added to it "which is bread"; and since they conceived that it was bread at that time, they also added the time to it. And so the word "this" formed this idea, "this which is bread at another moment." By the same token, when he said "this was his body," they conceived that "this was his body at that moment." Therefore the expression "this is my body" produced this complete proposition in them: "This which is bread at this moment, is my body at another moment." And since this expression is clear, the abbreviated proposition, taking nothing away from the idea, is also clear.

As for the difficulty alleged by the ministers, that the same thing cannot be both bread and the body of Jesus Christ, since it applies to the extended proposition: "This which is bread at this moment is my body at another moment," as well as the abbreviated proposition: "This is my body," clearly it can be nothing but a frivolous objection similar to the one that could be made against this proposition: this church burned at a certain time and was rebuilt at another time. They should all be analyzed in this same way, as conceiving [149] several distinct subjects under the same idea, which causes the same term to be taken sometimes for one subject and sometimes for another, without the mind being conscious of passing from one subject to another.

As for the rest, we do not claim to have settled the important question of how these words "This is my body" ought to be understood, whether in a metaphorical or literal sense. For it is not enough to prove that a proposition can be taken in a certain sense; we also have to show that it has to be taken that way. But because there are ministers who stubbornly maintain, by principles of a quite fallacious logic, that the words of Jesus Christ cannot admit the Catholic sense, it is not out of place to have shown here, briefly, that the Catholic sense is nothing other than clear, reasonable, and in conformity with the language common to all people.

CHAPTER 13

Other observations for recognizing whether propositions are universal or
particular

We can make several similar and equally necessary observations concerning
universality and particularity.

I. OBSERVATION
We must distinguish two kinds of universality, one which we may call metaphysical,
the other moral.

Metaphysical universality occurs when a universal proposition is perfect and
without exception, as in "every human being is living." This admits of no
exception.

I call universality moral when it admits of some exception, because in moral
matters we are satisfied if things are usually so, *ut plurimùm* [for the most part], as
in this proposition which St. Paul reports and approves of:

> *Cretenses semper mendaces, malae bestiae, ventres pigri.*[1] [Cretans are always liars,
> evil brutes, and gluttons.]
> Or in another one by the same Apostle: *Omnia quae sua sunt quaerunt, non quae
> Jesu Christi.*[2] [They seek all their own things, not those of Jesus Christ.]

Or as Horace says. [150]

> *Omnibus hoc vitium est cantoribus, inter amicos ut nunquam inducant animum cantare
> rogati, injussi nunquam desistant.*[3] [All singers have this fault: if asked to sing
> among their friends they are never so inclined; if unasked, they never stop.]

Or as in the usual sayings:

> All women love to talk.
> All young people are inconstant.
> All old people praise the past.

In all these sorts of propositions it is enough if things are usually this way, and
so we should not draw any strict conclusions from them.

Since these propositions are not so general that they do not admit of exceptions,
the conclusion might be false. For example, we could not infer that each particular
Cretan is a liar and an evil brute, even though the Apostle generally accepts this
verse by one of their poets: "Cretans are always liars, evil brutes, and gluttons,"
because some people from this island might not have the vices common to
others.

Thus with respect to propositions having only moral universality, we ought to be

[1] Titus 1:12.
[2] Philippians 2:21; read *Omnes enim quae ...*
[3] *Satires*, I.iii.1–2, *Satires, Epistles and Ars Poetica*, p. 33.

cautious enough, on the one hand, to draw particular conclusions from them only very judiciously, and, on the other, not to contradict them or reject them as false, even though we can find counterexamples to them. Instead, we should be satisfied to show that they should not be taken so strictly when they are too broad.

II. OBSERVATION

Some propositions ought to be considered metaphysically universal even though they admit of exceptions, since these extraordinary exceptions do not fall within the scope of the universal terms in ordinary practice. For example, when I say: "All humans have only two arms," this proposition ought to be considered true in ordinary speech. It would be quibbling to counter it by saying that there have been monsters who were just as human even though they had four arms, because it is clear that we are not referring to monsters in these general propositions, and that we simply mean that humans have only two arms in the order of nature. [151] Similarly, we can say that all humans use sounds to express their thoughts but they do not all use writing. It would not be a reasonable objection to use the counterexample of mute people to show that this proposition is false. For it is obvious enough, without being made explicit, that this can only refer to people who lack a natural impediment to using sounds, either one that prevents them from learning them, as in the case of deaf people, or one that prevents them from making them, as with people who are mute.

III. OBSERVATION

Some propositions are universal only because they ought to be understood *de generibus singulorum*, and not *de singulis generum*, as the philosophers say, i.e., of all the species of some genus, and not of all the individuals of these species. Thus we say that all the animals were saved by Noah's Ark because he saved some of each species. Christ also says about the Pharisees that they paid a tenth of all herbs, *decimatis omne olus*,[4] not because they paid a tenth of all the herbs in the world, but because there is no kind of herb of which they did not pay a tenth. So too St. Paul says: *Sicut et ego: omnibus per omnia placeo*[5] [Even as I please all people in all things]: that is, he accommodated himself to all kinds of people, Jews, Gentiles, and Christians, although he did not please his persecutors, who were quite numerous. Thus we say of someone that he passed through all offices, that is, through every kind of office.

IV. OBSERVATION

Some propositions are universal only because the subject ought to be considered as restricted by part of the attribute. I say by a part, for it would be absurd for it to be restricted by the entire attribute, as if someone claimed that this proposition is true:

---

4   Luke 11:42.
5   1 Corinthians 10:33.

"All people are just," because it means that all just people are just, which would be foolish. But when the attribute is complex and has two parts, for example in this proposition: "All people are just by the grace of Jesus Christ" it is right to claim that the term "just" is implicitly understood in the subject [152] although it is not expressed there, because it is clear that it means only that all people who are just are just only by the grace of Jesus Christ. So this proposition is strictly true, although it appears false if we consider only what is explicit in the subject, since so many people are wicked and sinners and consequently have not been made just by the grace of Jesus Christ. Scripture contains a great many propositions that should be taken in this sense, among them what St. Paul said: "As we all die by Adam, so shall we all be resurrected by Jesus Christ."[6] For it is certain that countless pagans who died as infidels will not be resurrected by Jesus Christ, and that they will have no part in the life of glory St. Paul refers to in this passage. Hence the Apostle means that just as all those who die, die by Adam, all those who are resurrected, are resurrected by Jesus Christ.

Many propositions are also morally universal only in this way, as when people say: "The French are good soldiers"; "the Dutch are good sailors"; "the Flemish are good painters"; "the Italians are good actors." This means that the French who are soldiers are usually good soldiers, and so on for the others.

V. OBSERVATION

We should not suppose that there is no other indication of particularity than the words *quidam, aliquis,* "some," and the like. For, on the contrary, we use them rarely enough, especially in our language.

According to a recent remark in the *General Grammar*,[7] when the particle "some" is the plural of the article "a," it causes the noun to be taken particularly, whereas usually they are taken generally with the article "the."[8] This is why there is a clear difference between these two propositions: "Doctors now believe that it is good to drink during the height of a fever," and "Some doctors now believe that blood is not made in the liver." For "doctors" in the first example indicates what is common to doctors nowadays, and "some doctors" in the second example indicates only some particular doctors. [153]

But we often put "there is" or "there are" before "some" or "a" in the singular, as in "there are some doctors," and this occurs in two ways.

The first is by putting only a substantive for the subject of the proposition and an adjective for its attribute after "some" or "a," whether it is first or last, as in: "There are healthy pains"; "There are mortal pleasures"; "There are false friends"; "There

---

6   Ibid. 15:22.
7   See *Grammar*, Pt. II, ch. 7, pp. 86–7.
8   In French, the particles "des" and "de" indicate the indefinite "some," whereas the articles "les" and "le" indicate the definite "the." In the plural, "les" means "all." The difference in the two examples which follow, then, is between "Les médecins" [the doctors = all doctors] in the first, and "Des médecins" [some doctors] in the second.

is a generous humility"; "There are vices concealed by the appearance of virtue." This is how in our language we express what is expressed by "some" in the Scholastic style: "Some pains are healthy," "Some humility is generous," etc.[9]

The second way is to join the adjective to the substantive by "that" or "who": "There are fears that are reasonable." But the "that" does not prevent these propositions from being simple in meaning, although they are complex in expression. For it is as if we simply said: "Some fears are reasonable." These ways of speaking are even more ordinary than the previous ones: "There are people who love only themselves"; "There are Christians who are unworthy of the name."

Sometimes a similar turn of phrase is used in Latin. (Horace)

Sunt quibus in satyra videor nimis acer et ultra
Legem tendere opus.[10]
[There are some critics who think that I am too savage in my satire
and strain the work beyond lawful bounds.]

This is the same as saying:

Quidam existimant me nimis acrem esse in satyra.
There are some who think me too pointed in my satire.
Similarly in Scripture: *Est qui nequiter se humiliat;*[11] There are some who humble themselves wickedly.

Omnis, "all," "every" combined with a negation also makes a proposition particular, with this difference, that in Latin the negation precedes *omnis,* and in our language it follows "all," "every." *Non omnis qui dicit mihi, Domine, Domine, intrabit in regnum caelorum.*[12] "Everyone who calls me Lord, Lord, will not enter the kingdom of heaven." *Non omne peccatum est crimen.* "All sin is not a crime."

In Hebrew, however, *non omnis* often replaces *nullus,* as in the Psalm: *Non justificabitur in conspectu tuo omnis vivens,*[13] "No living person will be made just before God." This happens because the negation affects only the verb, and not *omnis.*[a] [154]

---

[9] The difference here in French is equivalent to the difference in English, between "Il y a des douleurs salutaires" [There are healthy pains], and "Quelques douleurs sont salutaires" [Some pains are healthy].

[10] *Satires,* II.i.1–2, *Complete Works,* p. 57.

[11] Ecclesiasticus 19:23.

[12] Matthew 7:21.

[13] Psalm 143:2.

[a] ... *omnis;* whereas ordinarily in these ways of speaking it affects both, which perhaps has never been noticed. For when we say *non omnis amicus est fidelis,* Every friend is not faithful, if the negation affected only the verb, we would be denying the attribute "faithful" of every friend, which we do not wish to do. If it did not affect the verb at all, but only *omnis,* the proposition would be affirmative, and we would be affirming the attribute "faithful" of some friend, which is not the intention of anyone who says that all friends are not faithful, since it is clear that he does not want to say that some friend is faithful, but that some friend is not faithful. – VI. OBSERVATION ... (I)

VI. OBSERVATION

These are fairly useful observations when there is a universal term such as "all," "none," etc. But when there is no such term, and also no term of particularity, as for example in "Humans are reasonable"; "Humans are just," it is a well-known question among philosophers whether these propositions, which they call *indefinite*, ought to be considered universal or particular. This question should be understood to arise when nothing follows, or when what follows does not determine either of these meanings. For it is indubitable that when there is any ambiguity, we ought to interpret the proposition by the context in which it occurs.

Considering the proposition in itself, most philosophers say that it ought to be considered universal in necessary matters and particular in contingent matters.

I find this maxim accepted by some very astute persons, and yet it is false. We should say, to the contrary, that when some quality is attributed to a common term, the indefinite proposition ought to be considered universal regardless of the subject matter. So in contingent matters it should not be considered particular, but rather a universal proposition that is false. And this is the judgment people make naturally, since they reject them as false when they are not generally true, at least with the moral generality satisfying most people in ordinary speech about mundane matters.

Who could stand to hear someone say: "bears are white," "humans are black," "Parisians are gentlemen," "the Polish are Socinians,"[14] "the English are Quakers"? According to the philosophers' distinction, however, these propositions ought to be considered true since, being indefinite with respect to contingent matters, they should be taken particularly. Now it is quite true that there are some white bears, such as those of Novaja Zemla, that some people are [155] black like the Ethiopians, some Parisians are gentlemen, some Polish are Socinians, and some English are Quakers. It is clear, therefore, that in any subject matter whatever, indefinite propositions of this kind are taken universally. But in contingent matters we settle for moral universality, which allows us to say: "the French are valiant," "Italians are suspicious," "Germans are tall," and "Orientals are sensuous," although this is not true of all individuals, because we are satisfied if it is true of the majority.

There is, then, another distinction on this subject which is more reasonable. This is that indefinite propositions are universal in matters of doctrine, as when people say angels have no bodies, and they are particular only in relation to facts and narratives. When the Gospel says *Milites plectentes coronam de spinis, imposuerunt capiti ejus*[15] [The soldiers plaited a crown of thorns and placed it on his

---

14 Socinians professed the doctrines of the Italian Lelio Sozzini or Laelius Socinus (1525–62) and his nephew Fausto Sozzini or Faustus Socinus (1539–1604). The main founder of Socinianism was Faustus, who went to live in Poland in 1579. The Socinians affirmed that the Father alone is God, that Jesus Christ was only a man given by him to other men to be their model and their master. They attributed to the punishments of hell only a limited duration followed by the destruction of the body and the soul, refusing to admit original sin and the efficacy of the sacraments.

15 John 19:2.

head], clearly this should be taken to apply to only some soldiers, and not to all soldiers. The reason for this is that in the case of individual actions, especially when they are limited to a particular time, they can usually be expressed by a common term only by virtue of some particulars whose distinct idea is in the minds of the people forming these propositions. Consequently, to analyze them properly, these propositions are more singular than particular, as can be judged by what was said about terms which are complex in meaning in Part I, chapter 7, and Part II, chapter 6.

VII. OBSERVATION

The nouns "body," "community," and "people," when taken collectively as they usually are for the entire body, an entire community, and all the people, cause the propositions they occur in, properly speaking, to be neither universal nor, even less, particular, but rather singular. For instance when I say: "the Romans conquered the Carthaginians," "the Venetians are making war on Turkey," and "the judges of a certain place condemned a criminal," these propositions are not universal at all. Otherwise we could infer that each Roman conquered the Carthaginians, which would be false. They are also not particular. For it means more than if I said that some Romans conquered [156] the Carthaginians. But they are singular, because each people is considered as a moral person who endures for several centuries, which subsists insofar as it makes up a state, and which acts at all times by those who compose it, just as people act by the members of their bodies. As a result, we say that the Romans, who were conquered by the Gauls who took Rome, conquered the Gauls in Caesar's time. Thus we attribute to this same term "Romans" both being conquered at one time and being victorious at another, although there were no Romans living at one of those times who lived at the other time. This exposes the grounds of vanity people derive from the fine actions of their nation in which they took no part, which is as foolish as for a deaf ear to glory in the eye's liveliness or in the skill of the hand.

CHAPTER 14

Propositions in which signs are given the names of things[1]

We said in Part I that some ideas have things for objects, others have signs. Now when ideas of signs are attached to words and form propositions, something happens that is important to examine here, and which properly speaking belongs to logic – namely sometimes the things signified are affirmed of these ideas of signs. The question is: when is it right to do so, especially with respect to conventional

---

[1] In this chapter the authors develop the remarks in vol. 2, Bk. I, chapters 12–15 of *La Perpétuité de la foi*, by Arnauld, which were largely reserved for the religious domain.

signs? There is no problem with natural signs, because the obvious connection between this kind of sign and things clearly indicates that when we affirm the thing signified of the sign, we mean not that the sign is this thing in reality, but only metaphorically and in signification. Hence, without any introduction or ceremony, we will say about a portrait of Caesar that it is Caesar, and about a map of Italy that it is Italy.

There is no need, then, to examine the rule permitting us to affirm the things signified of their signs except in the case of conventional signs, which do not indicate by any obvious connection in which sense these propositions are to be understood. This has given rise to no end of controversy. [157]

For some people think that we can do this whenever we like, and that in order to show that a proposition is reasonable when taken metaphorically, as a sign, it is enough to say that signs are commonly given the names of the things signified. Yet this is not true; for countless propositions would be preposterous if signs were given the names of the things signified, and this is never done because they are preposterous. So someone who had fixed ideas about what things certain things signified would look ridiculous if, without warning anyone, he took the liberty of giving these capricious signs the names of these things, for example, if he said that a rock were a horse, and a donkey were the king of Persia, because he had established these signs in his mind. The first rule to follow on this subject, then, is that we are not allowed to give just any signs the name of things.

The second rule, which follows from the first, is that an obvious incompatibility between terms alone is not a sufficient reason for giving a term the sense of the sign, and for inferring that a proposition that cannot be understood literally ought therefore be explained metaphorically. Otherwise there would be no preposterous propositions, and the more impossible they were in the strict sense, the more easily we would fall into the metaphorical sense, which, however, is not the case. Who would put up with it if, without any warning, and solely from some secret motive, someone said that the sea is the sky, the earth is the moon, or a tree is a king? Who could fail to see that there would be no faster way to acquire a reputation for insanity than to talk this way? We must, then, prepare our hearers in some way before we have the right to use these sorts of propositions. We should also note that some preparations are clearly insufficient and others are clearly sufficient.

1. Remote relations that are not apparent to the senses, nor to the first view of the mind, and that are discovered only by reflection, are not enough for immediately giving signs the names of things signified. For there is practically nothing between which these sorts of connections cannot be found. It is clear that the connections that are not immediately apparent are not sufficient to lead to the metaphorical sense.

2. To give a sign the name of the thing signified in the first institution, it is not enough to know that those to whom one is speaking already consider it a sign of [158] something entirely different. We know, for example, that the laurel tree is a

sign of victory and the olive branch a sign of peace. But this knowledge in no way prepares the mind to accept it when someone who wants to make the laurel tree a sign of the king of China and the olive branch a sign of the Great Lord, says abruptly, while walking in the garden: see this laurel tree, it is the king of China, and this olive branch is the Great Turk.

3. Any warning that leads the mind to expect only something important, without preparing it to consider something specifically as a sign, is not at all sufficient to give us the right to call the sign by the name of the thing signified in its first institution. The reason for this is clear, because there is no direct and proximate inference between the idea of greatness and the idea of a sign, and consequently one does not lead to the other.

But it is certainly a sufficient introduction for giving signs the names of things, when we see that our listeners already view certain things as signs, and only need to know what they signify.

Thus Joseph could reply to Pharaoh that the seven fat cows and seven full ears of corn he saw in his dream were seven years of abundance, and that the seven lean cows and seven sparse ears of corn were seven years of famine,[2] because he saw that this was all Pharaoh needed to know. For he had already asked himself: What is signified by these fat and lean cows, these full and sparse ears of corn?

And it was reasonable for Daniel to reply to Nebuchadnezzar that he was the golden head, because Nebuchadnezzar had described his dream of a statue that had a head of gold, and had asked Daniel about its meaning.[3]

So whenever we have told a parable and are explaining it, since our listeners already consider everything as signs, we have the right to give the sign the name of the thing signified in explaining each part.

Because the prophets distinguished visions from realities and were accustomed to taking them for signs, when God gave the prophet Ezekiel the vision, *in spiritu* [spiritually], of a field full of dead bodies,[4] God spoke very intelligibly when he told him that these bones were the house of Israel, that is, that they signified it.

These are clear preparations. Since only in cases like these is it appropriate to give the sign the name of the thing signified, we can derive this maxim of common sense: to give signs the names of things only when we have the right to assume [159] that they are already viewed as signs, and when it is clear that others need to know not what they are, but only what they signify.

But most moral rules have exceptions, so we might wonder whether we should not make one to this rule in a single case. This occurs when the thing signified in some sense must be indicated by a sign, so that as soon as the name of the thing is uttered, the mind immediately conceives that the subject thereby named is meant to signify it. Thus since covenants are ordinarily indicated by external signs, if we

2   Genesis 41:17.
3   Daniel 2:31–8.
4   Ezekiel 37:1–11.

affirm the word "covenant" of some external thing, the mind could be led to conceive that it is affirmed of it as its sign. For example, it would probably not be peculiar for Scripture to say "circumcision is a covenant," for a covenant carries with it the idea that the thing to which it is connected is a sign. Because whoever hears a proposition conceives the attribute and the qualities of the attribute before joining them to the subject, we can assume that anyone who hears this proposition: "circumcision is a covenant" is sufficiently prepared to conceive that circumcision is only the sign of a covenant. This is because the word "covenant" allows us to form this idea, not before it is uttered, but before it is joined in the mind to the word "circumcision."

I just said that we could take the things reason requires to be marked by signs as exceptions to the established rule prescribing a prior preparation to make us view the sign as a sign in order to be able to affirm the thing signified. It is also possible, however, to think the contrary. For first, this proposition, "circumcision is a covenant," is not in Scripture, which contains only: "Here is the covenant that you shall observe among yourselves, your posterity and me: Every male among you shall be circumcised."[5] Now these words do not say that circumcision is the covenant, but circumcision is commanded here as a condition of the covenant. It is true that God required this condition in order for circumcision to be the sign of the covenant, as the following verse says: *ut sit in signum foederis* [that it may be a sign of a covenant]. But in order for it to be a sign, it was necessary to command its observance and to make it the condition of the covenant, and this is what the preceding verse says.

Second, these words of St. Luke: "This chalice is the new covenant in my blood," which are also cited, provide even less evidence for confirming this exception. For when translated literally, [160] St. Luke says: "This chalice is the new Testament in my blood."[6] Now since the word "Testament" signifies not only the last will of the testator, but even more properly the instrument that marks it, there is nothing metaphorical about calling the chalice of Christ's blood a "Testament," since properly speaking it is the mark, the guarantee, and the sign of the last will of Jesus Christ, the instrument of the new covenant.

Be that as it may, since this exception is doubtful on the one hand, and extremely rare on the other, and since there are very few things that in themselves must be indicated by signs, these things do not prevent us from applying the rule to everything else lacking this quality, which people are not used to indicating by conventional signs. We must remind ourselves of this principle of impartiality, that although most rules have exceptions, they remain in force in matters not included in the exceptions.

These are the principles we should use to settle this important issue, whether these words, "This is my body," can be given a metaphorical sense. Rather, it is by

5 Genesis 17:10.
6 Luke 22:20.

these principles that the whole world settled it, since all the nations of the world were naturally led to take it in the literal sense, and to exclude the metaphorical sense. Since the Apostles did not view the bread as a sign and were not wondering what it signified, Christ could not have given signs the names of things without speaking contrary to common practice and deceiving them. They may perhaps have viewed what was done as something important, but that is not enough.

I have nothing more to note on the subject of signs that are given the names of things, except that we must distinguish carefully between expressions in which we use the name of the thing to indicate the sign, such as when we call a painting of Alexander "Alexander," and those in which the sign is indicated by its proper name or a pronoun, and we affirm the thing signified of it. For the rule that our listeners must already view the sign as a sign, and that they need to know what it is the sign of, does not apply to the first kind of expression but only to the second, in which we intentionally affirm the thing signified of the sign. For we use these expressions only to tell our listeners what the sign signifies. And we do it this way only when they are adequately prepared to conceive that the sign is the thing signified only in signification and metaphorically. [161]

CHAPTER 15

Two kinds of propositions used widely in the sciences: classification and definition. First, classification

It is necessary to say something in more detail about two kinds of propositions that are widely used in the sciences: classifications and definitions.

Classifications divide a whole into what it contains.

But since there are two kinds of *wholes*, there are also two kinds of classifications. There is a whole composed of several really distinct parts, called a *totum* in Latin, whose parts are called *integral parts*. A classification of this whole is properly called a *partition*, as when we divide a house into its rooms, a city into its neighborhoods, a kingdom or a state into its provinces, a human being into body and soul, and the body into its members. The only rule for this classification is to make accurate enumerations so that nothing is left out.

The other whole is called *omne* in Latin, and its parts are called *subjective parts* or *inferiors*, because this whole is a common term and its parts are the subjects included in its extension. For example, the word "animal" is a whole of this nature, whose inferiors, such as human and beast, which are included in its extension, are subjective parts. This classification properly speaking retains the name classification. We can note that there are four kinds.

The first is classifying the genus into its species. Every substance is a body or a mind. Every animal is a human or a beast.

The second is classifying the genus into its differences: Every animal is rational or irrational. Every number is even or odd. Every proposition is true or false. Every line is straight or curved.

The third occurs when we classify a common subject by the opposing accidents it may have, either in terms of its different inferiors or in terms of different times, such as: Every star is luminous in itself or only by reflection. Every body is in motion or at [162] rest. Every Frenchman is a noble or a commoner. Every person is healthy or sick. Every nation expresses itself either only by speech or by writing as well as speech.

The fourth is classifying an accident into its different subjects, such as classifying goods into mental goods and corporeal goods.

The rules of classification are these: First, it must be complete, that is, the members of the classification must include the entire extension of the term being divided, just as even and odd include the entire extension of the term "number," since there is no number which is neither even nor odd. Almost nothing causes as many fallacious inferences as lack of attention to this rule. What leads us astray is that often terms seem to be opposed in such a way that there is no room for a middle term, but in fact they do have one. So for example, between ignorant and learned, there is a certain intermediate state which takes a person out of the ranks of the ignorant but is not enough to put one into the ranks of the learned. Between evil and virtuous there is also a certain state of which we could say what Tacitus said of Galba: *magis extra vitia quam cum virtutibus*[1] [being free from faults rather than possessing virtues]. For there are people who have no crude vices and so are not called evil, but because they do no good they cannot be called virtuous, even though before God it would be a great vice to have no virtue. Between healthy and sick there is the state of an indisposed or convalescing person. Between day and night there is twilight. Between opposing vices there is the virtuous mean, for example, piety between impiety and superstition. And sometimes there are two means, as for instance between avarice and prodigality there is both generosity and laudable thrift. Between a timidity that fears everything and a rashness that fears nothing, there is both a bravery that is not at all daunted by perils, and reasonable caution which makes us avoid perils to which we should not expose ourselves.

The second rule, which is a consequence of the first, is that the members of the classification must be opposites, such as even and odd; rational and irrational. But we should recall what we already said in Part I, that it is not necessary for all the differences which make these members opposites to be positive, but it is enough if one of them is and if the other is only the genus with the negation of the other difference. This is how to make sure that the members are really opposites. Thus the difference between a beast and a human is only the privation of reason, which is nothing positive. Oddness is only the negation of divisibility into two equal parts. A

---

[1] *Histories*, Bk. I, ch. 49, p. 83.

prime number has nothing that a compound number lacks; since both [163] have the number one for a divisor, what is called a prime differs from a compound number only in having no other divisor than the number one.

Nevertheless, we must admit that it is better to express opposing differences by positive terms whenever possible, because it helps us understand better the nature of the members of the classification. This is why the classification of substances into those that think and those that are extended is much better than the usual classification into material and immaterial, or corporeal and incorporeal substances, because the words "immaterial" and "incorporeal" give us only a very imperfect and confused idea of what can be made clearer by the words "thinking substance."

The third rule, which follows from the second, is that no member should be contained in any other such that the other can be affirmed of it, although it may sometimes be contained in it in a different way. For example, the line is contained in the surface as the limit of the surface, and the surface is contained in the solid as the limit of the solid. But this does not preclude us from classifying extensions into lines, surfaces, and solids, because we cannot say that a line is a surface, or that a surface is a solid. By contrast, we cannot classify numbers into even, odd, and square. Since every square number is even or odd, it is already included in the first two members.

We also should not classify opinions into true, false, and probable, because every probable opinion is either true or false. But we can classify them first into true and false, and then classify each of these into certain and probable.

Ramus and his followers took great pains to show that all classifications should have only two members. Where this can be done conveniently, it is best: but since in the sciences we ought to consider clarity and ease above all, we should not reject classifications into three members, especially when they are more natural and when we would have to use artificial subdivisions to reduce them to two members. For in that case, rather than facilitating the mind, which is the main benefit of classification, it is encumbered by too [164] many subdivisions, which are even harder to remember than if all of a sudden we created more members to be classified. For example, is it not shorter, simpler, and more natural to say: "All extension is either a line, a surface, or a solid," than to say as Ramus does: *magnitudo est linea, vel lineatum: Lineatum est superficies, vel solidum*[2] [Extension is either a line or not a line; what is not a line is either a surface or a solid].

Finally, we may remark that it is just as bad not to make enough classifications as it is to make too many; one does not enlighten the mind enough, the other spreads it too thinly. Crassot, a philosopher admired by Aristotle's interpreters, ruined his book with too many classifications.[3] In doing so we fall into the confusion we claim

---

[2]   This refers to Ramus, *Arithmeticae libri tres*, Bk. I (1555).

[3]   Jean Crassot (d.1616) was a professor for more than thirty years at the University of Paris. His complete works were published in 1619 as *Totius philosophiae peripateticae corpus absolutissimum*. This reference is to *Éléments de physique et de logique*.

to avoid. *Confusum est quidquid in pulverem sectum est*[4] [Whatever is divided into dust is confused].

CHAPTER 16

The definition called a real definition

We have spoken at length in Part I about nominal definitions and we showed that they should not be confused with real definitions, since nominal definitions are arbitrary,[a] whereas real definitions do not depend on us at all, but on what is contained in the true idea of a thing. So they should not be taken for principles, but should be considered propositions which often must be supported by reasons and which are debatable. Here, then, we will discuss only the latter sort of definition.

There are two kinds of definitions: the more exact one, which retains the name definition, and the other, less exact, which is called a description.

The more exact definition explains the nature of a thing by its essential attributes, of which the common one is called the *genus*, and the proper one the *difference*.

Thus a human being is defined as a rational animal, the mind as a substance that thinks, the body as an extended substance, [165] and God as the perfect being. As much as possible, what we use for the genus in the definition should be the proximate genus of the defined, and not merely a remote genus.

Sometimes we also define in terms of integral parts, such as when we say that a human being is a thing composed of a mind and a body. But even in that case something takes the place of the genus, for example the term "composite thing," and the rest takes the place of the difference.

The less exact definition, called a description, provides some knowledge of a thing in terms of the accidents that are proper to it and determine it enough to give us an idea distinguishing it from other things.

This is the way we describe herbs, fruits, and animals, by their shape, size, color, and other such accidents. Descriptions by poets and orators are of this nature.

There are also definitions or descriptions in terms of cause, matter, form, purpose, and so on, for example when we define a clock as a machine made of iron, composed of various gears, whose regulated motion is used to indicate the time.

Three things are necessary for a good definition: it must be universal, it must be proper, and it must be clear.

1. It is necessary for a good definition to be universal, that is, to include

---

4   Seneca, Epistle 89, in *Ad Lucilium Epistulae Morales*, vol. 2, p. 379. The exact quotation is: *Simile confuso est, quidquid usque in pulverem sectum est.*
a   ... arbitrary and incontestable, whereas ... (I)

everything being defined. This is why the usual definition of time, that it is the measure of motion, is probably not good, because it is very likely that time measures rest no less than motion, since we can say that something was at rest for a certain time, just as we say that it was moving for a certain time. So it seems that time is nothing other than the duration of the creature, in whatever state it is.

2. A definition must be proper, that is, it must apply only to the defined. This is why the common definition of an element as a simple corruptible body does not seem good. Since by these philosophers' own admission the heavenly bodies are no less simple than the elements, there is no reason to deny that there are alterations in the heavens similar to those on earth. Without mentioning comets, which we now know are not formed of earthly exhalations, as Aristotle thought they were, we can cite as evidence sunspots which, we have discovered, are formed in the heavens and dissipate [166] the same way clouds do on earth, although they are much larger bodies.

3. A definition must be clear, that is, it must furnish us a more clear and distinct idea of the thing being defined, and it must help us understand its nature as much as possible, so that we can make sense of its principal properties. This is primarily what we should consider in definitions, and this is what is missing from a great many of Aristotle's definitions.

Who ever understood the nature of motion better from this definition: *Actus entis in potentia quatenus in potentia,*[1] the act of a being in potency insofar as it is in potency? Is not the idea of motion that nature provides a hundred times clearer than that? Who would ever find this idea useful for explaining any of the properties of motion?

The famous four definitions of these four primary qualities, the dry, the moist, the hot, and the cold, are no better.

The dry, he says, is that which is easily retained within its boundaries, and with difficulty within the boundaries of another body: *quod suo termino facilè continetur, difficulter alieno.*

And the moist, to the contrary, that which is easily retained in the boundaries of another body, and with difficulty in its own: *quod suo termino difficulter continetur, facilè alieno.*[2]

But in the first place, these two definitions apply better to hard and liquid bodies than to dry and moist bodies. For we say that one part of air is dry and another part of air is moist, even though air is always easily retained in the boundaries of another body, because it is always liquid. And further, we cannot see how, following this definition, Aristotle could have said that fire, that is flame, is dry, since it adapts itself easily to the boundaries of another body. This is also why Virgil calls fire liquid: *et liquidi simul ignis*[3] [and streaming fire

[1] Aristotle, *Metaphysics*, Bk. XI, ch. 9, *Complete Works*, vol. 2, p. 1683.
[2] *On Generation and Corruption*, Bk. II, ch. 2, *Complete Works*, vol. 1, pp. 539–40.
[3] *Eclogue*, VI.33, *Virgil*, vol. 1, p. 45.

withal]. And it is useless to agree with Campanella that when fire is confined, *aut rumpit, aut rumpitur*[4] [either it breaks out, or it is broken], for it is not at all due to its claimed dryness, but because it is smothered by its own smoke if there is no air. This is why it adapts itself quite easily to the boundaries of another body, provided there is an opening for it to emit whatever is continually given off.

As for the hot, he defines it as follows: that which unites similar bodies [167] and separates dissimilar ones: *quod congregat homogenea, et disgregat heterogenea*.

And he defines the cold as that which unites dissimilar bodies and separates similar ones: *quod congregat heterogenea, et disgregat homogenea*.[5] This sometimes applies to hot and cold bodies, but not always. Moreover, it is useless for explaining the true cause which leads us to call one body hot and another one cold. Chancellor Bacon was right to say that these definitions were similar to those we would produce if we defined a human being as an animal who makes shoes and who works the vineyards. The same philosopher defines nature: *Principium motûs et quietis in eo in quo est*:[6] the principle of motion and rest in whatever it is in. But this is based only on his imagining that natural bodies are different from artificial bodies in that natural bodies have their principle of motion in themselves, and artificial bodies have it only from outside. Rather, it is clear and certain that no body can cause its own motion, because matter is in itself indifferent to motion and rest, so it can be determined to one or the other state only by an external cause. Since this cannot go on to infinity, it is absolutely necessary that God imparted motion to matter, and that he conserves it there.

The famous definition of the soul appears even more defective: *Actus primus corporis naturalis organici potentiâ vitam habentis*.[7] The first form of a natural organic body, which has life potentially. We simply cannot tell what he wanted to define. If it is the soul insofar as it is common to humans and beasts, he defined a chimera, since nothing is common to these two things. Second, he explained one obscure term by four or five terms which are more obscure. To mention only the word "life," the idea we have of life is no less confused than our idea of the soul, since these two terms are equally ambiguous and equivocal.

These are some of the rules of classification and definition. But although nothing is more important in science than classifying and defining well, we need say no more about it here, because it depends much more on our knowledge of the subject matter being discussed than on the rules of logic. [168]

---

[4] Thomas Campanella, *De sensu rerum et magia*, Bk. III, ch. 5.
[5] Aristotle, *On Generation and Corruption*, Bk. II, ch. 2, *Complete Works*, vol. I, p. 539.
[6] *Physics*, Bk. II, ch. 1, *Complete Works*, vol. I, p. 329.
[7] *On the Soul*, Bk. II, ch. 1, *Complete Works*, vol. I, p. 656.

CHAPTER 17

The conversion of propositions: where we explain more thoroughly the nature of affirmation and negation, on which conversion depends. First the nature of affirmation[1]

The following chapters are a bit difficult to understand and are necessary only for philosophical speculation. This is why anyone who does not wish to wear himself out on impractical matters can skip them.

I have refrained from speaking about the conversion of propositions until now, because the whole foundation of argumentation, which we must discuss in the next part, depends on it. So it was better not to separate this topic from what we have to say about reasoning, although to treat it adequately we will have to repeat some of what was said about affirmation and negation, and explain the nature of both more thoroughly.[a]

It is certain that we can express a proposition to others only if we use two ideas, one for the subject and the other for the attribute, and another word that indicates the connection the mind conceives between them.

This connection can best be expressed only by the same words we use for affirming, when we say that one thing is another thing.

From this it is clear that the nature of affirmation is to unite and to identify, so to speak, the subject with the attribute, since this is what is signified by the word "is."

It also follows from this that it is the nature of affirmation to put the attribute in everything expressed in the subject [169] according to its extension in the proposition. For example, when I say "every human is an animal," I mean and I signify that everything that is a human is also an animal, and so I conceive animal in all humans.

If I say only "some people are just," I do not put "just" in all people, but only in some people.

But we should equally well keep in mind here what has already been said, that we have to distinguish the comprehension of an idea from its extension, and that the comprehension indicates the attributes contained in an idea, and the extension the subjects that[b] contain this idea.

For it follows that an idea is always affirmed according to its comprehension, because if we remove some of its essential attributes, the idea is destroyed and entirely annihilated, and is no longer the same idea. Consequently, it is always affirmed with respect to everything the idea contains. So when I say "a rectangle is a

---

[1]   Chapters 17–20, which end Part II, take up the Aristotelian rules of the conversion of propositions: see the *Prior Analytics*, Bk. I, chs. 2ff., *Complete Works*, vol. 1, pp. 40ff.

[a]   ... thoroughly.
      It is not easy to make clear nor even to understand what takes place in the mind whenever we affirm something, and to decide whether this is done by the simple view of the mind accompanied by consent, by which it represents something as containing a certain attribute by a single idea, or whether there really are two ideas, one for the subject and the other for the attribute, with a certain act of the mind which connects one with the other. – But it is certain ... (I)

[b]   ... that participate in and contain this idea according to its comprehension. – For ... (I)

parallelogram," I affirm of rectangles everything included in the idea of the parallelogram. For if some part of this idea did not apply to rectangles, it would follow that the whole idea would not apply to them, but only a part. In that case, the word "parallelogram," which signifies the total idea, should be denied and not affirmed of rectangles. We shall see that this is the principle of all affirmative arguments.

By contrast, it follows that the idea of the attribute is not taken according to its entire extension unless its extension is no greater than that of the subject.[c]

For when I say "all the immodest will be damned," I am not saying that they alone will be all the damned, but that they will be among those who are damned.

Thus because affirmation puts the idea of the attribute in the subject, it is properly speaking the subject that determines the extension of the attribute in the affirmative proposition. The identity it indicates takes the attribute as restricted to an extension equal to that of the subject, and not to its entire generality if it has one greater than the subject. For it is true that lions are all animals, that is, that each lion includes the idea [170] animal, but it is not true that they are all the animals.

I said that the attribute is not taken in its entire generality if it is greater than the subject. For since it is restricted only by the subject, if the subject is as general as the attribute then it is clear that the attribute will remain in its entire generality, since it will be as general as the subject, and, we are assuming, it will by its nature not be more general.

From this we can derive these four indubitable axioms.

FIRST AXIOM

The attribute is put in the subject by an affirmative proposition according to the entire extension of the subject in the proposition. That is, if the subject is universal, the attribute is conceived throughout the entire extension of the subject, and if the subject is particular, the attribute is conceived only in a part of the extension of the subject. Examples of this were given above.

SECOND AXIOM

The attribute of an affirmative proposition is affirmed according to its entire comprehension, that is, according to all its attributes. The proof of this is above.

THIRD AXIOM

The attribute of an affirmative proposition is not affirmed according to its entire extension if it is in itself greater than that of the subject. The proof of this is above.

FOURTH AXIOM

The extension of the attribute is restricted by that of the subject, such that it signifies no more than the part of its extension which applies to the subject. For example, when we

---

[c]   ... the subject. For when I say, for example, "all eagles fly," I do not mean that only eagles fly, but I am merely putting the attribute of flying in all eagles, without denying that it exists in other birds. – When I say ... (I)

say that humans are animals, the word "animal" no longer signifies all animals, but only those animals that are humans.

CHAPTER 18

The conversion of affirmative propositions

Converting a proposition is changing the subject into the attribute and the attribute into the subject without the proposition ceasing to be true if it was previously true. Rather, [171] it follows necessarily from the conversion that it is true, assuming it was previously.

Now what we have just said will make it easy to understand how conversions ought to be done. For it is impossible for one thing to be joined and united to another without this other thing also being joined to it, and it is evident that if *A* is joined to *B*, *B* also is joined to *A*. Hence it is clearly impossible for two things to be conceived as identified, which is the most perfect of all unions, if this union is not reciprocal, that is, if we cannot make a mutual affirmation of these two united terms, in the way in which they are united. This is known as conversion.

So in particular affirmative propositions, for example, when we say "some people are just," the subject and the attribute are both particular, since the subject "people" is particular by the mark of particularity added to it. The attribute "just" is also particular, because its extension is restricted by that of the subject, and so it signifies merely the justice found in some people. It is obvious that if some people are identified with some just things, some just things are also identified with some people. Thus to convert these propositions, all we have to do is simply change the attribute into the subject, keeping the same particularity.

The same cannot be said for universal affirmatives, because in these propositions only the subject is universal, that is, taken throughout its entire extension. The attribute, by contrast, is limited and restricted. Consequently, whenever we make it the subject by conversion, we must preserve this same restriction and add an indication to it that determines it, for fear that it will be taken generally. Thus when I say "a human is an animal," I am uniting the idea human with the idea animal, confined and restricted only to humans. And so when I want to envisage this union from another side, starting with animal and subsequently affirming human, it is necessary to preserve the restriction of this term, and, so that others will not be misled, to add some note of determination to it.[a] [172]

This being the case, from the fact that affirmative propositions can be converted only into particular affirmatives we should not conclude that they are less properly

---

[a] ... to it. For in the first proposition, "Every human is an animal," it is restricted by the subject. But when it becomes the subject, in order to retain the same restriction it is absolutely necessary to add to it some term that expresses it. This being ... (I)

converted than other propositions. But since they are composed of a general subject and a restricted attribute, it is clear that whenever we convert them by changing the attribute into the subject, they should have a limited and restricted subject, that is, a particular.

From this we can derive these two rules.

FIRST RULE
Universal affirmative propositions can be converted by adding a mark of particularity to the attribute which becomes the subject.

SECOND RULE
Particular affirmative propositions should be converted without any addition or change, that is, by retaining for the attribute which becomes the subject the mark of particularity which belonged to the former subject.

But it is easy to see that these two rules can be reduced to a single rule including both of them.

Given that the attribute is limited by the subject in all affirmative propositions, if we wish to make it the subject, we must preserve its restriction and, consequently, give it a mark of particularity, whether the original subject is universal or particular.

Nevertheless universal affirmative propositions can frequently be converted into other universals. But this happens only when the attribute in itself has no greater extension than the subject, for example, when the difference or the property is affirmed of a species, or the definition is affirmed of the defined. In that case, since the attribute is not at all restricted, it can be taken as generally as the subject in the conversion: Every human being is rational. Everything rational is a human being.

But since these conversions are legitimate only in particular cases, we cannot count them as true conversions which must be certain and infallible simply by rearranging the terms. [173]

CHAPTER 19

The nature of negative propositions

There is no clearer way to express the nature of a negative proposition than to say that it is to conceive that one thing is not another.

But in order for one thing not to be another, it is not necessary for it to have nothing in common with it. It suffices for it not to have everything the other thing has, just as, in order for a beast not to be a human, it is sufficient for it not to have everything a human has. It is not necessary for it to have nothing that is in a human. From this we can derive this axiom.

FIFTH AXIOM

A negative proposition does not separate all the parts contained in the comprehension of the attribute from the subject, but only the total and complete idea made up of all these attributes together.

If I say that matter is not a substance which thinks, I am not thereby saying that it is not a substance, but that it is not a *thinking* substance, which is the total and complete idea I am denying of matter.

It is completely opposite for the extension of the idea. For negative propositions separate from the subject the idea of the attribute taken throughout its entire extension. The reason for this is obvious. For to be the subject of an idea and to be contained in its extension is nothing more than to include that idea. Consequently when we say that one idea does not include another, which is known as denying, we are saying that it is not one of the subjects of that idea.

SIXTH AXIOM

The attribute of a negative proposition is always taken generally. This can also be expressed more distinctly in this way: *All* [174] *the subjects of an idea that is denied of another idea, are also denied of this other idea.* That is, an idea is always denied according to its entire extension. If triangle is denied of squares, everything that is a triangle will be denied of squares. In the School this rule is usually expressed in these terms, which have the same meaning: *If the genus is denied, the species is also denied.* For the species is a subject of the genus, human is a subject of animal, because it is contained in its extension.

Not only do negative propositions separate the attribute from the subject according to the entire extension of the attribute, but they also separate this attribute from the subject according to the entire extension of the subject in the proposition. That is, they separate it universally if the subject is universal, and particularly if it is particular. If I say "no evil person is happy," I am separating all happy persons from all evil persons. And if I say "some professor is not learned," I am separating learned from some professor. From this we can obtain this axiom.

SEVENTH AXIOM

Every attribute denied of a subject is denied of everything contained in the extension of the subject in the proposition.

CHAPTER 20

The conversion of negative propositions

Since it is impossible to separate two things completely without this separation being mutual and reciprocal, it is clear that if I say "no person is a rock," I can also say "no rock is a person." For if some rock were a person, this person would be a rock, and consequently it would not be true that no person was a rock. Therefore,

THIRD RULE

Universal negative propositions can be converted simply by changing the attribute into the subject, and preserving in the attribute which becomes the subject the same universality the original subject had.

For the attribute in negative propositions is always [175] taken universally because it is denied according to its entire extension, as we showed above.[a]

But for this same reason we cannot convert particular negative propositions. We cannot say, for example, "some physician is not a person" because it is said that "some person is not a physician." As I have said, this is due to the very nature of negation which we have just explained, namely that in negative propositions the attribute is always taken universally and throughout its entire extension. Consequently, when a particular subject becomes the attribute by converting a particular negative proposition, it becomes universal and changes its nature contrary to the rules of legitimate conversion, which should in no way change the restriction or the extension of the terms. Hence in this proposition, "Some person is not a physician," the term "person" is taken particularly. But in this false conversion, "some physician is not a person," the word "person" is taken universally.

Now it in no way follows from the fact that the quality of a physician is separated from some person in this proposition, "Some person is not a physician," and that the idea of the triangle is separated from that of some figure in this other proposition, "Some figure is not a triangle," it in no way follows, I say, that there are physicians who are not persons, or triangles that are not figures.[b] [177]

---

[a]   ... showed above. And in consequence we must not be surprised that in conversion it preserves the same generality it had before the conversion. – But ... (I)

[b]   ... figures.

It often happens, however, that these propositions are converted in ordinary usage, as when we say that some learned persons are not virtuous, and some virtuous persons are not learned. It is even always possible to do it, except for a single case, which is when we deny of a subject taken particularly a mode or an accident that applies only to this single subject: *quod convenit soli, sed non omni.* For if an attribute applied to an entire subject, we could not deny it of the subject, and if it applied to something other than this subject, we could take it for this other thing, and so the subject could be denied of it. For example, because being rich does not apply only to the virtuous, just as I can say that some virtuous people are not rich, I can also say that some rich persons are not virtuous.

Nevertheless, it is enough if there is a single case where these conversions are false to reject them absolutely, because, as we have already said, an authentic conversion should be such that, given the truth of the first proposition, the other is also necessarily true. For example, it follows necessarily that if no cruel person is virtuous, no virtuous person is cruel.

It would be these sorts of conversion that depend on the subject matter, which, properly speaking, should be called accidental. But in practice people have given this name to conversions in which the quantity of the proposition is changed, as we said happened with universal affirmative propositions. This has also taken place with universal negative propositions which can be converted not only into universal negatives, but also into particular negatives because the particular negative is contained in the universal negative. No evil person is a saint: Therefore no saint is evil. And for an even better reason: some saint is not evil ... (I)

Third part of the logic

On Reasoning

The part we now have to discuss, which includes the rules of reasoning, is considered the most important part of logic, and is almost the only one treated with some care. But there is reason to doubt whether it is as useful as is generally supposed. The majority of people's errors, as we have already said elsewhere, depend more on reasoning based on false principles, than from reasoning incorrectly from their principles. We rarely allow ourselves to be misled by arguments that are defective [178] merely because the conclusion is badly drawn. And those who could not recognize a fallacy by the light of reason alone would usually not be able to understand the rules behind it, much less to apply them. Nevertheless, when these rules are viewed merely as speculative truths, they are always useful for exercising the mind. Further, we cannot deny that they have some use now and then, with respect to some persons who, although naturally quick and discerning, still let themselves be misled occasionally by fallacious inferences only because of lack of attention, which could be remedied if they reflected on these rules. Be that as it may, here is what is usually said about them, and even a bit more than is usually said.

CHAPTER 1

The nature of reasoning, and the different kinds there can be

The necessity for reasoning is based only on the narrow limits of the human mind which, when called on to decide the truth or falsity of a proposition – in that case called the *question* – cannot always do so by considering the two ideas composing it. The idea that is its subject is also called the *minor term*, because the subject is usually less extended than the attribute. The idea that is its attribute is also called the *major term* for the opposite reason. Thus whenever the mere consideration of these two ideas is not sufficient for deciding whether we ought to affirm or deny one idea of the other, the mind has to have recourse to a third idea, whether noncomplex or complex (following what was said about complex terms). This third idea is called the *middle term*.

Now in order to compare two ideas by means of this third idea, it would serve no purpose to compare it with only one of the two terms. If I want to know, for example, whether the soul is spiritual, suppose that, not getting to the bottom of it [179] right away, I choose the idea of thinking to clarify the matter. It is clear that it will be useless to compare thinking with the soul if I do not conceive any connection between thinking and the attribute spiritual by which to judge whether

135

it does or does not apply to the soul. I can easily say, for example, that the soul thinks, but I could not infer from this, therefore it is spiritual, unless I conceive some connection between the terms "to think" and "spiritual."

Thus it is necessary to compare this middle term with the subject or the minor term as well as the attribute or the major term. This may be done separately with each term, as in syllogisms called *simple* for this reason, or with both terms at the same time, as in arguments called *conjunctive*.

But in both cases this comparison requires two propositions.

We will discuss conjunctive arguments in detail, but with respect to simple arguments, this much is clear: Because the middle term is compared once with the attribute of the conclusion (which can be done only by affirming or denying it), it forms the proposition called the *major proposition* because the attribute of the conclusion is called the *major term*.

When another comparison is made with the subject of the conclusion, it forms the proposition called the *minor proposition*, since the subject of the conclusion is called the *minor term*.

Then follows the conclusion, which is the very proposition to be proved, which before being proved is called the *question*.

It is helpful to know that the first two propositions are also called *premises* (*praemissae*) because they are placed, at least mentally, before the conclusion, which should follow necessarily from them if the syllogism is valid. That is, assuming the truth of the premises, the conclusion must necessarily be true.[a]

It is true that the two premises are not always expressed, because one alone is often enough to make us conceive two in the mind. When only two [180] propositions are expressed in this way, this kind of argument is called an *enthymeme*. This is an authentic syllogism in the mind because the mind supplies the proposition that is not expressed, but it is imperfect in expression and concludes only by virtue of this implicit proposition.

I said that there are at least three propositions in an argument, but there could be many more without its thereby being defective, provided that one always follows the rules. For suppose that, after consulting a third idea in order to know whether an attribute does or does not apply to a subject, and after comparing it with one of the terms I still do not know whether it does or does not apply to the second term. I can choose a fourth term to clear up the matter, and a fifth if that is not enough, until I come to a term that connects the attribute of the conclusion to the subject.

If I doubt, for example, whether misers are miserable, I could first consider that misers are full of desires and passions. If that does not allow me to conclude therefore they are miserable, I will examine what it means to be full of desires, and I will find that this idea contains the idea of lacking the many things one desires, and

[a]   ... be true, so that it could not reasonably be denied by anyone who has granted the premises. – It is true that these three propositions are not always expressed ... (I)

the misery of being deprived of the things one desires. This will allow me to form this argument: *Misers are full of desires. Those who are full of desires lack many things because it is impossible for all their desires to be satisfied. Those who lack what they desire are miserable. Therefore, misers are miserable.*

Arguments like this composed of several propositions, in which the second depends on the first, and so forth, are called *sorites*. These are most common in mathematics. But because it is more difficult for the mind to follow them when they are long, and since the scope of the mind is better adapted to three propositions, we have spent more time examining the rules of valid and invalid syllogisms, that is, arguments of three propositions. These are good to observe because the rules may be easily applied to all arguments composed of several propositions, insofar as they can all be reduced to syllogisms if they are valid. [181]

CHAPTER 2

The classification of syllogisms into simple and conjunctive, and of simple syllogisms into complex and noncomplex

Syllogisms are either *simple* or *conjunctive*. *Simple* syllogisms are those in which the middle term is connected each time to only one of the terms of the conclusion. *Conjunctive* syllogisms are those in which it is joined to both of them. Hence this argument is simple:

Every good prince is loved by his subjects.
Every pious king is a good prince.
Therefore every pious king is loved by his subjects;

because the middle term is joined separately to "pious king," which is the subject of the conclusion, and to "loved by his subjects", which is its attribute. But the following argument is conjunctive for the opposite reason:

If an elective state is subject to divisions, it will not last long.
Now an elective state is subject to divisions.
Therefore an elective state will not last long;

since "an elective state," which is the subject, and "last long," which is the attribute, both occur in the major premise.

Because these two kinds of syllogisms have separate rules, we will treat them separately.

Simple syllogisms, those in which the middle term is connected to each of the terms of the conclusion separately, are again of two kinds.

The first kind are those in which the middle term is connected to each term in its entirety, namely to the complete attribute in the major premise, and to the complete subject in the minor premise.

The others have a complex conclusion, that is, one composed of complex terms, and so only a part of the subject or attribute is connected to the middle term in one of the propositions. The remainder, which has now become [182] a single term, is connected to the middle term in the other proposition, as in the following example:

> *Divine law obliges us to honor kings.*
> *Louis XIV is a king.*
> *Therefore divine law obliges us to honor Louis XIV.*

We will call the first kind of argument unmixed or noncomplex, and the other complicated or complex, not that all those having complex propositions are of this latter type, but because none of this latter type lack complex propositions.

Now although the rules usually given for simple syllogisms can apply in reverse to all complex syllogisms, because the strength of the inference in no way depends on this reversal, here we will apply the rules of simple syllogisms only to noncomplex cases, reserving a separate discussion for complex syllogisms.

CHAPTER 3

General rules for simple, noncomplex syllogisms

This chapter and the following chapters up to chapter 12 are those mentioned in the Discourse as containing subtle points necessary for speculating about logic, but having little practical use.[a]

We have already seen in the preceding chapters that a simple syllogism should have only three terms, the two terms of the conclusion and a single middle term. Since each term occurs twice, it consists of three propositions: the major premise, made up of the middle term and the attribute of the conclusion, called the major term; the minor premise, which also contains the middle term and the subject of the conclusion, called the minor term; and the conclusion, in which the minor term is the subject and the major term the attribute.

But because we cannot draw just any conclusion whatever from any kind of premise, there are general rules showing that an inference cannot be correctly drawn in a [183] syllogism where these rules are not observed. The rules are based on the axioms established in Part II, concerning the nature of affirmative, negative, universal, and particular propositions, so we will only present them here, having proved them elsewhere.

---

[a]   ... use, if only for exercising the mind. – We have ... (I)

1. Particular propositions are contained in general propositions of the same nature, and not the general in the particular: **I** in **A**, and **O** in **E**, and not **A** in **I**, nor **E** in **O**.

2. The universality or particularity of a proposition depends on whether the subject is taken universally or particularly.

3. Since the attribute of an affirmative proposition never has a larger extension than the subject, it is always regarded as taken particularly, because it is only accidental if it is sometimes taken generally.

4. The attribute of a negative proposition is always taken generally.

These are the main axioms on which the general rules of syllogisms are founded, which we cannot violate without reasoning fallaciously.

RULE 1: *The middle term cannot be taken particularly twice, but must be taken universally at least once*

It is clear that the middle term could not unite or separate the two terms of the conclusion if it were taken for two different parts of the same whole, because it might not be the same part that is united to or separated from these two terms. Now if it is taken particularly twice, it could be taken for two different parts of the same whole. Consequently no conclusion could be drawn, at least necessarily. This is enough to make an argument defective since syllogisms are called valid, as we have just said, only when their conclusions could not be false, given true premises. So in this argument: *Some person is a saint; Some person is a thief; Therefore some thief is a saint*; the word "person," when taken for different parts of humanity, cannot unite "thief" with "saint," since it is not the same person who is both a saint and a thief.

The same cannot be said of the subject and the attribute of the conclusion. For even if they are taken twice particularly, we can still unite them by uniting one of these terms to the middle term taken throughout its entire extension. Thus it clearly [184] follows that if one part of the middle term is united to some part of the other term, the first term, which we said was joined to the whole of the middle term, will also be joined to the term that is joined to some part of the middle term. If there are some French people in every house in Paris, and there are Germans in some houses in Paris, there are houses where there are both French people and Germans.

If some rich persons are fools.[b]
And all rich persons are honored.
Some fools are honored.

For these rich people who are fools are also honored, since all rich people are honored, and consequently, in these foolish rich people who are honored the qualities of a fool and being honored are combined.

---

[b]   In I, "fools" (French "sots") was "cheats" ("fourbes").

RULE 2: *The terms of the conclusion cannot be taken more universally in the conclusion than in the premises*

This is why when either term is taken universally in the conclusion, the argument will be fallacious if the term is taken particularly in the first two propositions.

The reason is that we can infer nothing from the particular to the general (according to the first axiom). For from the fact that some human is black we cannot infer that all humans are black.

1st *Corollary*

The premises must always have one universal term more than the conclusion. For every term that is general in the conclusion must also be general in the premises. And further, the middle term has to be taken generally at least once.

2nd *Corollary*

When the conclusion is negative, the major term must necessarily be taken generally in the major premise. [185] For it is taken generally in a negative conclusion (by the fourth axiom) and consequently it must also be taken generally in the major premise (by the second rule).

3rd *Corollary*

The major premise of an argument whose conclusion is negative can never be a particular affirmative. For both the subject and attribute of a [particular] affirmative proposition are taken particularly (by the second and third axioms). So the major term would be taken only particularly, contrary to the second corollary.

4th *Corollary*

The minor term is always the same in the conclusion as in the premises. That is, just as it can only be particular in the conclusion when it is particular in the premises, it can nevertheless always be general in the conclusion when it is general in the premises. For[c] the minor term can be general in the minor premise when it is the subject, only if it is generally united to or separated from the middle term. And it can be the attribute of the minor premise and be taken generally only if the proposition is negative, because the attribute of an affirmative proposition is always taken particularly. Now negative propositions indicate that the attribute, taken in its entire extension, is separated from the subject.

Consequently, a proposition in which the minor term is general indicates either a

---

[c]   ... For the entire conclusion should be what it is by virtue of the premises. Now it is properly speaking of the minor term that we conclude that a certain thing does or does not apply to it. So it must always be taken in the same sense, and given the same extension. – 5th *Corollary* ... (I) In I an Addition is found at the end of the book which starts with "For" and continues to the end of p. [185] (p. 141:10), and includes the definitive text which takes its normal place in II.

union of the middle term with the whole minor term, or a separation of the middle term from the whole minor term.

Now if from this union of the middle with the minor term we conclude that another idea is joined to the minor term, we ought to conclude that it is joined to all of the minor term and not merely to part of it. For when the middle term is joined to the whole minor term, nothing can be proved by this union to one part that cannot also be proved of the other parts, since it is joined to all of them.

By the same token, if the separation of the middle term from the minor term proves anything about some part of the minor term, it proves it about all its parts, since it is equally separated from all of them. [186]

5th *Corollary*
When the minor premise is a universal negative, any legitimate conclusion that can be drawn from it can always be general. This is a consequence of the preceding corollary. For the minor term could not fail to be taken generally in the minor premise if it is a universal negative, whether it is its subject (by the second axiom), or its attribute (by the fourth).

RULE 3: *No conclusion can be drawn from two negative propositions*
For two negative propositions separate the subject from the middle term and the attribute from the same term. Now from the fact that two things are separated from the same thing, it follows neither that they are nor that they are not the same thing. From the fact that the Spanish are not Turks, and that the Turks are not Christians, it does not follow that the Spanish are not Christians. Neither does it follow that the Chinese are Christians, although they are no more Turks than the Spanish.

RULE 4: *A negative conclusion cannot be proved from two affirmative propositions*
For from the fact that the two terms of the conclusion are united with a third, it cannot be proved that they are separated from each other.

RULE 5: *The conclusion always follows the weaker part. That is, if one of the two propositions is negative, the conclusion must be negative; if one of them is particular, it must be particular*
The proof is that if there is a negative proposition, the middle term is separated from one part of the conclusion. So it is incapable of uniting the two parts, which is necessary for concluding in the affirmative.

And if there is a particular proposition, the conclusion cannot be general. For if the conclusion is a universal affirmative, since the subject is universal it must also be universal in the minor premise. Consequently it must be the subject of the minor premise, since the attribute is never taken generally in affirmative propositions. [187] Thus the middle term joined to this subject will be particular in the minor premise. Therefore it will be general in the major premise because otherwise it would be taken particularly twice. So it must be the subject of the major premise, and consequently the major premise will also be universal. Hence there cannot be a particular proposition in an affirmative argument whose conclusion is general.

This is even clearer in the case of universal negative conclusions. For it follows that there must be three universal terms in the two premises, according to the first corollary. Now since by the third rule there has to be an affirmative proposition, whose attribute is taken particularly, it follows that the other three terms are all taken universally and, consequently, so are the two subjects of the two propositions, and this makes them universal. This is what had to be proved.

4th *Corollary*[d]
Whatever implies the general implies the particular. Whatever implies A implies I. Whatever implies E implies O. But whatever implies the particular does not thereby imply the general. This is a consequence of the preceding rule and the first axiom. But we should note that people have been satisfied with classifying syllogisms only in terms of the nobler conclusion, which is the general. Accordingly they have not counted as a separate type of syllogism the one in which only a particular conclusion is drawn when a general conclusion is warranted.

This is why there is no syllogism in which the major premise is A, the minor premise E, and the conclusion O. For (by the fifth corollary) the conclusion of a universal negative minor premise can always be general. For if we cannot draw a general conclusion, this would be because we cannot draw any conclusion. Thus A.E.O. is never a separate syllogism, but only one insofar as it is implied by A.E.E.

RULE 6: *Nothing follows from two particular propositions*
For if they are both affirmative, the middle term will be taken particularly twice, whether it is the subject (by the second axiom) or the attribute (by the third axiom). Now by [188] the first rule, we can infer nothing from a syllogism whose middle term is taken particularly twice.

If there is a negative proposition, since the conclusion also is negative (by the preceding rule), there must be at least two universal terms in the premises (following the second corollary). Therefore there must be a universal proposition in these two premises, since it is impossible to arrange three terms in two propositions so that two terms are taken universally, unless either there are two negative attributes, which would be against the third rule, or one of the subjects is universal, which makes the proposition universal.

---

[d]   "6th *Corollary*" (I) which is preferable to "4th *Corollary*" in II–V.

CHAPTER 4

Figures and moods of syllogisms in general. That there can be only four
figures

After establishing the general rules that must be observed in all simple syllogisms,
it remains to be seen how many kinds of these syllogisms there may be.

In general we can say that there are as many kinds as there are different ways of
arranging the three propositions of a syllogism and the three terms of which they
are composed, while observing these rules.

The arrangement of the three propositions according to their four differences,
A.E.I.O., is called the *mood*.

The arrangement of the three terms, that is, the middle term with the two terms[1]
of the conclusion, is called the *figure*.

Now we can count how many conclusive moods[2] there may be, not considering
different figures by which the same mood can make different syllogisms. For by the
law of combinations, four terms (such as A.E.I.O.) when taken in threes, can be
arranged differently in only 64 ways. But of these 64 different ways, anyone who
would take the trouble to consider each one separately will find that:

> 28 are excluded by the third and sixth rules, that nothing can be inferred from
> two negatives and two particulars; [189]
> 18 are excluded by the fifth rule, that the conclusion follows the weakest part;
> 6 by the fourth rule, that no negative conclusion can be drawn from two
> affirmatives;
> 1, namely I.E.O., by the third corollary of the general rules;
> 1, namely A.E.O., by the sixth corollary of the general rules.

This makes 54 in all. And consequently there remain only ten conclusive moods.

					E.A.E.
		A.A.A.			A.E.E.
4 Affirmative	{	A.I.I.	6 Negative	{	E.A.O.
		A.A.I.			A.O.O.
		I.A.I.			O.A.O.
					E.I.O.

But it does not follow that there are only ten types of syllogism, because a single
one of these moods can form various types, according to the other way in which

---

[1] The French text says "trois termes," although the authors clearly mean two terms. Neither
Löringhoff/Brekle nor Clair/Girbal note this mistake.

[2] By "conclusive moods" the authors apparently mean moods that may be valid, depending on the
figure. In this chapter they argue, based on the general rules and corollaries for simple syllogisms
presented in the previous chapter, that there are ten conclusive moods. In chapters 5 through 8 they
present rules for each figure showing that not all of these ten moods are valid in every figure. When
the authors say an argument is conclusive outside the discussion of figures and moods of syllogisms,
the term appears to be synonymous with "valid."

syllogisms vary. This is the different order of the three terms which we have already said is known as the *figure*.

Now as for this arrangement of the three terms, it concerns only the first two propositions, because the conclusion is assumed before the syllogism is formed to prove it. Therefore, since the middle term can be arranged in only four different ways with the two terms of the conclusion, there are also only four possible figures.

For either the middle term is *the subject of the major premise and the attribute of the minor premise*, which makes the first *figure*.

Or it is *the attribute of the major and minor premises*, which makes the second *figure*.

Or it is *the subject of both*, which makes the third *figure*.

Or, finally, it is *the attribute of the major premise and the subject of the minor premise*, which can make a fourth *figure*, since it is certain that we can sometimes conclude necessarily this way, which is enough to make a true syllogism. We shall see some examples of this below.

Nevertheless, because we can conclude in this fourth way only in a manner which is extremely unnatural and to which the mind is never led, Aristotle and his followers did not call this form of reasoning a figure. [190] Galen maintained the contrary,[3] but it is clear that it is only a verbal dispute which ought to be settled by making each side say what they mean by the word "figure."

But people are undoubtedly mistaken who take, for a fourth figure, arguments of the first figure whose major and minor premises are transposed, which they accuse Aristotle of not having recognized. For example, when we say: *Every body is divisible; Everything that is divisible is imperfect. Therefore every body is imperfect.* I am amazed that Gassendi made this mistake.[4] For it is absurd to take the proposition that comes first for the major premise of a syllogism, and the second one for the minor premise. If that were so, it would often be necessary to take the conclusion itself for the major or minor premise of an argument, since it is frequently the first or second of the three propositions making up the argument. In these verses of Horace, for example, the conclusion is first, the minor premise is second, and the major premise is third.

Qui melior servo, qui liberior sit avarus;
In triviis fixum cùm se dimittit ad assem
Non video: nam qui cupiet metuet quoque; porro
Qui metuens vivit liber mihi non erit unquam.[5]
[How is the greedy person any more free than a slave, or more noble,

---

3   Galen, or Claudius Galenus, (c. 131–c. 201) was a Greek philosopher and physician who served as the court physician to Marcus Aurelius, and who made important discoveries about the nervous system and the heart. His physiology, like that of Hippocrates, rests on the theory of humors. His views had considerable influence until the seventeenth century.

4   *Institutio Logica*, Pt. III, "On the Syllogism," pp. 120–55.

5   *Epistles*, I.xvi.63–6, *Complete Works*, p. 287.

When he will stoop for a penny that street boys have glued to the pavement?
I see no difference. A person who is greedy is also in fear, and
Any person living in fear I will never regard as free.]

For this all comes down to the following argument:

Whoever is continually fearful is not free:
Every miser is continually fearful;
Thus no miser is free.

Consequently we should not take into account the merely local arrangement of the propositions, which changes nothing in the mind. But we ought to take for syllogisms of the first figure all those in which the middle term is the subject of the proposition where the major term is found (that is, the attribute of the conclusion), and the attribute of the proposition containing the minor term (that is, the subject of the conclusion). Hence for the fourth figure there remains only those where, to the contrary, the middle term is the attribute of the major premise and the subject of the minor premise. And this is how we label them, so no one can find anything wrong with it, since we are warning in advance that by the term "figure" we mean only a different arrangement of the middle term. [191]

CHAPTER 5

Rules, moods, and foundations of the first figure

The first figure, then, is the one in which the middle term is the subject of the major premise and the attribute of the minor premise. This figure has only two rules.

RULE 1: *The minor premise must be affirmative*
For if it were negative, the major premise would be affirmative by the third general rule, and the conclusion negative by the fifth rule. Therefore the major term would be taken universally in the conclusion, because it would be negative, and particularly in the major premise, because it is its attribute in this figure. And the major premise would be affirmative, violating the second rule which forbids inferring the general from the particular. This reasoning also holds in the third figure, where the major term is also the attribute of the major premise.[a]

[a] ... major premise.
   This rule can be proved by another, more essential argument, which I shall touch on only in a word, because it would take too long a discourse to make it intelligible to everyone, and because what I shall say about it will suffice to make it understood by those who handle these sorts of matters easily. This argument depends primarily on the axiom established in Part II, *the negative proposition does not separate from the subject every part contained in the comprehension of the attribute, but it separates only the total and complete idea composed of all the attributes it contains.* For in order for one thing not to be another thing, it is not necessary for it to have

RULE 2: *The major premise must be universal*
For since the minor premise is affirmative by the preceding rule, the middle term which is its attribute is taken particularly in it. Thus it must be universal in the major premise where it is the subject, which [192] makes this premise universal. Otherwise the middle term would be taken particularly twice, against the first general rule.

Proof:

That there can be no more than four moods of the first figure.
We saw in the preceding chapter that there can be only ten conclusive moods. But of these ten moods, A.E.E. and A.O.O. are excluded by the first rule of this figure, which is that the minor premise must be affirmative.

I.A.I. and O.A.O. are excluded by the second, which is that the major premise must be universal.

A.A.I. and E.A.O. are excluded by the fourth corollary of the general rules. For since the minor term is the subject of the minor premise, it can be universal only if the conclusion is also universal.

Consequently there remain only these four moods.

2 Affirmative	{	A.A.A.	2 Negative	{	E.A.E.
		A.I.I.			E.I.O.

This was what had to be demonstrated.

In order to remember these four moods more easily, they have been reduced to artificial words[1] whose three syllables indicate the three propositions, the vowel in each syllable indicating what the proposition should be. These words have been so convenient in the Schools, allowing a single word to indicate clearly a type of syllogism, which could not otherwise be done without a great deal of discourse.

nothing in common with the other thing, but it is enough if it does not have everything the other thing has.

This is how we can judge that from the fact that the minor term is not the middle term (which is what the negative minor premise shows), it does not follow that the major term, which is contained in the comprehension of the middle term (which is all the affirmative major premise can show in the first and third figures, where the middle term is its subject and the major term is its attribute), it does not follow, I say, that the major term may not apply to the minor term. From the fact that a horse is not a lion (this is the minor premise), and that a lion is an animal (this is the major premise in the first figure), we cannot infer that a horse is not an animal. – RULE 2 ... (I)

[1] These artificial words are attributed to Peter of Spain or Petrus Hispanus (1210/20–77), a logician, physician, and philosopher, who became Pope John XXI in 1276. His treatise *Summulae Logicales* (published not later than the 1230s) became the introductory logic textbook for the next three hundred years, although it was inferior to the works of other terminist logicians, notably those of his teacher, William of Sherwood. With respect to these artificial terms, however, it is known that the Byzantine theologian and writer Michael Psellus (1018–78) had already invented equivalent words in Greek.

BAR-^b *Whoever lets people whom he ought to feed die of hunger commits homicide.*

BA- *All wealthy persons who do not give alms for public needs let those they ought to feed die from hunger.*

RA. *Therefore they commit homicide.* [193]

CE- *No impenitent thief should expect to be saved.*

LA- *Everyone who dies after being enriched by the wealth of the Church without wanting to restore it is an impenitent thief.*

RENT. *Therefore none of them should expect to be saved.*

DA- *Everything which is an aid to salvation is beneficial.*

RI- *Some afflictions are aids to salvation.*

I. *Therefore some afflictions are beneficial.*

FE- *Nothing followed by just repentance is to be desired.*

RI- *Some pleasures are followed by just repentance.*

O. *Therefore some pleasures are not to be desired.*

Foundation of the first figure

Since in this figure the major term is affirmed or denied of the middle term taken universally, and in the minor premise this same middle term is subsequently affirmed of the minor term or the subject of the conclusion, it is clear that this figure is based on only two principles: one for affirmative moods, the other for negative moods.

The principle of affirmative moods: *Whatever applies to an idea taken universally also applies to everything of which this idea is affirmed, or which is the subject of this idea, or which is included in the extension of this idea*, for these expressions are synonymous.

Thus because the idea animal applies to all humans, it also applies to all Ethiopians. This principle has been explained so clearly in the chapter where we treated the nature of affirmative propositions that it is not necessary to say more about it here. It should be enough to warn that it is usually expressed in the Schools this way: *Quod convenit consequenti, convenit antecedenti* [Whatever applies to the consequent applies to the antecedent]. The term "consequent" means a general idea that is affirmed of another idea, and "antecedent" means the subject of which it is affirmed, because the attribute is actually derived as a consequent from the subject: if someone is a human, that person is an animal.

---

b   ...BAR- *Every wise person is subject to the will of God.*
BA- *Every good person is wise.*
RA. *Therefore every good person is subject to the will of God.*
CE- *No sin is praiseworthy.*
LA- *All vengeance is a sin.*
RENT. *Therefore no vengeance is praiseworthy.*
DA- ...(I)

The principle of negative moods: *Whatever is denied of an idea taken universally is denied of everything of which this idea is affirmed.*

Tree is denied of all animals, and thus it is denied of all [194] humans, because they are animals. This is expressed this way in the Schools: *Quod negatur de consequenti, negatur de antecedenti* [Whatever is denied of the consequent is denied of the antecedent]. What we said in treating negative propositions exempts me from saying more about it here.

We should note that only the first figure concludes in all propositions, **A.E.I.O.**

This is also the only figure which is conclusive in **A**, since in order for the conclusion to be a universal affirmative, the minor term must be taken generally in the minor premise. Consequently it must be its subject, and the middle term must be its attribute. From which it follows that the middle term is taken particularly in the minor premise. Thus it must be taken generally in the major premise (by the first general rule), and consequently it is its subject. Now this is what the first figure consists in, that the middle term is the subject of the major premise and the attribute of the minor premise.

CHAPTER 6

Rules, moods, and foundations of the second figure

The second figure is the one in which the middle term is an attribute twice. From this it follows that in order for it to conclude necessarily, two rules must be observed:

RULE 1: *One of the first two propositions must be negative, and consequently the conclusion must also be negative by the sixth general rule*
For if they were both affirmative, the middle term, which is always an attribute, would be taken particularly twice, contrary to the first general rule.

RULE 2: *The minor premise must be universal*
For since the conclusion is negative, the major term or the attribute is taken universally. Now this same term is the subject of the major premise. Therefore it must be universal, and this consequently makes the major premise universal.[a]
[195]

---

[a]   ... universal.
It would be easy to produce here examples of arguments which, since they violate these rules, are invalid and do not conclude. But it is more useful to let the readers find them so that they may apply themselves more to considering these rules. – *Proof* ... (I)

Proof:

That there can be only four moods in the second figure.

Of the ten conclusive moods, the four affirmative are excluded by the first rule of this figure, which is that one of the premises must be negative.

O.A.O. is excluded by the second rule, which is that the major premise must be universal.

E.A.O. is excluded for the same reason as in the first figure, because the minor term is also the subject of the minor premise.

Thus of these ten moods, only these four remain:

2 General $\begin{cases} \text{E.A.E.} \\ \text{A.E.E.} \end{cases}$ 2 Particular $\begin{cases} \text{E.I.O.} \\ \text{A.O.O.} \end{cases}$

This was what had to be proved.

These four moods are included under these artificial words.

CE-[b]	*No liar is believable.*
SA-	*Every good person is believable.*
RE.	*Therefore no good person is a liar.*
CA-	*All those who belong to Jesus Christ mortify their flesh.*
MES-	*No one who leads a soft and sensual life mortifies his flesh.*
TRES.	*Therefore, none of them belongs to Jesus Christ.*
FES-	*No virtue is contrary to the love of truth.*
TI-	*There is a love of peace contrary to the love of truth.*
NO.	*Therefore there is a love of peace that is not a virtue.* [196]
BA-	*All virtue is accompanied by discretion.*
RO-	*Some zeals are without discretion.*
CO.	*Therefore some zeals are not virtues.*

Foundation of the second figure

It would be easy to reduce all these different sorts of arguments to a single principle by some roundabout way. But it is better to reduce two of them to one principle

---

[b]	... CE-	*No matter thinks.*
	SA-	*The soul thinks.*
	RE.	*Therefore the soul is not matter.*
	CA-	*Every wise person is content with what he has.*
	MES-	*No miser is content with what he has.*
	TRES.	*Therefore no miser is wise.*
	FES-	*No harm is desirable.*
	TI-	*Some deaths are desirable.*
	NO.	*Therefore some deaths are not harms.*
	BA-	*All virtue is praiseworthy.*
	RO-	*Some magnificence is not praiseworthy.*
	CO.	*Therefore some magnificence is not a virtue.*
	Foundation ... .(I)	

and two to another, because their dependence on and connection to these two principles is clearer and more immediate.

1. Principle of arguments in *Cesare* and *Festino*

The first of these principles is the one that also serves as the foundation of negative arguments of the first figure, namely: *Whatever is denied of a universal idea is also denied of everything of which this idea is affirmed, that is, of all the subjects of this idea.* For it is clear that arguments in *Cesare* and in *Festino* are established on this principle. To show, for example, that no[c] good person is a liar, I affirmed "believable" of every good person, and I denied "liar" of every believable person, saying that no liar is believable. It is true that this manner of denial is indirect, since instead of denying "liar" of "believable," I denied "believable" of "liar." But since universal negative propositions convert simply, in denying the attribute of a universal subject we are denying this universal subject of the attribute.

This shows, however, that arguments in *Cesare* are in some sense indirect, since what ought to be denied is denied only indirectly in them. But because this does not prevent the mind from understanding the force of the argument easily and clearly, they can pass for direct arguments, taking this term to mean clear and natural arguments.

This also shows that these two moods, *Cesare* and *Festino*, differ from the two of the first figure, *Celarent* and *Ferio*, only in having the major premise reversed. But although we can say that the negative moods of the first figure are more direct, still it often happens that these two moods of the second figure which correspond to them are more natural, and that the mind is led to them more easily. This is why, for example, in the argument we just [197] presented, although the direct order of negation requires us to say: No[d] believable person is a liar, which would form an argument in *Celarent*, the mind is more naturally led to say that no liar is believable.

2. Principle of arguments in *Camestres* and *Baroco*

In these two moods the middle term is affirmed of the attribute of the conclusion and denied of the subject, which shows that they are directly established on this principle: *Nothing which is included in the extension of a universal idea applies to any subject of which the idea is denied, since the attribute of a negative proposition is taken throughout its entire extension, as was proved in Part II.*[e]

---

[c] ... that no human soul is matter, I affirmed "thinking" of all human souls, and I denied "matter" of everything that thinks, saying that no matter thinks. It is true that this form of denial is indirect, since instead of denying "matter" of that which thinks, I denied "that which thinks" of matter. But ... (I)

[d] ... No thinking thing is matter, which would form an argument in *Celarent*, the mind is more naturally led to say that no matter thinks. – Principle ... (I)

[e] ... *Part II*, the human soul is included in the extension of thinking substance, since the human soul is a thinking substance. Thinking substance is denied of matter, which forms this argument:

Every human soul is a thinking substance.

"True Christian" is included in the extension of "charitable," since every true Christian is charitable. "Charitable" is denied of "pitiless towards the poor." Thus "true Christian" is denied of "pitiless towards the poor," which forms this argument:

Every true Christian is charitable.
No one who is pitiless towards the poor is charitable.
Therefore no one who is pitiless towards the poor is a true Christian.

CHAPTER 7

Rules, moods, and foundations of the third figure

In the third figure the middle term is the subject twice. From this it follows:

RULE 1: *That the minor premise must be affirmative*
This was already proved by the first rule of the first figure, because in both cases the attribute of the conclusion is also the attribute of the major premise. [198]

RULE 2: *In this figure the conclusion can only be particular*
For since the minor premise is always affirmative, the minor term which is its attribute is particular. Thus it cannot be universal in the conclusion where it is the subject, because this would be inferring the general from the particular, against the second general rule.

Proof:
That there can be only six moods in the third figure.
Of the ten conclusive moods, A.E.E. and A.O.O. are excluded by the first rule of this figure, which is that the minor premise cannot be negative.
A.A.A. and E.A.E. are excluded by the second rule, which is that the conclusion cannot be general.
There thus remain only six moods.

3 Affirmative	A.A.I. A.I.I. I.A.I.	3 Negative	E.A.O. E.I.O. O.A.O.

This is what was to be proved.

No matter is a thinking substance.
Therefore no matter is a human soul.

If the minor premise were particular, we could form an argument in *Baroco* based on the same principle. [151:8] ... (I)

These six moods have been reduced to these six artificial words, albeit in another order.

DA-[a]   *The infinite divisibility of matter is incomprehensible.*
RAP-   *The infinite divisibility of matter is quite certain.*
TI.   *Therefore some quite certain things are incomprehensible.* [199]
FE-   *No one can get away from himself.*
LAP-   *Everyone is his own enemy.*
TON.   *Therefore there are enemies we cannot get away from.*
DI-   *Some wicked people are among the most fortunate.*
SA-   *All wicked people are miserable.*
MIS.   *Therefore some miserable people are among the most fortunate.*
DA-   *All servants of God are kings.*
TI-   *Some servants of God are poor.*
SI.   *Therefore some poor people are kings.*
BO-   *Some angers are not blameworthy.*
CAR-   *Every anger is a passion.*
DO.   *Therefore some passions are not blameworthy.*
FE-   *No idiocy is eloquent.*
RI-   *There are idiocies in metaphors.*
SON.   *Therefore some metaphors are not eloquent.*

Foundation of the third figure
Since in the two premises the two terms of the conclusion are attributed to a single term that serves as the middle term, the affirmative moods of this figure can be reduced to this principle:

[a]   .. DA-   *All true Christians are content with their condition.*
      RAP-   *All true Christians are persecuted.*
      TI.   *Therefore there are persecuted persons who are content with their condition.*
      FE-   *No saint is hated by God.*
      LAP-   *Every saint is afflicted in this world.*
      TON.   *Therefore there are persons afflicted in this world who are not hated by God.*
      DI-   *Some vicious persons are admired in the world.*
      SA-   *All vicious persons are worthy of scorn.*
      MIS.   *Therefore there are persons worthy of scorn who are admired in the world.*
      DA-   *All friendship is pleasant.*
      TI-   *Some friendships are dangerous.*
      SI.   *Therefore some dangerous things are pleasant.*
      BO-   *Some misers are not rich.*
      CAR-   *All misers are passionate for wealth.*
      DO.   *Therefore some persons passionate for wealth are not rich.*
      FE-   *No saint is contemptible.*
      RI-   *Some saints are ignorant.*
      SON.   *Therefore some ignorant persons are not contemptible.*
          Foundation .. . .(I)

The principle of affirmative moods: *Whenever two terms can be affirmed of the same thing, they can also be affirmed of each other taken particularly.*
Given that they are united with each other in this thing, since they apply to it, it follows that they are sometimes united with each other. Consequently we can affirm them of each other taken particularly. But in order to be sure that these two terms have been affirmed of the same thing, namely the middle term, we must take this middle term universally at least once. For if it were taken particularly twice, these could be two different parts of the common term which would not be the same thing.

The principle of negative moods: *For any two terms, whenever one is denied and the other affirmed of the same thing, they can be denied of each other taken particularly.*
For it is certain that they are not always united with each other, since they are not united in this thing. Thus we can sometimes deny one of the other, that is, we can deny one of the other taken particularly. But for the same reason, in order for this to be the same thing, the middle term must be taken universally at least once. [200]

CHAPTER 8

Moods of the fourth figure

The fourth figure is the one in which the middle term is the attribute of the major premise and the subject of the minor premise. But it is so unnatural that it is almost useless to give its rules. Nevertheless, here they are, so that nothing will be missing from our demonstration of all the simple forms of reasoning.

RULE 1: *When the major premise is affirmative, the minor premise is always universal*
For the middle term is taken particularly in the major affirmative premise, because it is its attribute. Thus (by the first general rule) the middle term must be taken generally in the minor premise, which is consequently made universal because the middle term is its subject.

RULE 2: *When the minor premise is affirmative, the conclusion is always particular*
For the minor term is the attribute of the minor premise, and consequently it is taken particularly in it when the minor premise is affirmative. From this it follows (by the second general rule) that the minor term must also be particular in the conclusion. This makes the conclusion particular because it is its subject.

RULE 3: *In negative moods the major premise must be general*
For since the conclusion is negative, the major term is taken generally in it. Thus (by the second general rule) it must also be taken generally in the premises. Now it

is the subject of the major premise here as well as in the second figure, and so, as in the second figure, being taken generally it must make the major premise general.

Proof:

That there can be only five moods in the fourth figure.

Of the ten conclusive moods, **A.I.I.** and **A.O.O.** are excluded by the first rule. [201]

> **A.A.A.** and **E.A.E.** are excluded by the second.
>
> **O.A.O.** by the third.
>
> There thus remain only these five moods.

2 Affirmative	{ A.A.I. I.A.I.	3 Negative	{ A.E.E. E.A.O. E.I.O.

These five moods can be contained in these artificial words.

BAR-[a]	*All miracles of nature are ordinary.*
BA-	*Everything that is ordinary does not strike us.*
RI.	*Therefore some things that do not strike us are miracles of nature.*
CA-	*All the evils of life are transitory evils.*
LEN-	*No transitory evils are to be feared.*
TES.	*Therefore none of the evils to be feared is an evil of this life.*
DI-	*Some madmen speak the truth.*
BA-[b]	*Whoever speaks the truth deserves to be followed.*
TIS.	*Therefore some who deserve to be followed are madmen.*
FES-	*No virtue is a natural quality.*
PA-	*Every natural quality has God for its first author.*
MO.	*Thus some qualities that have God for their author are not virtues.*
FRE-	*No unhappy person is content.*
SI-	*Some content persons are poor.*
SOM.	*Therefore some poor persons are not unhappy.* [202]

[a]   ...BAR- *Every [wise] person is moderate.*
     BA- *Every moderate person is an enemy of great fortunes.*
     RI. *Therefore some enemies of great fortunes are wise.*
     CA- *Every vice is blameworthy.*
     LEN- *Nothing blameworthy should be imitated.*
     TES. *Therefore nothing that should be imitated is a vice.*
[b]   BA- *Whoever speaks the truth deserves to be heard.*
     TIS. *Some who deserve to be heard are madmen.*
     FES- *No miser is content.*
     PA- *Every content person is rich.*
     MO. *Therefore some rich persons are not misers.*
     FRE- *No slave is free.*
     SI- *Some free persons are miserable.*
     SOM. *Therefore some miserable persons are not slaves.*

     We should . . . .(I)

We should caution that these five moods are ordinarily expressed this way: *Baralipton, Celantes, Dabitis, Fapesmo, Frisesomorum.* This came about because Aristotle did not make a separate figure of these moods. So they were generally viewed only as indirect moods of the first figure because, it was claimed, their conclusion was reversed and the attribute was the true subject. This is why those who held this opinion took the proposition introducing the subject of the conclusion as the first proposition, and the one introducing the attribute as the minor premise.

Hence they counted nine moods for the first figure, four direct and five indirect, which they included in these two verses:

> *Barbara, Celarent, Darii, Ferio, Baralipton,*
> *Celantes, Dabitis, Fapesmo, Frisesomorum.*

And for the other two figures:

> *Cesare, Camestres, Festino, Baroco, Darapti.*
> *Felapton, Disamis, Datisi, Bocardo, Ferison.*

But because the conclusion is always presupposed, since it is what we wish to prove, we cannot properly say that it is ever reversed. We thought it would always be better to take the proposition introducing the attribute of the conclusion as the major premise. Thus we were obliged, in order to put the major premise first, to reverse these artificial words. Accordingly, to remember them better, they are contained in this verse:

> *Barbari, Calentes, Dibatis, Fespamo, Frisesom.*

Summary

The different types of syllogisms
From all we have just said, we can conclude that there are nineteen types of syllogisms, which can be classified in different ways.

1. In terms of:

General $\qquad \left\{ \begin{array}{l} 5. \\ 14. \end{array} \right.$
Particular

2. In terms of:

Affirmative $\qquad \left\{ \begin{array}{l} 7. \\ 12. \end{array} \right.$
Negative

3. By their conclusions:

A. $\qquad \left\{ \begin{array}{l} 1. \\ 4. \\ 6. \\ 8. \end{array} \right.$
E.
I.
O.

4. According to different figures, subdivided by their moods, which was already done in the explanation of each figure. [203]

5. Or, by contrast, according to their moods, subdivided by figures,[c] which would still make nineteen kinds of syllogisms, because there are three moods which each conclude in only one figure, six moods which each conclude in two figures, and one mood which concludes in all four.[d]

---

[c] ... figures. – For since we showed in chapter 4 that there are only ten conclusive moods, not counting different arrangements of the middle term, and since a single mood used for different figures can make different kinds of syllogisms, we again arrive at the same number of 19 syllogisms by this sort of classification: because there are 3 moods that each conclude in only 1 figure, 6 moods that each conclude in 2 figures, and 1 mood that concludes in all 4 figures, which makes 19 kinds of syllogisms in all. I leave making a table of this to those who wish to take the trouble in order to relieve the memory. For it is not worth inserting here. – CHAPTER 9 ... (I)

[d] In I under the title CHAPTER 9 the following chapter ("The Reduction of Syllogisms") appeared, which was not included in the subsequent editions:

This chapter is extremely useless. To reduce a syllogism is to put it into a form that is more perfect, more evident, and more natural. Hence all reductions should be based on the fact that some arguments are clearer and more direct than others, and that less direct arguments can be reduced to more direct arguments, and less clear arguments to clearer arguments. This is done by changing some proposition, either simply, merely by making the subject the attribute and the attribute the subject, or by accident, also changing the quantity of the proposition. In the Schools it is usually assumed that since arguments of the first figure are the most direct, all others should be reduced to them. To do so, they note about the artificial words that include the moods of the other three figures:

1. The first consonant, namely C or D or F, which indicates that the moods which begin with C, namely *Camestres, Cesare, Calentes* are reduced to *Celarent*, etc., those which begin with D to *Darii*, and those with F to *Ferio*.

2. About the consonants which end the syllables, they note these three letters:
S, which indicates that the proposition containing it should be simply converted;
P, which indicates that the proposition that contains it should be converted by changing the quantity of the proposition;
M, which indicates that propositions should be transposed.

3. They note the syllables, and they attribute one to each proposition, the first to the major premise, the second to the minor premise, and the third to the conclusion. In order to remember all these rules more easily, they have created these two verses:

S. vult simpliciter verti, P. verò per acci
M. vult transponi, C. per impossibile duci.
[S. wants to be converted simply, but P. {wants to be converted} accidentally;
M. wants to be transposed, {and} C. {wants to be converted} impossibly.]

By following these rules, we can make all kinds of reductions, as is easily seen if one wishes to try with the examples we presented of each figure.

We made various new observations on this topic which are still to be found in the handwritten copies several persons had made of this *Logic*. But since these are useless and cannot be understood except by rather strict attention of the mind, we decided it was more appropriate to leave them out.

We will merely remark that we can indeed say that a conclusion is not directly derived from the premises, but we cannot properly say that it is indirect, because we assume that it was already formed before someone thought of proving it. Given, then, that it is already formed, we can of course apply to it the premises indirectly connected to it, but we cannot say for that reason that it is indirect.

CHAPTER 9

Complex syllogisms, and how they can be reduced to common syllogisms and judged by the same rules

We[a] must admit that if there are some people for whom logic is useful, there are many for whom it is harmful. At the same time we should acknowledge [204] that no one is harmed more than those who are most taken by it, and who pretend more vainly to be good logicians. For since this affectation is itself the mark of an inferior and unreliable mind, whenever they are more attached to the external form of the rules than to their meaning which is their soul, they [205] are easily led to reject as invalid some arguments that are quite valid. This happens because they do not have enough insight to adapt themselves to the rules, which function only to lead them astray because they understand them only imperfectly.

From this it follows that arguments that can be reduced only by changing the conclusion are not properly speaking reducible. And so *Calentes* and *Camestres* cannot be reduced to *Celarent*, nor *Disamis* and *Dibatis* to *Darii*, because the conclusion would have to be changed.

As for what is called reduction to absurdity, it consists in requiring a person who wrongly denies a conclusion to grant the contradictory of a previously accepted proposition. This is done by taking the contradictory of the conclusion which is denied, which, when connected with one of the premises, necessarily produces the contradictory of one of the accepted propositions. So, suppose someone denied the conclusion of this argument in *Bocardo*:

Some saints are not rich.
All saints are happy.
Therefore some happy persons are not rich.

We could take the contradictory of the conclusion which is denied, and say that if it is false that some happy persons are not rich, then it is true that all happy persons are rich.

Now all saints are happy, as is granted in the minor premise. Therefore all saints are rich, which is the contradictory of the major premise of the first argument.

If we connected the accepted major premise to it, we would form this other argument:

All happy persons are rich.
Now some saints are not rich.
Therefore some saints are not happy;

this is the contradictory of the accepted minor premise.

One can easily see by common sense how these propositions must be arranged to derive the contradictory of one of the accepted premises. This is why we will not take time to explain the rules given for them.

But we would be obliged to say about this kind of reduction what we said about the other kind, namely that it is practically useless. It is quite rare for someone to deny the conclusion of an argument made according to the rules. If it happened between persons who were acting in good faith, it could only be because of some confusion in the terms. In this case the middle term, which is ordinarily used to show that the argument being doubted is valid, is not used to cause the person who denied the conclusion to form a reductio ad absurdum, but to make another, similar argument composed of clearer and simpler terms which clearly appears valid. Just as the way to show that an argument is invalid is not to show that it is against the rules, which is always confusing and not very obvious, but to form another argument of the same kind that is obviously invalid. – CHAPTER 10 ... (I)

[a]   The first two paragraphs of this chapter were added in II. The first paragraph in I began: We have already said that some ordinary syllogisms can be called *complex*. This is not just because ... (I)

To avoid this defect, which reeks of the air of pedantry so unworthy of an educated person, we should instead examine the soundness of an argument by the natural light rather than the forms of reasoning. One means for succeeding, when we find some difficulty, is to form similar arguments from different subject matters. Whenever it is obvious to us that the argument concludes properly, taking into account only the meaning, if we find at the same time that it contains something that does not seem to conform to the rules, we should believe instead that it is due to some confusion rather than that the argument is actually contrary to them.

But the arguments that are the most difficult to judge properly, and where it is easiest to make mistakes, are those we said earlier can be called *complex*. This is not just because they contain complex propositions, but because the terms of the conclusion, being complex, are not always joined in their entirety to the middle term in each of the premises, but only to a part of one of these terms. As in this example:

> *The sun is an insensible thing.*
> *The Persians worshipped the sun.*
> *Therefore the Persians worshipped an insensible thing.*

Here we see that whereas the conclusion has "worshipped an insensible thing" for its attribute, only a part of it occurs in the major premise, namely, "an insensible thing," and "worshipped" appears in the minor premise.

Now we shall do two things concerning these sorts of syllogisms. We shall show, first, how they can be reduced to noncomplex syllogisms, which we have been discussing up to now, in order to judge them by the same rules.

And we shall show, second, that more general rules can be given for immediately judging the validity or invalidity of these complex syllogisms, without needing to reduce them in any way. [206]

It is rather strange that,[b] although people perhaps make more of logic than they should, going so far as to maintain that it is absolutely necessary for learning the sciences, they nevertheless treat it with so little care that they rarely say anything useful about it. For they are usually satisfied with giving the rules of simple syllogisms, and nearly all their examples are made up of noncomplex propositions, which are so clear that it never occurred to anyone to present them seriously in discourse. For who has ever heard anyone make syllogisms like this one: Every man is an animal; Peter is a man; therefore Peter is an animal?

But people rarely take the trouble to apply these rules of syllogisms to arguments with complex propositions, although this is often rather difficult, and there are several arguments of this nature that appear invalid but are nevertheless quite valid. Besides, this sort of argument is used much more frequently than are completely simple syllogisms. This will be easier to show by examples than by rules.

---

[b]   ... that the philosophers of the Schools, making more ... (I)

EXAMPLE 1

We said, for example, that all propositions composed of active verbs are complex in some way. From these propositions arguments are often constructed whose form and force is difficult to recognize, such as this one previously given as an example:

> *Divine law commands us to honor kings.*
> *Louis XIV is a king.*
> *Therefore divine law commands us to honor Louis XIV.*

Some fairly unintelligent persons have criticized these syllogisms as defective because, they say, they are composed of pure affirmatives in the second figure, which is an essential defect. But these persons have clearly demonstrated that they are consulting the letter and external form of the rules more than the light of reason, which is how these rules are discovered. [207] For this argument is so sound and conclusive, that if it were contrary to the rule it would prove that the rule was false, not that the argument was invalid.

I say first, then, that this argument is valid. For in the proposition "Divine law commands us to honor kings," the word "kings" is taken generally for all individual kings, and consequently Louis XIV is among the number of those whom the divine law commands us to honor.

In the second place, I say that "king," which is the middle term, is not at all the attribute of the proposition: "Divine law commands us to honor kings," even though it is joined to the attribute "commands," which is quite a different matter. For whatever is truly an attribute is affirmed and applies. Now "king" is not at all affirmed and does not apply to the law of God. Second, the attribute is restricted by the subject. Now the word "king" is not at all restricted in the proposition: "Divine law commands us to honor kings," since it is taken generally.

But if we are asked what it is, then, it is easy to answer that it is the subject of another proposition embedded in this one. For when I say that divine law commands us to honor kings, while I attribute "command" to the law, I am also attributing "honor" to kings. For it is as if I said: "Divine law commands that kings be honored."

The same is true of the conclusion, "Divine law commands us to honor Louis XIV." "Louis XIV" is not at all the attribute, although it is joined to the attribute. On the contrary, it is the subject of the embedded proposition. For it is just as if I said: "Divine law commands that Louis XIV be honored."

When these propositions are analyzed in this way:

> *Divine law commands that kings be honored.*
> *Louis XIV is a king.*
> *Thus divine law commands that Louis XIV be honored;*

it is clear that the entire argument consists in these propositions:

Kings ought to be honored.
Louis XIV is a king.
Thus Louis XIV ought to be honored.

Furthermore, the proposition "Divine law commands," which appears to be the principal proposition, is only a subordinate proposition in this argument, which is joined to the affirmation for which divine law serves as the proof.

Similarly, it is clear that this argument is in the first figure in *Barbara*, since singular terms such as "Louis XIV" can be viewed as universals, because they are taken in their entire extension, as we have already remarked. [208]

EXAMPLE 2

For the same reason this argument, which appears to be in the second figure and to conform to the rules of this figure, is worthless.

We ought to believe Scripture.
Tradition is not Scripture.
Therefore we ought not believe Tradition.

For it should be reduced to the first figure, as if it were:

Scripture ought to be believed.
Tradition is not Scripture.
Therefore Tradition ought not be believed.

Now nothing can be concluded in the first figure from a negative minor premise.

EXAMPLE 3 [c]

There are other arguments that appear to be pure affirmatives in the second figure and nonetheless are quite valid, such as this one:

All good pastors are ready to give their lives for their flocks.
Now few pastors at the present time are ready to give their lives for their flocks.
Therefore there are few good pastors at the present time.

What shows that this reasoning is valid is that the conclusion is only apparently affirmative. For the minor premise is an exclusive proposition, which contains this negation in its meaning: "Several pastors at the present time are not ready to give their lives for their flocks."

The conclusion also reduces to this negation: "Several pastors at the present time are not good pastors."

---

[c]   ... EXAMPLE 3 – It also happens with these complex, compound propositions, that arguments that are quite valid appear completely contrary to the common rules, such as this one: *Only the friends of God* ... (I). The third and fourth examples were added in II.

EXAMPLE 4

Here is still another argument which, although in the first figure, appears to have a negative minor premise, but is nevertheless valid.

> *All persons who cannot be robbed of what they love are beyond the reach of their enemies.*
> *Now when a person loves only God, he cannot be robbed of what he loves.* [209]
> *Therefore all persons who love only God are beyond the reach of their enemies.*

What makes this argument valid is that the minor premise only appears to be *negative*, but is actually *affirmative*.

For the subject of the major premise, which ought to be the attribute of the minor premise, is not "persons who can be robbed of what they love," but rather, "persons who cannot be robbed of it." Now this is what is affirmed of those who love only God, so that the minor premise means:

"Now all persons who love only God are among those who cannot be robbed of what they love," which is obviously an affirmative proposition.

EXAMPLE 5

This also happens when the major premise is an exclusive proposition, as in:

> *Only the friends of God are happy.*
> *Now some rich persons are not friends of God.*
> *Therefore some rich persons are not happy.*[d]

For the particle "only" makes the first proposition of this syllogism equivalent to these two: "The friends of God are happy"; and "all others who are not friends of God are not happy."

Now since the force of this argument depends on this second proposition, the minor premise which seemed negative becomes affirmative. This is because the subject of the major premise, which ought to be the attribute of the minor premise, is not "friends of God," but "persons who are not friends of God." Hence the entire argument ought to be understood as follows:

> *All persons who are not friends of God are not happy.*
> *Now some rich persons are among those who are not friends of God.*
> *Therefore some rich persons are not happy.*

But what makes it unnecessary to express the minor premise this way and leaves the appearance of a negative proposition, is that it is the same thing to say negatively [210] that a person is not a friend of God, and to say affirmatively that

---

[d] ... *happy.* – When examined according to the common rules, this argument would seem invalid because it appears to be in the first figure, in which nothing can be concluded from a negative minor premise. But since the first proposition is compound in meaning because of the particle "only" which makes it exclusive, it is equivalent to these two propositions: "The friends ... (I)

the person is a non-friend of God, that is, among the number of persons who are not friends of God.

EXAMPLE 6

There are many arguments like this, in which all the propositions appear negative, which nevertheless are valid, because one proposition is negative only in appearance and is actually affirmative, as we just saw, and as can be seen again in this example:

Whatever has no parts cannot perish by the dissolution of its parts.
The soul has no parts.
Therefore the soul cannot perish by the dissolution of its parts.

Some people offer these sorts of syllogisms to show that we should not claim that this axiom of logic, *Nothing can be concluded from pure negatives*, is true generally and without any exception. But they have not been attentive enough to see that the sense of the minor premise of this syllogism and others like it is affirmative, because the middle term, which is the subject of the major premise, is its attribute. Now the subject of the major premise is not "whatever has parts," but "whatever has no parts." So the sense of the minor premise is: "The soul is a thing which has no parts," which is an affirmative proposition with a negative attribute.

These same people also try to prove that negative arguments are sometimes conclusive, using these examples: "John is not rational, therefore he is not a person. No animal sees, thus no human sees." But they ought to consider that these examples are only enthymemes, and that no enthymeme concludes except by virtue of an implicit proposition, which consequently must be in the mind even if it is not expressed. Now in both of these examples the implicit proposition is necessarily affirmative. In the first one: "All people are rational, John is not rational, thus John is not a person." And in the other: "All humans are animals, no animal sees, thus no human sees." Now it cannot be said that these syllogisms are purely negative. Consequently enthymemes, which conclude only because these entire syllogisms are contained in the mind of the person who is forming them, cannot be offered as examples to show that purely negative arguments are sometimes conclusive. [211]

CHAPTER 10

A general principle by which the validity or invalidity of every syllogism can be judged, without any reduction to figures and moods

We have seen how to decide whether complex arguments are conclusive or defective, by reducing them to the form of more common arguments, in order to judge them subsequently by the common rules. But since it is not at all apparent that the mind needs such a reduction to make this judgment, we thought there must be more general rules on which even the common rules depend, by which we can recognize more easily the validity or defect of each kind of syllogism. Here is what occurred to us.

Whenever we want to prove a proposition whose truth is not obvious, it seems that all we have to do is to find a better known proposition confirming it, which for this reason can be called the *containing* proposition. But because this proposition cannot contain the first one explicitly and in the same terms – since if it did it would not differ from it in any way and so would not help make it clearer – there must be yet another proposition that shows that what we call the *containing* proposition actually does contain the one we wish to prove. This proposition can be called *applicative.*

In affirmative syllogisms it is often indifferent which of the two propositions is called *containing*, because in some sense they each contain the conclusion, and they function mutually to show that the other contains it.

For example, suppose I wonder whether an evil person is unhappy, and I reason this way:

Every slave of the passions is unhappy.
Every evil person is a slave of the passions.
Thus every evil person is unhappy. [212]

Whichever proposition you take, you could say that it contains the conclusion and that the other one shows this. For the major premise contains it because "slave of the passions" contains "evil" under itself. That is, "evil" is included in its extension and is one of its subjects, as the minor premise shows. And the minor premise also contains it, because the idea "slave of the passions" includes the idea "unhappy," as the major premise shows.

Since, however, the major premise is almost always more general, it is usually considered the containing proposition and the minor premise the applicative proposition.

For negative syllogisms, since there is only one negative proposition and since negation is properly contained only in a negative proposition, it seems that the negative proposition should always be taken as the containing proposition, and the affirmative proposition alone as the applicative proposition. This would be true whether the negative is the major premise, as in *Celarent, Ferio, Cesare,* and *Festino,* or whether it is the minor premise, as in *Camestres* and *Baroco.*

For suppose I prove by the following argument that no miser is happy:

Every happy person is content.
No miser is content.
Therefore, no miser is happy.

It is more natural to say that the minor premise, which is negative, contains the conclusion, which is also negative, and that the major premise shows that it contains it. For since the minor premise, "no miser is content," totally separates "content" from "miser," it also separates "content" from "happy," since according to the major premise, "happy" is entirely contained in the extension of "content."

It is not difficult to show that all the rules we have given function only to show that the conclusion is contained in one of the first propositions, and that the other one reveals this, and further, that arguments are defective only when we fail to observe this and that they are always valid when it is observed. For all these rules can be reduced to two principles, which are the foundation of the others. One is *that no term can be more general in the conclusion than in the premises.* Now this rule obviously depends on the general principle *that the premises must contain the conclusion.* This could not be the case if, when the same term is in the premises and the conclusion, it had a smaller extension in the premises than in the conclusion. For the less general does [213] not contain the more general; "some man" does not contain "all men."

The other general rule is that *the middle term must be taken universally at least once.* This again depends on the principle *that the conclusion must be contained in the premises.* For suppose that we have to prove that some friend of God is poor, and to do so we use the proposition,[a] "some saint is poor." I say that it will never be evident that this proposition contains the conclusion except by another proposition where the middle term "saint" is taken universally. For it is obvious that in order for the proposition "some saint is poor" to contain the conclusion, "some friend of God is poor," it is both necessary and sufficient for the term "some saint" to contain the term "some friend of God," since they have the other term in common. Now a particular term has no determinate extension, and it contains with certainty only what is included in its comprehension and its idea.

In consequence, in order for the term "some saint" to contain the term "some friend of God," it is necessary for "friend of God" to be contained in the comprehension of the idea "saint."

Now everything contained in the comprehension of an idea can be affirmed universally of it. Everything included in the comprehension of the idea triangle can be affirmed of every triangle. Everything included in the idea person can be affirmed of every person. And consequently, in order for friend of God to be included in the idea saint, it is necessary for every saint to be a friend of God. From this it follows that the conclusion "some friend of God is poor," can be contained in the proposition "some saint is poor," where the middle term "saint" is taken particularly, only by virtue of a proposition where it is taken universally, since it has to show that friend of God is contained in the comprehension of the idea saint. This can be shown only by affirming "friend of God" of "saint" taken universally: "every saint is a friend of God." And consequently none of the premises would contain the conclusion if the middle term, which is taken particularly in one of the propositions, were not taken universally in the other. This is what had to be demonstrated. [214]

[a]   ... proposition, where the middle term we take to prove it is taken particularly, namely, "some ... (I)

CHAPTER 11

The application of this general principle to several syllogisms that appear
confused

Given what we said in Part II, that the way to decide when a proposition does or
does not contain another is by the extension and comprehension of the terms, we
can judge the validity or invalidity of every syllogism without considering whether
it is simple or composite, complex or noncomplex, and without paying attention to
figures and moods, by this single general principle: *That one of the two propositions
must contain the conclusion, and the other must show that it contains it.* This will be
understood better by examples.

EXAMPLE 1

I wonder whether this reasoning is good.

> *The duty of a Christian is not to praise those who commit criminal acts.*
> *Now those who fight duels commit criminal acts.*
> *Thus the duty of a Christian is not to praise those who fight duels.*

I do not have to worry about knowing to what figure or mood this can be
reduced. It is enough to consider whether the conclusion is contained in one of the
first two propositions, and whether the other one shows it. And I find, first, that the
first proposition is no different from the conclusion except that one has "those who
commit criminal acts," and the other has "those who fight duels." The proposition
that has "commit criminal acts" will contain the one that has "fight duels,"
provided that "commit criminal acts" contains "fight duels."

Now it is obvious from the meaning that the term "those who commit criminal
acts" is taken universally, and that it means everyone who commits any such acts
whatever. So the minor premise, "those who fight duels commit criminal acts,"
which shows that "fight duels" is contained [215] under the term "commit criminal
acts," also shows that the first proposition contains the conclusion.

EXAMPLE 2

I wonder whether this reasoning is good.

> *The Gospel promises Christians salvation.*
> *Some wicked people are Christians.*
> *Therefore the Gospel promises some wicked people salvation.*

In order to decide, I only have to consider that the major premise cannot
contain the conclusion unless the word "Christians" is taken generally for all
Christians, and not just for some Christians. For if the Gospel promises salvation
only to some Christians, it would not follow that it promises it to wicked persons
who are Christians, because these wicked persons might not be among the number

of Christians to whom the Gospel promises salvation. This is why this argument is valid, but the major premise is false if the word "Christians" is taken there for all Christians. The argument is invalid if it is taken only for some Christians, for in that case the first proposition would not contain the conclusion.

In order to determine whether it should be taken universally, we have to decide by means of another rule which we gave in Part II, namely that *except in the case of facts, that of which something is affirmed is taken universally when it is expressed indefinitely*. Now although "those who commit criminal acts" in the first example, and "Christians" in the second example are each part of an attribute, they nevertheless function as subjects with respect to the other part of that same attribute. For in the first example, it is affirmed of those who commit criminal acts that they should not be praised, and in the second example, Christians are promised salvation. Consequently, since these terms are not restricted, they should be taken universally. So both arguments are valid in form. But the major premise of the second argument is false unless by the word "Christians" we understand only those who live in conformity with the Gospel, in which case the minor premise would be false, because there are no wicked persons who live in conformity with the Gospel.

EXAMPLE 3

It is easy to see by the same principle that this reasoning is invalid:

> *Divine law commands us to obey secular magistrates.*
> *Bishops are not secular magistrates.*
> *Therefore divine law does not command us to obey bishops.* [216]

For neither of the first propositions contains the conclusion, since it does not follow that because divine law commands one thing it does not command another. Hence the minor premise clearly shows that bishops are not included under the term "secular magistrates," and that the commandment to honor secular magistrates does not include bishops. But the major premise does not say that God made no other commandments besides that one, as it would have to in order to contain the conclusion by virtue of this minor premise. This shows that this other argument is valid:

EXAMPLE 4

> *Christianity requires servants to serve their masters only in matters that are not against God's law.*
> *Now improper commerce is against God's law.*
> *Therefore Christianity does not require servants to serve their masters in improper commerce.*

For the major premise contains the conclusion, since by the minor premise, improper commerce is contained in the many things against God's law, and because the major premise is exclusive, it is equivalent to saying, "divine law does not require servants to serve their masters in anything that is against God's law."

EXAMPLE 5

This common sophism can be easily explained by this single principle.

Whoever says you are an animal speaks the truth.
Whoever says you are a goose says you are an animal.
Thus whoever says you are a goose speaks the truth.

For it suffices to say that neither of the first two propositions contains the conclusion, since if the major premise contained it, given that it differs from the conclusion only in that "animal" occurs in the major premise, and "goose" in the conclusion, "animal" would have to contain "goose." But "animal" is taken particularly in the major premise, since it is the attribute of the subordinate affirmative proposition, "you are an animal." Consequently it could contain "goose" only in its comprehension. To show this we would have to take the word "animal" universally in the minor premise, by affirming "goose" of every animal, which we could not do. And in fact this is not done here, since "animal" is still taken particularly in the minor premise, because, as [217] in the major premise, it is the attribute of the subordinate affirmative proposition, "you are an animal."

EXAMPLE 6

By the same means we can again explain this ancient sophism reported by St. Augustine:

You are not what I am.
I am a person.
Therefore you are not a person.

This argument is invalid according to the rules of figures, because it is in the first figure, and the first proposition, which is its minor premise, is negative. But we only have to say that the conclusion is not contained in the first of these propositions, and that the other proposition ("I am a person") does not show it to be contained in it. For since the conclusion is negative, the term "person" is taken universally in it, and thus it is not at all contained in the term "what I am." This is so, because whoever speaks thus is not all people, but only some person, as is apparently said simply in the applicative proposition "I am a person," where the term "person" is restricted to a particular signification because it is the attribute of an affirmative proposition. Now the general is not contained in the particular.

CHAPTER 12[a]

Conjunctive syllogisms[b]

Conjunctive syllogisms are not all those whose propositions are conjunctive or composite, but only those whose major premise is composite in such a way as to contain the entire conclusion. They can be reduced to three kinds: *conditionals, disjunctives*, and *copulatives*.

Conditional syllogisms [218]
Conditional syllogisms are those in which the major premise is a conditional proposition containing the entire conclusion, for example:

> *If there is a God, we must love him.*
> *There is a God.*
> *Therefore we must love him.*

The major premise has two parts, the first, called the antecedent, "If there is a God"; the second, called the consequent, "we must love him."

This syllogism may be of two kinds, because from the same major premise two conclusions can be drawn.

The first kind occurs when, after affirming the consequent in the major premise, we affirm the antecedent in the minor premise, according to the rule: *In affirming the antecedent, one affirms the consequent.*

> *If matter cannot move itself, the first motion must have been given to it by God.*
> *Now matter cannot move itself.*
> *Thus the first motion must have been given to it by God.*

The second kind is when we deny the consequent in order to deny the antecedent, according to the rule: *In denying the consequent, we deny the antecedent.*

> *If[c] one of the elect perishes, God is mistaken.*
> *Now God is never mistaken.*
> *Thus none of the elect perishes.*

This is St. Augustine's argument: *Horum si quisquam perit, fallitur Deus: sed nemo eorum perit, quia non fallitur Deus*[1] [If one of us perishes, God lies; but none of us perishes because God does not lie].

Conditional arguments are fallacious in two ways. One is when the major

---

[1]   *On Admonition and Grace*, ch. 7, *Writings*, vol. 4, p. 262.
[a]   Here in I appears chapter 13, "*Dilemmas*," which in V is chapter 16.
[b]   ... Composite or Conjunctive Syllogisms. – It remains to explain only composite or conjunctive syllogisms, which do not ... (I)
[c]   *... If beasts think, matter thinks.*
      Now matter is incapable of thinking.
      Therefore beasts do not think.
      Conditional arguments are fallacious in two ways: the first occurs [169:8] ... (I)

premise is an unreasonable conditional, where the consequent is against the rules; for example, if I were to infer the general from the particular, saying: "If we are mistaken about something, we are mistaken about everything."

But the falsity of the major premise in syllogisms of this kind concerns the matter more than the form. Accordingly they are considered invalid in form only when a faulty inference is drawn from the major premise, whether it is true or false, reasonable or unreasonable. This can happen in two ways. [219]

The first occurs whenever the antecedent is inferred from the consequent, as if someone said:

If the Chinese are Mohammedans, they are infidels.
Now they are infidels.
Thus they are Mohammedans.

The second sort of invalid conditional argument occurs when the negation of the consequent is inferred from the negation of the antecedent, as in the same example:

If the Chinese are Mohammedans, they are infidels.
Now they are not Mohammedans.
Thus they are not infidels.[d]

Some conditional arguments, however, seem to have this second defect, but are nonetheless valid because there is an implicit exclusion in the major premise, although it is not expressed. Example: When Cicero published a law against buying votes and Murena was accused of having bought them, Cicero, who was defending him, justified his action against Cato's criticism that he was violating his own law by this argument: *Etenim si largitionem factam esse confiterer, idque rectè factum esse deffenderem, facerem improbè, etiam si alius legem tulisset; cùm verò nihil commissum contra legem esse deffendam, quid est quod meam deffensionem latio legis impediat?*[2] [Even if someone else had sponsored the law it would be immoral to admit that bribery had occurred while at the same time maintaining that what happened was correct and proper. But since my defense is that no illegal act has been committed, why should that law stop me from speaking for the defense?] This argument seems to be similar to one a blasphemer might make, who would say to excuse himself: "If I denied that there is a God, I would be wicked. But although I blaspheme, I do not deny that there is a God. Therefore I am not wicked." This argument is worthless, because there are crimes other than atheism that make a person wicked. But what shows that Cicero's argument is valid, although Ramus presented it as an example of bad reasoning,[3] is that its meaning contains an exclusive particle. So it should be reduced to these terms:

---

[2]   *Pro Murena*, III.5, *Speeches*, pp. 153–5.
[3]   Clair and Girbal note the source as Ramus's *Dialectic*, but remark that the argument has not been identified.
[d]   From here to "*Disjunctive syllogisms*" was added in II.

I could be rightly criticized for acting against my law only if I admitted that Murena had bought votes, and I continued to justify his action.
But I claim that he did not buy votes;
Consequently I am not acting against my law. [220]

The same thing should be said about Venus's argument in Virgil, in speaking to Jupiter:

Si sine pace tua, atque invito numine Troes
Italiam petiére, luant peccata, neque illos
Juveris auxilio: sin tot responsa secuti,
Quae superi manesque dabant: cur nunc tua quisquam
Flectere jussa potest, aut cur nova condere fata.[4]
[For if the Trojans have reached Italy without your leave,
against your will, then let them suffer for their crime,
do not bring help. But if they followed oracles of High Ones,
of gods above and gods below, then why can anyone
annul what you command or make new fates for them?]

For this argument comes down to these terms:

If the Trojans had come to Italy against the will of the gods, they would be subject to punishment.
But they did not come against the will of the gods.
Hence they are not subject to punishment.

Something else has to be supplied there, otherwise it would be similar to this argument, which is certainly invalid:

If Judas had become an Apostle without being called, he should have been rejected by God.
But he did not become an Apostle without being called.
Hence he should not have been rejected by God.

But what keeps Venus's argument in Virgil from being invalid is that the major premise has to be considered exclusive in meaning, as if it were:

The Trojans would be subject to punishment and unworthy of their help only if they had come to Italy against their will.
But they did not come against their will.
Therefore, etc.

Or else we should say, which is the same thing, that the affirmative premise, *si sine pace tua*, etc. includes this negation in its meaning:

If the Trojans had come to Italy only by the order of the gods, it is not just for the gods to abandon them.

---

[4] *Aeneid*, IX.32–6, *Virgil*, vol. 2, p. 115. (Löringhoff and Brekle give the location as X.31–5.)

Now they came only by the order of the gods.
Therefore, etc.

Disjunctive Syllogisms
Syllogisms are called disjunctive when their first proposition is disjunctive, that is, when their parts are joined by *vel*, "or," as in this syllogism of Cicero's:

Those who killed Caesar are either parricides or defenders of liberty.
Now they are not parricides.
Hence they are defenders of liberty. [221]

There are two kinds of disjunctive syllogisms. The first are those where we deny one part in order to retain the other, as in the one we just presented, or in this one:

All wicked persons must be punished either in this world or the other.
Now there are wicked persons who are not punished in this world.
Hence they will be in the other.

Sometimes there are three members in this sort of syllogism, and then two are denied to retain one, as in St. Augustine's argument in his book on *Lying*, chap. 8. *Aut non est credendum bonis, aut credendum est eis quos credimus debere aliquando mentiri, aut non est credendum bonos aliquando mentiri. Horum primum perniciosum est: secundum stu'tum: Restat ergo ut nunquam mentiantur boni.*[5] [Either we should not believe the good, or we should believe those whom we believe to lie occasionally, or we should believe that the good never lie. The first of these is dangerous, the second is foolish, so it remains that the good never lie].

The second but less natural kind occurs when we posit one of the parts in order to deny the other, as in the following:

In testifying that by His miracles God had confirmed his preaching about the crusade,
St. Bernard was either a saint or an impostor.
Now he was a saint.
Therefore he was not an impostor.

These disjunctive syllogisms are rarely unsound, except when the major premise is false, that is, when the division is not exact because there is a mean between opposed members; for example, if I were to say:

One must either obey princes in whatever they command against the law of God, or
revolt against them.
Now one must not obey them in whatever is against God's law.
Therefore one must revolt against them.

or

---

[5] *On Lying, Treatises*, p. 71. St. Augustine begins with *Quamobrem* ...

Now one must not revolt against them.
Therefore one must obey them in whatever is against God's law.

Both arguments are unsound, because there is a mean in this disjunction which was observed by the first Christians, namely to suffer all things patiently rather than doing anything against God's law, without however revolting against princes.

These false disjunctions are one of the most common sources of unsound arguments among people. [222]

Copulative syllogisms
There is only one kind of syllogism like this, which occurs when one takes a negative copulative proposition, and then establishes one part in order to deny the other.

A person cannot be both a servant of God and a worshipper of money.
Now a miser is a worshipper of money.
Therefore a miser is not a servant of God.

For this sort of syllogism is not necessarily valid when we deny one part in order to posit the other, as can be seen in this argument derived from the same proposition:

A person cannot be both a servant of God and a worshipper of money.
Now prodigals are not worshippers of money.
Hence they are servants of God.

CHAPTER 13

Syllogisms with conditional conclusions

We saw that a perfect syllogism can have no less than three propositions. But this is true only when we infer absolutely, and not when we do so only conditionally, because then the conditional proposition alone can contain one of the premises in addition to the conclusion, and even both of them.

Example: If I want to prove that the moon is an uneven body, and not smooth like a mirror, as Aristotle imagined, I can infer it absolutely only with three propositions.

Every body that reflects light from all its parts is uneven.
Now the moon reflects light from all its parts.
Hence the moon is an uneven body.

But I need only two propositions in order to infer conditionally as follows:

Every body that reflects light from all its parts is uneven.
Hence if the moon reflects light from all its parts, it is an uneven body. [223]

And I can even frame this argument in a single proposition thus:

If every body that reflects light from all its parts is uneven, and the moon reflects light from all its parts, it must be admitted that it is not a smooth body but uneven.

Or else by connecting one of the propositions by the causal particle "because," or "since," as in:

If every true friend ought to be ready to give his life for his friend, there are scarcely any true friends, since there are scarcely any who are ready to go so far.

This manner of reasoning is very common and quite superb, and it makes us realize that we should not suppose that reasoning occurs only when three propositions are separated and arranged as in the Schools. For it is certain that this single proposition includes an entire syllogism:

Every true friend ought to be ready to give his life for his friends:
Now there are scarcely any persons ready to give their lives for their friends:
Therefore there are scarcely any true friends.

The whole difference between absolute syllogisms and those whose conclusion is contained along with one of the premises in a conditional proposition, is that syllogisms of the first kind can be accepted in their entirety only if we agree with the conclusion. In the latter kind, however, we can grant everything without conceding anything to the person proposing the argument, because that person still has to prove that the condition on which the accepted consequence depends is true.

So these arguments are, properly speaking, only preparations for an absolute conclusion. But they are also very well suited for this, and we must admit that these forms of reasoning are quite common and quite natural. Moreover, they have this advantage, that because they are further removed from the atmosphere of the Schools, they are better received in the world.

We can make these kinds of inferences in all figures and moods, and hence there are no other rules to be observed than the same rules of figures.

We should remark only that the conditional conclusion always includes one of the premises in addition to the conclusion. Sometimes it is the major premise and sometimes the minor premise.

This will be seen in examples of several conditional conclusions that can be drawn from two general maxims, [224] one affirmative, the other negative, whether the affirmative is already proved or accepted without proof.

Every sensation of pain is a thought:

From this we can infer affirmatively.

1. *Therefore if all beasts feel pain,*
   All beasts think. Barbara.
2. *Therefore if some plant feels pain,*
   Some plant thinks. Darii.

3. *Therefore if every thought is an action of the mind,*
    Every sensation of pain is an action of the mind.   Barbara.
4. *Therefore if every sensation of pain is an evil,*
    Some thoughts are evils.   Darapti.
5. *Therefore if the sensation of pain is in the hand that is burned,*
    There is some thought in the hand that is burned.   Disamis.

We can infer negatively.

6. *Therefore if no thought is in the body,*
    No sensation of pain is in the body.   Celarent.
7. *Therefore if no beast thinks,*
    No beast feels pain.   Camestres.
8. *Therefore if some part of a person does not think,*
    Some part of a person does not feel pain.   Baroco.
9. *Therefore if no motion of matter is a thought,*
    No sensation of pain is a motion of matter.   Cesare.
10. *Therefore if no sensation of pain is pleasant,*
    Some thoughts are not pleasant.   Felapton.
11. *Therefore if some sensations of pain are not voluntary,*
    Some thoughts are not voluntary.   Bocardo.

Still other conditional conclusions can be drawn from this general maxim: "Every sensation of pain is a thought," but since they would be fairly unnatural, they are not worth discussing.

Among the conditionals we have derived, some contain the minor premise in addition to the conclusion, namely, the first, second, seventh, and eighth. The others contain the major premise, namely the third, fourth, fifth, sixth, ninth, tenth, and eleventh.

Similarly, we can note the various conditional conclusions that can be derived from a general negative proposition. For example, let us take this one: [225]

No matter thinks.

1. *Therefore if every beast's soul is matter,*
    No beast's soul thinks.   Celarent.
2. *Therefore if some part of a human is matter,*
    Some part of a human does not think.   Ferio.
3. *Therefore if the soul thinks,*
    The soul is not matter.   Cesare.
4. *Therefore if some part of a human thinks,*
    Some part of a human is not matter.   Festino.
5. *Therefore if everything that feels pain thinks,*
    No matter feels pain.   Camestres.

6. *Therefore if all matter is a substance,*
    Some substance does not think.   Felapton.
7. *Therefore if some matter is the cause of several effects that appear quite marvelous,*
    Not everything that is the cause of marvelous effects thinks.   Ferison.

Among these conditionals only the fifth includes the major premise in addition to the conclusion. All the others include the minor premise.

The best use of this sort of argument is to require the people you want to persuade of something to recognize, first, the validity of an inference they can admit without committing themselves to anything, since it is presented to them only conditionally and, so to speak, as separated from the material truth of its content.

In that way they are better disposed to admit the absolute conclusion drawn from it, either by affirming the antecedent in order to affirm the consequent, or by denying the consequent in order to deny the antecedent.

So if anyone grants me that "no matter thinks," I will infer "Therefore, if a beast's soul thinks, it must be distinct from matter."

And since I could not be denied this conditional conclusion, I could draw one or the other of these two absolute consequences:

Now a beast's soul thinks,
Therefore it is distinct from matter.

Or else the contrary:

Now the soul of a beast is not distinct from matter.
Therefore it does not think. [226]

From this we see that four propositions are necessary to make this sort of argument complete, and to establish something absolutely. But they should not, however, be classified as composite syllogisms, because these four propositions contain no more meaning than these three propositions of a common syllogism:

No matter thinks.
Every beast's soul is matter.
Therefore no beast's soul thinks.

CHAPTER 14

Enthymemes and enthymematic sentences

We said earlier that the enthymeme is a perfect syllogism in the mind but imperfect in expression, because one of its propositions is suppressed as too clear and well known, and as easily supplied by the minds of one's listeners. This kind of argument is so common in speech and writing that it is rare, by contrast, for all the propositions to be expressed, because some are usually clear enough to be presupposed. The nature of the human mind is such as to prefer something to be left to be supplied, rather than for others to suppose that it needs to be taught everything.

Hence this suppression flatters the vanity of one's listeners by leaving something to their intelligence and, by abbreviating speech, it makes it stronger and livelier. For example, consider this verse from Ovid's *Medea*, which contains a very elegant enthymeme:

> *Servare potui, perdere an possim rogas?*[1]
> *I was able to save you, could I thus lose you?*

It is certain that if an argument were made from it in this form: *Whoever can save can lose. Now I was able to save you, therefore I can lose you*, all the grace would be removed. The reason is that, since one of the principal attractions of discourse is to be full of meaning and to allow the mind to form a thought that is more comprehensive than the expression, it is, by contrast, one of its greatest defects to be devoid of sense and to [227] include very few thoughts, which is almost inevitable in philosophical syllogisms. For since the mind is faster than the tongue, whenever one proposition is enough to make us think of two, expressing the second becomes superfluous, since it does not add any new meaning. This is what makes these kinds of arguments so rare in our lives, because even without reflecting on it, we distance ourselves from what is annoying, and confine ourselves to precisely what is required to make ourselves understood.

Enthymemes are, then, the way people usually express their arguments, by suppressing the proposition they think should be easily supplied. This proposition is sometimes the major premise, sometimes the minor premise, and sometimes the conclusion. In the latter case, however, it is not properly called an enthymeme, since the entire argument is in some sense contained in the first two propositions.

It also happens, sometimes, that the two propositions of the enthymeme are included in a single proposition. For this reason Aristotle calls it an enthymematic sentence, and he illustrates it by this example:

> Ἀθάνατον ὀργὴν μὴ φύλαττε θνητὸς ὤν.[2]
> *Mortal, do not cherish an immortal hatred.*

The entire argument would be: *Whoever is mortal should not preserve an immortal hatred. Now you are mortal. Therefore, etc.*, and the perfect enthymeme would be: *You are mortal. Therefore let your hatred not be immortal.*

[1] This verse, the only one we have from Ovid's tragedy, is cited by Marcus Fabius Quintilianus in *De Institutio Oratoria*, VIII.v.6. See *The Institutio Oratoria*, vol. 3, p. 285.
[2] *Rhetoric*, Bk. II, ch. 21, *Complete Works*, vol. 2, p. 2222.

CHAPTER 15

Syllogisms composed of more than three propositions

We have already said that syllogisms composed of more than three propositions are generally called *sorites*.[1]

We can distinguish three types of *sorites*. First, gradations, about which it is not necessary to say anything more than has already been said in chapter 1 of Part III.

Second, dilemmas, which we will discuss in the following chapter.

Third, the syllogisms the Greeks called epicheiremata,[2] which contain a proof of one or both of the first two [228] propositions. These are the ones we will discuss in this chapter.

Just as we are often bound to suppress certain very clear propositions in discourse, it is also often necessary, when asserting doubtful propositions, to put forward their proofs at the same time, in order to prevent one's listeners from becoming impatient. People are sometimes offended when others try to persuade them with reasons that appear to be false or doubtful, because even if these doubts are remedied in what follows, it is nevertheless dangerous to produce this aversion in their minds for even a short time. Hence it is better for the proofs to follow such doubtful propositions immediately, rather than be separated from them. This separation produces yet another troublesome problem, which is that we have to repeat the proposition we want to prove. This is why, although the Scholastic method is to present the entire argument and then prove the proposition that causes difficulty, the method followed in ordinary discourse is to connect doubtful propositions to the proofs that establish them. This forms an argument composed of several propositions, for the major premise is connected to its proofs, the minor premise to its proofs, and then the conclusion is drawn.

Thus the entire oration on behalf of Milo can be reduced to a composite argument whose major premise is that it is permissible to kill people who set up ambushes against us. The proofs of this major premise are taken from natural law, human laws, and examples. The minor premise is that Claudius attempted to ambush Milo, and the evidence for the minor premise is Claudius's equipment, his retinue, etc. The conclusion is that Milo is therefore permitted to kill him.[3]

The suffering of children could be used to prove original sin by the dialectic method, in the following way:

Children could suffer only as a punishment for some sin they inherit from their birth. Now they do suffer; therefore, it is because of original sin. Next the major and minor premises need to be proved, the major premise by this disjunctive

---

[1] In antiquity, "sorite" designated the sophism of the heap, σωρός, due to Chrysippus or Eubulid the Megarian. From the fifteenth century, the word was used to designate an accumulation of syllogisms.

[2] *Epicheirema* (επι, χειρ) had a wide variety of uses in antiquity, which Quintilian reviews in Bk. v, ch. 14, *Institutio Oratoria*, vol. 2, p. 351–65.

[3] This refers to Cicero's *Pro Milone*, translated as *The Speech on Behalf of Titus Annius Milo* in *The Speeches*.

argument: the suffering of children could proceed only from one of these four causes: 1. from sins committed previously in another life; 2. from the impotence of God who did not have the power to safeguard them from it; 3. from the injustice of God who subjects them to it without cause; 4. from original sin. Now it is impious to say that it comes from the first three causes. Therefore it [229] could arise only from the fourth, which is original sin.

The minor premise, "that children suffer," would be proved by enumerating their miseries.

But we can readily see how St. Augustine presented this proof of original sin with more grace and force, by framing it in a composite argument this way:

> Consider how many and how great are the evils that befall children, and how the first years of their lives are filled with futility, suffering, illusions, and fears. Later, when they have grown and even when they begin to serve God, error tempts them in order to seduce them, labor and pain tempt them to weaken them, lust tempts them to enflame them, grief tempts them to defeat them, and pride tempts them to make them vain. Who could explain so easily all the different pains that weigh like a yoke on Adam's children? The evidence of these miseries compelled pagan philosophers, who had no knowledge or belief in the sin of our first father, to say that we were born only to suffer the punishment we deserve from crimes committed in another life, and that our souls were attached to corruptible bodies in the same kind of torture that Etruscan tyrants made people suffer whom they bound, alive, to dead bodies. But this opinion, that souls are joined to bodies in punishment for previous faults from another life, is rejected by the Apostle. What remains, then, if not that the cause of these dreadful evils is either the injustice or impotence of God, or the pain of the first sin of humanity? But because God is neither unjust nor impotent, there remains only what you are unwilling to acknowledge, but which you must, however, in spite of yourselves. Namely that this yoke, so heavy, which the children of Adam are obliged to bear from the time their bodies leave their mothers' wombs until the day they return to the womb of their common mother, which is the earth, would not have existed if they had not deserved it by the offense that proceeds from their origin.[4] [230]

CHAPTER 16

Dilemmas[a]

A dilemma can be defined as a composite argument in which, after a whole has been divided into its parts, we conclude affirmatively or negatively from the whole what was concluded from each part.

[4]   *Against Julian*, Bk. IV, ch. 16, *Writings*, vol. 16, p. 240.

[a]   ... Dilemmas. – We said in chapter 1 that there are arguments composed of more than three propositions, which are generally called *Sorites*.
Now since, among this kind of argument, scarcely any but dilemmas need any particular reflection, we thought it would be appropriate to explain them here. A dilemma ... (I)

I say what was concluded from each part, and not only what would have been affirmed from it. For an argument is properly called a dilemma only when what is said about each part is supported by its specific reason.

For example, we could prove that it is not possible to be happy in this world, by this dilemma.

> *We can live in this world only by abandoning ourselves to our passions or by combating them.*
> *If we abandon ourselves to them, this is an unhappy state because it is shameful, and we cannot be content with it.*
> *If we combat them, this is also an unhappy state because nothing is more painful than having to wage internal war against ourselves.*
> *Therefore there can be no true happiness in this life.*

If we want to prove that bishops who do not work for the salvation of the souls committed to them cannot be excused before God, we can do so by a dilemma.

> *Either they are capable of this charge or they are incapable of it.*
> *If they are capable of it, they cannot be excused for not working at it.*
> *If they are incapable of it, they cannot be excused for having accepted such an important charge of which they cannot acquit themselves.*
> *Consequently, in either case, they cannot be excused before God if they do not work for the salvation of the souls committed to them.*

But we can make several observations about this kind of argument.

The first is that we do not always express all the propositions [231] that occur in them. For example, the dilemma we just presented is contained in very few words in a speech by St. Charles, at the opening of one of his Provincial Councils: *Si tanto muneri impares, cur tam ambitiosi: si pares, cur tam negligentes?*[1] [If you are not equal to such an important office, why are you so ambitious? If you are equal, why so negligent?]

Similarly there are many implicit ideas in the famous dilemma an ancient philosopher used to prove that one should never get involved in the affairs of the Republic.[2]

> *If one acts well, he will offend people; if one acts badly, he will offend the gods. Thus one ought never get involved in them.*

And the same is true of the argument someone else used to prove that a man should never marry: *If the woman one marries is beautiful, she will cause jealousy; if she is ugly she will be displeasing. Therefore a man should never marry.*

In each of these dilemmas, the proposition that has to contain the division is

---

[1]   St. Charles Borromeo (1538–84) was the Archbishop of Milan.
[2]   Cicero reports that this view is common to many ancient philosophers, but that Antisthenes appears to have taught it first.

implicit. This is fairly common, because they are easily understood, being sufficiently indicated by the specific propositions treating each part.

Moreover, in order for the conclusion to be contained in the premises, what is implicit must be something general that can apply to everything, as in the first example:

If one acts well, one will offend people, which is unfortunate.
If one acts badly, one will offend the gods, which is also unfortunate.
Therefore it is unfortunate in both cases to get involved in the affairs of the Republic.

It is important to keep this advice in mind in order to judge the force of a dilemma properly. What makes the previous argument unsound, for example, is that it is not at all unfortunate to offend people, when we can avoid it only by offending God.

The second observation is that a dilemma can be fallacious primarily through two defects. One occurs when the disjunctive premise on which it is based is defective, because it does not include all the members of the whole it divides.

So the dilemma against marrying is unsound because there could be women who are not so beautiful that they cause jealousy, nor so ugly that they are displeasing.

For the same reason the dilemma ancient philosophers used against fearing death is also unsound. *Either the soul,* they say, *perishes with the body and thus, no longer having sensations, we will be beyond harm. Or if the soul survives the body, it will be happier than it was in* [232] *the body. Therefore death is not to be feared.*[3] As Montaigne rightly remarked, we have to be quite blind not to see that there is a possible third state between these two, namely that the soul, surviving the body, finds itself in a state of torment and misery, which is a good reason to fear death, for fear of falling into this state.[4]

The other defect that makes dilemmas invalid is when the particular conclusions drawn from each part are not necessary. Hence it is not necessary for a beautiful woman to cause jealousy, because she might be so wise and virtuous that there would be no reason to suspect her fidelity.

It is also not necessary for her to displease her husband if she were ugly, since she could have other qualities of mind and virtue that are so beneficial that she could not fail to please him.

The third observation is that people who use a dilemma ought to be careful not to let it be used against them. Thus Aristotle shows that the dilemma used to justify his case can be turned against the philosopher who was unwilling to become involved in public affairs, for we can say:

If we govern according to the corrupt rules of people, we shall please people.

---

[3] Cicero, *Tusculan Disputations*, I.xi.24–5, pp. 29–31.
[4] *Essays*, Bk. II, ch. 12, *Complete Works*, p. 413.

If we maintain true justice, we shall please the gods.
Therefore we ought to get involved in public affairs.

Nonetheless this counterargument is not reasonable, for it is not beneficial to please people by offending God.

CHAPTER 17

Topics, or the method of finding arguments. How useless this method is

What the rhetoricians and the logicians call topics, *loci argumentorum*, are certain general headings for classifying all the proofs we use in the different subjects we discuss. The part of logic they call *invention* is nothing other than what they teach about these topics.

Ramus quarrelled with Aristotle and the Scholastic philosophers [233] on this subject, because they discuss the topics after giving the rules of arguments. He maintains against them that it is necessary to explain the topics and whatever pertains to invention before discussing these rules.

The reason Ramus gives is that it is necessary to have the subject matter first, before thinking about how to organize it. Now the theory of the topics teaches how to find this subject matter, whereas the rules of arguments can only teach us how to organize it.

But this argument is very weak, because even if it is necessary to have the subject matter in order to organize it, it is not, however, necessary to learn how to find the subject matter before learning how to organize it. In order to learn how to organize the subject matter, it is sufficient to have some general subjects to use as examples. Now the mind and common sense always furnish enough of these without needing to borrow from any art or any other method. It is true, then, that we must have some subject matter in order to apply the rules of arguments to it, but it is false that this matter has to be found by the method of topics.

We could say, on the contrary, that because people claim to teach the art of forming arguments and syllogisms in the topics, it is necessary to know first what arguments and syllogisms are. But we could equally well reply, perhaps, that nature alone furnishes us a general knowledge of reasoning that is sufficient for us to understand what is said about it in the topics.

So it is fairly useless to worry about the order for treating the topics, since it is rather unimportant. But it might be more useful to examine whether it may not be more appropriate not to discuss them at all.

We know that the ancients made a great mystery of this method, and that Cicero even preferred it to all of dialectic as the Stoics taught it, because they never spoke about the topics. Let us leave aside, he says, all this science that tells us nothing about the art of finding arguments and only produces too much discourse for teaching us how to judge them. *Istam artem totam relinquamus quae in excogitandis argumentis muta nimiùm est, in judicandis nimiùm loquax.*[1] [Let us completely relinquish the art that has too little to say when it comes to careful argumentation, and too much to say when it comes to passing judgment]. Quintilian and all the other rhetoricians, and Aristotle and all the philosophers spoke about it in the same way, so it would be difficult not to share their view if general experience did not appear entirely opposed to it.

We could take as witnesses almost all the people who have passed through the ordinary course of study, and [234] who learned what is taught in the colleges about this artificial method for finding proofs. Is there a single person who can truly say that when he was required to deal with some subject, he reflected on these topics and looked to them for the arguments he needed? Consult as many lawyers and preachers as there are in the world, as many people who speak and write, and who always have material remaining, and I do not know if you could find among them anyone who ever thought of making an argument *à causa, ab effectu,* or *ab adjunctis* [from a cause, from an effect, from an accompanying circumstance], for proving whatever he wanted to persuade others of.

Further, although Quintilian appears to respect this art, he is nonetheless obliged to acknowledge that when we are treating some subject, we do not have to knock at the door of all these topics in order to derive arguments and proofs. *Illud quoque,* he says, *studiosi eloquentiae cogitent, non esse cùm proposita fuerit materia dicendi scrutanda singula et velut ostiatim pulsanda, ut sciant an ad id probandum quod intendimus, fortè respondeant.*[2] [I would also have students of oratory consider that all the forms of argument I have just set forth cannot be found in every case, and that when the subject on which we have to speak has been propounded, it is no use considering each separate type of argument and knocking at the door of each with a view to discovering whether they may chance to be useful for proving our point, except while we are in the position of mere learners without any knowledge of actual practice].

It is true that any argument that could be made on any subject may be brought under these headings and the general terms called topics. But they are not found by this method. Nature, the attentive consideration of the subject, and knowledge of various truths enable us to produce them, and afterwards art relates them to certain genres. Accordingly we can truly say about the topics what St. Augustine says in general about the precepts of rhetoric. We find, he says, that the rules of eloquence are observed in the speech of eloquent people, although they never think about them when they talk, whether they know them or whether they are ignorant of

---

[1]   Cicero, *De Oratore*, II.xxxviii.160, p. 313.

[2]   *Institutio Oratoria*, Bk. V, ch. 10, vol. 2, p. 269. The passage actually reads: *Illud quoque studiosi eloquentiae cogitent, neque omnibus in causis, quae demonstravimus, cuncta posse reperiri; neque, cum proposita fuerit materia dicendi, scrutanda singula et velut ostiatim pulsandum, ut sciant, an ad probandum id, quod intendimus, forte respondeant, nisi cum discunt et adhuc usu carent.*

them. They practice these rules because they are eloquent, but they do not use them in order to be eloquent: *Implent quippe illa quia sunt eloquentes, non adhibent ut sint eloquentes.*[3]

We walk naturally, as this same Father remarks in another place, and in walking we make certain regular motions of the body. But it would be useless for learning to walk to say, for example, that you have to send the animal spirits into certain nerves, move certain muscles, make certain motions in the joints, put one foot in front of the other, and lean on one while the other goes forward. It is easy to form rules by observing what nature causes us to do, but we never use these rules in performing these actions. Thus people use all the topics in most ordinary discourse, and nothing could be said that is not related to them. But these thoughts are not produced by reflecting explicitly on the topics, [235] since reflection serves only to slow the ardor of the mind and to prevent us from finding lively and natural reasons, which are the true ornaments of all kinds of speech.

In the ninth book of the *Aeneid*, Virgil represents Eurial as taken by surprise and surrounded by his enemies, who were about to avenge the death of their companions whom Eurial's friend Nisus had killed. He then puts these words, full of emotion and passion, in Nisus's mouth:

> *Me me adsum, qui feci, in me convertite ferrum,*
> *O Rutuli! mea fraus omnis; nihil iste nec ausus,*
> *Nec potuit. Coelum hoc et sidera conscia testor.*
> *Tantum infelicem nimium dilexit amicum.*[4]
> [On me – on me – here am I who did the deed– on me turn your steel,
> O Rutulians! Mine is all the guilt; he neither dared
> nor could have done aught; this heaven be witness and the all-seeing stars!
> He but loved his hapless friend too well.]

Ramus says this is an argument *à causa efficiente* [from an efficient cause], but we could swear with equal confidence that when Virgil wrote these verses he never thought of the topic of efficient cause. He would never have written them had he stopped to look for this thought. To produce such noble and lively verses, he would have had not only to forget these rules if he had known them, but in some sense to forget himself to be swept away by the passion he was portraying.

In fact, the little use people have made of the method of topics for as long as it has been known and taught in the Schools is clear proof that it is not very helpful. But when we set out to extract from it all the fruit we can, it is impossible to see how to arrive at something that is truly practical and valuable. For the most we can claim to find in each subject by this method are various general, ordinary, and remote thoughts, such as those the Lullists find by means of their tables. Now this

---

[3] *On Christian Instruction*, Bk. IV, ch. 3, *Writings*, vol. 4, p. 171.
[4] *Aeneid*, Bk. IX.427–30, *Virgil*, vol. 2, p. 141.

sort of abundance is not only far from useful, but there is nothing more damaging to our judgment.

Nothing stifles good seeds more than an abundance of weeds; nothing renders a mind more devoid of exact and sound thoughts than this poisonous fertility of common thoughts. The mind becomes accustomed to this facility, and no longer makes an effort to find the appropriate, specific, and natural reasons, which are discovered only by considering the subject attentively.

We ought to consider that the abundance sought [236] through the topics is a rather small benefit. It is not what most people need. We sin much more by excess than by defect, and our speeches are only too crammed with material. Hence to teach people judicious and serious eloquence, it would be much more useful to teach them to remain silent rather than to speak, that is, to suppress and cut out their base, common, and false thoughts, rather than to produce as they do a confused mass of good and bad arguments, which fill up books and speeches.

Since the topics are rarely useful except for finding these sorts of thoughts, we could say that if it is good to know what is said about them – because so many famous persons have spoken of them that they have created a type of necessity not to be ignorant of such a common matter – it is even more important to be convinced that there is nothing more ridiculous than using them to expound about everything as far as the eye can see, as the Lullists do by means of their general attributes which are a kind of topics. In addition, this harmful facility of discussing everything and finding reasons everywhere, which gives rise to so much vanity, is such a bad mental trait that it is much worse than stupidity.

This is why the entire benefit we can derive from the topics comes down, at best, to taking on, unwittingly, a general tendency that may be slightly useful to consider the subject under discussion by more of its aspects and parts.

CHAPTER 18

The classification of topics into topics of grammar, logic, and metaphysics

Those who have treated the topics have classified them in various ways. The system followed by Cicero in his books on invention and in the second book on the *Orator*, and by Quintilian in the fifth book of his *Institutions* is less methodical. But it is also more appropriate for use in judicial discourse, to which they specifically refer it. Ramus's method is too complicated by subdivisions. [237]

Here is a system of classification that seems reasonably useful, created by a very judicious and reliable German philosopher named Clauberg, whose *Logic* fell into my hands after we had already begun to have this book printed.[1]

Topics are taken from either grammar, logic, or metaphysics.

Topics of grammar

Topics of grammar are etymology and words derived from the same root, which are called *conjugata* in Latin, and παρόνυμα in Greek.

We argue from etymology when we say, for example, that many people in the world never engage in amusements or diversions, properly speaking, because to engage in diversions is to be distracted from serious occupations, and they are never seriously occupied at anything.

Words derived from the same root are also useful for finding thoughts.

> *Homo sum, humani nil à me alienum puto.*[2] [I am human, I regard nothing human as alien to me.]
>
> *Mortali urgemur ab hoste, mortales.* [Being mortal, we flee from the mortal enemy.]
>
> *Quid tam dignum misericordiâ quàm miser? quid tam indignum misericordiâ quàm superbus miser?* What is more worthy of commiseration than a miserable person? What is less worthy of commiseration than a miserable person who is proud?

Topics of logic

Topics of logic are the universal terms: genus, species, difference, property, accident, definition, and classification. Since all these points have been explained previously, it will not be necessary to discuss them further here.

We should only note that it is good to know certain common maxims usually connected with these topics, not because they are particularly useful but because they are common. We have already discussed some of them under other terms. But it is good to know them under their usual terms.

1. Whatever is affirmed or denied of the genus is affirmed or denied of the species. *Whatever applies to all people applies to the great. But they cannot claim privileges that are beyond people.*

2. In destroying the genus one also destroys the species. *Anyone who does not judge at all does not judge badly; anyone who does not speak at all never speaks indiscreetly.* [238]

3. When all the species are destroyed, the genus is destroyed. *The forms called substantial (except for the rational soul) are neither body nor spirit; therefore they are not substances.*

---

[1] Clauberg (1622–?) was the first to propagate Cartesianism in Germany. He published the *Logica vetus et nova* in 1654.

[2] Terence, *Heautontimorumenos*, I.i.25. This verse is cited by St. Augustine in *Against Julian*, Bk. IV, ch. 16, *Writings*, vol. 16, p. 240.

4. If we can affirm or deny the entire difference of something, we can affirm or deny the species of it. *Extension does not apply to thinking; therefore thought is not matter.*

5. If we can affirm or deny the property of something, we can affirm or deny the species of it. *Since it is impossible to envision half a thought, or a round or square thought, it is impossible for a thought to be a body.*

6. The defined may be affirmed or denied of that of which the definition is affirmed or denied. *There are few just persons, because few persons have a firm and constant will to render to each what belongs to them.*

Topics of metaphysics

Topics of metaphysics are certain general terms that apply to all beings, to which various arguments are referred, such as causes, effects, the whole, the parts, and opposite terms. What is most useful here is to know several general classifications, and primarily the causes.

The Scholastic definitions of cause in general, that *a cause is that which produces an effect*, or *that through which a thing exists*, are so imprecise, and it is so hard to see how they apply to all types of cause, that it would be better to leave this word undefined since our idea of it is as clear as these definitions.

But the classification of causes into four species, namely final, efficient, material, and formal, is so famous that everyone ought to know it.

The FINAL CAUSE is the end for which a thing exists.

There are *principal ends*, which are those we mainly take into consideration, and *incidental ends*, which are considered merely as additional.

Whatever one claims to do or obtain is called *finis cujus gratia*. Thus health is the end of medicine, because it claims to procure it.

The one for whom we labor is called *finis cui*. People are the end of medicine in this sense because they are the ones for whom the cure is intended. [239]

Nothing is more common than deriving arguments from the end, either to show that something is imperfect, for example, that a speech is badly formed when it is not appropriate for persuading; or to show that it is likely that someone did or will do some action because it promotes the end one usually sets for oneself. This is the source of the famous phrase by a Roman judge, that first of all we should look for *cui bono*, that is, who would benefit by an action, because people ordinarily act according to their interests. Or we can show, to the contrary, that people should not be suspected of committing an action because it would have been contrary to their purposes.

There are still other ways of reasoning from the end, which good sense will teach better than any precept. This could also be said for the other topics.

The EFFICIENT CAUSE is that which produces something else. Arguments are derived from this by showing that an effect does not exist because there was not a sufficient cause, or that it is or will exist, by showing that all its causes exist. If these causes are necessary, the argument is necessary; if they are free and contingent, it is only probable.

There are various species of efficient cause, whose names are useful to know.

When God created Adam, He was his *total* cause because nothing else contributed to it. But the father and mother are each only *partial* causes of the child because they each need the other.

The sun is a *proper* cause of light, but it is only an *accidental* cause of the death of a person killed by heat who is unable to cope with it.

The father is the *proximate* cause of his son.

The grandfather is only a *remote* cause.

The mother is a *productive* cause.

The nurse is only a *preserving* cause.

The father is a *univocal* cause with respect to his children, because they are similar in nature to him.

God is merely an *equivocal* cause with respect to his creatures, because they do not have God's nature.

A worker is the *principal* cause of the work, the instruments being only the *instrumental* cause.

The air that fills an organ is a *universal* cause of its harmony.

The particular disposition of each pipe and the person who plays the organ are the *particular* causes that determine the universal cause. [240]

The sun is a *natural* cause.

People are the *intellectual* cause with respect to whatever they do using their judgment.

The fire that burns wood is a *necessary* cause.

A person who walks is a *free* cause.

The sun shining in a room is the *proper* cause of its illumination, whereas the open window is only a cause or condition without which the effect would not take place, *conditio sine qua non.*

The fire that burns a house is the *physical* cause of the blaze; the person who sets the fire is its *moral* cause.

Further, we can also classify as an *efficient* cause the *exemplary* cause, which is the model one has in mind in creating a work. An example would be the blueprint of a building which guides the architect, or in general whatever causes the objective being of an idea or any other image, as King Louis XIV is the exemplary cause of his portrait.

The MATERIAL CAUSE is that out of which things are formed, for example, gold is the matter of a gold vase. Whatever does or does not apply to the matter does or does not apply to the things which are composed of it.

The FORM is whatever makes something to be what it is and distinguishes it from other things, whether it is a being really distinct from the matter, as the Scholastics think, or merely the arrangement of its parts.

There are as many different effects as causes, since these words are reciprocal. The usual way of deriving arguments from them is to show that if the effect exists, the cause exists, since nothing can exist without a cause. This is also the way to show that a cause is good or bad, when its effects are good or bad. But this is not always true of accidental causes.

We have said enough about the whole and its parts in the chapter on classification, and so we need not add anything more about it here.

There are four kinds of opposite terms:

Relatives: such as father and son, master and servant.

Contraries: such as cold and hot, healthy and sick.

Privatives: such as life and death, sight and blindness, hearing and deafness, knowledge and ignorance.

Contradictories, which consist of a term and the simple negation of this term: for example, to see and not to see. The difference between these last two kinds of oppositions is that [241] privative terms contain the negation of a form in a subject having the capacity for it, whereas negatives do not indicate this capacity. This is why we do not say that a stone is blind or dead, because it is capable of neither sight nor life.

Because these terms are opposed, we use one to deny the other. Contradictory terms have the property that, in denying one, we affirm the other.

There are several sorts of comparisons, for things can be compared either as equal or unequal, or as similar or dissimilar. We can prove that what does or does not apply to an equal or similar thing does or does not apply to something else to which it is equal or similar.

With unequal things we can prove negatively that if what is more probable does not exist, whatever is less probable does not exist for a stronger reason. Or we can show affirmatively that if what is less probable exists, whatever is more probable also exists. Differences or dissimilarities are generally used to refute what others try to establish by similarities, just as we refute an argument based on a judicial decision by showing that it applied to a different case.

That, in outline, is part of what is said about the topics. Some things are best known only in this way. Anyone who would like to know more about them can find it in the authors who have discussed them in more detail. We would not, however, advise anyone to go looking in Aristotle's *Topics*, since these are strangely confused books. But there is something rather nice on the subject in the first book of his *Rhetoric*, where he teaches different ways of showing that something is useful, pleasant, nobler, or more trivial. It is true, however, that by this path we will never arrive at any truly reliable knowledge.

CHAPTER 19[1]

Different ways of reasoning badly, which are called sophisms

Although it is not difficult to recognize bad arguments if we know the rules of good reasoning, nevertheless, examples of mistakes to be avoided are often more striking than [242] the examples to be imitated. So it will be helpful to describe the main sources of bad reasoning, which are called *sophisms* or *paralogisms*, since that will make it even easier to avoid them.

I will limit them to only seven or eight kinds, since some are so obvious that they are not worth mentioning.

I. *Proving something other than what is at issue*
Aristotle calls this sophism *ignoratio elenchi*, that is, ignorance of what must be proved against one's adversary.[2] This is a very common mistake in our disputes. We argue heatedly, and often we do not listen to each other. Passion or bad faith causes us to attribute to our adversaries something remote from their views to gain an advantage over them, or to impute to them consequences we imagine can be drawn from their doctrines, although they disavow and deny them. All this can be classified under this first kind of sophism, which good and sincere people should avoid above all.

We would have hoped that Aristotle, who went to such pains to warn us about this error, had taken as much care to avoid it. For we cannot conceal the fact that in his arguments against several ancient philosophers he reports their views dishonestly. He criticizes Parmenides and Melissus for admitting only a single principle of everything, as if they meant by that the principle out of which things are composed, when they actually meant the sole and unique principle from which everything originates, which is God.[3]

He accuses all the ancients of not recognizing privation as a principle of natural things, and for that reason he treats them as rustic and crude. But how could anyone fail to see that what he represents as a great mystery, unknown up to his time, could never have been ignored by anyone, since it is impossible not to see that the matter from which a table is made must be deprived of the form of the table, that is, not be a table, before it is made into a table? It is true that the ancients did not take it into their heads to use this knowledge to explain the principles of natural things, because in fact nothing is less useful for that purpose. It is obvious enough

---

[1] This chapter was entirely rewritten, beginning with II. Only the final passages are completely identical in all editions. Fouillée, the editor of an edition in 1877, attributes this chapter to Nicole.
[2] *Sophistical Refutations*, ch. 5, *Complete Works*, vol. 1, pp. 281–3.
[3] Parmenides (c. 515–c. 450 BC) was the most original and important philosopher before Socrates, and the founder of the Eleatic School. Considered the father of ontology, he is best known for his poem *On Nature*, which argues for the unity and eternal changelessness of reality. Melissus of Samos (fifth century BC) was perhaps a student of Parmenides. In any case, his writings conform to Parmenides' general views.

that we do not know more about how to make a clock [243] when we know that the matter from which it is made could not have been a clock before being made into a clock.

It is unfair, then, for Aristotle to criticize these ancient philosophers for not having known something that is impossible not to know, and to accuse them of not explaining nature by means of a principle that explains nothing. It is an illusion and a sophism to represent the principle of privation to the world as a rare secret, since this is not at all what we need when we try to discover the principles of nature. We assume as given that something does not exist before it is created. But we want to know what principles compose it and what cause produced it.

Was there ever a sculptor, for example, who, when teaching someone how to make a statue, gave for the first lesson this instruction, which Aristotle thinks all explanations of the works of nature should begin with: My friend, the first thing you should know is that to make a statue you have to select a piece of marble which is not yet the statue you want to make.

II. *Assuming as true what is at issue*

Aristotle calls this *begging the question*, which is clearly entirely contrary to good reason, since in all arguments what is used as proof has to be clearer and better known than what we want to prove.

Galileo accuses him, however, and rightly so, of having himself fallen into this fallacy when he wanted to prove by the following argument that the earth is at the center of the universe:

> *The nature of heavy things is to tend toward the center of the universe, and of light things to go away from it.*
> *Now experience shows that heavy things tend toward the center of the earth, and that light things go away from it.*
> *Therefore the center of the earth is the same as the center of the universe.*

It is clear that the major premise of this argument contains a manifest begging of the question. For it is obvious that heavy things move to the center of the earth, but how did Aristotle learn that they tend toward the center of the universe if he did not assume that the center of the earth is the same as the center of the universe? This is the very conclusion he wants to prove by this argument.

Most of [244] the arguments used to prove the existence of a certain bizarre type of substance the Schools call *substantial forms* are completely question-begging. They claim these are corporeal even though they are not themselves bodies, which is pretty difficult to understand. If there were no substantial forms, they say, there would be no generation. Now there is generation in the world. Therefore there are substantial forms.

But all we have to do to see that this argument is nothing but pure question-begging is to identify the equivocation in the word "generation." For if the word "generation" means the natural production of a new whole in nature, such as the way a chicken is produced in an egg, it is right to say that there is generation in this sense. But we cannot infer that there are substantial forms from this, since nature can produce these new wholes and new natural beings merely by rearranging the parts. But if the word "generation" is taken to mean, as it usually is, the production of a new substance which did not previously exist, namely this substantial form, we will be assuming precisely what is at issue, since it is obvious that anyone who denies the existence of substantial forms cannot agree that nature produces them. Far from being swayed by this argument to assert that there are such things, we ought to draw the completely contrary conclusion, as follows: If there were substantial forms, nature could produce substances that did not previously exist. Now nature cannot produce new substances since this would be a type of creation. Consequently there are no substantial forms.

Here is another inference of the same nature: If there were no substantial forms, they also say, natural beings would not be the wholes which are called *per se, totum per se* [in itself, whole in itself], but beings by accident. Now there are wholes *per se.* Therefore there are substantial forms.

Again we have to ask those who use this argument to try to explain what they mean by a whole *per se, totum per se.* For if they mean, as they do, a being composed of matter and form, it is clear that this is begging the question, since it is the same as saying: If there were no substantial forms, natural beings would not be composed of matter and substantial forms. Now they are composed of matter and substantial forms. Therefore there are substantial forms. If they mean something else, they should say what it is, and it will be obvious that they are not proving anything.
[245]
We have taken some time in passing to show the weakness in these arguments the Schools use to establish these sorts of substances, which are discovered neither by the senses nor the mind, and about which nothing else is known except that they are called substantial forms. The reason is that although those who defend them do so with good intentions, the foundations they use and their ideas of these forms obscure and interfere with the sound and convincing proofs of the immortality of the soul, which are based on the distinction between bodies and minds, and on the impossibility for an immaterial substance to perish by changes taking place in matter. For in these substantial forms we unwittingly provide libertines with examples of substances which perish, which are not properly material, and to which are attributed countless thoughts, that is, purely mental actions, in animals. This is why, for the sake of religion and for persuading the impious and the libertine, it is useful to deprive them of this response, by showing them that nothing is more badly founded than these perishable substances called substantial forms.

We can also classify under this sort of sophism all proofs based on a principle different from that which is at issue, but known to be no less contested by one's opponent. There are, for example, two equally firm dogmas among Catholics: one is that not all the articles of faith can be proved by Scripture alone; the other is that it is an article of faith that children can be baptized. So it would be a fallacy for an Anabaptist to argue against Catholics that they are wrong to believe that children can be baptized because we see nothing about it in the Scripture, since this proof assumes that we ought to take on faith only what is in Scripture, which is what Catholics deny.

Finally, we can classify under this sophism all arguments in which something unknown is proved by something which is equally or even more unknown, or something uncertain by something else which is equally or more uncertain.

III. *Taking for a cause what is not a cause*
This sophism is called *non causa pro causa*. It is very common among people, and we commit it in several ways. One is by simple ignorance of the true causes of things. Thus philosophers have attributed to the horror of a vacuum a thousand effects [246] which were recently demonstrated, by very ingenious experiments, to be caused only by air pressure, as may be seen in the excellent treatise by Pascal which just appeared.[4] These same philosophers typically teach that vases full of water break when the water freezes because the water compacts and thus leaves a void that nature cannot allow. But we now recognize that they break only because, to the contrary, when water is frozen it occupies more space than before it was frozen, which is also what causes ice to float on water.

The same sophism occurs when remote causes that prove nothing are used to prove things that are clear enough in themselves, or false, or at least doubtful. This happened, for example, when Aristotle wanted to prove that the world is perfect using this argument: "The world is perfect because it contains bodies. Body is perfect because it has three dimensions. Three dimensions are perfect because three are all there are (*quia tria sunt omnia*), and three are all there are because the word 'all' is not used when only one or two things exist, but only when there are three."[5] By this argument we can show that the least atom is as perfect as the world, because together with the world, it has three dimensions. But instead of proving that the world is perfect, it proves, on the contrary, that every body insofar as it is a body is essentially imperfect, and that the perfection of the world consists primarily in its containing creatures that are not bodies.

This same philosopher proves that there are three simple motions because there are three dimensions. It is difficult to see the inference from one to the other.

He also proves that the heavens are unchangeable and incorruptible because they move circularly, and because there is nothing contrary to circular motion.[6] But 1. it

---

4   *On the Weight of the Air, Physical Treatises,* pp. 27–75. This essay was probably written about 1651 but was not published until 1663.
5   *On the Heavens,* Bk. I, ch. 1, *Complete Works,* vol. 1, p. 445.
6   Ibid., Bk. I, ch. 2, *Complete Works,* vol. 1, p. 448.

is not clear what the contrariety of motion has to do with the corruption or alteration of a body. 2. It is even less clear why a circular motion from east to west would not be contrary to a different circular motion from west to east.

The other cause making people fall into this sophism is the foolish vanity that makes us ashamed to acknowledge our ignorance. This is why we prefer to fabricate imaginary causes of things we are asked to explain, rather than admitting that we do not know their [247] causes. Moreover, the way we escape confessing our ignorance is rather amusing. Whenever we see an effect whose cause we do not know, we imagine that we have discovered it if we connect the general word "power" or "faculty" to this effect. This word produces no other idea in the mind except that this effect has some cause, which we knew quite well before finding the word. There is no one, for example, who does not know that the pulse beats, that when iron is brought near a magnet it moves towards it, that senna purges, and that the poppy causes sleep. People who do not profess to have knowledge, and to whom ignorance is not shameful, frankly admit that they know these effects but that they do not know their causes. By contrast, the learned, who would blush to say as much, cope with it another way by claiming that they have discovered the true causes of these effects, namely that there is a pulsing power in the pulse, a magnetic power in the magnet, a purgative power in the senna, and a soporific power in the poppy. This is how they resolve the problem quite conveniently. There is no Chinese who could not as easily have made himself admired when clocks were brought to that country from Europe. For all he had to say was that he knew perfectly well the reason behind what others found so marvelous, which was simply that this apparatus had an *indicative* power which marked the hours on the quadrant, and a *sonorific* power which made it chime. He would thereby have rendered himself as learned in the science of clocks as these philosophers are in the science of the beating of the pulse and the properties of magnets, senna, and poppies.

There are still other words that function to make people learned at little expense, such as "sympathy," "antipathy," and "occult qualities." But again, all these would convey nothing false if people contented themselves with giving the words "power" and "faculty" the general notion of cause, of whatever kind, internal or external, dispositional or active. For it is certain that a magnet has some disposition that causes the iron to go to it rather than to some other stone, and we are permitted to call this disposition, whatever it consists in, "magnetic power." Accordingly, if people are mistaken, it is only in imagining themselves to be more knowledgeable for having found this word, or else in wanting us to take this to mean a certain imaginary quality by which the magnet attracts the iron, which neither they nor anyone else has ever understood. [248]

But there are others who would give us pure chimeras for the true causes of nature, such as astrologers who relate everything to the influence of the stars, and who have even discovered by this means that there had to be an immobile heaven above everything to which they attribute motion because the earth produces different things in different countries. *Non omnis fert omnia tellus. India mittit ebur; molles sua thura Sabaei*[7] [Every country does not provide everything; India sends us her ivory, the soft Sabaeans their frankincense]. The cause of this could only be the influence of the heavens which, since they are immobile, always present the same aspects to the same places on earth.

Thus when one of these astrologers undertook to prove the immobility of the earth from physical reasons, he based one of his main demonstrations on the mysterious argument that if the earth turned around the sun, the influences of the stars would cross one another, which would cause a great disorder in the world.

Astrologers use these influences to terrify people when some comet appears or some great eclipse occurs, as in 1654, which was supposed to throw the whole world into confusion, especially in the city of Rome. This was explicitly mentioned in Helvicus's chronology, *Romae fatalis*.[8] But there is no reason either for comets and eclipses to have any significant effect on the earth, or for general causes such as these to act on one place more than on another, and to threaten a king or prince more than an artisan. So we see a hundred of these events that are not followed by any unusual effects. If it sometimes happens that wars, deaths, plagues, or the death of some prince occurs after comets or eclipses, they also occur without comets or eclipses. Besides, these effects are so general and so common that it would clearly be odd if they did not happen every year in some part of the world. So those who say vaguely that a certain comet threatens some great person with death are not taking a big risk.

It is even worse when they cite these chimerical influences as causes of people's inclinations, whether evil or virtuous, and even of particular actions and events in their lives, without any other grounds except that out of a thousand predictions, some happen by chance to be true. But if we want to judge things using good sense, we will admit that a lit torch in the room of a woman giving birth ought to have a greater effect on the body of her child [249] than does the planet Saturn, regardless of the aspect it presents and whatever conjunction it is in.[a]

Finally, there are people who offer chimerical causes for chimerical effects.

[7]   Virgil, *Georgics*, 1.56–7, *Virgil*, vol. , p. 85. *Non omnis fert omnia tellus* does not occur in this passage.
[8]   Helvicus (1581–1616) was a German scholar and the author of the *Chronologia universalis*, (1618).
[a]   ... is in. – So we see people often attributing effects to the moon in which experience shows that it plays no part, as very precise persons have assured me of having proved. People say, for example, that there is a great deal of marrow in animals' bones during a full moon, and little or none during the new moon. Let them make the experiment and they will find that this is false, and that in all phases of the moon some bones have a great deal of marrow, and others have very little.
       It is also said that the moon eats some rocks, because these are the rocks exposed to the moon that erode more than others. But since they could not be exposed to the moon without also being exposed to the south winds which, being very humid, are very corrosive, it is much more reasonable to attribute this effect to the winds than to the moon. – Finally ... (I)

People who suppose, for example, that nature abhors a vacuum and that she makes efforts to avoid it (which is an imaginary effect, for nature abhors nothing, and all the effects attributed to this horror depend solely on air pressure), continually propose reasons for this imaginary horror that are even more imaginary. Nature abhors a vacuum, says one of them, because it needs continuity in bodies to make influences work and to propagate qualities. It is a strange sort of science that proves something that does not exist by something else that does not exist.

This[b] is why, when it is a question of seeking causes for extraordinary effects asserted by someone, we should first examine carefully whether these effects are real. For people often wear themselves out to no purpose seeking reasons for things that do not exist at all. Countless problems ought to be solved the way Plutarch solved this problem he posed. Why are the colts chased by wolves faster than the others? After he said that it might be because the slower ones were caught by wolves and so those that escaped were the fastest, or that fear gave them an unusual speed which they retained by habit, he finally related another solution, which is apparently the right one. Perhaps, he says, it is not true. This is the way we ought to explain a great number of effects attributed to the moon, such as, for example, that bones are full of marrow [250] when it waxes and empty when it wanes, and that the same is true of crayfish. For all we have to say is that this is all false, since some very precise persons have assured me of having tested it, finding it equally likely that bones and crayfish are sometimes full and sometimes empty during all phases of the moon. The same is true of a number of observations made about cutting wood, reaping or sowing grain, grafting trees, and taking medicine. Little by little the world will be delivered from all these constraints that have no foundation other than conjectures no one ever seriously thought were true. This is why people are wrong who claim that, provided they allege an experience or a fact taken from some ancient author, it ought to be accepted without question.

Further, this kind of sophism is also committed in the common fallacy of the human mind, *post hoc, ergo propter hoc*: This happened following a certain thing, hence that thing must be its cause. This is how people concluded that a star called the Dog-Star causes the extraordinary heat we feel during the period called dog days, which prompted Virgil to say about this star, which in Latin is called *Seirius*:

> *Aut Seirius ardor:*
> *Ille sitim morbosque ferens mortalibus aegris*
> *Nascitur, et laevo contristat lumine coelum.*[9]
> [... or as the blazing Dog Star,

---

9   Virgil, *Aeneid*, x.273ff., *Virgil*, vol. 2, p. 189
b   This paragraph was added in II.

bringer of diseases and drought to tired mortals,
when it rises with light and menace, saddening the skies.]

Nevertheless, as Gassendi quite rightly observed, nothing is less plausible than this supposition, for since this star is on the other side of the equator, its effects ought to be stronger in places where it is more perpendicular. The days we call dog days here, however, occur during the winter on that side of the equator. Accordingly, in a country on the other side of the equator they have more reason to believe that the Dog-Star causes cold than we have to believe that it causes us heat.

IV. *Imperfect enumeration*[c]

There is hardly any defect of reasoning that capable persons fall into more easily than making imperfect [251] enumerations, and not sufficiently considering all the ways a thing could exist or could happen. This leads them to conclude hastily either that it does not exist because it does not exist in a certain way although it could exist in another, or that it exists in such-and-such a way although it could exist in still another way that they have not considered.

We can find examples of these defective inferences in the proofs Gassendi uses to establish the principle of his philosophy, which is the void dispersed among particles of matter, which he calls *vacuum disseminatum*. I am all the more willing to recount them as Gassendi was a famous man who had a store of rather curious knowledge. So even the mistakes that may be scattered throughout the many works published since his death are not to be scorned and are worth knowing about, whereas it is quite useless to burden the memory with mistakes found in authors who have no reputation.

The first argument Gassendi uses to prove this scattered void, which he claims in one place can be considered as clear a demonstration as those used in mathematics, is this.[10]

If there were no void and everything were filled by bodies, motion would be impossible, and the world would be only a large mass of rigid, inflexible, and immobile matter. For if the universe were entirely filled, no body could be moved unless it took the place of another body. Thus if body *A* moves, it has to displace another body at least equal to itself, namely *B*, and in order to move, *B* must also displace another. Now this could happen in only two ways: one is if this displacement of bodies goes on to infinity, which is absurd and impossible; the other is if it occurs in a circle, so that the last body displaced occupies the place of *A*.

Up to this point there has not yet been an imperfect enumeration. It is true, moreover, that it is ridiculous to imagine that when one body moves, motion must go on to infinity, each body displacing another. Let us claim only that motion takes

---

[10]   *Physicae*, Sect. I, chs. 2 and 3, *Opera Omnia*, vol. I, pp. 185–6, 192–6.
[c]   This section was added in II.

place in a circle, and that the last body to be moved occupies the place of the first body, which is A, and so all places are filled. Gassendi also tries to refute this view by the following argument: The first body to be moved, which is A, cannot move if the last body, which is X, cannot be moved. Now X cannot be moved, since [252] for it to be moved it must take the place of A, which is not yet vacant. Consequently, if X cannot be moved, neither can A. Therefore everything remains at rest. This entire argument depends only on the assumption that body X, which is immediately adjacent to A, can be moved only on the condition that A's place is already vacant when it begins to move. Accordingly, before the instant X occupies this place, there would be another instant when it could be said to be empty. But this assumption is false and imperfect, because there is still another condition under which X may move, which is that A leaves its place at the same instant X occupies A's place. In this case there is no difficulty in A's pushing B, B's pushing C, and so on up to X, and in X's occupying A's place in the same instant. This way there would be motion without a void.

Now that this is possible, namely that one body could occupy the place of another body at the same instant this other body leaves it, is something we are obliged to recognize whatever our hypothesis, provided only that we admit some continuous matter. So, for example, if we distinguish two parts of a stick that are immediately adjacent, it is clear that whenever it is moved, at the same instant the first part leaves a space, this space is occupied by the second part. There is no point where we could say that this space is vacated by the first part and not filled by the second part. This is even clearer with a ring of iron that rotates around its center. For in that case each part occupies the space vacated by the part preceding it at the same instant, without our needing to imagine any void. Now if this is possible with a ring of iron, why could it not happen with a ring that is part wood and part air? And if body A, which we assume to be made of wood, pushes and displaces body B, which we assume to be made of air, why could not body B displace another, and this in turn another, up to X, which takes A's place at the same time A leaves it?

So it is clear that Gassendi's error in reasoning arises from his belief that in order for one body to occupy the place of another, this place must first be vacant, and in a preceding instant. He did not consider that it would suffice if it were empty at the same instant.

His other proofs are derived from various [253] experiments by which he rightly shows that air can be compressed and that more air can be made to enter a space that already appears to be completely full, as we can see in balloons and harquebuses.

Based on these experiments he constructs this argument: if space A, which is already completely filled with air, is capable of admitting more air by compression, either this additional air which is introduced must enter by penetrating a space already occupied by air, which is impossible, or the air contained in A must not fill it entirely, but among the particles of air there must exist empty spaces that admit the additional air. He says: This second hypothesis proves what I maintain, which is that there are void spaces among the particles of matter, capable of being filled by new bodies. But it is rather odd that Gassendi does not realize that he is arguing from an imperfect enumeration. For in addition to the hypothesis of penetration, which he is right to consider naturally impossible, and the hypothesis of voids scattered among the parts of matter which he wants to establish, there is a third hypothesis that he does not mention which, being possible, makes his argument invalid. For we can suppose that there is a more subtle and delicate matter among the coarsest particles of air which, since it is capable of exiting through the pores of bodies, causes a space that seems to be filled with air capable of receiving still more air, because when this subtle matter is pushed out by the particles of air which are forced in, it makes room for them by exiting through the pores.

Gassendi was even more obliged to refute this hypothesis, given that he himself admits the existence of this subtle matter that penetrates bodies and passes through all the pores, since he wants cold and heat to be corpuscles entering the pores. He says the same thing about light, and he even acknowledges the famous experiment made with mercury that remains suspended, at a height of two feet three-and-a-half inches, in tubes that are longer than that, leaving above it a space that appears to be void and which is certainly not filled by any sensible matter. He recognizes, I say, that we could not reasonably claim that this space is absolutely empty, since light, which he takes for a body, passes through it.

By thus filling these spaces that he claims are void with a subtle matter, he will find as much room for new bodies to enter as if they really were void. [254]

V. *Judging something by what applies to it only accidentally*

In the Schools this sophism is called *fallacia accidentis* [fallacy of the accident]. It happens whenever we draw an absolute, simple, and unconditional conclusion from what is true only accidentally. This is what so many people do who inveigh against antimony because it produces bad effects when it is misapplied. The same is true of other people who attribute to eloquence all the bad effects it produces when it is abused, or to medicine the faults of certain ignorant doctors.

This is how some recent heretics led so many deluded people to believe that they ought to reject as inventions of Satan the invocation of the Saints, the veneration of relics, and prayer for the dead, because these holy practices were riddled with abuse and superstition from antiquity, as if the bad use people can make of the best things renders them bad.

People also often fall into bad reasoning like this when they take mere occasions for true causes. An example is someone who might accuse the Christian religion of having caused the massacre of countless persons who preferred to suffer death rather than renounce Jesus Christ. On the contrary, these murders should be attributed neither to the Christian religion nor to the constancy of martyrs, but solely to the injustice and cruelty of pagans.[d]

We also see an important example of this sophism in the ridiculous reasoning of the Epicureans, who concluded that the gods must have human form because only humans, among all the creatures in the world, use reason. *The gods, they say, are very happy. No one could be happy without virtue. There is no virtue without reason; and reason is found nowhere except in what has human form. Therefore we must admit that the gods have a human form.* But they must have been completely blind not to see that although in a human being the substance that thinks and reasons is connected to a human body, it is not, however, the human shape which makes a person think and reason. It is ridiculous to imagine that reason and thought could depend on something's having [255] a nose, a mouth, cheeks, two arms, two hands, and two feet. And so it was a puerile sophism for these philosophers to conclude that reason could exist only in human form because it is accidentally connected to the human form in human beings.

VI. *Passing from a divided sense to a composite sense, or from a composite sense to a divided sense*

One of these sophisms is called *fallacia compositionis* [fallacy of composition], and the other *fallacia divisionis* [fallacy of division]. We will understand them better by examples.

Christ says in the Gospel, in speaking of miracles: "The blind see, the lame walk upright, the deaf hear."[11] This could be true only by taking these things separately and not conjointly, that is, in a divided sense and not in a composite sense. For the blind do not see insofar as they are blind, and the deaf do not hear while remaining deaf. But those persons see who were formerly blind and are no longer so, and similarly for the deaf.

This is also the same sense in which Scripture says that God justifies the impious.[12] For this cannot mean that he takes those who are still impious as just, but that he makes just by his grace those who were previously impious.

By contrast, some propositions are true only in a sense opposed to the divided sense. For example, when St. Paul says: Let the defamers, the fornicators, and the miserly not enter the kingdom of heaven.[13] This does not mean that none of those who had these vices will be saved, but only that those who remain attached to them

---

[11] Matthew 11:5
[12] Romans 4:5.
[13] Ephesians 5:5.
[d]   ... pagans.
         This is the sophism by which people often attribute to worthy persons the cause of all the evils they could have avoided by doing things that would have wounded their consciences, because if they had wanted to relieve themselves of observing God's law exactly, these evils would not have happened. – We also ... (I)

and will not give them up by converting to God will have no part in the kingdom of heaven.

It is easy to see that we cannot pass from one of these senses to the other without committing a sophism. People reason badly, for example, who promise themselves heaven while persisting in their crimes because Christ came to save sinners, and because he says in the Gospel that women of ill repute will precede the Pharisees into the kingdom of God.[14] For[e] he [256] did not come to save sinners who remain sinners, but to make them stop being sinners.

VII. *Passing from what is true in some respect to what is absolutely true*
This is what the Schools call *a dicto secundum quid ad dictum simpliciter* [from what is said conditionally to what is said absolutely]. Here are some examples. The Epicureans, again, argued that the gods had to have human form because nothing was more beautiful, and everything that is beautiful should belong to God. This is very bad reasoning. For the human form is not beautiful absolutely, but only with respect to bodies. Hence being a perfection only in some respect and not simply, it in no way follows that it has to exist in God because all perfections exist in God. Only simple perfections, that is, those which contain no imperfection, belong necessarily to God.

We also see in Cicero, in the third book of *The Nature of the Gods*, a ridiculous argument by Cotta against the existence of God, which can be related to the same mistake. "How," he says,

> could we conceive of God, not being able to attribute any virtue to Him? For should we say that he has prudence? But since prudence consists in the choice of goods and evils, what need could God have of this choice, not being capable of any evil? Should we say that He has intelligence and reason? But reason and intelligence are useful for discovering what is unknown by what is known. Now nothing could be unknown to God. Justice also could not exist in God since it concerns only human society; nor temperance, since there is nothing lustful to be moderated, nor force, because he is susceptible to neither pain nor travail, and he is exposed to no peril. How, therefore, could God exist, who would have neither intelligence nor virtue?[15]

It is difficult to conceive anything more impertinent than this kind of argument.

---

[14] Matthew 21:31.
[15] Cicero, *De Natura Deorum*, Bk. III, sec. xv, *De Natura Deorum, Academica*, pp. 321ff. Aurelius Cotta belonged to the party of conservative reform. He became consul in 75 BC and died the following year.
[e] ... God. Or, to the contrary, people who, having lived badly, would despair of salvation, having nothing more to expect than punishment for their crimes, because it is said that God's anger is reserved for those who live badly and that all vicious persons will have no part in Christ's inheritance. The former pass from the divided sense to the composite sense by promising themselves, while remaining sinners, what is promised only to people who cease to be sinners by true conversion. The latter go from the composite sense to the divided sense, applying to those who were sinners and who cease to be so by converting to God, what concerns only sinners who persist in their sins and the bad life. – VI. *Passing* ... (I)

It resembles the thought of a peasant who, never having seen houses covered with anything but thatch [257] and having heard that in cities there are no thatched roofs, would infer from this that there were no houses in cities, and that people who live there are very unhappy since they are exposed to all the ills of the weather. This is how Cotta or rather Cicero reasons. God could have no virtues similar to those in humans. Therefore there could be no virtue in God. What is amazing is that he concludes that there is no virtue in God only because the imperfection found in human virtue could not exist in God. Accordingly this proves to him that God has no intelligence because nothing is hidden from him, that is, that he sees nothing because he sees everything; that he can do nothing because he can do everything; and that he enjoys no good because he possesses all goods.

VIII. *Abusing the ambiguity in words, which can be done in different ways*
We can classify under this sophism all syllogisms that are fallacious because they have four terms, either because the middle term is taken twice particularly, or because it is taken in one sense in the first proposition and in another sense in the second, or finally because the terms of the conclusion are not taken in the same sense in the premises as in the conclusion. We are not restricting the word "ambiguity" only to words that are grossly equivocal, which is almost never misleading. But we understand it to mean anything that can change the meaning of a word, especially when people are not readily aware of this change, because when different things are signified by the same sound they take them for the same thing. On this topic we can refer to what was said near the end of Part I, where we also discussed how to remedy the confusion in ambiguous words by defining them so precisely that no one could be mistaken.

Hence I will content myself with presenting some examples of this ambiguity which sometimes misleads competent people. One example is found in words signifying some whole that can be taken either collectively, for all its parts [258] together, or distributively, for each of its parts. This is how we should resolve the Stoics' sophism that concluded that the universe was an animal endowed with reason. *Whatever uses reason is better than whatever does not. Now nothing*, they said, *is better than the universe: therefore, the universe uses reason.* The minor premise of this argument is false, because they attribute to the universe what applies only to God, which is to be such that nothing can be conceived to be better and more perfect. When we limit the argument to creatures, although we could say that nothing is better than the universe, taking it collectively for the universality of all the beings God created, all that can be inferred from this is that reason is used in some parts of the universe, such as in angels and humans, and not that the whole taken together is an animal using reason.

It would be an equally bad argument to say: Human beings think; now a human being is composed of a body and a soul; therefore the body and the soul think. For in order to attribute thought to a human being as a whole, it is sufficient for one of the parts to think, from which it in no way follows that the other part thinks.[f]

IX. *Drawing a general conclusion from a faulty induction*
Induction occurs whenever an examination of several particular things leads us to knowledge of a general truth. Thus when we experience several seas in which the water is salty, and several rivers in which the water is fresh, we infer that in general sea water is salty and river water is fresh. Different experiments conducted to show that gold does not diminish when heated have led us to judge that this is true of all gold. And since no people have ever been found who do not speak, [259] we believe it to be quite certain that all people speak, that is, use sounds to signify their thoughts.

This is even the beginning of all knowledge, because singular things are presented to us before universals, although afterwards universals are used to know the singulars.

It is true, however, that induction alone is never a certain means of acquiring a perfect science, as we will show elsewhere, since the consideration of singular things serves only as an occasion for the mind to pay attention to its natural ideas, by which it judges the truth of things in general. It is true, for example, that I might never have taken it into my head to consider the nature of a triangle if I had not seen a triangle that gave me the occasion to think of it. Nevertheless, it is not the particular examination of all triangles which makes me draw the general and certain conclusion about all of them, that their area is equal to that of a rectangle having their entire base and half their height (for this investigation would be impossible), but the mere consideration of what is contained in the idea of the triangle which I find in my mind.

Be that as it may, and reserving the discussion of this topic for another place, it suffices to say here that defective inductions, that is, those which are not complete, often fall into error. I will be content to report one notable example.

All philosophers have believed up to now, as an indubitable truth, that it is impossible to draw out the piston of a syringe that is completely sealed without making it collapse, and that it is possible to make water rise as high as we like by suction pumps. And what made them believe this so firmly was that they imagined

---

[f]   ... thinks. – Aristotle's arguments for the eternity of the world are also based only on the ambiguity in some words. He says: "There could be no first instant in time, because every instant is the end of a preceding time and the beginning of a following one. Therefore time is eternal. Therefore motion is also eternal." We could prove by this reasoning that there is no motion of a millstone which is not eternal. But this is to equivocate on the word "instant."

There is also an equivocation on the word "privation" when he says, "That the mover could not precede the motion, because it would have been at rest. Thus it would have been necessary before this for there to have been a motion of which this rest was a privation." It is as if there were no other privation than to lose what one already had, and that those who are born blind are not deprived of sight, although they have never seen the light of day. – VIII. *Drawing* ... (I)

these were confirmed by very certain inductions based on numerous experiments. But both beliefs were found to be false, because new experiments were performed which showed that the piston of a syringe, however it was sealed, can be drawn out provided one uses a force equal to the weight of a column of water the width of the syringe and more than thirty-three feet high, and that we cannot raise water by a suction pump higher than thirty-two to thirty-three feet.[16] [260]

CHAPTER 20

Fallacies committed in everyday life and in ordinary discourse

We have seen examples of the most common errors committed in reasoning[a] about scientific matters. But since the main use of reason is not in these sorts of subjects, which have little to do with the conduct of life and in which it is less dangerous to be mistaken, it would doubtless be much more useful to consider what usually leads people to make false judgments on all sorts of topics, mainly in morality and other matters important to everyday life, which are the usual topics of conversation. But because this plan would require a separate work that would include practically all of ethics, we will be satisfied here to indicate generally some of the causes of these false judgments that are so common among people.

We have not made it a point to distinguish false judgments from unsound arguments, and we have paid equal attention to the causes of each. This is as much because false judgments are the source of unsound arguments and necessarily result in them, as because in fact there is almost [261] always a hidden inference embedded in what appears to be a simple judgment, since there is always some reason or principle behind this judgment. For example, when we judge that a stick that appears bent in water really is bent, this judgment is based on the general and

---

[16] This was an observation that intrigued the people who took care of fountains in Florence in 1643. It was the starting point for the experiments by Torricelli and Pascal on the void and air pressure: see Pascal, *On the Weight of the Air, Physical Treatises*, pp. 48–9.

[a]   ... reasoning. It would be desirable for people to pay as much attention to noticing them in matters concerning morals and the conduct of life as they do for discovering them in scientific matters, since, on the one hand, people make bad arguments in morals even more frequently, and, on the other, these arguments are much more dangerous, since they are not only errors, but also rather important faults.

It would doubtless be not only a very useful study, but also a very pleasant one, to consider in detail what leads people into all the false judgments they make about moral matters. But because this subject would require a separate work considerably longer than this one, we will be content to note here various ways of reasoning badly that are common in people's lives, of which each person can subsequently find countless specific examples, however little the attention paid to them.

I. One of the common human defects is to judge [217:4up] ... (I)
This chapter was considerably rewritten in II. The greater part of the text in I is found after 217:4, although certain developments present in I were located elsewhere in II or their order of presentation was modified. The long passage 207:7–217: 6 up was added in II.

false proposition that what appears bent to our senses is bent in reality. Here there is an embedded inference, although it is not made explicit. When we consider the general causes of our errors, then, it seems they can be classified under two main headings: one internal, namely a disorder of the will that disturbs and confuses our judgment; the other external, arising from the objects we are judging, which misleads the mind by false appearances. Now although these causes almost always go together, one is more apparent than the other in certain errors, and this is why we will discuss them separately.

Sophisms of self-love, interest, and passion

I

If we examine carefully why people usually adopt one view rather than another, we will find that it is not the penetration of truth or the force of reason, but some connection to self-love, interest, or passion. This is what carries weight and what causes most of our doubts. It both unsettles our judgments and fixes us most firmly to them. We judge things not by what they are in themselves, but by what they are in relation to us. For us truth and utility are the same thing.

We[b] need no other proof of this than what we see every day, that things considered doubtful or even false everywhere else are held to be quite certain by people of one nation or profession or institute. Since it is not possible for what is true in Spain to be false in France, or for all Spanish minds to be so [262] different from all French minds that, to judge only by the rules of reason, what appears generally true to one nation appears generally false to the other, it is obvious that this difference in judgment can have no other cause than that it pleases some people to take as true what is advantageous to them, and others, who have no stake in it, to judge it otherwise.[1]

What could be less reasonable, however, than taking our interest as a motive for believing something? The most it can do is to make us pay more attention to the reasons that could reveal the truth to us about what we want to be true. But we should be persuaded only by this truth, which must be found in the thing itself independently of our desires. I am from such-and-such a country, hence I ought to believe that a certain Saint preached the Gospel. I am of such-and-such an order, therefore I ought to believe that a certain privilege is authentic. These are not reasons. Whatever order or country you come from, you ought to believe only what is true and what you would be disposed to believe if you were from another country or order or profession.

---

[1] Pascal, *Pensées*, no. 294, *Pensées and the Provincial Letters*, pp. 100–2.
[b] In I this passage was immediately preceded by:
     We see clearly enough how ridiculous this mistake is, and yet nothing is more common. People believe what is false because they want to; what pleases us appears true to us, and our interests and our passions usually unsettle our judgments most. This is what carries weight and what causes most of our doubts ...

II

But this illusion is even more obvious when it arises from some change in the passions, for although everything stays the same, it nevertheless seems to those who are moved by some new passion that the change that has taken place merely in their hearts has changed everything external which is related to it in some way. How many people do we see who can no longer recognize any good quality, either natural or acquired, in people for whom they feel some aversion or who have in some way frustrated their feelings, desires, or interests? This is enough to make others suddenly become reckless, proud, ignorant, without faith, without honor, and without conscience in their eyes. Their affections and desires are no more fair or moderate than their hatreds. Anyone they love is exempt from every kind of defect. Everything they desire is fair and easy; everything they do not desire is unjust and impossible, without their being able to give any reason for these judgments but the passion itself [263] that possesses them. So even though they do not make this formal inference in their minds – I love him, therefore he is the most competent person in the world; I hate him, therefore he is without merit – instead they do it in some sense in their hearts. This is why these sorts of aberrations are called sophisms and illusions of the heart, because they consist in transferring our passions onto the objects of our passions, and judging that they are what we wish or desire them to be. This is obviously quite unreasonable, since our desires change nothing in what exists outside us, and since only God's will is so efficacious as to make things exactly as he wills them.

III

We can relate this same illusion of self-love to the illusion suffered by people who decide things based on a very general and convenient principle, namely that they are right and that they know the truth. From here it is not difficult for them to conclude that people who do not share their views are mistaken. Indeed, the conclusion follows necessarily.[c]

Their mistake arises only from the high opinion they have of their insight, which makes them view all their thoughts as so clear and evident that they imagine they only have to assert them to make everyone accept them. This is why they take so little trouble to prove them. They rarely hear other people's arguments; they want authority to carry all the weight, because they never distinguish their authority from reason. They treat everyone rashly who does not share their opinions, without realizing that if others do not share their views, they also do not share the views of the others, and that it is not reasonable to assume without proof that we are right, when it is a question of convincing people who hold opinions different from ours only because they are convinced that we are wrong. [264]

[c] ... necessarily. But the mistake of these persons is not believing that they are right, since this is something common to everyone who is convinced of something, but using this principle with respect to others who have a different opinion from theirs, only because they are convinced that the others are not right. – The same is true ... (I)

IV

The same is true of those who have no other basis for rejecting certain views than this pleasing argument: if that were the case, I would not be clever; but I am clever; therefore it is not the case. This is the main reason why some very useful remedies and quite certain experiments were rejected for so long, because those who were not yet informed about them thought that they would have been mistaken up to then. What? If, they said, the blood circulated in the body, if food were not carried to the liver by the mesenteric veins, if the venous artery carried blood to the heart, if blood rose by the descending vena cava, if nature did not abhor a vacuum, if air were heavy and had a downward motion, I would be ignorant of important facts of anatomy and physics. So these things must not be the case. But to cure them of this fantasy, we only have to point out to them that it is a very slight inconvenience to be mistaken, and that they are competent in other matters, although they were not well-informed about these recent discoveries.

V[d]

Nothing is more common than seeing people make the same criticisms of each other, and treat each other, for example, as opinionated, hotheaded, or quarrelsome whenever they hold different views. There are practically no litigants who do not [265] accuse each other of lengthening the trial and concealing the truth by artificial maneuvers. Hence those who are right and those who are wrong speak almost the same language and make the same complaints, attributing the same faults to each other. This is one of the most disagreeable aspects of people's lives, since it casts truth and error, justice and injustice, into such obscurity that most people are incapable of telling the difference between them. From this it happens that some people take sides with one of the parties by chance and without good reason, and others condemn both of them as equally wrong.

All this peculiar behavior results from the same passion, which makes us take as a principle that we are right. For from here it is not difficult to infer that anyone who resists us is opinionated, because to be opinionated is to fail to surrender to reason.

It is true, however, that these accusations of passion, blindness, and quibbling, which are quite unjust on the part of people who are mistaken, are just and legitimate on the part of those who are not mistaken. Nevertheless, because these accusations presuppose that truth is on the side of the person making them, wise and judicious persons who are discussing some contested subject ought to avoid making them before sufficiently establishing the truth and justice of their cause. So they would never accuse their adversaries of being opinionated or rash, or of lacking common sense, before proving it. They would not say, if they had not previously shown it, that their opponents are sliding into absurdities and untenable exaggerations, for the others would say the same on their side. This gets them nowhere, and hence they would prefer to abide by this rule of St. Augustine which

---

[d]   This section was considerably shorter in I and was located elsewhere.

is so fair: *Omittamus ista communia, quae dici ex utraque parte possunt, licèt verè dici ex utraque parte non possint* [We say nothing that both sides can accept, but only what the opposing side cannot accept]. They would be satisfied to defend the truth by weapons appropriate to it – weapons that falsehood cannot borrow – namely clear and sound reasons.

VI

The human mind is not only naturally enamored of itself, but it is also naturally jealous, envious, and malicious towards others. It allows others to have advantages only with [266] difficulty, because it desires all of them for itself. Since it is an advantage to know the truth and bring insight to others, people develop a secret passion to rob others of this glory, which often leads them to criticize others' opinions and discoveries for no reason.

Hence self-love often causes them to construct this ridiculous argument: This is an opinion I discovered, it is the view of my order, it is a view convenient for me; therefore it is true. Their natural malevolence often causes them to make this other argument which is no less absurd: Someone else said it, therefore it is false; it was not I who wrote this book, therefore it is bad.

This is the source of the spirit of contradiction so common among people, which, when hearing or reading something by someone else, causes them barely to consider the reasons that might be persuasive, and to concentrate only on those they think they can refute. They are always on guard against the truth, and they think only about how to suppress it and obscure it, in which they almost always succeed, given the inexhaustible fertility of the human mind for producing poor arguments.

When this vice is excessive it constitutes one of the main traits of the spirit of pedantry, which takes its greatest pleasure in quibbling with others over the most trivial matters and contradicting everything with a base malevolence. But frequently it is less obvious and more hidden, and we could even say that no one is entirely exempt from it, since it has its roots in the self-love which is always alive in people.

Our acquaintance with this malicious and envious disposition residing deep in the human heart shows us that one of the most important rules we can observe, to avoid leading our audience into error and taking them away from the truth of which we want to persuade them, is to provoke their envy and jealousy as little as possible when speaking of ourselves and presenting objects to which they can become attached.

Since people love scarcely anyone but themselves, they are very impatient when others make them pay attention to them and want to be respected. Anything they cannot relate back to themselves is odious and annoying, and they usually pass from hating persons to hating their opinions and reasons. This is why wise people avoid as much as possible exposing their advantages to the eyes of others. [267] They refrain from presenting themselves face to face and making themselves particularly visible. They try, rather, to hide themselves in the crowd so as not to be noticed, so that people will see only the truth they assert in their speech.

The late M. Pascal, who knew as much about true rhetoric as anyone has ever known, carried this rule so far as to claim that honest people ought to avoid referring to themselves, and even using the words "I" and "me." On this subject he was accustomed to saying that Christian piety nullifies the human "me" and human civility hides and suppresses it.[2] This rule ought not be taken to extremes, for there are occasions when trying to avoid these words would cause us unnecessary difficulties. But it is always good to keep it in mind, in order to distance ourselves from the miserable habit some people have who speak only about themselves and constantly quote themselves when their own views are not at issue. This causes their listeners to suspect that this repeated attention to themselves arises from a secret complacency that often leads them to this object of their love. And it quite naturally provokes in their listeners a hidden aversion for these people and everything they say. This shows that one of the most ignoble traits of an honest person is the one Montaigne affected, of entertaining his readers with all his moods, inclinations, fancies, passions, virtues, and vices. This arises from a lack of judgment as well as an extreme love for oneself.[3] True, he tries as much as possible to avoid being suspected of a low and vulgar vanity by speaking as freely of his faults as of his good qualities. This has something appealing about it, appearing to come from sincerity. But obviously it is all only a game and a stratagem that ought to make it even more odious.[4] He speaks of his vices in order to make them known and not to make them detested. He does not claim that he ought to be respected less; he regards them somewhat dispassionately, and as daring rather than shameful. If he reveals them, it is because he does not care very much about them, and he thinks that he will not be more vile or contemptible on that account. But when he learns that something tarnishes him a little, he is as adroit as anyone at hiding it. This is why a famous recent author[5] remarks appropriately that although he took rather pointless pains to advise us in two places [268] in his book that he had a page – who is a fairly useless servant in the house of a gentleman with six thousand pounds income a year – he was not as careful to tell us that he also had a clerk, since he had been Counsellor to the Parliament of Bordeaux. This office, although quite honorable in itself, did not sufficiently satisfy his vain desire to appear everywhere in the guise of a gentleman and cavalier, and to distance himself from the legal profession and the courts.

Apparently, however, he would not have been silent about this circumstance of his life had he been able to find some Marshal of France who had been Counsellor

---

[2] *Pensées*, no. 455, *Pensées and the Provincial Letters*, p. 151.
[3] Ibid., no. 62, *Pensées and the Provincial Letters*, pp. 19–20.
[4] Nicolas Malebranche, *Search After Truth*, Bk. II, Pt. iii, ch. 5, "On Montaigne's Book," pp. 184–90.
[5] Jean-Louis Guez de Balzac, Dissertation 19, "De Montaigne et de ses écrits," *Œuvres*, vol. 2, pp. 658–61.

of Bordeaux, since he obviously wanted us to know he had been Mayor of this city, but only after advising us that he succeeded the Marshal of Biron in this office, and that he left it to the Marshal of Matignon.

But vanity is not this author's greatest vice. He is full of so many shameful infamies and Epicurean and impious maxims, that it is amazing that everyone has put up with him for so long. There are even some rather acute persons who do not recognize the poison in him.

No other evidence is needed to judge his libertinism than the very manner in which he speaks of his vices. For acknowledging in many places that he had engaged in a great number of criminal excesses, he nevertheless declares in other places that he repents none of it and that if he had to live it over again, he would live as he did. "As for me," he says,

> I cannot desire in general to be other than I am. I can condemn my universal form, be displeased with myself and beg God to reform me completely and to forgive my natural weakness. But I should not call that repentance, any more than my dissatisfaction with being neither an angel nor Cato. My actions are ruled by and conform to what I am and to my condition. I can do no better, and repenting does not properly affect things that are not in our power. I never expected to create a monster by joining the tail of a philosopher to the head and body of a lost man, nor that this puny scrap of life should disavow and deny the most beautiful, most complete, and longest part of my life. If I had to live it over again, I would live it as I have lived it, neither complaining about the past, nor fearing the future.[6]

Horrible words, which indicate the complete extinction of any religious feeling, but which are [269] worthy of the person who says this in another place:[7] "I plunge into death, my head lowered stupidly, without considering and recognizing it, as into mute and obscure depths, which engulf me suddenly and instantly suffocate me, full of a powerful sleep, insipid and insolent." And in another place: "Death, which is only a quarter of an hour's passion, without consequence or harm, does not deserve its own precepts."[8]

Although this digression seems somewhat removed from the subject, it is nevertheless relevant for the reason that no book inspires us more to the bad habit of speaking about ourselves, being concerned for ourselves, and wanting others to be similarly concerned. This corrupts reason in a strange way, both in us, by the vanity that always accompanies this discourse, and in others, by the contempt and aversion they feel for it. The only persons permitted to speak of themselves are persons of eminent virtue, who testify by the way they publicize their good actions

---

[6] Montaigne, *Essays*, Bk. III, ch. 2, *Complete Works*, p. 617. This quotation is inexact.
[7] Ibid., Bk. III, ch. 9, *Complete Works*, p. 742.
[8] The exact citation has not been found, but Bk. I, ch. 20 of the *Essays* contains "Nothing can be grievous that happens only once. Is it reasonable so long to fear a thing so short?" (*Complete Works*, p. 64).

that they do so only to move others to praise God or to edify others. If they make their faults public, it is only to humble themselves before us and to turn others away from these faults. But it is a ridiculous vanity for ordinary persons to want to inform others about their petty merits. Further, it is an arrogance deserving condemnation to reveal their disturbances to the world without testifying to being affected by them, since the ultimate excess of abandoning ourselves to vice is not to be embarrassed by it, not to be troubled by it nor to repent,[9] but instead to speak about it as indifferently as about everything else. This is, properly speaking, Montaigne's mentality.

VII

We can to some extent distinguish this malicious and envious contradiction from another sort of temperament that is not as bad but commits the same errors of reasoning. This is the spirit of contention, which is still a fault that substantially injures the mind.

It is not that we can generally condemn disputes. On the contrary, we can say that provided they are used properly, nothing is better for giving us an opportunity either to find the truth or to convince others of it. The activity of a mind that is completely absorbed in investigating some matter is [270] usually too cold and too languid. It needs a certain ardor to excite it and awaken its ideas. When people take different positions against us we discover where the difficulties in persuading them and the obscurity lie, which prompt us to make the effort to overcome them.

But it is true that as helpful as this exercise is when we use it properly and with complete detachment, it is just as dangerous when it is used badly and when we invest our reputations in maintaining our views at any price and contradicting the views of others. Nothing is more likely to distance us from the truth and lead us astray than this sort of temperament. Without realizing it, we get used to finding reasons for everything and putting ourselves above arguments by never surrendering to them. Little by little this leads us to take nothing for certain, and to confuse truth with error, viewing both as equally probable. This is why it is so rare for an issue to be settled by argument, and it almost never happens that two philosophers end up agreeing. We find them always starting over and defending themselves, because their goal is not to avoid error, but to avoid silence. They think it is less shameful to remain in error than to admit they are mistaken.

Thus unless we are accustomed by long experience to having perfect control over ourselves, it is very difficult not to lose sight of the truth in these disputes, because there is practically no action that provokes greater passion in us. What vice do they not awaken in us, says a famous author,[10] since they are almost always

---

[9] Pascal, *Pensées*, no. 63, *Pensées and the Provincial Letters*, p. 20. See also *Entretien avec M. de Saci*, *Œuvres Complètes*, pp. 291–7, esp. pp. 293–5.

[10] Montaigne, *Essays*, Bk. III, ch. 8, *Complete Works*, p. 706. In general the authors of the *Logic* take some liberties in citing Montaigne as they do here, but they never go so far as to falsify the citations.

governed by anger? We become hostile first to reasons, then to persons. We learn to argue only for the sake of contradicting, and since each person both contradicts and is contradicted, the upshot of the dispute is to annihilate the truth. One person goes to the east, the other to the west. They lose the main point and get lost in a multitude of details. After an hour of stormy debate they no longer know what they are looking for. One is below, another above, and another to the side. One latches onto a word or a comparison, the other does not listen and no longer hears the opposing view. One is so committed to a line of argument that they think only of following it and not you. There are some people who, aware of their weakness, fear and reject everything, and confuse the discussion from the beginning. Or else they rebel in silence in the middle of the debate, affecting a contemptuous pride or the absurd modesty [271] of avoiding contention. As long as they are attacking they do not care how they look to others. Others count their words carefully and weigh them as arguments. Still others take advantage of their voice and lungs. Some even argue against themselves, and others weary and daze everyone with introductions and useless digressions. Finally, there are some who arm themselves with injuries and who quarrel pointlessly in order to avoid confronting a mind that is too powerful for them. These are the common vices of our disputes, which are rather ingeniously represented by this writer who, never having known the authentic greatness in people, knew their faults well enough. We can judge from this how liable these sorts of encounters are to disorder the mind, unless we are extremely careful not only not to be the first to leave the straight and narrow, but also not to follow others who do. We should also govern ourselves in such a way that we can watch them stray without going astray ourselves, and without wandering from the goal we ought to set for ourselves, which is to be enlightened by the truth we are investigating.

VIII

There are persons, primarily among those who haunt the court, who, recognizing quite clearly how inconvenient and unpleasant this contradictory mentality is, go to the other extreme, which is never to contradict anything and to praise and approve of everything equally. This is called complacency, which is a temperament more suitable for success, but just as damaging to our judgment. For just as contradictory people take the contrary of whatever is said to them to be true, complacent people seem to take everything said to them to be true. This habit first corrupts their speech and then their minds.

This is why praise has become so common and is given so indifferently to everyone that we no longer know what to make of it. There is no preacher described in the *Gazette* who is not the most eloquent and who does not delight his listeners by the profundity of his knowledge. Everyone who dies is renowned for piety; the least important authors could publish books of the eulogies they receive from their friends. Given this profusion of praise which is made so indiscriminately, it is amazing that there are still persons who desire it so greatly that they treasure the praises they receive. [272]

It is impossible for this confusion in language not to produce the same confusion in the mind, and for those who are used to praising everything to become used to approving of everything as well. But if falsity existed only in words and not in the mind, this would be enough to make those who sincerely love the truth distance themselves from it. It is not necessary to criticize all the evil one sees, but it is necessary to praise only what is truly praiseworthy. Otherwise we create illusions in the people we praise this way, we mislead those who judge these persons by this praise, and we harm people who deserve genuine praise by making it common to those who do not deserve it. Finally, we destroy all the fidelity of language, and we muddle our ideas of words, so that they are no longer signs of our judgments and thoughts, but merely signs of the outward civility we want to show toward those we are praising, as if it were a form of reverence. For this is all we ought to conclude from everyday praise and compliments.

IX

Among the different ways in which self-love leads us into error, or rather entrenches us in it and prevents us from getting out of it, we must not forget one that is probably among the principal and most common ones. This is our commitment to maintain some opinion to which we are attached by considerations other than the truth. For this goal of defending our opinions causes us to stop considering whether our reasons are true or false, and to consider only whether they are useful for convincing others of what we believe. We use all sorts of arguments, good and bad, in order to have one for everybody. And we sometimes go so far as to say things we know are absolutely false, as long as they serve the end we have in view. Here are some examples.

An intelligent person would never suspect Montaigne of having believed all the fantasies of judicial astrology. When he needs them to degrade mankind foolishly, however, he uses them as good reasons: "When we consider," he says, "the dominion and power these bodies have, not only on our lives and the state of our fortunes, but even on our inclinations that are governed, moved, and agitated thanks to these influences, why should we deprive them of a soul, of life, and of speech?"[11] [273]

Would he destroy the advantage of communication through language which humans have over beasts? He tells ridiculous stories, whose extravagance he recognizes better than anyone, and he draws even more ridiculous conclusions from them. "Some people," he says, "boast of understanding the language of beasts, such as Apollonius, Thyaneus, Melampus, Tiresias, Thales, and others.

---

[11]   Ibid., Bk. II, ch. 12, *Complete Works*, pp. 329–30. The citation appears to have been "arranged."

Since it is true, as the cosmographers say, that there are nations that accept a dog as their king, they must interpret his voice and movements a certain way."[12]

By the same reasoning we will infer that when Caligula made his horse a Consul, others must have understood the orders it gave in exercising this charge. But we would be wrong to accuse Montaigne of this bad inference. He has no intention of speaking reasonably, but only of creating a confused mass of everything that might be said against mankind. This is, nevertheless, a vice quite contrary to the mental accuracy and sincerity of a good person.

Likewise, who would put up with this other argument by the same author on the subject of the omens pagans derived from the flight of birds, which the wisest among them mocked: "Of all the predictions of times past," he says,

> the most ancient and the most certain were those derived from the flight of birds.
> We have nothing similar nor as admirable. That regularity, that order in flapping
> their wings, by which people make inferences about things to come, must be
> directed by some excellent means to so noble an operation. For it is insufficient
> to attribute this great effect to some natural ordinance, without the intelligence,
> the consent, and the discourse that produces it, and this is an obviously false
> view.[13]

Is it not rather amusing to see someone who thinks nothing is evidently true or evidently false, in a treatise intentionally written to establish Pyrrhonism and to destroy evidence and certitude, seriously recite these fantasies as certain truths and treat the contrary opinion as evidently false? But he mocks us when he speaks this way. It is inexcusable to play this way with his readers, telling them things he does not believe and only a fool could believe.

It was doubtless a philosopher as good as Virgil who did not attribute to whatever intelligence is found in birds the regular changes we see in their motions, according to different air currents, from which conjectures can be made about [274] rain and good weather, as can be seen in these admirable verses in the *Georgics*:

> *Non equidem credo quia sit divinitùs illis*
> *Ingenium, aut rerum fato prudentia major;*
> *Verùm ubi tempestas et coeli mobilis humor*
> *Mutavere vias, et Jupiter humidus austris*
> *Densat erant quae rara modò, et quae densa relaxat;*
> *Vertuntur species animorum, ut corpora motus*
> *Nunc hos, nunc alios: dum nubila ventus agebat,*
> *Concipiant, hinc ille avium concentus in agris,*
> *Et laetae pecudes, et ovantes gutture corvi.*[14]
> [Not, methinks, that they have wisdom from on high,
> or from Fate a larger foreknowledge of things to be;

---

[12] Ibid., p. 331.
[13] Ibid., p. 344.
[14] 1.415–23, *Virgil*, vol. 1, p. 109.

but that when the weather and fitful vapors of the sky
have turned their course, and Jove, wet with the south winds,
thickens what just now was rare, and makes rare what now was thick,
the phases of their minds change, and their breasts now conceive impulses,
other than they felt, when the wind was chasing the clouds.
Hence that chorus of the birds in the fields, the gladness of the
cattle, and the exulting cries of the rooks.]

But when these deviations are willful, we need only a little good faith to avoid them. The most common and the most dangerous are those we do not recognize, because our commitment to defend an opinion disturbs the mind's perspective and makes us take as true everything serving this end. The only remedy for this is to take as our goal only the truth, and to examine the arguments so carefully that this commitment itself cannot mislead us.

Fallacious arguments arising from the objects themselves
We previously remarked that it is not necessary to separate the internal causes of our errors from those that originate in the objects, which we may call external, because the false appearances of these objects could not lead us into error if the will did not push the mind to make a hasty judgment when it is not yet sufficiently enlightened.

But because the will also cannot exercise this power over the understanding in matters that are completely evident, it is clear that the obscurity of objects contributes greatly to errors. There are even occasions when the passion that leads us to reason badly is almost imperceptible. This is why it is useful to consider separately these illusions arising principally from the things themselves.

I

It is a false and impious opinion that truth is so similar to falsehood and virtue so similar to vice that it is impossible to tell them apart. But it is true that in most matters there is a mixture of error and truth, vice and virtue, perfection and imperfection, and this mixture is one of the most common sources of our false judgments. [275]

Because of this misleading mixture the good qualities of people we admire lead us to approve of their faults, and the faults of those we do not admire make us condemn what is good in them. For we do not consider that even the most imperfect people are not completely imperfect, and that God leaves imperfections even in the most virtuous. Since these imperfections are the remnants of human infirmity, they ought not be the objects of imitation or esteem.

The reason is that since people hardly ever consider matters in detail, they judge only according to their strongest impression and feel only what is most striking. So whenever they are aware that a speech contains a great many truths, they do not notice the errors mixed in among them. On the contrary, if there are truths mixed in among many errors, they pay attention only to the errors, the strong prevailing over the weak, the more vivid impression stifling the more obscure.

It is, however, manifestly wrong to judge this way: there can be no good reason for rejecting reason. The truth is no less the truth for being mixed in with lies. The truth never belongs to people, although they assert it. So although people deserve to be condemned for their lies, the truths they advance do not deserve condemnation.

This is why justice and reason require that in everything containing a mixture of good and evil we distinguish them. Exactness of mind is particularly apparent in this judicious separation. This is how the Church fathers took excellent points on morality from books written by pagans, and how St. Augustine had no difficulty borrowing seven rules for understanding the Scripture from a Donatist heretic.

This is what reason obliges us to do whenever we can make this distinction. But because we do not always have time to examine the good and evil in each matter in detail, it is right on these occasions to give them the label they deserve according to the more substantial part. Hence we ought to say that people are good philosophers when they usually reason well, and that a book is good whenever there is noticeably more good than bad in it.

Again, this is what frequently misleads people in their judgments. For they often admire or condemn things only according to what is less important in them, since their lack of insight keeps them from grasping [276] the main idea whenever it is not the most obvious.

So although those who are knowledgeable about painting value the design infinitely more than the color or delicacy of line, the ignorant are more affected by a canvas whose colors are vivid and dazzling than by a more somber one whose design would be admirable.

We must admit, however, that false judgments are not so common in the arts, because those who know nothing about them defer more readily to the views of more informed people. But they are much more frequent in matters such as eloquence, which are within everyone's jurisdiction, and about which the world takes the liberty of judging.

Preachers are called eloquent, for example, whenever their phrases are exact and when they use no inappropriate words. On this basis de Vaugelas said in one place that a bad word does more harm to a preacher or an attorney than a bad inference.[15] We ought to believe that this is a factual truth he is reporting and not an opinion he is defending. Indeed there are people who judge this way, but it is also true that nothing is less reasonable than these judgments. For the purity of language and the number of figures are to eloquence as color is to painting, that is, they are only the lowest and most material part. But the important point is to form powerful conceptions and to express them in such a way that we evoke in our listeners' minds a vivid and luminous image that does not just present the

---

[15]   Claude Favre, Baron of Peroges, Lord of Vaugelas (1585–1650), author of *Remarques sur la langue française* (Paris, 1647).

bare idea of these things, but also expresses the emotions we feel for them. This can happen with people who speak imprecisely, using few elegant figures. It is rarely encountered in those who pay too much attention to words and embellishments, because their view distracts them from things and diminishes the vigor of their thought. Painters remark, similarly, that artists who excel in colors do not usually excel in design, since the mind is not capable of this double attention, one aspect detracting from the other.

We can generally say that most things in the world are admired only externally, because hardly anyone penetrates to the core and the foundation of things. Everything is judged by appearances, and woe to those who do not have a favorable appearance. They may be as clever, intelligent, and solid as you like, but if they do not speak fluently and do not handle a compliment [277] well, let them be resigned to being little admired all their lives by the common folk, and to seeing countless petty minds preferred to them. It is not a great evil not to have the reputation one deserves. But it is a considerable evil to follow false judgments and to view things only by their outer shell. This is what we ought to try to avoid.

II

Among the causes that lead us into error by a false brilliance that prevents us from recognizing it, we ought to put a certain pompous and magnificent eloquence, which Cicero calls *abundantem sonantibus verbis uberibusque sententiis* [full of resonant words and copious sentences]. For it is strange how a fallacious inference can slide gently by us following a phrase that is pleasing to the ear or a figure that is startling and delightful to consider.

Not only do these flourishes rob us of our view of the falsehoods mixed in with speech, but they entice us into them insensibly, because they are often necessary to make the phrase or the figure precise. Thus when we see orators beginning a long peroration or an antithesis of several members, we are right to be on guard, because it is rare for them to emerge from it without twisting the truth to some extent for the sake of the figure. They usually use truth as one would use rocks to make a building or metal to make a statue: they size it, extend it, shorten it, and disguise it as needed to fit it into the vain works they want to create out of words.[16]

How many false thoughts have been produced from the desire to make a point? How often has rhyme tempted us to lie? How often has the affectation to use Cicero's words, which is called pure Latinity, made certain Italian authors write idiocies? Who would not laugh to hear Bembo say that a Pope was elected by the favor of the immortal gods, *Deorum immortalium beneficiis?*[17] There are even poets

---

[16] Pascal, *Pensées*, no. 27, *Pensées and the Provincial Letters*, p. 11.

[17] Pietro Bembo (1470–1547), secretary to Pope Leo X and later a cardinal, was the author of many Latin poems, sonnets, and letters. He published editions of Petrarch's lyrics and Dante's *Divine Comedy*. His most famous works were *De Imitatione* (1513), a manifesto for Ciceronian humanism, and the *Rime* (*Rhymes*, 1530).

who imagine that it is the essence of poetry to introduce pagan divinities. A German poet, as good a versifier as he is an injudicious writer, who was rightly criticized by Francis Pico della Mirandola[18] for putting all the pagan divinities into a poem where he describes the wars of Christians against Christians, [278] and for mixing Apollo, Diana, and Mercury in with the Pope, the Electors, and the Emperor, maintains flatly that without this he would not have been a poet. To prove this he offers the bizarre reason that the verses of Hesiod, Homer, and Virgil are filled with the names and stories of these gods, from which he concludes that he is permitted to do the same.

These bad inferences are often imperceptible to those who make them, and mislead them first of all. They are stunned by the sound of their words and dazzled by the brilliance of their figures. The magnificence of certain words draws them, without their realizing it, to thoughts that are so unsound that they would doubtless reject them if they reflected on them even a little.

It is easy to believe, for example, that it was the word "vestal" which charmed a contemporary author, moving him to tell a lady, to prevent her from being ashamed for knowing Latin, that she should not blush to speak a language that the vestal virgins spoke. For if he had thought about it, he would have seen that it would have been just as reasonable to tell her that she ought to blush to speak a language that was previously spoken by the courtesans of Rome, who were clearly more numerous than the vestal virgins, or that she ought to blush to speak another language than that of her country, since the ancient vestals spoke only their natural language. All these arguments, which are completely worthless, are as good as that author's. The truth is that the vestal virgins can no more be used to justify than to condemn girls who learn Latin.

Fallacious arguments of this sort, which are so often encountered in the writings of those who affect the most eloquence, show how most people who speak or write need to be thoroughly convinced of this excellent rule: Nothing is more beautiful than the truth. This would remove countless useless flourishes and false thoughts from their speech. Now it is true that precision makes the style drier and less pompous. But it also makes it livelier, more serious, clearer, and more worthy of an honest person. The impression it makes is stronger and lasts much longer, whereas the impression that arises merely from these heavily labored phrases is so superficial that it vanishes almost as soon as we have heard them. [279]

III

It is a very common fault among people to judge others' actions and intentions rashly. People almost always make this mistake by a bad inference in which, not knowing distinctly enough all the causes that might produce some effect, they attribute this effect to one specific cause when it could have been produced by

---

[18] A mystical philosopher and the nephew of the Italian humanist Giovanni Pico della Mirandola.

several others. Or else they suppose that a cause that accidentally had a certain effect on one occasion, when it was combined with certain circumstances, must have it all the time.

Suppose a writer is found agreeing with a heretic on a point of criticism that is independent of any religious controversy. A malevolent adversary will infer from this that the writer has an inclination for heretics, but this is rash and malicious, because his view might be based on reason and truth.

A writer will speak forcefully against an opinion he thinks dangerous. Based on this he will be accused of hatred and animosity against the authors who advanced it. But this would be unjust and reckless, since his vigor might arise as much from zeal for the truth as from hatred for others.

Someone is a friend of a wicked person. So, another infers, the former's interests are tied up with the latter's, and he participates in his crimes. This does not follow. Perhaps he does not know about them, and perhaps he has nothing to do with them.

Someone fails to render some civility to those to whom it is owed. This person is, they say, proud and insolent. But it might be only an oversight or simple forgetfulness.[e]

All these external things are only equivocal signs, that is, signs that could signify several things, and it is judging rashly to determine such a sign to be a sign of a particular thing without having a specific reason. [280] Silence is sometimes a sign of modesty and judgment, and sometimes a sign of stupidity. Slowness sometimes indicates prudence and sometimes dullness. Change is sometimes a sign of inconstancy and sometimes sincerity. So it is bad reasoning to conclude that a person is inconstant merely because he changed his mind, for he might have a good reason for changing it.

IV

Faulty inductions in which general propositions are derived from several particular instances are one of the most common sources of people's fallacious reasoning. They need only three or four examples to form a maxim or a platitude, which they then use as a principle for judging everything.

Many diseases are hidden from the most competent doctors, and often their remedies do not work. Hasty minds conclude from this that medicine is absolutely useless, and that it is a profession of charlatans.

There are flighty and fickle women. This is enough for jealous persons to

---

[e]   ... forgetfulness.
    Some persons do not share the opinions of someone else. He concludes from this that they are stubborn, that they betray their consciences, that they are cowardly, interested, vain, and presumptuous. All these judgments are manifestly unfair, for perhaps these persons are right not to share his view because it is false. Or if it is true, perhaps it is only a simple lack of insight and not any bad motive which prevents them from embracing it. – All these ... (I)

suspect the most honest women unjustly, and for licentious writers to condemn all of them generally.

Frequently people hide great vices behind an appearance of piety. Libertines conclude from this that all devotion is only hypocrisy.

Some matters are obscure and hidden, and people often make great mistakes. Everything is obscure and uncertain, say the ancient and modern Pyrrhonists, and we can know the truth about nothing with certainty.

There is inequality in some of our actions. This is enough to form a truism from which no one is excepted:[f] "Reason," they say, "is so weak and so blind, that there is nothing so clear that it is clear enough for it, the easy and the hard are all the same to it. All subjects equally, and nature in [281] general, disavow its jurisdiction. We think of what we want only at the instant we will it; we will nothing freely, nothing absolutely, nothing constantly."

Most people can describe others' defects or good qualities only by general and excessive propositions. From some particular actions they infer habits; they make a custom out of three or four faults. What happens once a month or once a year happens every day, every hour, every moment in people's speech, given the little care they take to keep their words within the limits of truth and justice.

V

It is a weakness and an injustice, often condemned but rarely avoided, to judge decisions by events, and to hold people who make a prudent resolution, from the point of view of foreseeable circumstances, responsible for all the bad consequences that ensue, either merely by chance, or from the malice of those who obstructed it, or from some other incident they could not have foreseen. Not only do people love being happy as much as they love being wise, they make no distinction between happiness and wisdom, nor between misfortune and guilt. This distinction appears too subtle for them. People are ingenious in identifying the faults that, they assume, explain failure. Just as astrologers who know of a certain happening never fail to find the aspect of the stars that produced it, people likewise never fail to find that those who fall into disgrace and unhappiness deserve it for some imprudence. Some people were not successful; therefore they were wrong. This is how people reason in the world, and how they have always reasoned, because there has always been little fairness in their judgments.[g] Not knowing the true causes of things, they substitute others for them according to events, praising those who succeed and blaming those who do not. [282]

[f]   ... excepted. It is only inconstancy, they say, only instability in human conduct, even in the wisest. "We think of ... constantly." There are philosophers who are hardly religious. All philosophers are libertines and impious, say some rash and indiscreet persons. – Most people ... (I)

[g]   ... judgments.

   V. – Passion is more a general source of bad reasoning than a particular way of reasoning badly. Nevertheless, we can relate to it certain false judgments that seem to result merely from passion itself, without the intermediary of any other error ... (I) Here follows the important passage moved in II to the first part of chapter 19.

VI

But no fallacies are more frequent than those people commit, either by judging the truth of things hastily based on some authority insufficient to assure us of it, or by deciding what is essential to something by appearances. We call the first the sophism of authority,[19] and the second the sophism of manner.

To understand how common they are, we only have to consider that most people are determined to believe one opinion rather than another, not by the sound and essential reasons which make the truth known to us, but by certain external and alien marks that are more fitting – or that they think are more fitting – to truth than to falsity.

The reasons are that the internal truth of things is often fairly well hidden, and that our minds are usually weak and obscure, full of clouds and shadows, whereas these external marks are clear and visible. This being the case, since people are readily led to do what is easiest, they almost always support the view where they see these external marks that are easily discernible.

These marks can be reduced to two main kinds: the authority of whoever presents something, and the manner in which it is presented. These two ways of persuading are so powerful that they influence almost everyone.

For this reason God, who wanted the simplest among the faithful to be able to acquire certain knowledge of the mysteries of faith, was benevolent in accommodating himself to this weakness in people's minds, by not making them depend on a particular examination of all the points presented for our belief. Instead, he gave us as a certain rule of the truth, the authority of the universal Church which presents these points to us and which, being clear and evident, removes from the mind all the perplexity arising from particular discussions of these mysteries.

Thus in matters of faith the authority of the universal Church is entirely decisive. Far from being an occasion for error, we fall into error only when we depart from her authority and refuse to submit to it.

Convincing arguments about religious matters are also derived from the manner in which they are presented. Throughout various centuries of Church history, and primarily in the [283] last, when people were seen trying to instill their views by bloodshed and the sword; when they were seen raising arms in schism against the Church and in revolt against temporal powers; when people without the customary divine orders, without miracles, without any external marks of piety, and instead, visibly disordered, were seen undertaking to change the faith and discipline of the Church: such criminal manners were more than enough to make all reasonable persons reject them and to prevent the crudest from listening to them.

But in matters where knowledge is not absolutely necessary and God has left more to the rational discernment of each individual, authority and manner are not

---

[19] Pascal, *Preface to the Treatise on the Vacuum, Pascal, Selections*, pp. 62–6.

so important. They often function to lead some people into judgments contrary to the truth.

We will not attempt to give rules and precise limits here for the deference owed to authority in human affairs, but only to indicate several gross errors people commit in these matters.

People often consider only the number of witnesses, without thinking about whether the number makes it more probable that they have discovered the truth. This is not reasonable. As a modern author has wisely observed, in difficult matters where each person has to find his own way, it is more likely that a single individual will find the truth than that several will discover it.[20] Thus it is not a good inference to argue: Such-and-such an opinion is accepted by the majority of philosophers, therefore it is the truest.

People are often persuaded by certain qualities that are irrelevant to the truth of the issue being discussed. Thus there are a number of people who unquestioningly believe those who are the oldest and more experienced, even in matters that depend neither on age nor experience, but only on mental insight.

Piety, wisdom, and moderation are probably the qualities most admired in the world, and they ought to give more authority to people who possess them in matters that depend on piety, sincerity, and even on divine illumination, which God most likely communicates best to those who serve him most purely. But there are countless matters that depend only on human insight, human experience, and human discernment. [284] In these matters those who have the advantage of intellect and study are more deserving of belief than others. The contrary often happens, however, and some people think that in these matters it is safer to follow the opinion of the greatest number of good people.

This is due in part to the fact that these mental advantages are not as visible as the external discipline apparent in pious people, and in part also to the fact that people simply do not like to make distinctions. Discriminations confuse them; they want things to be all or nothing. If they give credence to one person on some topic, they believe him in everything. If they do not on another, they believe him in nothing. They like short, decisive, abbreviated ways. But this temperament, however common, is no less contrary to reason, which shows us that the same people are not believable all the time because they are not eminent in all matters. So it is bad reasoning to infer: This is a serious person, who is therefore intelligent and competent in everything.

VII

It is true that if there are pardonable errors, they are those that lead people to defer more than they should to the opinions of those deemed to be good people. But there is an illusion much more absurd in itself, although quite common, which is to

---

[20] Descartes, *Discourse on the Method*, Pt. II, *Philosophical Writings*, vol. 1, pp. 116–17.

believe that people speak the truth because they are of noble birth or wealthy or in high office.

Not that people explicitly reason as follows: They have an income of a hundred thousand pounds, therefore they are right; they come from a noble lineage, therefore we ought to believe what they claim to be true; they are without wealth, therefore they are wrong. Nevertheless something similar occurs in the minds of most people, that influences their judgment without their realizing it.

Let the same view be presented by a noble person and a nobody; people will often accept it in the mouth of the person of distinction while not even deigning to listen to the person of lowly estate. Scripture tries to teach us about this human temperament, by portraying it perfectly in the book of Ecclesiasticus: If the rich speak, it says, all the world is silent and praises their [285] words to the skies. If the poor speak, people ask who is that person? *Dives locutus est, et omnes tacuerunt, et verbum illius usque ad nubes perducent: pauper locutus est, et dicunt: Quis est hic?*[21]

It is certain that complacency and flattery play a significant role in the approval given to the actions and words of the nobility. These people also often attract approval by a certain outward grace and manner of acting nobly, freely, and naturally, which is sometimes so distinctive that it is almost inimitable by persons of lowly birth. But it is also certain that there are many persons who approve everything the great do and say by internally abasing their minds, which fold under the weight of grandeur and do not have a firm enough view to stand up under brilliance. The external pomp that surrounds the great always imposes a little on others and makes an impression even on the strongest souls.

The reason for this deception comes from the corruption in people's hearts, for, given their fervent passion for honor and pleasure, they necessarily become enamored of wealth and other qualities by which these honors and pleasures are obtained. Now the love people have for anything the world admires makes them judge their owners to be happy, and in judging them happy people look up to them and consider them as eminent and exalted. This habit of viewing them with respect passes imperceptibly from their fortunes to their minds. We do not ordinarily do things by half. So we think they have souls as elevated as their rank and we defer to their opinions. This is the reason for the credibility they usually acquire in the matters they discuss.

But this illusion is even stronger among the nobility themselves than in their inferiors, for the nobility take no pains to correct the impression their fortunes naturally leave in their minds. Few persons do not take their estate and wealth for reasons, and do not claim that their opinions ought to prevail over those of their inferiors. They cannot allow those they view with contempt to claim to have as much judgment and reason as they have. This is what makes them so impatient with the slightest contradiction.

---

[21] Ecclesiasticus 13:23.

All this arises, again, from the same source, namely the false ideas of their grandeur, nobility, and wealth. Rather than considering these as things [286] entirely foreign to their being, which do not prevent them from being perfectly equal to the rest of humanity in terms of body and soul, and from having a judgment as weak and capable of error as everyone else, they in some way incorporate into their essence all these qualities of greatness, nobility, wealth, mastery, of a lord, or of a prince. They exaggerate their ideas of themselves, and never think of themselves without all their titles, all their trappings, and all their retinue.

They are accustomed from childhood to seeing themselves as a species set off from others. They never imagine themselves mixed in with the crowd of humanity. They are always counts or dukes in their own eyes and never simply people. Thus they fashion souls and judgment for themselves according to the size of their fortunes,[h] and believe that they are as elevated above others in mind as in status and fortune.

The stupidity of the human mind is such that there is nothing they will not use to aggrandize their ideas of themselves. A beautiful house, magnificent clothes, a full beard make them think themselves more clever. And there are few who do not consider themselves better on horseback or in a carriage than on foot. It is easy to convince everyone that nothing is more ridiculous than these judgments, but it is very difficult to safeguard ourselves completely from the secret impression all these external things make on the mind. All we can do is to accustom ourselves as much as possible to giving no authority to any of the qualities that contribute nothing to discovering the truth, and to giving none even to those that do contribute to it, except insofar as they actually have some effect. Age, knowledge, study, experience, intellect, energy, discipline, precision, and work are useful for finding the truth in hidden things. So these qualities deserve our consideration. But we must, however, weigh them with care, and compare them later with opposing reasons. For from each of these items in particular, nothing can be concluded with certainty, since some quite false opinions have been accepted by persons of very sound intellect who have a good number of these qualities. [287]

VIII

There is something even more misleading in the mistaken inferences that arise from appearances. For we are naturally led to believe that people are right when they speak with grace, fluency, seriousness, moderation, and gentleness, and to believe, by contrast, that they are wrong whenever they speak disagreeably or when they allow anger, bitterness, or presumption to appear in their actions and words.[i]

If we judge the fundamentals only by these external and visible appearances,

---

h   ... their fortunes. This is what Scripture tries to indicate to us in these words: *Facultates et virtutes exaltant cor*, wealth and power raise the soul in its own eyes, and make it consider itself greater. – The stupidity ... (I)

i   ... words, since it is difficult to recognize a truth surrounded by so many marks of falsehood, and to reject a falsehood covered by the natural colors of the truth. – If we ... (I) however, it is impossible not to be frequently mistaken. For there are persons who seriously and modestly spread idiocies, and others by contrast who, being naturally quick or even possessed of some passion apparent in their expression and words, nonetheless have truth on their side. There are very mediocre and superficial minds who, because they were educated at court, where the art of pleasing is studied and practiced better than anywhere else, have quite pleasant manners that make many of their false judgments acceptable. Others, by contrast, lack polish altogether, but still have fundamentally a large and sound mind. Some speak better than they think, and others think better than they speak. Hence reason dictates that people who can do so should not judge by these externals and should not fail to surrender themselves to the truth, not only when it is presented in an offensive and disagreeable manner, but even when it is mixed in with a number of falsehoods. For the same person may speak truly on one topic and falsely on another; someone may be right on this point and wrong on that one.

Therefore we have to consider each item separately, that is, we must judge appearances by appearances and the essentials by the essentials, and not the essentials by appearances nor appearances by the essentials. A person is wrong to speak with anger, and right to tell the truth; by contrast someone else is right to speak calmly and civilly, and wrong to assert falsehoods.

But since it is reasonable to be on guard not to conclude that something is true or false because it is presented in such-and-such a way, it is also right for those [288] who want to persuade others of some truth to study how to clothe it in favorable appearances that are suitable for making it accepted, and to avoid odious appearances that can only repel others.

They should remember that when it is a question of persuading people of something, it is a small thing merely to be right, and it is a great misfortune merely to be right and to lack what is required to make reason appetizing.

If they seriously honor the truth, they should not dishonor it by covering it with marks of falsity and lies. If they love it sincerely, they should not attract people's hatred and aversion to it by presenting it in an offensive manner. This is the greatest precept of rhetoric, which is all the more useful since it serves to rule the soul as well as our words. For even though being wrong in presentation and being wrong in essence are two different things, mistakes in presentation are nevertheless often worse and more important than essential mistakes.

Actually, all of these proud, presumptuous, bitter, opinionated, and angry manners always spring from some mental disorder that is often more serious than the defect of intelligence or insight we criticize in others. Moreover, it is always unjust to want to persuade people this way. For it is clearly right to surrender to the truth when we know it, but it is wrong to demand others to take as true everything we believe and to defer merely to our authority. And nevertheless this is what people do when they present the truth in these offensive ways. For the way in which a speech is made usually enters the mind before the reasons, since the mind is quicker to recognize appearances than to understand the soundness of the proofs, which it often does not understand at all. Now when the impression of a speech is separated from the evidence in this way, it indicates only the authority the speaker attributes to himself. Accordingly, people who are bitter and imperious necessarily antagonize others' minds because it appears they want to win by authority and a kind of tyranny what should be earned only by persuasion and reason.

The injustice is even worse if someone tries to use these offensive ways of arguing to refute common and received opinions. One individual's argument could easily be preferred to those of several others whenever it is more sound, [289] but an individual should never claim that his authority ought to prevail over the authority of all the others.

Thus not only modesty and prudence, but justice itself requires us to take on a muted air when we argue against common opinion or accepted authority, because otherwise we cannot avoid unjustly opposing an individual's authority to a public authority or to one that is greater and better established. We cannot show too much moderation when it is a question of disturbing the grip of a received opinion or a belief acquired from long ago. This is so true that St. Augustine extends it even to truths of religion, giving this excellent rule to all those who are obliged to instruct others.

"Here is the way," he says, "wise and religious Catholics teach what they ought to teach others: if they are common and authorized matters, they present them in a manner full of assurance which testifies to no doubts, accompanying them with all the gentleness they can. But if they are extraordinary matters, although they know the truth very clearly, they present them more as doubts and questions to be examined than as dogmas and decided opinions, in order to accommodate the weakness of their listeners."[22] If a truth is so lofty that it surpasses the powers of their audience, they prefer to retain it for a while, to give them a chance to grow and make themselves capable of it, rather than to reveal it to them in their state of weakness where it would only overwhelm them. [291]

[22] This passage has not been identified.

Fourth part of the logic
On Method

It remains to explain the last part of logic, concerning method, which is doubtless one of the most useful and important parts. We thought we ought to add this to the discussion of demonstrations, because usually a demonstration consists not of a single argument, but of a series of several inferences by which some truth is conclusively proved; and because, to demonstrate things well, there is little value in knowing the rules of syllogism, which knowledge we rarely lack. But the whole point is to order our thoughts well, using those that are clear and evident to get to the bottom of what appears more obscure.[a]

Since the aim of demonstration is scientific knowledge, it is necessary first to say something about that.

CHAPTER 1

On scientific knowledge. That there is such a thing. That the things known by
the mind are more certain than whatever is known by the senses. That there
are things the human mind is incapable of knowing. The utility we can derive
from this necessary ignorance

Whenever we consider some maxim, if we recognize its truth in itself and by the evidence we perceive in it that convinces us without any other reason, this sort of knowledge [292] is called intelligence. This is how we know first principles.

But if the maxim is not convincing in itself, we need some other motive for surrendering to it. This motive is either authority or reason. If authority makes the mind embrace what is presented to it, it is called faith. If it is reason, then there are two possibilities: either reason does not produce complete conviction, but still leaves some doubt; mental acquiescence accompanied by doubt is called opinion.

Or, if reason convinces us completely, then either this reason is clear only apparently and from lack of attention, and the persuasion it produces is an error if the reason is in fact false; or it is at least a hasty judgment if, although the reason is true in itself, it is still not good enough for us to believe it to be true.

But if the reason is not merely apparent but cogent and reliable, which is recognized by longer and more exact attention, firmer persuasion, and the quality of the clarity, which is livelier and more penetrating, then the conviction this reason produces is called scientific knowledge. Various questions have been raised about it.

The first is whether there is such a thing, that is, whether we have knowledge

---

[a] ... obscure. Now, properly speaking, this is what true method is useful for. – CHAPTER ... (I)

based on clear and certain reasons, or generally, whether we have clear and certain knowledge. This question concerns the understanding as much as science.

There have been philosophers who professed to deny it, and who even established their entire philosophy on this foundation. Among these philosophers, some are satisfied with rejecting certainty while admitting probability. These are the new Academicians. The others, who are Pyrrhonists, reject even probability and claim that everything is equally obscure and uncertain.

But the truth is that all these opinions that have made such a splash in the world have never been alive except in speeches, debates, and writings, and that no one was ever seriously convinced of them. They were games and amusements for idle and clever people. But they were never views that they inwardly endorsed and on which they tried to act. This is why the best way to convince these philosophers is to recall them to their consciences and good faith, and to ask them, after all the speeches in which they tried to show that sleeping could not be distinguished from waking, or madness from sanity, if they were not persuaded despite [293] all these arguments that they were not sleeping and that they were of sound mind. If they were at all sincere, they would reject all their useless subtleties, frankly admitting that they could not believe any of these things when they tried to do so.

If there were people able to doubt that they were not sleeping or were not mad, or who could even believe that the existence of everything external was uncertain, and that it is doubtful whether there is a sun, a moon, or matter, at least no one could doubt, as St. Augustine says, that one exists, that one is thinking, or that one is alive.[1] For whether one is sleeping or awake, whether one's mind is healthy or sick, whether one is mistaken or not, it is certain at least that since one is thinking, one exists and is alive. For it is impossible to separate being and life from thought, and to believe that what thinks does not exist and is not alive. From this clear, certain, and indubitable knowledge one can form a rule for accepting as true all thoughts found to be as clear as this one appears to be.

Likewise it is impossible to doubt one's perceptions, separating them from their objects. Whether there is or is not a sun or an earth, I am certain that I imagine seeing one. I am certain that I am doubting when I doubt, that I believe I am seeing when I believe I am seeing, that I believe I am hearing when I believe I am hearing, and so on. So confining ourselves to the mind alone, and considering what takes place there, we will find countless clear instances of knowledge that is impossible to doubt.

This consideration can help us settle another issue raised on this subject, namely whether the things we know only by the mind are more or less certain than those known by the senses. For it is clear from what we have just said, that we are more sure of our perceptions and our ideas when we see them only by mental reflection than we are of all the objects of the senses. We could even say that although the

---

[1]   There are numerous texts in St. Augustine on this point. See in particular *Soliloquies*, Bk. II, ch. I, *Basic Writings*, vol. I, p. 277; *City of God*, Bk. XI, ch. 26, *Writings*, vol. 7, pp. 228–9; *Free Will*, Bk. II, chs. 3 and 5, *The Teacher*, pp. 114, 120; *The Trinity*, Bk. X, ch. 10, *Writings*, vol. 18, p. 308.

senses are not always misleading in what they report to us, nonetheless, our certainty that they are not deceiving us comes not from the senses, but from a reflection of the mind by which we distinguish when we should and when we should not believe the senses.

This is why we must acknowledge that St. Augustine was right [294] to maintain, following Plato, that judging the truth and the rule for discerning it do not belong to the senses at all but to the mind – *Non est judicium veritatis in sensibus* [Judgment about the truth is not in the senses][2] – and even that the certainty that may be derived from the senses does not extend very far. There are several things we think we know by the senses about which we cannot say we are entirely sure.

For example, we can easily know by the senses that a particular body is larger than another body, but we cannot know with certainty what the true and natural size of each body is. To understand this, we only have to consider that if we had all seen external objects only through magnifying glasses, it is certain that we would represent bodies and all their measurements only in terms of the size in which these lenses represented them. Now our eyes themselves are lenses. We do not know at all precisely whether they diminish or enlarge the objects we see, or whether the artificial lenses that we think diminish or enlarge them do not, on the contrary, establish their true size. Consequently we cannot know with any certainty the absolute and natural size of any body.[3]

We also do not know whether we are seeing bodies the same size as other people see them, for although two persons measuring them might agree that a particular body is, for example, only five feet long, nevertheless what one person conceives by a foot may not be at all what the other one conceives. For the first one conceives what his eyes report to him, and likewise for the other. Now it could be that one person's eyes do not report the same thing as that represented by the other's eyes, because they are lenses of different sizes.

It is more likely, however, that this diversity is not great, because we see no difference in the structure of the eye that could produce such a notable change. Besides, although our eyes are lenses, still they are lenses fashioned by God's hand. So we have reason to believe that they depart from the truth of objects only because of defects that corrupt or disturb their natural shape.

Be that as it may, even if our judgments about the size of objects are uncertain in some way, it is scarcely necessary, and we must in no way conclude, that there is no more certainty in all the other reports of the senses. For even if I do not know precisely, as I said, what the absolute and natural size [295] of an elephant is, I do know, however, that it is larger than a horse and smaller than a whale, which is enough for day-to-day living.

---

[2] St. Augustine: *Veritatis judicium in sensibus corporis posuerunt (Epicuri et Stoïci)* [The Epicureans and Stoics located the judgment of truth in the bodily senses], *City of God*, Bk. VIII, ch. 7, *Writings*, vol. 7, p. 34.

[3] Malebranche, *Search After Truth*, Bk. I, ch. 6, pp. 28–30.

There is, therefore, certainty and uncertainty both in the mind and the senses. It would be equally mistaken to try to make everything pass either for certain or for uncertain.

Reason, on the contrary, obliges us to recognize three types of things.

Some things can be known clearly and certainly. Some things we do not in fact know clearly, but we can hope to come to know them. Finally, some are virtually impossible to know with certainty, either because we lack the principles to lead us to them, or because they are too disproportionate to the mind.

The first type includes everything known by demonstration or by the understanding.

The second is the object of study by philosophers. But it is easy for them to waste a lot of time on such issues if they do not know how to distinguish them from the third, that is, if they cannot distinguish things the mind can come to know from those that are beyond its grasp.

The best way to limit the scope of the sciences is never to try to inquire about anything beyond us, which we cannot reasonably hope to be able to understand. Of this type are all questions concerning God's power, which it is ridiculous to try to confine within the narrow limits of the mind, and generally anything having to do with infinity. Because the mind is finite, it gets lost in and is dazzled by infinity, and remains overwhelmed by the multitude of contrary thoughts that infinity furnishes us.

There is a very practical and simple solution for steering clear of a great number of issues that we could always debate as long as we liked, because we would never arrive at knowledge clear enough to decide them and to make up our minds. Is it possible for a creature to have been created from eternity? Could God make a body infinitely large, a motion infinitely fast, a multitude infinite in number? Is an infinite number even or odd? Is one infinity larger than another? Whoever immediately says I do not know, will have instantly made as much progress as anyone who spends twenty years reasoning [296] about these sorts of topics. The only difference between the two is that the person who tries to penetrate these issues is in danger of falling to a level even lower than simple ignorance, namely believing that one knows what one does not know.

Similarly, there are countless metaphysical questions that are too vague, too abstract, and too removed from clear and known principles ever to be resolved. The safest thing is to get rid of them as quickly as possible, and after studying cursorily how they arise, to resolve in good faith to ignore them.

Nescire quaedam magna pars sapientiae. [Some ignorance is a great part of wisdom.]

By this means, delivering ourselves from inquiries in which it is impossible to succeed, we will be able to make more progress in matters more proportional to the mind.

But we must remark that there are things that appear incomprehensible but certainly exist. We cannot conceive how they might exist, but nevertheless it is certain that they do.

What is more incomprehensible and at the same time more certain than eternity? Accordingly, people who out of a horrible blindness have destroyed the knowledge of God in their minds are obliged to attribute eternity to the most vile and contemptible of all beings, namely matter.

How to understand that the smallest bit of matter is infinitely divisible and that one can never arrive at a part that is so small that not only does it not contain several others, but it does not contain an infinity of parts; that the smallest grain of wheat contains in itself as many parts, although proportionately smaller, as the entire world; that all the shapes imaginable are actually to be found there; and that it contains in itself a tiny world with all its parts – a sun, heavens, stars, planets, and an earth – with admirably precise proportions; that there are no parts of this grain that do not contain yet another proportional world?[4] What part of this little world could correspond to the volume of a grain of wheat, and what an enormous difference must there be in order for us to say truthfully that, what a grain of wheat is with respect to the entire world, this part is with respect to a grain of wheat? Nonetheless, this part whose smallness is already incomprehensible to us, contains still another proportional world, and so on to infinity. So there is no particle of matter [297] that does not have as many proportional parts as the entire world, whatever size we give it.[5]

All these things are inconceivable, and yet they must necessarily be true, since the infinite divisibility of matter has been demonstrated. Geometry provides proofs of it as clear as proofs of any of the truths it reveals to us.

For this science shows us that there are certain lines having no common measure, that for this reason are called incommensurable, such as the diagonal of a square and its sides. Now if the diagonal and the sides were made up of a certain number of indivisible parts, one of these indivisible parts would be a measure common to these two lines. Consequently it is impossible for these two lines to be made up of a certain number of indivisible parts.

Second, this science also demonstrates that it is impossible for the square of one number to be twice the square of another number. It is quite possible, however, for the area of one square to be twice the area of another square. Now if these two square areas were composed of a certain number of finite parts, the large square would contain twice as many parts as the small one, and since both of them are squares, there would be a number whose square is twice the square of another number, which is impossible.

Finally, nothing is clearer than this reasoning, that two things having zero extension cannot form an extension, and that every extension has parts. Now taking

---

[4]   Pascal, *Pensées*, "The Disproportion of Man," no. 72, *Pensées and the Provincial Letters*, pp. 22–3.
[5]   Ibid., p. 23. "For finally what is man in nature? A non-being with respect to the infinite..."

two of these parts that are assumed to be indivisible, I ask whether they do or do not have any extension. If they have some extension, then they are divisible, and they have several parts. If they do not, they therefore have zero extension, and hence it is impossible for them to form an extension.

We would have to renounce human certainty to doubt the truth of these demonstrations. But to help us conceive the infinite divisibility of matter as much as possible, I will add still another proof that presents, at the same time, an infinite division and a motion that slows to infinity without ever arriving at a state of rest.

Certainly, while we might doubt whether extension can be infinitely divided, at least we cannot doubt that it can be increased to infinity, and that we can join to a surface of a hundred thousand leagues another surface of a hundred thousand leagues, and so on to infinity.[6] Now this infinite increase in extension proves its infinite divisibility. To understand this we only have to [298] imagine a flat sea that is increased infinitely in extent, and a vessel at the shore that leaves the port in a straight line. It is certain that when the bottom of this vessel is viewed from the port through a lens or some other diaphanous body, the ray that ends at the bottom of this vessel will pass through a certain point of the lens, and the horizontal ray will pass through another point of the lens higher than the first. Now as the vessel goes further away, the point of intersection with the lens of the ray ending at the bottom of the vessel will continue to rise, and will divide space infinitely between these two points. The further away the vessel goes, the more slowly it will rise, without ever ceasing to rise. Nor can it reach the point of the horizontal ray, because these two lines that intersect at the eye will never be parallel nor the same line. Thus this example provides at the same time proofs of the infinite divisibility of extension and of an infinite decrease in motion.

From this infinite decrease in extension that arises from its divisibility, we can solve problems that look impossible when stated in the following terms: To find an infinite space equal to a finite space, or that is only half, third, etc. of a finite space. These can be solved in various ways. Here is one that is fairly crude but very easy. If we take half of a square, and half of this half, and so on to infinity, and then we join all these halves along their longest sides, we will form a space of an irregular shape that will continually decrease to infinity along one end, but that will be equal to the entire square. For a half and half of the half, plus half of this second half, and so on to infinity, make the whole. A third and a third of the third, and a third of the new third, and so on to infinity, make the half. Fourths taken the same way make a third, and fifths make a fourth. Joining these thirds or fourths end to end, we will create a figure containing half or a third of the area of the whole, that will be infinitely long on one side while decreasing proportionally in width.

6   Descartes, *Principles of Philosophy*, Pt. II, art. 21, *Philosophical Writings*, vol. 1, p. 232.

The benefit we can derive from these speculations is not just to acquire this kind of knowledge, which in itself is fairly sterile, but to teach us to recognize the limits of the mind, and to make us admit in spite of ourselves that some things exist even though we cannot understand them. This is why it is good to tire the mind on these subtleties, in order to master its presumption and to take away its audacity ever to oppose our feeble insight to the truths presented by the Church, under the pretext that we cannot understand them. [299] For since all the vigor of the human mind is forced to succumb to the smallest atom of matter, and to admit that it clearly sees that it is infinitely divisible without being able to understand how that can be, is it not obviously to sin against reason to refuse to believe the marvelous effects of God's omnipotence, which is itself incomprehensible, for the reason that the mind cannot understand them?

But just as it is beneficial to make the mind sometimes feel its own weakness by considering these objects that surpass it and in surpassing it abase and humiliate it, it is also certain that it is usually necessary to try to choose subjects and topics to occupy it that are more proportional to it. These are subjects whose truth it is capable of finding and understanding, either by proving effects by their causes, which is called an *a priori* proof, or, on the contrary, by demonstrating causes by their effects, which is called an *a posteriori* proof. We have to extend these terms a bit to reduce all kinds of demonstrations to them. But it is good to indicate them in passing so that we may understand them and will not be surprised to see them in books or in philosophical discourse. Because these arguments are ordinarily composed of several parts, in order to make them clear and conclusive it is necessary to arrange them in a certain order and by a certain method. This is the method we shall discuss in the greater part of this book.

CHAPTER 2

Two kinds of method, analysis and synthesis. An example of analysis

The art of arranging a series of thoughts properly, either for discovering the truth when we do not know it, or for proving to others what we already know, can generally be called method.

Hence there are two kinds of method, one for discovering the truth, which is known as *analysis*, or the *method of resolution*, and which can also be called the *method of discovery*. The other is for making the truth [300] understood by others once it is found. This is known as *synthesis*, or the *method of composition*, and can also be called the *method of instruction*.[a]

---

a ... *instruction.* – In analysis or the method of discovery, we assume that what we are looking for is not completely known, but that it can be known by examining it more particularly and using the knowledge from this examination to reach what we are looking for. Suppose we wondered [237:3] ... (I); long addition in II.

Analysis does not usually deal with the entire body of a science, but is used only for resolving some issue.*

Now all issues concern either words or things.

Here[1] I am calling "issues about words," not issues in which we look for words, but those in which we investigate things by words, for example when it is a question of finding the meaning of an enigma or explaining what an author meant by some obscure or ambiguous words.

Issues concerning things can be reduced to four main types.

The first is when we look for causes by effects. We know, for example, the different effects of a lodestone, so we look for its cause. We know the different effects usually attributed to the horror of a vacuum; we investigate whether it is the true cause, and we find that it is not. We know the ebbs and flows of the sea, so we ask what might be the cause of such a great and regular motion.

The second is when we seek effects by their causes. Since ancient times it has been known, for example, that wind and water have a great force capable of moving bodies. But the ancients did not sufficiently investigate what the effects of these causes might be. They did not apply them, as has been done since by means of mills, to a great number of things that are very useful to human society and noticeably lighten human labor – which should be the result of a true physics. So we could say that the first kind of question, where we investigate causes by effects, constitutes speculation in physics, and that the second kind, where we seek effects by their causes, constitutes its practice.

The third kind of question is that in which we try to find the whole from the parts, as when we find the sum of several numbers by adding one to another, or when we have two numbers [301] and we find the product by multiplying one by the other.

The fourth is when we have the whole and some part, and we look for another part, such as when from a number and what is to be subtracted from it, we find the remainder, or when we have a number and we find its nth part.

But we should note that to extend these last two sorts of questions further, and in order for them to include what could not, properly speaking, be related to the first two questions, we have to take the word "part" more generally, for everything a thing includes – its modes, limits, accidents, properties, and in general all its attributes. Accordingly, an example of finding a whole by its parts would be finding the area of a triangle by its height and its base. And by contrast, it would be finding a part by the whole and another part if we looked for the side of a rectangle based on knowledge of its area and one of its sides.

Now regardless of the nature of the issue we set out to resolve, the first thing we

---

* The greater part of what is said here about issues was taken from a manuscript by the late Descartes, which Clerselier was kind enough to lend us. [Authors' note.]

[1] At this point a free translation of Rule Thirteen begins from Descartes' *Rules for the Direction of the Mind, Philosophical Writings*, vol. 1, pp. 51–6.

must do is to conceive clearly and distinctly precisely what it is we are asking, that is, the precise point of the question.

For it is necessary to avoid what happens to some people who, from mental haste, set out to resolve what someone presents to them before sufficiently considering the signs and marks by which they might recognize what they are looking for when they encounter it. For example, it is as if a valet whose master had ordered him to find one of his friends hurried to go looking for him before finding out more precisely from his master which friend it was.

Now even though there is something unknown in every question – otherwise there would be nothing to investigate – it is still necessary to indicate and designate this same unknown by certain conditions. These determine us to investigate one thing rather than another and may enable us to decide when we have found what we are looking for.

These are the conditions we first ought to contemplate properly, taking care not to add anything to them that is not contained in what is presented, and not to omit from them anything they contain, for we can commit an error either way.

We would be erring in the first way if, for example, when someone asks us what animal walks on four feet in the morning, on two feet at noon, and on three feet in the evening, we thought [302] we were required to take all the words "feet," "morning," "noon," and "evening" in their proper and natural meaning. For anyone who proposes this enigma does not make it a condition that we have to take them this way. But it is enough if these words may be related metaphorically to other things, and so the question is properly answered when we say that this animal is a human being.

Suppose, moreover, someone asks us what ingenuity could have created the figure of a Tantalus which, when set on a column in the middle of a vase in the posture of a man who is bending over to drink, can never do it because the water may easily rise in the vase up to his mouth, but flows out as soon as it reaches his lips, without leaving any in the vase.[2] We would be committing an error if we added conditions that are absolutely worthless for finding the solution to this problem, if we were diverted by looking for some amazing secret in the figure of the Tantalus that caused the water to flow out as soon as it touched his lips, for this is not contained in the question. If we think about it carefully, we have to analyze it in these terms: to make a vase that holds water only when filled up to a certain height and lets it out if it is filled further. This is quite easy, for we only need to hide a siphon in the column that has a small hole in the bottom where the water enters, and whose longer leg has an opening under the foot of the base. So when the water put into the vase approaches the top of the siphon it stays there, but

---

[2] The enigma of the Sphinx and the mechanism of the Tantalus are taken from Rule Thirteen of Descartes' *Rules for the Direction of the Mind, Philosophical Writings*, vol. 1, pp. 54–5. The charlatan water-drinker is mentioned in the letter from Descartes to Mersenne of 11 March 1640, *Œuvres*, vol. 3, p. 42.

when it reaches it, it all runs out through the longer leg of the siphon, which is open under the foot of the vase.

We are also asked what could be the secret of the water drinker who appeared in Paris twenty years ago, and how, by spitting water from his mouth, he could fill five or six different glasses with different colored water at the same time. If we assume that water of different colors had been in his stomach, and that in spitting he separated them, one into one glass, another into another, we would be looking for a secret we would never find, because it is impossible. Instead, we only have to inquire why water coming out of the same mouth at the same time appears with different colors in each of these glasses. It is much more likely that it comes from some coloring he put in the bottom of each glass.

It is also a trick of people who pose problems they do not want us to be able to solve easily, to embed what has to be found in so many irrelevant conditions [303] that are not at all helpful for finding it, that we cannot easily discover the true point of the question. So we lose time and tire our minds to no purpose by concentrating on things contributing nothing to resolving them.

The other way of erring in examining the conditions of whatever we are looking for is by omitting some conditions essential to the question under consideration. For example, someone proposes to find perpetual motion by human design, for we know very well that there are perpetual motions in nature, such as the motions of fountains, rivers, and stars. There are people who imagined that the earth turns around its center and that it is only a large magnet whose properties are all shared by lodestone. They thought it would be possible to position a magnet in such a way that it would rotate forever. But if this were so, we would not have solved the problem of finding perpetual motion by human design, since this motion would be as natural as the motion of a wheel exposed to the current of a river.

Thus when we have properly examined the conditions that designate and indicate whatever is unknown in a problem, it is necessary next to examine what is known in it, since this is how we must arrive at knowledge of the unknown. For we should not suppose that we have to find some new type of being, but rather that our insight can extend only as far as recognizing that what we are looking for participates in such-and-such a way in the natures of the things known to us. For example, we would die in vain looking for arguments and proofs to give a person blind from birth the true ideas of colors as we know them by the senses. Similarly, if magnets and other bodies whose natures we are investigating were new types of beings, such that the mind had never conceived anything similar, we should never expect to come to know them by reasoning. To do that we would need a different mind from ours. Hence we ought to think that we have found everything that can be found by the human mind if we can distinctly conceive a certain combination of beings and natures that are known to us so as to produce all the effects we see in magnets.

Now analysis consists primarily in paying attention to what is known in the issue we want to resolve. The entire art is to derive from this examination many truths that can lead us to the knowledge we are seeking. [304]

Suppose we wondered whether the human soul is immortal, and to investigate it we set out to consider the nature of the soul. First we would notice that it is distinctive of the soul to think, and that it could doubt everything without being able to doubt whether it is thinking, since doubting is itself a thought. Next we would ask what thinking is. Since we would see nothing contained in the idea of thought that is contained in the idea of the extended substance called body, and since we could even deny of thought everything belonging to body – such as having length, width, and depth, having different parts, having a certain shape, being divisible, etc. – without thereby destroying the idea we have of thought, from this we would conclude that thought is not at all a mode of extended substance, because it is the nature of a mode not to be able to be conceived while the thing of which it is a mode is denied. From this we infer, in addition, that since thought is not a mode of extended substance, it must be the attribute of another substance. Hence thinking substance and extended substance are two really distinct substances. It follows from this that the destruction of one in no way brings about the destruction of the other, since even extended substance is not properly speaking destroyed, but all that happens in what we call destruction is nothing more than the change or dissolution of several parts of matter which exist forever in nature. Likewise it is quite easy to judge that in breaking all the gears of a clock no substance is destroyed, although we say that the clock is destroyed. This shows that since the soul is in no way divisible or composed of parts, it cannot perish, and consequently is immortal.[3]

That is what we call *analysis* or *resolution*. We should notice, first, that in this method – as in the one called *composition* – we should practice proceeding from what is better known to what is less well known. For there is no true method which could dispense with this rule.

Second, it nevertheless differs from the method of composition in that these known truths are taken from a particular examination of the thing we are investigating, and not from more general things as is done in the method of instruction. Thus in the example we presented, we did not begin by establishing these general maxims: that no substance [305] perishes, properly speaking; that what is called destruction is only a dissolution of parts; that therefore what has no parts cannot be destroyed, etc. Instead we rose by stages to these general notions.

Third, in analysis we introduce clear and evident maxims only to the extent that we need them, whereas in the other method we establish them first, as we will explain below.

Fourth and finally, these two methods differ only as the route one takes in

---

[3] This passage on the immortality of the soul refers to the synopsis of the *Meditations* (of the Second) and the *Principles of Philosophy*, Pt. I, arts. 63 and 64, *Philosophical Writings*, vol. 2, pp. 9–10 and vol. 1, pp. 215-16.

climbing a mountain from a valley differs from the route taken in descending from the mountain into the valley, or as the two ways differ that are used to prove that a person is descended from St. Louis. One way is to show that this person had a certain man for a father who was the son of a certain man, and that man was the son of another, and so on up to St. Louis. The other way is to begin with St. Louis and show that he had a certain child, and this child had others, thereby descending to the person in question. This example is all the more appropriate in this case, since it is certain that to trace an unknown genealogy, it is necessary to go from the son to the father, whereas to explain it after finding it, the most common method is to begin with the trunk to show the descendants. This is also what is usually done in the sciences where, after analysis is used to find some truth, the other method is employed to explain what has been found.

This is the way to understand the nature of analysis as used by geometers. Here is what it consists in. Suppose a question is presented to them, such as whether it is true or false that something is a theorem, or whether a problem is possible or impossible; they assume what is at issue and examine what follows from that assumption. If in this examination they arrive at some clear truth from which the assumption follows necessarily, they conclude that the assumption is true. Then starting over from the end point, they demonstrate it by the other method which is called *composition*. But if they fall into some absurdity or impossibility as a necessary consequence of their assumption, they conclude from this that the assumption is false and impossible.

That is what may be said in a general way about analysis, which consists more in judgment and mental skill than in particular rules. The following four rules, however, which Descartes [306] presents in his *Method*, may be useful for guarding against error when we try to find the truth in the human sciences,[b] although in fact, they are general enough for all kinds of methods, and not specific to analysis alone.[4]

The first is *never to accept anything as true that is not known evidently to be so; that is, to take care to avoid precipitation and preconceptions, and to include nothing more in our judgments than what is presented so clearly to the mind that we would have no occasion to doubt it.*

The second is *to divide each of the difficulties being investigated into as many parts as possible, and as may be required for resolving them.*

The third is *to proceed by ordering our thoughts, beginning with the simplest and the most easily known objects, in order to rise step by step, as if by degrees, to knowledge of the most complex, assuming an order even among those that do not precede one another naturally.*

The fourth is *always to make enumerations so complete and reviews so comprehensive that we can be sure of leaving nothing out.*

---

[4] *Discourse on the Method*, Pt. II, *Philosophical Writings*, vol. 1, p. 120. This statement of the rules is a paraphrase of Descartes' text.

[b] ... human sciences, which depend only on reason, although ... (I)

It is true that it is often difficult to follow these rules, but it is always helpful to bear them in mind, and to heed them as much as possible whenever we try to find the truth by means of reason, and insofar as the mind is capable of knowing them.

CHAPTER 3

The method of composition, and in particular the method followed by geometers

What we said in the preceding chapter has already given us some idea of the method of composition. It is the most important method, since it is the one used to explain all the sciences.

This method consists primarily in beginning with the most general and the simplest things, in order to go on to the less general and the more complex. This is how to avoid repetition, since if we were to discuss the species before the genus – because it is [307] impossible to know a species properly without knowing the genus – we would have to explain the nature of the genus several times, in explaining each species.

There are still many things to note to perfect this method and make it entirely appropriate to the goal it ought to set for itself, which is to yield clear and distinct knowledge of the truth. But because general precepts are more difficult to understand when they are completely separated from any subject matter, we will consider the method followed by geometers as the one always judged most suitable for persuading us of the truth and completely convincing the mind. We will show, first, what is good in it, and second, what appear to be its defects.

Since geometers have as their goal to assert only what is convincing, they thought they could achieve it by observing three general rules.

The first is *never to leave any ambiguity in terms*, which they achieve by the definitions of words we spoke about in Part I.

The second is *to base their reasoning only on clear and evident principles*, which cannot be disputed by anyone having any intelligence. That is why, first of all, they posit the axioms they need to have granted, as being so clear that one would only obscure them by trying to prove them.

The third is *to prove demonstratively all the conclusions they put forward*, using only the definitions presented, the principles granted them as quite evident, and the propositions already derived from them by the force of reason, which subsequently become almost like principles.

Hence we can reduce to three headings everything geometers use to convince the mind, and include everything under these five very important rules.[1]

---

[1]   Pascal, *The Art of Persuasion, Pascal, Selections*, pp. 189-90.

Necessary rules

For definitions
  1. *Leave no term even slightly obscure or equivocal without defining it.*
  2. *Use in definitions only terms that are perfectly known or already explained.*
  [308]
For axioms
  3. *Require in axioms only things that are perfectly evident.*
For demonstrations
  4. *Prove all slightly obscure propositions, using in the proof only preceding definitions, axioms that have been granted, propositions that have already been demonstrated, or the construction of the thing itself that is in question whenever there is some operation to be done.*
  5. *Never take advantage of the equivocation in terms by failing to substitute mentally the definitions that restrict and explain them.*

This is what geometers have considered necessary to make proofs convincing and conclusive. We must admit that the attention paid when following these rules is sufficient to avoid making faulty inferences when we are treating scientific matters, which is doubtless the main point, since everything else may be called useful rather than necessary.

CHAPTER 4

A more detailed explanation of these rules; first, rules regarding definitions

Although we have already spoken in Part I about the usefulness of defining one's terms, this is, however, so important that we cannot bear it too much in mind, since this is how countless disputes are cleared up whose cause is often merely an ambiguity in terms that one person takes one way and another person another way. Accordingly, some very serious arguments would cease in an instant if either of the disputants took the care to indicate clearly, in a few words, the meanings of the terms that are the subject of dispute.

Cicero remarked that the majority of disputes among ancient philosophers, and especially between the Stoics and the Academics, was based only on this ambiguity in words, for the Stoics took pleasure, in order to raise themselves in public esteem, to take moral terms in another sense than other philosophers did. This made people [309] think that their ethics was considerably more strict and more perfect, although actually this claimed perfection existed only verbally and not in fact. This was because the Stoic sage was no less taken by the pleasures of life than philosophers of other sects, who appeared less rigorous, and was just as careful to avoid evils and inconveniences. The only difference was that whereas other philosophers used ordinary words for goods and evils, the Stoics, in enjoying pleasures, did not call them goods but only preferable things, προηγμένα, and in avoiding evils did not call them evils, but only things to be avoided, ἀποπροηγμένα.[1]

So it is very practical advice to remove from disputes everything based only on the equivocation in words, by defining them in other terms that are so clear that they cannot be misunderstood.

This is the purpose of the first rule we just presented: *Not to leave any term slightly obscure or equivocal without defining it.*

But to obtain all the use we should from these definitions, it is necessary as well to add the second rule: *To use in definitions only terms that are perfectly known or already explained*; that is, only terms that designate as clearly as possible the idea we want to signify by the word we are defining.[a]

For when we have not designated clearly and distinctly enough the idea we wish to connect with a word, it is almost impossible in what follows not to pass imperceptibly to another idea than the one designated. That is, rather than substituting mentally the same idea we have designated each time we use the word, we substitute another idea provided by nature. This is easy to check by explicitly substituting the definition for the defined term. For nothing should be changed in the proposition if we keep the same idea, whereas it will be changed if we do not keep it. [310]

We can understand all this better by some examples. Euclid defines the plane straight-line angle this way: "The intersection of two straight lines inclined on the same plane."[2] If we consider this definition as a simple definition of a word, so that we take the word "angle" as having been deprived of all meaning in order to mean nothing more than the intersection of two lines, we should find nothing more to say on the matter. For Euclid was allowed to call the intersection of two lines an angle. But he was then obligated to remember this, and to continue to take the word "angle" only in this sense. Now to decide whether he did this, we only have to substitute the definition he gave for the word "angle" every time he mentions an angle. If in substituting this definition there exists some absurdity in whatever he says about the angle, it will follow that he did not keep the same idea he designated, but passed imperceptibly to another idea, which is the natural idea. He instructs us, for example, how to bisect an angle. Substitute the definition. Who cannot see that

---

[1]   Cicero, *De Finibus Bonorum et Malorum*, Bk. III, chs. 14 and 15, p. 271.
[2]   *Euclid's Elements*, Bk. I, def. 8, p. 1.
[a]   ... defining. – For we must note that although definitions are properly speaking not contestable, as we showed in Part I, they may still be defective whenever they do not have the effect for which they were introduced. Now the effect they should have is to indicate distinctly the idea to which a word is connected. Consequently, it is useless to define a word if after defining it we leave it in the same confusion it was in previously. This will happen if the designated idea to be connected to the word is not clearly and distinctly designated. But further, when we have not ... (I)

it is not the intersection of two lines that is bisected, that it is not the intersection of two lines that has two sides and a base or subtending side, but that all of this applies to the space enclosed between the lines, and not to the intersection of the lines.

It is obvious that what confused Euclid and prevented him from designating the angle by the words "space enclosed between two intersecting lines," is that he saw that the space could be larger or smaller when the sides of the angle are longer or shorter, without the angle being larger or smaller. But he should not have concluded from this that the plane angle is not a space, but only that it is a space enclosed between two intersecting straight lines, indeterminate according to the dimension corresponding to the length of these lines, and determinate according to the other dimension by the proportional part of a circumference that has for its center the point where these lines intersect.

This definition designates the idea everyone has of an angle so clearly that it is simultaneously a definition of a word and a real definition, except that the word "angle" in ordinary speech also includes a solid angle, whereas in this definition it is restricted to signifying a plane straight-line angle. When the angle is defined thus, it is indubitable that everything that could subsequently be said about the [311] plane straight-line angle, such as is found in all straight-lined figures, will be true of the angle so defined, without having to change our idea or without ever finding any absurdity in substituting the definition for the defined term. For it is the space as explained that can be divided into two or three or four parts. It is the space that has two sides enclosing the angle. It is the space that can be limited on the side, in itself indeterminate, by a line called the base or the subtending line. It is this space that is not considered as larger or smaller when enclosed between longer or shorter lines. Since it is indeterminate according to this dimension, this is not the way to take its largeness or smallness. This is the definition that enables us to decide whether one angle is equal to another angle, or larger or smaller than it. Since the size of this space is determined only by the proportional part of a circumference having for its center the point where the two lines enclosing the angle intersect, when two angles are each measured by an equal proportion of the circumference, such as a tenth, then they are equal. If one is a tenth and the other a twelfth, the one that is a tenth is larger than the one that is a twelfth. Whereas by Euclid's definition, we could not understand what the equality of two angles consists in. This creates a terrible confusion in his *Elements*, as Ramus remarked, although he himself scarcely did any better.

Here are some other definitions by Euclid, where he makes the same mistake as in the definition of an angle. "A ratio," he says, "is a disposition of two magnitudes of the same kind, compared to one another in terms of quantity." A proportion is a similarity of ratios.[3]

---

[3] *Euclid's Elements*, Bk. v, defs. 3 and 6, p. 134.

From these definitions the term "ratio" ought to include the disposition between two magnitudes, when we consider how much greater one is than the other. For we cannot deny that this is a disposition of two magnitudes compared according to quantity. In consequence, four magnitudes will be proportional when the difference between the first and second is equal to the difference between the third and fourth. Thus nothing remains to be said about these definitions of Euclid's, provided he always keeps the ideas he has designated by these words, and to which he gives the names "ratio" and "proportion." But he does not keep them, since throughout the rest of his book these four numbers, 3, 5, 8, and 10, [312] are not at all proportional, although the definition he gives of the word "proportion" applies to them, since between the first and second numbers compared according to quantity there is a disposition similar to that between the third and the fourth.

In order to avoid this difficulty, then, he should have noted that we can compare two magnitudes in two ways: one, by considering how much greater one is than the other; the other, by the way one is contained in the other. Since these two dispositions are different, it is necessary to give them different names, calling the first the difference, and reserving the name "ratio" for the second. He should subsequently have defined "proportion" as the equality of either of these kinds of dispositions, that is, of either the difference or the ratio. Since this makes two species, he should also have distinguished them by two different names, calling the equality of differences the "arithmetic proportion" and the equality of ratios the "geometric proportion." Because the latter is much more useful than the former, we could always state that whenever we say simply "proportion" or "proportional magnitude," we mean geometrical proportion, and that we mean arithmetic proportion only when it is said explicitly. This would have gotten rid of all the obscurity and removed all the equivocation.

All this shows us that it is necessary not to abuse the maxim that definitions of words are arbitrary. But we must be very careful to designate so precisely and clearly the idea with which we want to connect the word being defined that no one could be misled in the rest of the discourse into changing this idea, that is, by taking the word in a sense other than that given by the definition. In that case they could not substitute the definition for the defined term without falling into some absurdity.

CHAPTER 5

Geometers seem not always to have clearly understood the difference between verbal definitions and real definitions

Although no other authors have made as much use of verbal definitions as geometers, I nevertheless feel obliged to remark here that they have not always heeded [313] the distinction that ought to be drawn between definitions of things and definitions of words, which is that the first are disputable and the others are not. For I have seen some geometers contest verbal definitions as heatedly as if it were a question of the things themselves.

Thus we can see in Clavius's commentaries on Euclid a long and quite heated debate between Peletier and himself, concerning the space between the tangent and the circumference, which Peletier claimed was not an angle, whereas Clavius maintained that it was.[1] But who cannot see that all this could be ended in a word, by asking each of them what he means by the word "angle"?

Again, we see Simon Stevin,[2] the very famous mathematician to the Prince of Orange, defining number thus: "Number is that by which the quantity of each thing is explained." He then became quite angry with people who would not recognize the unit as a number, going so far as to make rhetorical comments, as if it were a very serious argument. It is true that he mixes a question of some importance in this discourse, which is whether the unit is to a number as the point is to a line. But he should have distinguished these questions in order not to confuse two quite different things. So, treating these two questions separately – one, whether the unit is a number; the other, whether the unit is to a number as the point is to a line – he should have said about the first that it was only a verbal dispute, and that the unit either is or is not a number depending on how one wishes to define a number. If you define it as Euclid did – "Number is a multitude of units put together" – it is obvious that the unit is not a number. But since Euclid's definition was arbitrary, and it is permissible to define the term "number" differently, we could give another definition such as Stevin's, according to which the unit is a number. This way the first question becomes vacuous, and nothing more can be said against those who are not happy calling the unit a number without manifestly begging the question, as can be seen by examining Stevin's alleged demonstrations. The first is:

> *The part has the same nature as the whole.*
> *The unit is part of a multitude of units.*
> *Therefore the unit has the same nature as a multitude of units and, consequently, is a number.* [314]

This argument is utterly worthless. For even if the part always had the same nature as the whole, it would not follow that it always had the same name as the whole. On the contrary, it quite often happens that the part does not have the

---

[1] Clavius (Christoph Klau) (1537–1612) was a German Jesuit and mathematician who organized the scientific instruction of Jesuits at Rome and worked on the Gregorian calendar. Jacques Peletier du Mans (1517–1582) was a French humanist and mathematician; he translated Horace and wrote on the art of poetry.

[2] Simon Stevin (d. 1635) was interested in statics and hydrostatics. He left a treatise on arithmetic, from which passages in this chapter are drawn: see Definition II in Bk. 1 of *L'Arithmétique, Principal Works*, vol. IIB, p. 495.

same name. A soldier is part of an army but is in no way an army. A room is part of a house but is not a house. A semicircle is not a circle; part of a square is not a square. This argument, then, proves at the most that since the unit is part of a multitude of units, it has something in common with the whole multitude of units, according to which we could say that they have the same nature. But this does not prove that we are required to give the same name "number" to the unit and the multitude of units, since we could, if we wanted, keep the name "number" for the multitude of units, and give the unit its own name, "unit" or "part of a number."

Stevin's second argument is no better:

> *If no number is subtracted from a given number, the given number remains.*
> *Therefore if the unit were not a number, in subtracting one from three the given number would remain, which is absurd.*

But this major premise is ridiculous and assumes what is at issue. Euclid will deny that the given number remains whenever no number is subtracted, since it is enough for it not to stay the same to subtract either a number or a part of a number, such as the unit. If this argument were sound, we could prove in the same way that in removing a semicircle from a given circle, the given circle would have to remain, because no circle was removed from it.

Thus all Stevin's arguments prove at most that number can be defined in such a way that the word "number" applies to the unit, because the unit and a multitude of units have enough in common to be signified by the same name. But they certainly do not prove that we cannot also define number by restricting this word to a multitude of units, so as not to be obliged to except the unit every time we explain the properties that belong to all numbers besides the unit.

But the second question, namely whether the unit is to other numbers as the point is to the line, is not at all of the same nature as the first, and is not a verbal dispute [315] but a real one. For it is absolutely false that the unit is to the number as the point is to the line, since when added to a number the unit makes it larger, whereas when added to a line the point does not make it larger. The unit is part of a number, but the point is not part of a line. When the unit is subtracted from a number, the given number no longer remains. But when the point is removed from a line, the given line remains.

This same Stevin is full of similar disputes over definitions of words, for example when he becomes heated over proving that number is not a discrete quantity, that the proportion of numbers is always arithmetic and not geometric, and that every root of any number whatever is a number. This shows that he lacked a proper understanding of verbal definitions, and that he took verbal definitions, which cannot be contested, for real definitions, which often can rightly be contested.

CHAPTER 6

Rules concerning axioms, that is, propositions which are clear and evident in
themselves

Everyone agrees that some propositions are so clear and evident in themselves that
they do not need to be demonstrated, and that all propositions that are not
demonstrated ought to be similarly clear and evident in order to be principles of an
authentic demonstration. For if they were even slightly uncertain, obviously they
could not be the foundation of a completely certain conclusion.

But many people do not understand well enough in what the clarity and evidence
of a proposition consist. For in the first place, we should not suppose that a
proposition is clear and certain only when no one contradicts it, and that we should
consider it doubtful, or at least needing proof, whenever someone denies it. If this
were so, nothing would be certain or clear, since there are philosophers who have
made a career out of doubting everything generally, [316] and there are even some
who have claimed that no proposition is more likely than its contrary. So we should
not judge certainty or clarity by people's disputes, for there is nothing that cannot
be contested, especially verbally. But we should take as clear whatever appears so to
everyone who is willing to take the trouble to consider things attentively and is
sincere in saying what is inwardly thought. This is why what Aristotle says is very
meaningful,[1] that a demonstration, properly speaking, concerns only internal
discourse and not external discourse, because nothing is demonstrated so well that
it may not be denied by an obstinate person who is committed to disputing verbally
even things of which they are inwardly persuaded. This is a very bad disposition
and quite unworthy of a well-formed mind, although it is true that this humor
often takes hold in philosophical schools through the custom they have of disputing
everything and making it a point of honor never to give up. There the person
judged more mentally apt is the one who is quickest to find the way to avoid defeat,
whereas the character of an honest person is to put one's weapons in the service of
the truth as soon as one perceives it, and to want to hear it even in the mouth of
one's adversary.

In the second place, the same philosophers who hold that all our ideas come
from the senses also maintain that all the certainty and evidence of propositions
comes either immediately or mediately from the senses. They say: For even this
axiom, "the whole is greater than its part," which passes for the clearest and the
most evident one could wish for, finds credence in the mind only because ever
since childhood we have noticed in particular that every man is larger than his
head, every house larger than a room, every forest larger than a tree, and every sky
larger than a star.

This fantasy is as false as the one we refuted in Part I, that all our ideas come

---

[1]   *Posterior Analytics*, Bk. I, ch. 10, *Complete Works*, vol. I, p. 124.

from the senses. For if we were sure of this truth, that the whole is greater than its part, only from the various observations we have made since childhood, we would be sure only of its probability, since induction is a certain means for knowing something only when we are sure that the induction is complete. Nothing is more common than discovering the falsity of something we thought was true based on inductions that appeared so general that we could not imagine finding any exception to them. [317]

Thus, only two or three years ago it was thought indubitable that the water contained in a curved vessel with one side larger than another would always remain level, not being higher on the smaller side than on the larger side, because we were sure of it by numerous observations. Nevertheless, only a short while ago this was found to be false when one of the two sides is extremely narrow, because in that case the water remains higher on that side than on the other side. All this shows that mere inductions cannot give us complete certainty of any truth, unless we are sure that they are general, which is impossible. Consequently, we could be sure only of the probability of this axiom, "the whole is greater than its part," if we were sure of it only because we had seen that a man was larger than his head, a forest larger than a tree, a house larger than a room, and the sky larger than a star, since we would always have reason to wonder whether there was not some other whole to which we had not paid attention, that might not be larger than its part.

The certainty of this axiom, then, does not depend on observations we have made since childhood. On the contrary, nothing is more capable of leading us into error than limiting ourselves to these childhood prejudices. Certainty, rather, depends solely on the fact that our clear and distinct ideas of a whole and a part clearly imply both that the whole is greater than its part, and that the part is smaller than the whole. All that our different observations of a man larger than his head and a house larger than a room can do, is to give us an occasion to pay attention to the ideas of a whole and a part. But it is absolutely false that they cause the absolute and unshakable certainty we have of the truth of this axiom, as I believed I have demonstrated.

What we have said about this axiom can be said about all the others. Hence I believe that the certainty and evidence of human knowledge about natural things depends on this principle:

Everything contained in the clear and distinct idea of a thing can be truthfully affirmed of that thing.

So, because animal is included in the idea human, I can affirm of human beings that they are animals. Because having all its diameters equal is included in the idea of a circle, I can affirm of every circle that all its diameters are equal. [318] Because having all its angles equal to two right angles is included in the idea of a triangle, I can affirm it of every triangle.

This principle cannot be contested without destroying everything evident in human knowledge and establishing a ridiculous Pyrrhonism. We can judge things only by our ideas of them, since we have no other means of conceiving them except as they are in the mind, and since they exist there only by means of their ideas. Now suppose the judgments we form in considering these ideas did not concern things themselves, but only our thoughts. In other words, suppose that from the fact that I see clearly that having three angles equal to two right angles is implied in the idea of a triangle, I did not have the right to conclude that every triangle really has three angles equal to two right angles, but only that I think this way. It is obvious that we would know nothing about things, but only about our thoughts. Consequently, we could know nothing about things except what we were convinced we knew most certainly, but we would know only that we thought them to be a certain way, which would obviously destroy all the sciences.

We should not fear that there are people who seriously agree with the conclusion that we do not know what is true or false about anything in itself. For some things are so simple and evident – such as: "I think, therefore I am"; "the whole is greater than its part" – that it is impossible to doubt seriously whether they are in themselves the way we conceive them to be. The reason is that we could not doubt them without thinking of them, and we could not think of them without believing them to be true, and consequently we could not doubt them.

This principle alone, however, is not sufficient for deciding what ought to be accepted as an axiom. Some attributes truly contained in the ideas of things nevertheless may be and ought to be demonstrated, such as the equality of all the angles of a triangle to two right angles, or of all the angles of a hexagon to eight right angles. But we must be alert to whether we only need to consider the idea of something with moderate attention in order to see clearly whether a certain attribute is contained in it, or whether it is also necessary to connect some other idea to it to recognize this connection. When we only need to consider the idea, the proposition can be taken for an axiom, especially if this consideration requires only the moderate attention of which all ordinary minds are capable. But if we need [319] some other idea besides the idea of the thing, the proposition must be demonstrated. Thus we can give these two rules for axioms:

RULE I

In order to show clearly that an attribute applies to a subject – for example, to see that being larger than its part applies to the whole – whenever we need only to consider the two ideas of the subject and the attribute with moderate attention, so that we cannot do it without recognizing that the idea of the attribute is truly included in the idea of the subject, then we have the right to take this proposition for an axiom, not needing to be demonstrated. This is because it has in itself all the evidence that could be given in a demonstration, for a demonstration could do nothing more than show that this attribute applies to the subject by using a third idea to show this connection, which is already seen without the aid of a third idea.

But we should not confuse a mere explanation, even if it is in the form of an argument, with a true demonstration. Some axioms need to be explained to be better understood although they do not need to be demonstrated, since an explanation is nothing more than saying in other terms and at more length what is contained in the axiom, whereas a demonstration requires some new middle term which the axiom does not clearly contain.

RULE 2

When the mere consideration of the ideas of the subject and attribute is not enough to show clearly that the attribute applies to the subject, the proposition that affirms it should not be taken for an axiom. But it must be demonstrated, by using some other ideas to show the connection, as, for example, the idea of parallel lines is used to show that the three angles of a triangle are equal to two right angles.

These two rules are more important than people realize. One of the most common mistakes of people is not to reflect enough on what they affirm or deny. Instead, they refer to what they have heard said or what they have previously thought without paying heed to what they themselves would think if they paid more attention to what occurred in the mind. They focus more on the sounds of words than on their true ideas. They affirm that something that is impossible to conceive is clear and evident, and they deny as [320] false what it would be impossible not to believe true if they took the trouble to think seriously about it.

For example, people who say that in a piece of wood, besides its parts and their arrangement, their shape, motion, or rest, and the pores existing among them, there is also a substantial form distinct from all that, believe that they are saying nothing that is not certain. Nevertheless they are saying something that neither they nor anyone else has ever understood or will ever understand.

By contrast, if we try to explain to them the effects of nature in terms of the insensible particles composing bodies, and the variations in their arrangement, size, shape, motion, or rest, and the pores existing among these particles which are open or closed to the passage of other material particles, they think they are just being told fantasies, although nothing is being said that they may not conceive very easily. By an even stranger mental perversion, the ease with which they conceive these things leads them to think that they are not the true causes of natural effects, but that the true causes are more mysterious and hidden. Accordingly they are more disposed to believe people who explain things to them by principles they do not conceive at all, than people who use only principles they understand.

What is even more amusing is that when someone mentions insensible particles, they think they are justified in rejecting them because they cannot be seen or touched. They are satisfied, however, with substantial forms, weight, attractive powers, etc., which not only cannot be seen or touched, but cannot even be conceived.

CHAPTER 7

Some important axioms that may be used as principles of great truths

Everyone agrees that it is important to have in mind several axioms and principles that, being clear and indubitable, can function as a foundation for knowing the most obscure things. But the axioms usually mentioned [321] are so useless that they are hardly worth knowing. What is known as the first principle of knowledge, *It is impossible for the same thing to be and not to be*, is very clear and certain. But I do not see any way it could possibly be used to give us knowledge. Therefore I believe that the following principles could be more useful. I shall begin with the one we just explained.

1st Axiom: *Everything contained in the clear and distinct idea of a thing can truthfully be affirmed of it.*

2nd Axiom: *At least possible existence is contained in the idea of everything we conceive clearly and distinctly.*

From the fact that something is clearly conceived, we cannot avoid viewing it as being able to exist, since only a contradiction between ideas makes us think that something cannot exist. Now there can be no contradiction in an idea when it is clear and distinct.[a]

3rd Axiom: *Nothingness cannot be the cause of anything.*

From this axiom arise several others that can be called corollaries, such as the following.

4th Axiom, or 1st Corollary of the 3rd Axiom: *No thing, nor any perfection of an actually existing thing, can have nothingness or a nonexistent thing for the cause of its existence.*

5th Axiom, or 2nd Corollary of the 3rd Axiom: *All the reality or perfection in something exists formally or eminently in its first and total cause.*

6th Axiom, or 3rd Corollary of the 3rd Axiom: *No body is capable of moving itself,* that is, of giving itself motion when it has none. [322]

This principle is naturally so evident that it was responsible for introducing substantial forms and the real qualities of heaviness and lightness. For when philosophers saw, on the one hand, that it was impossible for something that had to be moved to move itself, and they were falsely convinced, on the other hand, that there was nothing outside a falling rock that pushed it downwards, they thought they had to distinguish two things in the rock. One was the matter which receives the motion, the other was the substantial form, aided by the accident of weight, which gave it the motion. By not taking care, either they run into the difficulty they want to avoid if this form is itself material, that is true matter, or, if it is not matter, the form has to be a substance really distinct from the matter.

---

[a]   ... distinct, and consequently at least possible existence is contained in the idea of everything we conceive clearly and distinctly. – 3rd Axiom ... (I)

The latter would be impossible to conceive clearly unless it is conceived as a mind, that is, a substance that thinks, as the form of a human really is, but not the form of all other bodies.

7th Axiom, or the 4th Corollary of the 3rd Axiom: *No body can move another body if it is not itself in motion.* For if a body at rest cannot impart motion to itself, it is even less able to impart it to another body.

8th Axiom: *We should never deny what is clear and evident because we cannot understand what is obscure.*

9th Axiom: *It is the nature of a finite mind not to be able to understand the infinite.*

10th Axiom: *The testimony of an infinitely powerful, wise, good, and true person should have more power to persuade the mind than the most convincing reasons.*

For we ought to be more sure that he who is infinitely intelligent is not mistaken and that he who is infinitely good does not deceive us, than we are sure that we are not mistaken about the clearest things. [323]

These last three axioms are the foundation of faith, which we will say something about below.

11th Axiom: *When the facts that the senses can easily judge are witnessed by a great number of persons from different times, different nations, and diverse interests, who speak about them as if from personal experience, and who cannot be suspected of having conspired to maintain a lie, they should be considered as constant and indubitable as if we had seen them with our own eyes.*

This is the foundation of most of our knowledge, since we know infinitely many more things this way than we do from personal experience.

CHAPTER 8

Rules concerning demonstrations

A true demonstration requires two things: one, that the content include only what is certain and indubitable; the other, that there is nothing defective in the form of the argument. Now we will certainly satisfy both of these if we observe the two rules we have laid down.

The content will include only what is true and certain if all the propositions asserted as evidence are:

Either definitions of words that have been explained, which, since they are arbitrary, cannot be disputed;

Or axioms that have already been granted and should not be assumed if they are not clear and evident in themselves, by the 3rd rule;

Or previously demonstrated propositions that have consequently become clear and evident by virtue of the demonstration;

Or the construction of the thing itself in question, whenever there is some operation to be performed. This should also be as indubitable as the rest, since the construction should have been [324] previously shown to be possible, if there had been any doubt about it.

It is clear, then, that by observing the first rule we will never offer as evidence any proposition that is not certain and evident.

It is also easy to show that we will never commit an error in the form of an argument as long as we observe the second rule, which is never to exploit the equivocation in terms by failing to substitute mentally the definitions that restrict and explain them.

For whenever we violate the rules of syllogisms, it is by being misled by the equivocation in some term, taking it in one sense in one of the propositions and in another sense in the other proposition. This mainly happens with the middle term of the syllogism, which when taken in two different senses in the first two propositions is the most common defect of invalid arguments. Now it is clear that we will avoid this defect if we observe the second rule.

It is not that there are no other defects of argumentation besides those arising from the equivocation of terms. But it is almost impossible for a person of average intelligence who has some insight ever to fall into them, especially in speculative matters. Thus it would be pointless to warn us to pay attention to them and to give rules for them. It would even be harmful, because the attention we might pay to these superfluous rules could distract us from the attention we ought to pay to necessary things. So we never see geometers worrying about the form of their arguments, nor thinking about whether they conform to the rules of logic. They are not missing anything, however, because this happens naturally and does not need to be studied.[a]

There is one more observation to be made about propositions that need to be demonstrated. It is that we should not include among them propositions that can be demonstrated by applying the rule of evidence to every evident proposition. For if we did, there would be almost no axiom that did not need to be demonstrated, since they can almost all be demonstrated by that axiom which we said may be taken as the basis of all evidence: *Everything we clearly see to be contained* [325] *in a clear and distinct idea can be truthfully affirmed of it.* We could say, for example:

> *Everything we clearly see to be contained in a clear and distinct idea can be truthfully affirmed of it.*
> *Now we clearly see that the clear and distinct idea we have of the whole contains being greater than its part.*
> *Therefore we can truthfully affirm that the whole is greater than its part.*

---

[a]   ... studied. – But there are two observations to be made about propositions that need to be demonstrated. The first is that we should not ... (I)

Although this proof is quite sound it is unnecessary, because the mind supplies the major premise without needing to pay any particular attention to it. Thus it sees clearly and evidently that the whole is greater than its part without needing to reflect on where this evidence comes from. For it is two different things to know something evidently and to know the source of the evidence.[b]

CHAPTER 9

Some common mistakes in the geometers' method

We have seen what is good in the geometers' method, which we reduced to five rules that cannot be kept too much in mind. We must admit that nothing is more admirable [326] than to have discovered so many hidden things, and to have demonstrated them by such firm and invincible arguments, using so few rules. So among all the philosophers, geometers alone have the advantage of having banished controversies and disputes from their school and their books.[a]

Nevertheless, if we want to judge things without prejudice, just as we cannot take away from geometers the glory of having followed a much surer path to truth

---

[b] ... evidence. – The second observation is that when a proposition has been generally demonstrated, it is supposed to have been demonstrated in its particular cases. That is, what was demonstrated of the genus is supposed to have been demonstrated of all the species and all the individuals of each species. For it would be absurd to claim that after having demonstrated that every quadrilateral has four angles equal to four right angles, we still need to demonstrate that a parallelogram has four angles equal to four right angles, although it could be done this way:

Every quadrilateral has four angles equal to four right angles;
Now every parallelogram is a quadrilateral; therefore, etc.

From this we see that every time we prove the generic difference or a generic property of some species, which logicians often give as examples of the best arguments – for example, when we say:

Every animal has sensations.
Every human being is an animal.
Therefore every human being has sensations –

these are worthless arguments and absolutely useless in the sciences. It is not that they are not true, but that they are too true and they prove only what is already known. So without going to such lengths, we ought to assume that what was proved of the genus is proved of each species. Hence to show that a right triangle has one of its angles equal to two others, I would say only that since all three together are equivalent to two right angles, and one of them is a right angle, it is necessary for the other two also to be equal to a right angle. Here I assume without proof that all the angles of a right triangle are equivalent to two right angles, because it is generally proved for triangles. So it would be an irrelevant detour to prove it again for the right triangle by this Scholastic argument:

Every right triangle has three angles equal to two right angles;
Now a right triangle is a triangle; Therefore, etc. – CHAPTER ... (I)

[a] ... books, professing to assert nothing that is not convincing and incontestable. – Nevertheless ... (I)

than everyone else, we also cannot deny that they have made some mistakes that do not divert them from their purpose, but merely cause them not to reach it by the straightest and most convenient route. This is what I shall try to show by taking examples of these mistakes from Euclid himself.

MISTAKE I. *Paying more attention to certainty than to evidence, and to convincing the mind than to enlightening it.*
Geometers are praiseworthy for wanting to assert only what is convincing. But they seem not to have noticed that in order to have perfect knowledge of some truth, it is not enough to be convinced that it is true if we do not also discern why it is true by reasons taken from the nature of the thing itself. Until we reach this point, the mind is not fully satisfied and continues to seek more knowledge than it has, which is an indication that it still does not have scientific knowledge. We could say that this defect is the source of nearly all the others we shall note. Hence it is not necessary to explain it further, since we shall say enough about it in what follows.

MISTAKE II. *Proving things that do not need to be proved.*
Geometers admit that we should not try to prove what is clear in itself. They often do it, however, [327] because they are more attached to convincing the mind than enlightening it, as we just said. And they think they will convince it better by finding some proof, even of the most evident things, than by simply presenting them and leaving it up to the mind to recognize their evidence.

This is what led Euclid to prove that two sides of a triangle taken together are larger than a third,[1] although this is evident from the mere notion of a straight line, which is the shortest distance that can be given between two points, and the natural measure of the distance from one point to another. This would not be the case if it were not also the shortest of all the lines that could be drawn from one point to another point.

This also led him to make not a postulate, but a problem to be demonstrated, of drawing a line equal to a given line, although this is as easy as or easier than drawing a circle having a given radius.

This mistake probably arises from not having considered that all the certainty and evidence of our knowledge in the natural sciences comes from this principle: *That we can affirm of a thing everything contained in the clear and distinct idea of it.* From this it follows that if in order to know whether an attribute is contained in an idea, we need only the simple consideration of the idea without involving any others, it should be considered clear and evident, as we have already said above.

I know that certain attributes are more easily seen in ideas than others. But I think it is enough that they can be seen clearly with moderate attention, and that no one with any intelligence could seriously doubt them, to view the propositions derived thus from the mere consideration of ideas as principles that do not need

---

[1]   *Euclid's Elements*, Bk. I, prop. 20, p. 23.

proof but at most need some explanation and a little discussion. Hence I maintain that we cannot pay a little attention to the idea of a straight line, not only without conceiving that its position depends only on two points (which Euclid took for one of his postulates), but also without understanding easily and quite clearly that if[b] one [328] straight line intersects another, and if there are two points on the intersecting line that are each equidistant from two points on the intersected line, there will be no other point on the intersecting line that is not equally distant from these two points on the intersected line. From this it is easy to decide when a line is perpendicular to another without using angles or triangles, which should be discussed only after having established many things that could be demonstrated only by means of perpendicular lines.

It is also noteworthy that some excellent geometers use as principles propositions that are less clear than these, as when Archimedes based his most elegant demonstrations on this axiom: *If two lines on the same plane have common endpoints, and are convex or concave in the same direction, the line that is contained will be smaller than the line that contains it.*

I admit that this defect of proving what does not need proof does not appear important, and also that in itself it is not a great defect. But it has important consequences, because this is how the reversal of the natural order, which we will discuss below, usually arises. This desire to prove what should be assumed as clear and evident in itself often obliged geometers to discuss some things that, according to the natural order, should only have been dealt with subsequently, in order to use them as proof of what they ought never have proved.

MISTAKE III. *Demonstrations by impossibility.*
This kind of demonstration, which shows that something is such-and-such not by its principles but by some absurdity that would follow if it were otherwise, is very common in Euclid. It is obvious, however, that it can convince the mind but it cannot enlighten it, which ought to be the main result of science. For the mind is not satisfied unless it knows not only that something is, but why it is, which is certainly not learned from a proof by reduction to absurdity.

It is not that we ought to reject these demonstrations altogether. We can sometimes use them to prove negatives that are properly speaking only corollaries of other propositions that are clear in themselves or previously demonstrated by another way. In that case this kind of demonstration [329] by reduction to absurdity is more like an explanation than a new demonstration.

---

b   ... if two points of a line are equally distant from another line extended as needed, all the other points will be equally distant from it. – From this it follows that after showing, as it is easy to do, that the distance from a point to a line is measured by the perpendicular, and that two lines are called equidistant and parallel whenever all the points of each line are equally distant from the other line when extended as needed, it will be enough to find on one line two points that are equally distant from the other to conclude that all the others are too, and that thus they are parallel. – It is also noteworthy ... (I)

We can say, finally, that these demonstrations are acceptable only when others cannot be given, and that it is a fault to use them to prove what can be proved positively. Now there are many propositions in Euclid he proved only this way, that can be proved otherwise without any great difficulty.

MISTAKE IV. *Demonstrations derived by routes that are too remote.*
This mistake is very common among geometers. They never bother themselves about where the proofs they supply are taken from as long as they are convincing. However, this is to prove things only imperfectly, to prove them by foreign paths on which their natures do not depend.

We will understand this better by some examples. At Proposition 5 of Book I, Euclid proves that an isosceles triangle has two equal angles on its base by extending the sides of the triangle equally and making new triangles that he compares with each other.

But is it not incredible that something as easy to prove as the equality of these angles needs so much contrivance to be proved, as if there were nothing more ridiculous than imagining that this equality depended on these foreign triangles? Instead, by following the true order, there are several very easy, short, and natural routes for proving this same equality.

The 47th proposition of Book I, where he proves that the square of the base subtending a right angle is equal to the squares of the two sides, is one of the mostly highly esteemed of Euclid's propositions. Yet it is fairly clear that the way it is proved is not at all natural, since the equality of these squares in no way depends on the equality of the triangles used as a means in this demonstration, but on the proportion of the lines. This is easy to demonstrate without using any line other than the perpendicular from the summit of the right angle to the base.

All of Euclid is full of demonstrations by these unfamiliar ways. [330]

MISTAKE V. *Not to be careful about the true order of nature.*
This is the greatest of the geometers' mistakes. They suppose that there is almost no order to observe except that the first propositions may be used to demonstrate the ones that follow. And so, without worrying about the rules of the true method, which is always to start with the simplest and most general things, to proceed next to the more composite and particular, they mix everything together and treat pell-mell lines and surfaces, triangles and squares. They prove the properties of simple lines by figures, and make countless other reversals that deform this beautiful science.

Euclid's *Elements* is full of this defect. After treating extension in the first four books, he has a general discussion of the proportions of all kinds of magnitudes in the fifth book. He takes up extension again in the sixth, and treats numbers in the seventh, eighth and ninth, to begin again in the tenth by speaking of extension. So much for the overall disorder. But in addition it is filled with countless confused details. He begins the first book by constructing an equilateral triangle, and twenty-two propositions later he gives a general procedure for forming any triangle from three given straight lines, provided that two are greater than a third, which entails the particular construction of an equilateral triangle on a given line.

He proves nothing about perpendicular and parallel lines except by triangles. He mixes the dimensions of surfaces with the dimension of lines.

In Proposition 16 of Book I he proves that when the side of a triangle is extended, the external angle is greater than either internal angle of the opposing sides. Sixteen propositions later he proves that the external angle is equal to the two opposing angles.

We would have to transcribe all of Euclid to give all the examples that could be produced as evidence of this disorder.

MISTAKE VI. *Not making use of classifications and divisions.*

It is yet another mistake in the geometers' method not to make use of classifications and divisions. It is not [331] that they do not indicate all the species of the genera they treat. But it is simply that in defining terms and putting all the definitions in a sequence, they do not indicate that a genus has so many species and cannot have more because the general idea of the genus can admit only so many differences. This is very illuminating for getting to the bottom of the nature of a genus and its species.

For example, in Book I of Euclid we find definitions of all the species of triangles. But who could doubt that it would not be clearer to say it as follows:

Triangles can be classified in terms of their sides or their angles. For the sides are either: all equal, which is called *equilateral*; or two equal, which is called *isosceles*; or all three unequal, which is called *scalene*.

The angles are either: all three acute, which is called *acute*; or only two acute, and then the third is either: right, which is called *right*; or obtuse, which is called *obtuse*.

It is even much better to give this classification of triangles only after having explained and demonstrated all the properties of triangles in general. From this we shall have learned that it is necessary for at least two angles of a triangle to be acute, because the three together cannot be greater than two right angles.

This mistake runs afoul of order, which would require us not to discuss nor even to define the species until after knowing enough about the genus, especially when there are many things to say about the genus that can be explained without discussing the species.

CHAPTER 10

A reply to what geometers say on this subject

There are geometers who think they have excused these mistakes, saying that they do not worry about all this, that it is enough to say nothing that they cannot prove in a convincing way, [332] and that by this means they are sure of having found the truth, which is their only aim.

We also admit that these mistakes are not so important that they must be acknowledged, and that of all the human sciences, none has been treated better than those included under the general name of mathematics. But we claim only that something more could be added to them that would make them more perfect, and that although the main thing to be considered in them is not to assert anything but the truth, it nonetheless would have been desirable for geometers to have paid more attention to the most natural way to convey the truth to the mind.

For it is vain to say that they are not concerned about true order nor about proving things, whether by natural or remote routes, provided that they do what they claim, which is to convince. They cannot change the nature of the mind that way, nor can they change the fact that we have a much more accurate, complete, and perfect knowledge of the things we know by their true causes and principles than of those we have proved only by indirect and unfamiliar ways.

Similarly, it is indubitable that we learn much more easily and that we retain the things taught in their true order much better, because ideas having a natural sequence are better arranged in memory and prompt each other more easily.

We could even say that whatever is once known by the grasp of right reason is retained not by memory but by judgment, and that we appropriate it so that it cannot be forgotten. On the other hand, whatever we know only by demonstrations that are not based on natural reasons easily escapes us and is recovered with difficulty once it has left the memory, because the mind furnishes no way to recover it.

Thus we must agree that it is much better in itself to preserve this order than not to preserve it. But the most that could fairly be said is that we must overlook a small difficulty whenever we cannot avoid it without falling into a greater one. Hence not always preserving the true order is a difficulty. Nevertheless, it is better not to preserve it than to fail to prove invincibly whatever we are asserting, or to expose ourselves to falling into some error or paralogism by seeking [333] certain proofs that might be more natural but are not as convincing nor as exempt from all suspicion of error.

This reply is very reasonable. I admit that we must prefer the assurance of not being mistaken to everything else, and that it is necessary to overlook the true order if we cannot follow it without losing much of the force of demonstration and exposing ourselves to error. But I do not agree that it is impossible to observe both.[a] I think that all the elements of geometry could be treated so that everything would be discussed in its natural order, all propositions would be proved by very simple and natural routes, and everything would nonetheless be quite clearly demonstrated. [We have since carried this out in the *New Elements of Geometry*, and particularly in the new edition which has just appeared.][b]

---

[a] ... both, provided one is satisfied with reasonable certainty; that is, that we grant as true what no one could believe to be false, provided he pays even a little attention in considering it. – For I think ... (I)

[b] This sentence was added in IV. It refers to Arnauld's *Nouveaux éléments de géométrie* (Paris, Savreux, 1667), in vol. 40 of his *Œuvres*.

CHAPTER 11

The scientific method reduced to eight main rules

We can conclude from all we have just said that in order to have a method even more perfect than the one practiced by geometers, we should add two or three rules to the five we presented in chapter 2. Accordingly all these rules can be reduced to eight.

The first two concern ideas, and can be referred to Part I of this *Logic*.

The third and fourth concern axioms and can be referred to Part II.

The fifth and sixth concern arguments and can be referred to Part III.

The last two concern order, and can be referred to Part IV. [334]

Two rules concerning definitions

1. Leave no term even slightly obscure or equivocal without defining it.

2. In definitions use only terms that are perfectly known or have already been explained.

Two rules for axioms

3. In axioms require everything to be perfectly evident.

4. Accept as evident what needs only a little attention to be recognized as true.

Two rules for demonstrations

5. Prove all propositions that are even slightly obscure, using in their proofs only definitions that have preceded, axioms that have been granted, or propositions that have already been demonstrated.

6. Never exploit the equivocation in terms by failing to substitute mentally the definitions that restrict and explain them.[1]

Two rules for method

7. Treat things as much as possible in their natural order, beginning with the most general and the simplest, and explaining everything belonging to the nature of the genus before proceeding to particular species.[2]

8. Divide each genus as much as possible into all its species, each whole into all its parts, and each difficulty into all its cases.[3]

I have added "as much as possible" to these two rules, because it is true that there are many occasions where they cannot be strictly observed, either because of the limits of the human mind or because of limits we are obliged to set for each science.

This frequently causes us to discuss a species without being able to discuss

---

[1] Cf. Pascal, *The Art of Persuasion, Pascal, Selections*, pp. 189–90.

[2] This rule is adapted from Rules Five and Six of Descartes' *Rules for the Direction of the Mind, Philosophical Writings*, vol. 1, pp. 20–4.

[3] Descartes, *Discourse on the Method*, Pt. II, *Philosophical Writings*, vol. 1, p. 120.

everything belonging to the genus, as when circles are discussed in ordinary geometry without anything being said specifically about curves, which is their genus, which people are content simply to define.

It is also not possible to explain everything that could be said about a genus because that would often take too long. But it [335] suffices to say everything about it we wish to say before passing on to the species.

But I believe that we can treat a science perfectly only by paying special attention to these last two rules as well as to the others, and by resolving not to dispense with them except when necessary or for a greater benefit.[a]

CHAPTER 12

What we know by faith, whether human or divine

Everything we have just said up to now concerns knowledge that is exclusively human and based on rational evidence. But before ending it will be good to discuss another kind of knowledge that often is no less certain nor less evident in its own way, namely knowledge derived from authority.

For there are two general paths that lead us to believe that something is true. The first is knowledge we have of it ourselves, from having recognized and examined the truth either by the senses or by reason. This can generally be called *reason*, because the senses themselves depend on a judgment by reason, or *science*, taking this name here more generally than it is taken in the Schools, to mean all knowledge of an object derived from the object itself.

The other path is the authority of persons worthy of credence who assure us that a certain thing exists, although by ourselves we know nothing about it. This is called faith or belief, [336] following this saying of St. Augustine: *Quod scimus, debemus rationi; quod credimus, autoritati*[1] [What we know we owe to reason; what we believe, to authority].

But since this authority can have two sources, God or people, there are also two kinds of faith, divine and human.

Divine faith cannot be subject to error, because God can never deceive us nor be deceived.

---

[1]   *The Advantage of Believing*, ch. 11, *Writings*, vol. 2, p. 425.

[a]   ... benefit. – We admit, however, that we were not greatly constrained in this work. If anyone complains, we will confess frankly that since this *Logic* was augmented almost by half since the first essays, which were written in four or five days, no one should be surprised if the different passages added at different times, and even while it was being printed, are not always as well placed as they might have been if they had been inserted from the start. This is why we said in the Discourse at the beginning that many persons might be satisfied with Parts I and IV, thereby classifying all of Part III under things that are more subtle than pleasant. Since then, however, we have made additions that render the last half as useful as and more amusing than any other part. – CHAPTER ... (I)

Human faith is in itself subject to error because all humans are liars, according to Scripture, and it can happen that people who assure us that something is true may themselves be mistaken. As we have already indicated above, however, some things we know only by human faith, which we ought to consider as certain and as indubitable as if we had mathematical demonstrations of them. Such are the things we know from the constant testimony of so many people that it is morally impossible that they could have conspired to assure us of the same thing if it were not true. For example, people naturally have some trouble in conceiving that there are antipodes. However, even though we have never been there, and thus we know nothing about them except by human faith, we would have to be insane not to believe in them.[a] Similarly we would have to have lost all sense to wonder whether Caesar, Pompey, Cicero, or Virgil ever existed, or whether they were only imaginary characters, such as those of the *Amadis*.[2]

It is true that it is often fairly difficult to mark precisely when human faith has attained this certainty and when it has not. This leads us astray in two opposite ways. One way is taken by people who believe too readily based on the least rumor; the other is taken by people who absurdly set their mental powers to not believing the best testified things whenever they conflict with their prejudices. We can, however, mark certain limits that must be reached in order to attain this human certainty, and others beyond which we definitely have it, leaving a middle ground between these two kinds of limits which is closer to certainty or uncertainty, depending on whether it approaches one or the other set of limits.

If we compare the two general routes – reason and faith – that [337] make us believe that something exists, it is certain that faith always presupposes some reason. As St. Augustine says in letter 122 and many other places,[3] we could not be led to believe what is beyond reason if reason itself had not persuaded us that there are things that it is good to believe although we are not yet capable of understanding them. This is mainly true with respect to divine faith, because true reason teaches us that since God is truth itself, he could not deceive us in what he reveals to us about his nature or his mysteries. From this it appears that even though we are obligated to hold our understanding captive to obey Jesus Christ, as St. Paul says,[4] still we do not do it blindly and irrationally, which is the origin of all false religions. Rather, we do it knowing the cause and because it is reasonable to be a captive in this way to God's authority whenever he has given us sufficient evidence, such as miracles and other prodigious events, which oblige us to believe that he himself has revealed to us the truths we ought to believe.

---

[2] The *Amadis* is a Spanish chivalric romance, whose text goes back to the beginning of the fourteenth century, but which was published in 1508 by Montalvo. The text was a model for *Don Quixote*.

[3] Letter 120: *Consentio ad quaestiones de Trinitate sibi propositas*, ch. 1, no. 3, *Writings*, vol. 10, pp. 301–3. This letter was formerly numbered "222" and not "122," as the authors claim.

[4] Romans 6:16-18.

[a] ... in them, or to doubt whether there is a kingdom called Peru, where the Spanish are masters, and a strait in that region to which Magellan gave his name. Similarly ... (I)

In the second place, it is certain that divine faith should have more power over the mind than our own reason. This is because reason itself shows us that we must always prefer what is more certain to what is less certain, and that it is more certain that what God says is true than what our reason convinces us of, because God is less capable of misleading us than our reason is of being misled.

Nevertheless, considering things exactly, whatever we see evidently and by reason, or by the faithful testimony of the senses, is never opposed to what divine faith teaches us. But we believe it is because we do not pay attention to the limits of the evidence of reason and the senses. For example, in the Eucharist the senses clearly show us roundness and whiteness, but they do not inform us whether it is the substance of bread that causes our eyes to perceive roundness and whiteness in it. Thus faith is not at all contrary to the evidence of the senses when it tells us that it is not the substance of bread, which is no longer there, since it has been changed into the body of Jesus Christ by the [338] mystery of Transubstantiation, and that we see in it only the species and the appearance of the bread which remain, although the substance is no longer there.

Likewise, reason shows us that a single body is not in different places at the same time, nor two bodies in the same place. But this should be understood as a natural condition of bodies, because it would be a defect of reason to suppose that, given that the mind is finite, it could understand the extent of God's power, which is infinite. Hence when, in order to destroy the mysteries of faith such as the Trinity, the Incarnation, and the Eucharist, heretics set in opposition these alleged impossibilities derived from reason, in doing so they visibly depart from reason, claiming that their minds are able to understand the infinite extent of God's power. This is why it is sufficient to reply to all these objections what St. Augustine said on the same subject about the penetration of bodies, *sed nova sunt, sed insolita sunt, sed contra naturae cursum notissimum sunt, quia magna, quia mira, quia divina, et eò magis vera, certa, firma*[5] [But these are new, these are strange, these are against the natural course which we are familiar with, because they are great, they are marvelous, they are divine, and so are more true, certain, and enduring].

CHAPTER 13

Some rules for directing reason well in beliefs about events that depend on human faith

The most common use of good sense and the power of the soul that makes us distinguish truth from falsehood is not in the speculative sciences, to which so few persons are obliged to apply themselves; but there are hardly any occasions where it is used more frequently, and where it is more necessary, than in judgments we make about what takes place every day in human affairs.

---

[5] This passage has not been identified.

I am not speaking about judgments we make concerning whether an action is good or bad, or praiseworthy or blameworthy, because it is up to morality to determine this, but only about the judgments we make concerning the truth or falsity of human events, which alone can concern logic. This is so whether they are viewed as in the past, when it is a question only of knowing whether we [339] ought to believe in them or not, or whether they are viewed as in the future, as when we are afraid that they will happen or when we want them to happen, which determines our hopes and fears.

It is certain that we can make several reflections on this subject that may not be useless and might at least help us avoid the mistakes several persons make when they do not consult the rules of reason sufficiently.

The first reflection is that it is necessary to draw a sharp distinction between two sorts of truths. First are truths that concern merely the nature of things and their immutable essence, independently of their existence. The others concern existing things, especially human and contingent events, which may or may not come to exist when it is a question of the future, or which may not have occurred when it is a question of the past. I am referring in this context to the proximate causes of things, in abstraction from their immutable order in God's providence, because on the one hand, God's providence does not preclude contingency, and on the other, since we know nothing about it, it contributes nothing to our beliefs about things.

For the first kind of truth, since everything is necessary, nothing is true that is not universally true. So we ought to conclude that something is false if it is false in a single case.[a]

But if we try to use the same rules for beliefs about human events, we will always judge them falsely, except by chance, and we will make a thousand fallacious inferences about them.

Since these events are by their nature contingent, it would be absurd to look for some necessary truth in them. Hence a person would be completely irrational who would refuse to believe anything except after having been shown that it was absolutely necessary for something of that sort to have happened.

And it would be no less irrational if someone tried to require me to believe in some event, such as the conversion of the king of China to the Christian religion, merely for the reason that it [340] is not impossible. Since someone else who would assure me of the contrary event could use the same reason, it is clear that this reason alone could not determine me to believe in one event rather than the other.

[a]   … case. On the contrary, possibility is a sure mark of the truth with respect to what is recognized as possible, whenever it is a question only of the essence of things. For the mind cannot conceive anything as possible unless it conceives it as true according to its essence.

   Thus when a geometer conceived that a line could be described by four or five different motions, he never took the trouble actually to draw the line, because it was enough for it to be possible in order for him to consider it as true, and to reason based on this assumption. – But if … (I)

It is necessary, then, to take as a certain and indubitable maxim in this case that the mere possibility of an event is not a sufficient reason to believe in it, and that we may also be right to believe in it even if we judge that it is not impossible for the contrary to happen. Consequently, of two events I can be right to believe in one and not the other, although I believe them both to be possible.

But what, then, would determine me to believe in one rather than the other if I judge them both possible? It would be the following maxim.

In order to decide the truth about an event and to determine whether or not to believe in it, we must not consider it nakedly and in itself, as we would a proposition of geometry. But we must pay attention to all the accompanying circumstances, internal as well as external. I call those circumstances internal that belong to the fact itself, and those external that concern the persons whose testimony leads us to believe in it. Given this attention, if all the circumstances are such that it never or only rarely happens that similar circumstances are consistent with the falsity of the belief, the mind is naturally led to think that it is true. Moreover, it is right to do so, above all in the conduct of life, which does not require greater certainty than moral certainty, and which even ought to be satisfied in many cases with the greatest probability.

But if, on the contrary, these circumstances are such that they are often consistent with the falsity of the belief, reason would require either that we remain in suspense, or that we view as false whatever we are told when its truth does not look likely, even if it does not look completely impossible.

Suppose, for example, someone asks us whether the story of Constantine's baptism by St. Sylvester is true or false. Baronius thinks it is true; Cardinal du Perron, Bishop Sponde, Father Petau, Father Morin,[1] and the most competent churchmen think it is false. If we focus on its mere possibility we would be wrong to reject it, for it contains nothing absolutely impossible. It is even possible, speaking absolutely, that Eusebius, who testifies to the [341] contrary, wanted to lie to favor the Arians and that the Fathers who followed him were misled by his testimony. But if we use the rule we just established, namely to consider the circumstances of both accounts of the baptism of Constantine,[b] and which ones have the most indications of truth, we will find that it is the circumstances of the latter. On one hand, there is no good reason to depend on the testimony of a writer who is as much a fabulist as was the author of the acts of St. Sylvester, who was the only ancient to speak of Constantine's baptism at Rome. On the other hand, it is unlikely that anyone as competent as Eusebius would have dared lie in recounting something as famous as the baptism of the first emperor who gave freedom to the

---

[1]   Pope Sylvester I (314–46) was a friend of Constantine. Cardinal du Perron (Jacques Davy du Perron) was born in Switzerland in 1556, and died at Paris in 1618; he was a converted Calvinist, and became the Archbishop of Sens in 1606. Henri de Sponde (1568–1643) was the Bishop of Pamiers. Petau (1583–1652) was a professor of theology at Paris. Jean Morin (1591–1659) was a priest of the Oratory. Eusebius (267–338) was a bishop of Cesarea and the author of an ecclesiastical history.

[b]   ... Constantine, at Rome or at the end of his life, which ones ... (I)

Church, which would have been known to all the world when he wrote it, since it was only four or five years after the death of that emperor.

There is, however, an exception to this rule, when we ought to be satisfied with possibility and likelihood. This is when a fact that is otherwise sufficiently confirmed is beset by difficulties and apparent contradictions with other stories. In that case it is enough if the solutions brought to these contradictions are possible and likely. It is acting against reason to require positive evidence of them, because when the fact is sufficiently proved in itself, it is not right to require similar proof of all the circumstances. Otherwise we could doubt a thousand well-established histories that can be reconciled with other histories that are no less certain only by conjectures that are impossible to prove positively.

We could, for example, reconcile what is reported in the *Book of Kings* and in *Chronicles* about the reigns of different kings of Judea and Israel, only by giving some of these kings two beginnings to their reigns, one during their fathers' lifetime, the other after their fathers' death. If someone asks what proof we have that a certain king reigned for some time with his father, we have to admit that there is nothing positive. But it is enough if it is something possible that has happened often enough in other cases for us to have [342] the right to assume it as a circumstance necessary for reconciling these otherwise well-confirmed histories.

This is why nothing is more absurd than the efforts several heretics of the last century made to prove that St. Peter was never in Rome. They could not deny that this truth was attested to by all the ecclesiastical authors, even the most ancient, such as Papias, St. Denis of Corinth, Cajus, St. Irenaeus, and Tertullian, without finding any authors who denied it. Nevertheless, they imagine they can refute it by conjectures such as, for example, that St. Paul does not mention St. Peter in his letters written from Rome. When someone replies that St. Peter might have been outside Rome at the time, because no one claims that he was so attached to Rome that he did not leave frequently to preach the Gospel in other places, they answer that this is being said without evidence. This is irrelevant. Since the fact they are contesting is one of the surest truths of church history, it is up to those who argue against it to show that it contradicts Scripture. It is sufficient for those who maintain it to resolve these claimed contradictions, as is done with apparent contradictions in Scripture itself, for which we have shown that possibility suffices.

CHAPTER 14

Application of the preceding rule to beliefs about miracles

The rule we have just explained is doubtless quite important for guiding reason properly in beliefs about particular facts. If we fail to observe it we are in danger of falling into the dangerous extremes of credulity and skepticism.

There are some people, for example, who make it a point of conscience not to doubt any miracle, because they have taken it into their heads that they are obligated to doubt all miracles if they doubt any. They are convinced that it is enough for them to know that everything is possible for God, in order to believe everything told to them about the effects of his omnipotence. [343]

Others, by contrast, suppose absurdly that there is strength of mind in doubting all miracles, without having any other reason than that frequently miracles were reported that were found not to be authentic, and that there is no more reason to believe in some than in others.

The disposition of the former is much better than that of the latter. But it is still true that both reason equally badly.

In both cases they take refuge in banalities. The former do this with respect to the power and goodness of God, the indubitable miracles they introduce as evidence for those that are doubtful, and the blindness of libertines who want to believe only what is commensurate to reason. All this is quite good in itself, but very weak for convincing us of some particular miracle: because God does not do everything he is capable of; it is not an argument that a miracle has happened because similar ones have happened on other occasions; and since we may be quite strongly disposed to believe what is beyond reason without being obliged to believe everything people enjoy recounting to us as beyond reason.

The latter engage in banalities of another kind. One of them says:

> The truth and the lie have similar faces, a similar demeanor, flavor, and appearance. We look at them with the same eye. I have seen the birth of several miracles in my time. Although they were stifled at birth, we nonetheless foresee the course they would have taken had they come of age. For we only have to find the end of the string, to unwind it as much as we want, and it is farther from nothing to the smallest thing in the world than it is from the smallest to the greatest. Now the first people who are immersed in a strange fact, as they come to spread their story, sense by the opposition they meet where the difficulty in persuasion lies and hurry to close up this gap with some false patch. Their private error first produces a public error. And later, the public error in turn produces private error. So goes the entire edifice, taking shape and being formed from hand to hand, so that the most remote witness is better informed about it than the nearest, and the last to know is more convinced than the first.[1]

This discourse is ingenious and may be useful for not letting oneself be carried away by all kinds of rumors. But it would be an exaggeration to conclude from it generally that we ought to view everything said about miracles as suspect. For it is certain that this pertains at most only to what is known merely by [344] common rumors whose origins have not been investigated. We have to admit that there is no good reason to be sure of what is known only this way.

[1] Montaigne, *Essays*, Bk. III, ch. 11, *Complete Works*, pp. 785–6. This quotation is exact, but cut and edited.

But who does not see that we can also produce a rule opposed to this one that would be at least as well founded? Just as there are some miracles we would hardly be sure of were we to go back to the source, there are also some that have faded from people's memories or find little credence in their minds, because they do not want to take the trouble to inform themselves about them. The mind is not subject to a single kind of disorder; there are different and completely contrary kinds. There is an idiotic simplicity that believes in the least credible things. But there is also a foolish presumption that condemns as false everything surpassing the narrow limits of the mind. People are often curious about frivolities but not about important things. False stories are spread everywhere, and true ones have no currency.

How few people know about the miracle that happened in our time at Faremonstier, in the person of a nun who was so blind that she barely had the shape of eyes. She recovered her sight instantly by touching the relics of St. Fare, as I know from a person who saw her in both conditions.

St. Augustine says that in his time there were many quite certain miracles that few persons knew about which, although quite remarkable and astonishing, did not travel from one end of the city to the other. This is what led him to have those that had been verified written up and recounted before the people. He remarks in Book 22 of the *City of God*[2] that in the city of Hippo alone, nearly seventy miracles were produced in the two years after a chapel was built in honor of St. Stephen, not to mention many others that were not written about, which he nevertheless testifies to having known quite certainly.

Thus it is clear enough that nothing is less reasonable than being led by platitudes in these cases, either for embracing all miracles or for rejecting them [345] all. But we must investigate their particular circumstances and the reliability and insight of the witnesses who report them.

Piety does not oblige a person of good sense to believe all the miracles reported in the *Lives of the Saints* or in Metaphrastes,[3] because these authors are full of so many fables that there is no reason to be sure of anything based merely on their testimony, as Cardinal Bellarmine readily admitted about the latter.

But I maintain that persons of good sense, even if they are devoid of piety, ought to recognize as authentic the miracles St. Augustine relates in his *Confessions* or in the *City of God* as having taken place before his eyes, or about which he testifies to having been particularly informed by the persons themselves to whom these things happened. For example, there is one about a blind man cured at Milan in the presence of everyone, by touching the relics of St. Gervasius and St. Protasius,

---

[2]   *Writings*, vol. 8, p. 445.

[3]   The *Lives of the Saints*, also known as the *Golden Legend*, was written by Iacopo Da Varazze (1228/30–98), an Italian Dominican; the work abounds with legends and miracles, and was the most famous hagiographic compilation of the Middle Ages. Symeon Metaphrastes was a Byzantine writer living at the end of the tenth century. He was a typical exponent of tenth-century encyclopedism, and compiled hagiographic legends in *The Menologion*, a collection of 148 texts on the lives of the saints and acts of martyrs, which became an official tool for church services.

which he reports in his *Confessions*. He says about it in Book 22, chapter 8 of the *City of God*: *Miraculum quod Mediolani factum est cùm illic essemus, quando illuminatus est coecus, ad multorum notitiam potuit pervenire; quia et grandis est civitas, et ibi erat tunc Imperator, et immenso populo teste res gesta est concurrente ad corpora Martyrum Gervasii & Protasii*[4] [Many people could come to know about a miracle that was performed in Milan when I was there (a blind man regained his sight), because Milan is a large city, and the Emperor was there at the time, and a huge crowd that had gathered at the bodies of the martyrs Protasius and Gervasius witnessed the miracle].

Another one concerns a woman in Africa, cured by flowers that had touched the relics of St. Stephen, as he testifies in the same place.

Also a noble woman was cured of a cancer judged to be incurable, by the sign of the cross that she had a newly baptized woman make on it, according to a revelation she had had.

Finally, there was a miracle concerning an infant who died without baptism, whose mother obtained his resurrection by her prayers to St. Stephen, telling him with her great faith: "Holy Martyr, give me back my son. You know that I am asking for his life only so that he will not be eternally separated from God."[a]

---

[4]   No. 2, *Writings*, vol. 8, p. 433.

[a]   ... God." This saint reports this as something he was quite sure about in a sermon he gave his people about another very conspicuous miracle that had occurred in the church at the very time he was preaching, which he describes at great length in this passage from the *City of God*.

He says that when seven brothers and three sisters from an honorable family of Cesarea in Cappadocia were cursed by their mother for treating her badly, God punished them by making them continually agitated, even in sleep, with terrible convulsions throughout the body. This deformed them so much that they could no longer stand for their acquaintances to see them, and so they all left their country to go in different directions. Hence one of the brothers, named Paul, and one of the sisters, named Palladia, came to Hippo, and when they were noticed by the entire city, people learned from them the cause of their misfortune. On Easter Day itself, the brother, who was praying to God before the altar rail of the Chapel of St. Stephen, suddenly fell into a stupor. During this time people perceived that he was no longer trembling, and he awoke from it perfectly healthy. It caused a great clamor in the church, from the people praising God for the miracle and running to St. Augustine, who was preparing to say Mass, to tell him what had happened.

He says:

After these cries of joy were over, and the Holy Scripture was read, I told them a little bit about the celebration and the great reason for joy, because I preferred to let them not only hear but meditate on God's eloquence in this divine deed. Then I took the brother who had been cured to dine with me. I had him recount the entire story. I made him write it down, and the next day I promised the people that I would have him recite it the day after. So the third day after Easter, after putting the brother and sister on the steps of the choir, so that all the people could see in the horrible convulsions which the sister still had, what evil the brother was delivered of by God's goodness, I had the account of their story read before the people and then I let them go. I began to preach on this subject (we have the sermon on it), and all of a sudden while I was still speaking, a great cry of joy arose from the direction of the Chapel. They brought me the sister who, after she had left me, went away and was completely

Assuming these things happened as he reports them, [346] there is no reasonable person who should not recognize the hand of God. So the only remaining basis for skepticism would be to doubt the testimony itself of St. Augustine, and to suppose that he altered the truth to legitimize the Christian religion in the minds of pagans. Now no one can say this with the slightest plausibility.

First, it is not at all likely that a judicious person would have wanted to lie about such public things when he could have been convicted of lying by countless witnesses, which could only have brought disgrace on the Christian religion. Second, no one was a greater enemy of lies than this Saint, especially in religious matters, since he wrote entire books proving not only that it is never permissible to lie, but that it is a horrible crime to do it under the pretext of attracting people to the faith more easily.[b]

We ought to be completely astonished at the way [347] the heretics of our time, who view St. Augustine as a very enlightened and sincere man, have not considered how their way of speaking of the invocation of the Saints and the veneration of relics, as superstitious worship that supports idolatry, would lead to the downfall of all religion. For it is obvious that it removes one of its most solid foundations to take away from true miracles the authority they should have to confirm the truth. It is clear that it completely undercuts the authority of miracles to say that God produces them to reward a superstitious and idolatrous cult. Now, properly speaking, this is what heretics do when, on the one hand, they treat the veneration Catholics offer the saints and their relics as a criminal superstition, and, on the other, they cannot deny that the greatest friends of God, such as St. Augustine, have by their own admission assured us that God cures incurable evils, gives sight to the blind, and resuscitates the dead in order to reward the devotion of those who invoke the saints and revere their relics.

Indeed, this consideration alone ought to make everyone of good faith recognize the falsity of the so-called reformed religion.

I have spoken at some length about this famous example of judgments we ought to make concerning factual truths, in order to use this rule in similar cases, because people go astray in those cases in the same way. Each person thinks that, in order to decide them, it is sufficient to produce a platitude that often consists only of maxims that not only are not universally true but are not even probable when they are joined with the particular circumstances of the facts under examination. It is

cured as her brother had been. This caused such rejoicing among the people that one could hardly stand the din they were making. [*City of God*, Bk. xxii, ch. 8, *Writings*, vol. 8, pp. 448–50]

I wanted to report all the details of this miracle to convince the most skeptical that it would be insane to doubt it, along with so many others this Saint recounts in the same passage. For assuming these things ... (I)

[b] ... easily. – Someone, then, as strongly convinced of this maxim as St. Augustine was, could not reasonably be suspected of having altered the least thing in the accounts of the miracles he reports having seen with his own eyes or otherwise knowing about quite certainly. We ought ... (I)

necessary to connect them with the circumstances and not to separate them, because it often happens that a fact that is improbable in relation to a single circumstance usually indicating falsity, should be deemed certain with respect to other circumstances. By contrast, a fact that might appear true in relation to a certain circumstance that is usually connected with the truth, should be judged false according to others that weaken that circumstance, as we shall explain in the following chapter. [348]

CHAPTER 15

Another remark on the same subject of beliefs about events

There is still one other very important remark to be made concerning beliefs about events. It is that among the circumstances we ought to consider in order to decide whether we should or should not believe in events, are some we may call common circumstances, because they are encountered in many facts and they are found more often than not joined to truth than to falsehood. In that case, if they are not counterbalanced by other particular circumstances that weaken or destroy in the mind the grounds for belief that the mind derives from common circumstances, we are right to believe in these events, if not with certainty, at least with high probability. This is enough when we are required to judge them. Since we should be satisfied with moral certainty in matters not susceptible of metaphysical certainty, so too when we cannot have complete moral certainty, the best we can do when we are committed to taking sides is to embrace the most probable, since it would be a perversion of reason to embrace the less probable.

But if, on the contrary, these common circumstances that would have led us to believe something are connected to other particular circumstances that, as we have just said, destroy in the mind the grounds for belief that it derives from these common circumstances, or that themselves are such that similar circumstances are rarely unaccompanied by falsehood, we no longer have the same reason for believing in the event. Either the mind must remain in suspense if the particular circumstances only weaken the weight of the common circumstances, or it is led to believe that the fact is false if they are such as usually indicate falsehood. Here is an example that may clarify this remark.

It is a common circumstance for many deeds to be [349] signed by two notaries, that is, by two public persons who ordinarily have a great interest in not saying something false, because not only do their conscience and honor depend on it, but also their welfare and livelihood. This consideration alone suffices, if we know no other details of a contract, to make us believe that it was not antedated. Not that there could not be antedated contracts, but because it is certain that out of a thousand contracts, 999 are not antedated. Consequently it is considerably more likely that the contract I see is one of the 999 than that it is the unique one among a thousand that is antedated. If the probity of the notaries who signed it is perfectly well known to me, I will then take it to be very certain that they committed no falsehood.

But if this common circumstance of being signed by two notaries – which when it is not refuted by others is a sufficient reason for me to have faith in the date of the contract – is connected with other particular circumstances, such as that these notaries have been accused of being without honor and conscience, or that they may have had a great interest in falsifying this contract, this would still not make me conclude that the contract is antedated. But it would diminish the weight that the signature of two notaries would otherwise have had in my mind to make me believe it was not antedated. If, further, I can discover other positive evidence that it was antedated, either through witnesses or strong arguments, such as the inability of someone to have lent twenty thousand crowns at a time when it is shown that he was not worth a hundred crowns, I will then be determined to believe that this contract is false. It would be a highly irrational expectation to require me either not to believe the contract antedated, or to acknowledge that I was wrong to suppose that the other contracts where I did not see the same indications of falsity were not antedated, since they might have been like this one.

All this can be applied to matters that often cause disputes among the learned. People ask whether a book is really written by an author whose name it has always carried, or whether the acts of a Council are true or fictitious.

It is certain that the presumption is in favor of the author who has been in possession of a work for a long time, and for the truth of the acts of a Council that we read about every day. There must be [350] some significant reasons to make us believe the contrary, notwithstanding this bias.

This is why, when a quite competent man of our time[1] wanted to show that the letter of St. Cyprian to Pope Stephen on the subject of Martien, Bishop of Arles, was not written by this holy martyr, he could not convince the learned, since his conjectures did not appear strong enough to take away from St. Cyprian something that had always borne his name and resembled perfectly the style of his other works.

It was also in vain for Blondel and Saumaise, who could not reply to the argument derived from the letters of St. Ignatius for the superiority of the Bishop over priests since the beginning of the Church,[2] to try to claim that all these letters were fraudulent, inasmuch as they were printed by Isaac Vossius and Usserius on the ancient Greek manuscript of the library of Florence. They were refuted by

---

[1] This refers to Jean de Launoy, nicknamed the *dénicheur de saints* (exposer of saints). The letter by St. Cyprian on Martien, the Bishop of Arles, is numbered 48, *Cyprianus Stephano Fratri, salutem, S. Coecilii Cypriani opera* (3rd edition, Amsterdam, 1700).

[2] This concerns St. Ignatius of Antioch, who lived in the first century A.D. The text of the *Letters* was established by two scholars Usserius (Jean Usher) and Vossius, but its authenticity was hotly debated between Catholics and Protestants.

their own supporters[3] because, admitting as they do that the same letters are cited by Eusebius, St. Jerome, Theodoret, and even Origen, there is no reason to think that when the letters of St. Ignatius were collected by St. Polycarp, the authentic letters disappeared and others were substituted in the time between St. Polycarp and Origen or Eusebius. Furthermore, the letters of St. Ignatius we now possess have a certain character of holiness and simplicity so appropriate to Apostolic times, that they provide in themselves a defense against these worthless accusations of fraud and falsehood.

Finally, all the difficulties that Cardinal du Perron presented against the letter of the Council of Africa to Pope St. Celestine, concerning the appeals to the Holy See,[4] have not prevented us from thinking since then, as we had previously, that they really were written by this Council.

There are, however, other occasions where particular arguments prevail over the general argument of long possession.

Hence although the letter by St. Clement to St. James, the Bishop of Jerusalem, was translated by Ruffin almost thirteen [351] hundred years ago, and although a Council of France alleged that it was written by St. Clement more than twelve hundred years ago,[5] it is difficult, all the same, not to admit that it is fraudulent. Since St. James the Bishop of Jerusalem was martyred before St. Peter, it is impossible for St. Clement to have written him after the death of St. Peter, as this letter presupposes.

Similarly, although the commentaries on St. Paul attributed to St. Ambrose were often cited under his name by a great many authors, as well as the imperfect work on St. Matthew under the name of St. Chrysostom, still everyone today agrees that they were not written by these saints, but by other ancient authors who made many mistakes.

Finally, the Acts we have from the Councils of Sinuesses under Marcellinus, two or three Councils of Rome under St. Sylvester, and another Roman Council under Sixtus III, would be sufficient to convince us of their authenticity if they contained only what was reasonable and related to the times attributed to these Councils. But they contain so much that is unreasonable and inappropriate to those times, that it is much more likely that they are false and fraudulent.

These are some remarks that may be helpful in making judgments of this kind. But we should not suppose that they are so useful that they will always prevent us from making mistakes. The most they can do is to make us avoid the crudest errors, and to accustom the mind not to let itself be carried away by banalities that,

---

3   This probably alludes to the attacks by the Protestant Daillé in 1666 against the authenticity of the letters of St. Ignatius.

4   This refers to a synodal letter from the bishops of Africa to Pope Celestine in 426, on the subject of reestablishing the priest Apiarius in their community. While waiting for clarifications on the canons of the Council of Nicea, these bishops did not want to have to make appeals to Rome.

5   This Council of France was at Vaison-la-Romaine. The sixth canon of this Council "cites with great respect the (alleged) letter by Pope Saint Clement to St. James."

although they contain some general truth, are nonetheless false on many specific occasions, which is one of the greatest sources of human error.

CHAPTER 16

The judgments we ought to make concerning future accidents

These rules, which are helpful for judging about past events, can easily be applied to future events. For as we ought to believe it probable that an event has happened whenever certain circumstances [352] we know about are ordinarily connected with that event, we also ought to believe that it is likely to happen whenever present circumstances are such that they are usually followed by such an effect. This is how doctors can decide the good or bad outcome of diseases, how military leaders judge the future course of a war, and how we in the world judge most contingent matters.

But with respect to accidents in which we play a part, and that we can bring about or prevent in some sense by our care in exposing ourselves to them or avoiding them, many people happen to fall into an illusion that is all the more deceptive as it appears more reasonable to them. This is that they consider only the greatness and importance of the benefit they desire or the disadvantage they fear, without considering in any way the likelihood or probability that this benefit or disadvantage will or will not come about.

So whenever they are apprehensive about some great harm, such as loss of life or all their wealth, they think it prudent not to neglect any precaution to safeguard themselves against it. And if it is some great good, such as gaining a hundred thousand crowns, they think they are acting wisely by trying to obtain it if the risks are slight, however unlikely they are to succeed.

It was reasoning of this kind that led a princess, who heard that some persons were crushed by a falling ceiling, not to enter a house ever afterwards without having it inspected first. She was so convinced she was right that it seemed to her that everyone who acted otherwise was imprudent.

This is also the form of reasoning that leads various people into troublesome and excessive precautions for protecting their health. This is what makes others overly distrustful in the smallest matters because, having been mistaken on a few occasions, they assume they will also be wrong about everything. This is what attracts so many people to lotteries: Is it not highly advantageous, they say, to win twenty thousand crowns for one crown? Each person thinks he will be the happy person who will win the jackpot. No one reflects that if it is, for example, twenty thousand crowns, it may be thirty thousand times more probable for each individual [353] to lose rather than to win it.

The flaw in this reasoning is that in order to decide what we ought to do to obtain some good or avoid some harm, it is necessary to consider not only the good or harm in itself, but also the probability that it will or will not occur, and to view geometrically the proportion all these things have when taken together. This can be clarified by the following example.

There are games in which, if ten persons each put in a crown, only one wins the whole pot and all the others lose. Thus each person risks losing only a crown and may win nine. If we consider only the gain and loss in themselves, it would appear that each person has the advantage. But we must consider in addition that if each could win nine crowns and risks losing only one, it is also nine times more probable for each person to lose one crown and not win the nine. Hence each has nine crowns to hope for himself, one crown to lose, nine degrees of probability of losing a crown, and only one of winning the nine crowns. This puts the matter at perfect equality.

All games of this sort are fair, as much as games can be, and those that are otherwise are manifestly unfair. This is how we can show that there is an obvious injustice in the type of games called lotteries because, with the operator of the lottery usually taking a tenth for his share in advance, the whole group of players is duped in the same way as if someone made an equal wager, that is, where the likelihood of winning is as great as that of losing, of ten pistoles against nine. Now if this is disadvantageous to the whole group, it is also disadvantageous to each person in it, since from this it follows that the probability of loss exceeds the probability of winning by more than the advantage desired exceeds the disadvantage to which one is exposed, namely of losing what he has put in.

Sometimes the success of something is so unlikely that however advantageous it may be, and however little risk there is in obtaining it, it is preferable not to chance it. Thus it would be foolish to play twenty sous against ten million pounds, or against a kingdom, on the condition that one could win only in case a child arranging the letters in a printer's shop at random immediately composed the first twenty verses of Virgil's *Aeneid*. So without thinking about it, there is no moment in life in which we [354] would risk life any more than a prince would risk his kingdom in wagering on this condition.[1]

These reflections appear trivial, and in effect they are if we go no further. But we can make them useful for more important things. The main use we ought to derive from them is to make us more reasonable in our hopes and fears. Many people, for example, are exceedingly frightened when they hear thunder. If thunder makes them think of God and death and happiness, we could not think about it too much. But if it is only the danger of dying by lightning that causes them this unusual apprehension, it is easy to show that this is unreasonable. For out of two million people, at most there is one who dies this way. We could even say that there is hardly a violent death that is less common. So, then, our fear of some harm ought to be proportional not only to the magnitude of the harm, but also to the probability

---

[1] Here Arnauld borrows from Pascal the premises of his famous argument, "Pascal's wager," concerning the existence of God. See the *Pensées*, "Infini rien," No. 233, *Pensées and the Provincial Letters*, pp. 79–84.

of the event. Just as there is hardly any kind of death more rare than being struck by lightning, there is also hardly any that ought to cause us less fear, especially given that this fear is no help in avoiding it.

Not only is this how we should set straight these people who take extraordinary and bothersome precautions to safeguard their life and health, by showing them that these precautions are a greater harm than is the danger of such a remote accident as the one they fear. But it is also necessary to disabuse other people who reason almost the same way in their undertakings – there is danger in this affair, therefore it is bad; there is an advantage in that one, therefore it is good – since it is neither by the danger nor the advantages, but by the proportion between them that we should judge them.

It is the nature of finite things, however great they are, to be able to be surpassed by the smallest things if they are multiplied often, whether the little things surpass the largest in the likelihood of their occurring more than they are surpassed in magnitude. Thus the smallest gain can surpass the largest that could be imagined if the lesser one is often duplicated, or if the greater good is so difficult to obtain [355] that it surpasses the small one in size by less than the small one surpasses it in ease of acquisition. The same is true of the harms we dread, that is, that the smallest harm can be more important than the greatest harm that is not infinite, if it surpasses it by this proportion.

Only infinite things such as eternity and salvation cannot be equalled by any temporal benefit. Thus we ought never balance them off against anything worldly. This is why the slightest bit of help for acquiring salvation is worth more than all the goods of the world taken together. And the least peril of being lost is more important than all temporal harms considered merely as harms.

This is enough to make all reasonable people draw this conclusion, with which we will end this *Logic*: that the greatest of all follies is to use one's time and life for something other than what may be useful for acquiring a life that will never end, since all the goods and harms of this life are nothing in comparison to those of the other life, and the danger of falling into those harms, as well as the difficulty of acquiring these goods, is very great.

Those who draw this conclusion and who follow it in the way they lead their lives are prudent and wise, however inexact they are in reasoning about scientific matters. Those who do not draw it, however exact they are in everything else, are treated in Scripture as foolish and senseless persons, and they misuse logic, reason, and life.[a]

The end.

[a]   I ends with the following:

> Addition. –
>
> In rereading this *Logic*, we found that the proof of the fourth corollary of Part III, chapter 3, p. 226, was not clear enough. Thus we can put line 27, which follows: ... [next comes the text 140:7up–141:11 added in II at the normal place; cf. p. 140 n. c.]

Index

Index

Cambridge texts in the history of philosophy

Titles published in the series thus far

Conway *The Principles of the Most Ancient and Modern Philosophy* (edited by Allison P. Coudert and Taylor Corse)

Descartes *Meditations on First Philosophy*, with selections from the *Objections and Replies* (edited with a new introduction by John Cottingham)

Antoine Arnauld and Pierre Nicole *Logic or the Art of Thinking* (edited by Jill Vance Buroker)

La Mettrie *Machine Man and Other Writings* (edited by Ann Thomson)

Schleiermacher *On Religion: Speeches to its Cultured Despisers* (edited by Richard Crouter)

Kant *The Metaphysics of Morals* (edited by Mary Gregor with an introduction by Roger Sullivan)